Cambridge Studies in Early Mod

ALGERNON SII
AND THE ENGLISH REPU

Cambridge Studies in Early Modern British History

Series editors

ANTHONY FLETCHER
Professor of Modern History, University of Durham

JOHN GUY
Reader in British History, University of Bristol

and JOHN MORRILL
*Lecturer in History, University of Cambridge, and
Fellow and Tutor of Selwyn College*

This is a series of monographs and studies covering many aspects of the history of the British Isles between the late fifteenth century and the early eighteenth century. It includes the work of established scholars and pioneering work by a new generation of scholars. It includes both reviews and revisions of major topics and books which open up new historical terrain or which reveal startling new perspectives on familiar subjects. It is envisaged that all the volumes will set detailed research into broader perspectives and the books are intended for the use of students as well as of their teachers.

Titles in the series

The Common Peace: Participation and the Criminal Law in Seventeenth-Century England
    CYNTHIA B. HERRUP
Politics, Society and Civil War in Warwickshire
    ANN HUGHES
London Crowds in the Reign of Charles II: Propaganda and Politics from the Restoration to the Exclusion Crisis
    TIM HARRIS
Criticism and Compliment: The Politics of Literature in the England of Charles I
    KEVIN SHARPE
Central Government and the Localities: Hampshire, 1649–1689
    ANDREW COLEBY
John Skelton and the Politics of the 1520s
    GREG WALKER
Algernon Sidney and the English Republic, 1623–1677
    JONATHAN SCOTT

ALGERNON SIDNEY AND THE ENGLISH REPUBLIC, 1623–1677

JONATHAN SCOTT

Lecturer in History, Victoria University of Wellington

The right of the
University of Cambridge
to print and sell
all manner of books
was granted by
Henry VIII in 1534.
The University has printed
and published continuously
since 1584.

CAMBRIDGE UNIVERSITY PRESS

Cambridge

New York   New Rochelle   Melbourne   Sydney

PUBLISHED BY THE PRESS SYNDICATE OF THE UNIVERSITY OF CAMBRIDGE
The Pitt Building, Trumpington Street, Cambridge, United Kingdom

CAMBRIDGE UNIVERSITY PRESS
The Edinburgh Building, Cambridge CB2 2RU, UK
40 West 20th Street, New York NY 10011–4211, USA
477 Williamstown Road, Port Melbourne, VIC 3207, Australia
Ruiz de Alarcón 13, 28014 Madrid, Spain
Dock House, The Waterfront, Cape Town 8001, South Africa

http://www.cambridge.org

First published 1988
First paperback edition 2004

A catalogue record for this book is available from the British Library

Library of Congress cataloguing in publication data

Scott, Jonathan, 1958–
Algernon Sidney and the English republic. 1623–1677 / Jonathan
Scott.
p.   cm. – (Cambridge studies in early modern British history)
Includes index.
ISBN 0 521 35290 8 hardback
1. Sidney, Algernon, 1622–1683.   2. Politicians – Great Britain –
Biography.   3. Political scientists – Great Britain – Biography.
4. Great Britain – History – Puritan Revolution, 1642–1660.   5. Great
Britain – History – Charles II. 1660–1685.   6. Great Britain – Politics
and government – 1603–1714.   I. Title.   II. Series.
DA407.s6s43   1988
941.06 6′0924–dc19   87–33391 CIP
[B]

ISBN 0 521 35290 8 hardback
ISBN 0 521 61195 4 paperback

Nothing is farther from my intention than to speak irreverently of kings...

Discourses p. 160

... and I presume no wise man will think I do so, if I profess ... what history, and daily experience teach us concerning the virtues and religions, that ... have been from the beginning of the world supported by monarchs ... their moral as well as their theological graces, together with what the Scriptures tell us of those, who in the last days will principally support the throne of antichrist ... [and] conclude ... that monarchy can be said to be natural in no other sense, than that our depraved nature is most inclined to that which is worst.

Discourses p. 160

For Lindsey

CONTENTS

PREFACE

This is the first of two books on the life and political thought of the English republican Algernon Sidney (1623–83). In one sense – chronologically – the two works may be regarded as volumes of a single intellectual biography separated by the dates of their titles: *Algernon Sidney and the English Republic 1623–1677*; *Algernon Sidney and the Restoration Crisis 1677–1683*. Since Sidney himself proved a good deal more popular in two pieces than he had been in one this would not be inappropriate.

Biographical chronology, however, and the resulting narrative, provides only part of the content and purpose of each book. In another sense each is a separate work in its own right and neither is bounded by the date limits of its title. For each addresses a wider question about Sidney's thought and experience in its historical context and in each case it is the nature of this question rather than that narrative which gives the book its final shape.

Thus the question asked by the present work (following its preliminary: 'What did Sidney believe?') is '*How did Sidney come to hold* the beliefs he expressed?' – beliefs which were to prove so influential in the eighteenth century and which remain influential today. The answer to this question, in so far as it can be provided, calls for a combination of analysis and narrative which takes us well beyond the date limits of the book's title. Chapters 1–4 and 11–13 in particular involve substantial examination of aspects of the period 1677–83 as well. Similarly, in its turn, *Algernon Sidney and the Restoration Crisis 1677–1683* will use its central focus on Sidney's activities within those years to argue a wider case about Restoration (and indeed seventeenth-century) political structures as a whole.

In addition to this central question and its subsidiary object of locating Sidney's thought in some sort of intellectual context, this present work has a secondary historiographical purpose as well. One of the ironies of the whig historiography of Sidney was that his biographers were writing the life of someone whose life in the public eye began with his death. Accordingly the spectacle of that death and its immediate political context traditionally occupied a greatly disproportionate share of their attention. The result was not only a relative neglect of the first fifty-four years of Sidney's life – the subject of this book – but a misrepresentation in the process of that life's political fulcrum. This was not the so-called 'Exclusion Crisis'[1] though this and its aftermath made his name. It was the age of the English Republic (1649–53, and 1659) and the period from 1635 to 1677 generally. It was through the disorder, hard choices, struggle, and eventually loss of this period that Sidney developed all the attitudes that were to motivate the rest of his life and writing.

In short it is one purpose of my work on Sidney in general to show that he was a republican – an historical product of the first of England's seventeenth-century 'revolutions' (1649), not an 'exclusionist Whig' who may be ahistorically appropriated for the second (1688). The construction of this revised picture will be the object of this book; we will see in the next what happened when such a creature was transplanted back to the political world of the later Restoration. It will be time at that stage, from the standpoint of the crisis of 1678–83, to make some more general remarks about the relationship between those two 'revolutions' themselves, and between the first and second halves of the seventeenth-century English political experience in general.

---

[1] The grounds for my objections to this term will be fully explained in the book to follow.

ACKNOWLEDGEMENTS

This work, and much of that which follows, was completed in my time at Cambridge University, first as a research student at Trinity College, and then as a research fellow at Magdalene College. I would like to express my gratitude to the Commonwealth Scholarship Commission, to the Master and Fellows of Trinity College and, above all, to the Master and Fellows of Magdalene College, for making that time possible, and for making it so enjoyable.

It is impossible to adequately record all of the obligations incurred in the writing of this book. To the many archive, record office, and library staffs who have helped me over the years I can only express my thanks for assistance often well beyond the call of duty. I am grateful to Viscount De L'isle, by whose kind permission I was able to use the Sidney family papers at Maidstone; and to Lord Bath, and the Duke of Devonshire, who also allowed me to see manuscripts in their private possession.

Graduate research can be lonely; that mine was never so I owe above all to John Morrill. For his unflagging interest, support, and generosity over almost five years this book is a very inadequate return. To J. C. Davis, who first introduced me to Sidney, and who has continued to teach me about him since, I also owe more than even he knows. It was Blair Worden who rediscovered not only Sidney's *Court Maxims*, but the historical Sidney himself. For the stimulus and kindness he has seen fit to offer my subsequent arrival on the same shores I feel the deepest gratitude.

Others who have read my work in manuscript and tried to save me from error include Mark Goldie, Johann Sommerville, Richard Tuck, Eamon Duffy, and Glenn Burgess. For whatever scholarship exists in this account I am indebted to them also; the errors which remain are, of course, my own. I would also like to thank John Carswell, Alan Houston, Paul Hopkins, and John Adamson – the first two working on their own studies of Sidney – for information about manuscript material I would otherwise have missed. Finally I owe a great deal to all those Cambridge historians and friends upon whose knowledge, conversation, and criticism over the years I have relied.

My greatest debt is to Lindsey, who in marrying me found herself married to the ghost of Algernon as well. A glance at the text will show the disruption to domestic harmony which could have resulted. Yet one strong character took the measure of another, and allowed the scholarly exorcism to take its due course. I dedicate this book to her.

All references to Sidney's works in the text are in italics; the *Court Maxims* has not, however, been published. References to the *Court Maxims* are to the manuscript at the Warwickshire Record Office. References to the *Discourses Concerning Government, Apology, Last Paper*, and *Works* are to *The Works of Algernon Sydney* (London 1772). *Of Love* was published in *Tracts . . . of the Late Lord Somers* (1809–15) volume 8; the manuscript is in the British Museum, add. MS 34,100. *The Character of Henry Vane jnr* was published in V. Rowe, *Sir Henry Vane the Younger* (London 1970) Appendix F.

$$\text{---}\!\!\!\ll\!\!\!1\!\!\!\gg\!\!\!\text{---}$$

Introduction: the man and the myth

Anyone attempting a large-scale study of Algernon Sidney at the moment has to contend with two historiographical problems: eighteenth- and nineteenth-century distortion, and twentieth-century neglect. Both stem, paradoxically, from the same source: Sidney's fame as the foremost English martyr and patriot-figure in the political mythology of both England and America, in the century and a half following his death on the scaffold in 1683.[1]

During his heyday as a whig hero Sidney was the subject of a string of biographies, the collective scholarship of which failed to assert itself over the terms of party political debate. Without exception the eighteenth- and nineteenth-century biographers of Sidney were writing the life of a living contemporary symbol rather than a historical man. They wrote to reinforce an existing mythology in response to the political needs it was required to serve, rather than investigate the facts about the man from whose memory it was derived. The resulting rigid formula, which one can encounter with increasing *déjà vu* in any of the nineteenth-century biographies, was insular, two-dimensional, and self-perpetuating, built around a few key incidents in Sidney's life (at least half of which never occurred),[2] the neglect or ignorance of many writings and an emphasis on others (the most important of which was forged after his death),[3] and a point-blank refusal to accept new evidence from outside the mythology.[4]

[1] See Karsten P., *Patriot-Heroes in England and America* (Wisconsin 1978); Robbins C., 'Algernon Sidney's *Discourses Concerning Government*; Textbook of Revolution' in *William and Mary Quarterly* ser. 3, vol. 4 (1947); Kenyon J.P., *Revolution Principles* (Cambridge 1977), esp. pp. 51–3.

[2] Celebrated episodes in Sidney's life for which there is no evidence include (1) His shooting his horse in France when the King asked to ride it; (2) The French ambassador Terlon's tearing his inscription out of the Copenhagen commonplace book; (3) His 'gallantry' in Ireland; (4) His 1650s trips to Holland; (5) His playing Brutus in a staging of *Julius Caesar* in 1656. The first two at least were whig (anti-French) fabrications (Sidney got on well with both the French King and Terlon).

[3] In particular, neglect of much of the *Discourses*; ignorance of the *Court Maxims* and many letters; and an emphasis on the forged letter 'Algernon Sidney to His Friends...' (1660), reprinted in *Tracts ... of the Late Lord Somers* ed. W. Scott (1809–15), vol. 8 pp. 6ff.

[4] The principal biographies of Sidney are by Meadley (1813), Chase Sidney (1835), Van

1

Consequently the Sidney myth got the man seriously wrong. It did so because it needed to portray him as a whig and, as time went on, as an increasingly respectable one; a 'philosophical liberal' and a 'reformer', not a 'radical'; as one who would have hailed the moderate constitutional amendment of 1688, and had nothing to offer those who, in Ewald's words (1873), 'disgrace the name of Republicanism in Trafalgar Square'. In fact he had never been a whig; he was the product of a previous age; a violent civil war era insurrectionary of an entirely different order. Executed five years before the 'Revolution' of 1688, he was subsequently adopted as the most newsworthy of its early martyrs; but in fact his entire political life from the civil war to the Exclusion Crisis had been devoted to a perspective, alliances, and policies which worked in a very different direction. The 1688 settlement marked the triumph of Sidney's most hated enemy (William Prince of Orange), and sounded the historical death knell for the linked causes of Dutch and English republicanism, in opposition to both Stuart and Orange, to which Sidney had devoted most of his political life. During the 'Exclusion Crisis', which whig history teaches was focused on the Duke of York (thus prefacing 1688), Sidney was telling the French ambassador Barillon that he 'feared the Prince of Orange more than the Duke of York'. The whig mythology of Sidney was a vehicle for eighteenth- and nineteenth-century political sensibilities, not the seventeenth-century realities of Sidney's own. By the time his last biographer Blackburne came to write (1885) he could be described as 'merely an anachronism . . . a man of the nineteenth century . . . who, by some mischance found himself put back into the seventeenth century'.[5]

The real nature of Sidney's political career was never examined, partly because, in whig terms, one didn't need to scratch far beneath the surface to be threatened with disturbing evidence. It was more prudent, as well as pertinent, for biographers to concentrate on his death instead, a Stoic martyrdom the background and character of which conventionally occupied 50 per cent of Sidney biographies. Sidney was consequently portrayed travelling through life upright upon the scaffold, a cool 'inflexible patriot' who, for the benefit of post-1688 audiences, 'pretended to little or no religion', but whose principles were modelled upon 'the stern heroes of antiquity', thankfully free from 'that fanaticism and coarseness which strongly characterised his age'. Van Saantvoord noted approvingly his 'calm and placid disposition', and Blackburne concluded with evident

---

Saantvoord (1851), Ewald (1873), and Blackburne (1885). Meadley's, written early and so lacking much of the evidence used by the later biographers, is nevertheless still the best, with its compact text and careful footnotes.

[5] Blackburne G., *Algernon Sidney: A Review* (1885) p. 13; PRO Baschet Corresp. 150 fol. 261 (1681).

relief: 'we can now know Algernon Sidney . . . as the moderate man'.[6]

This is a peculiar way to describe someone who was clearly one of the most passionate and bellicose rebels of his age, even judged by civil war rather than Restoration standards. His own time delivered their judgement on his *Discourses* by executing him for the mere possession of the manuscript, when no reliable evidence of either intention to publish or other actual insurrectionary activity could be found. It contained, as Judge Jeffreys observed (and as the *Court Maxims* before it had contained) 'all the malice, revenge and treason mankind can be guilty of . . . there is not a line in the book scarce but what is treason' (and this was the result of a deliberate attempt by Sidney to restrain himself). Informed by Sidney's scepticism, the *Discourses* was concerned above all to emphasise the variety and mutability of particular political forms, in a world characterised by the presence – as God, its creator was characterised by the absence – of change. The result was a vision of history and politics which made the inevitability of change the informing spirit of the whole theory. In the process Sidney not only produced a powerful and influential revolution ideology, but did so with insights which mark a crucial development between the sixteenth-century scepticism of Machiavelli, and the eighteenth-century idea of progress.

Far from being the 'inflexible patriot' of whig martyrology, Sidney was, in practice as in theory, a French-educated Sceptic and relativist whose (literally Machiavellian) flexibility in the application of means to political ends ruffled even his own plotting colleagues and would have made Ewald's hair stand on end. Far from being a moderate constitutional reformer, Sidney wrote his first major tract in the process of preparing to invade England at the head of a French army, and his second in the process of attempting to tip a crisis in which royal policy and religion were being debated, into a second civil war in which the question of monarchy itself would be submitted afresh to the arbitration of the sword. Far from being 'the perfect Englishman' admired by insular, anti-French, whig culture, Sidney spent half of his life outside England, in France, Ireland, Scandinavia, Italy, the Netherlands, and Germany, engaged among 'forrein princes' and republics in a variety of (in whig and English terms) internationalist exercises in treason. Consequently he died 'much admired by the French'[7] and much the worse for wear at the hands of the English. Sidney's later influence as a theorist, stronger outside England

---

[6] Meadley p. 291; Karsten, *Patriot-Heroes* p. 65; Blackburne, *Algernon Sidney* p. 238. This view of Sidney as the sober Victorian rationalist, relatively unconcerned with religion, was challenged strongly in the nineteenth century in the face of clear evidence to the contrary by both Winthrop in America and Blencowe in England. Nevertheless, its substance has survived through to the modern day. See, for instance, Ashley, *John Wildman: Plotter and Postmaster* (1947) p. 11; Robbins, *Two Republican Tracts* (1969) p. 41.
[7] HMC Rep. no. 7 Graham MSS p. 343.

than in it, was to be as international as his own education and perspective had been.

Not only were Sidney's politics not whiggish, he was also, contrary to the mythology, a deeply religious thinker, whose range of expression on the subject ran from the classical piety of the *Discourses* to the turbulent enthusiasm of the *Maxims* and of his final *Apology*. For Sidney, 'political science' or the study of the world of man was second in importance only to 'Theology, or the knowledge of God', and all political struggles took their root from 'the contrariety of principles' between 'God, and the impulse of the Devil, whose devices and designs are against God'.[8] While his political thought drew more extensively on scripture than any other source, Sidney himself showed a particular tendency towards political and personal friendships with quakers, or the friends of quakers, like Vane, Furly, and Penn, men who combined inward spirituality with outward political action to protect it. Indeed Sidney's religious and political action took shape against a pedigree of family religion and involvement in the European struggle for liberty of conscience which stretched back to the huguenot cause in the sixteenth-century French civil wars; a background which helped set the tone for Sidney's (fundamentally, though not simply) religious conception of the issues involved in England's own seventeenth-century civil conflict. After a lifetime of struggle with 'God's people' against persecution of every form, Sidney went to the scaffold not a Roman but a saint, openly modelling himself not upon Brutus or Cato but upon Henry Vane jun., patron of the sects, whose death Sidney said had given him 'a never perishing crown'. There Sidney offered prayers to God, 'glorifying thee for all thy mercies ... that at the last thou hast permitted me to be singled out as a witness of thy truth'.[9]

Eventually the eighteenth-century picture of Sidney the popular whig patriot-hero became harassed by the Dalrymple discoveries; documentary evidence that Sidney had used money during the Exclusion Crisis from the French ambassador; no greater blow could have been struck to the whig world view.[10] This line of evidence, if pursued, might have led scholars irretrievably to the truth that Sidney had been, in his own lifetime, in whig terms, neither popular, nor a whig, nor a patriot. They might have discovered, for instance, that Sidney had not only actually encouraged Charles II's infamous policy of a French alliance, in conjunction with liberty of conscience for all religions including catholics, from Paris as early as mid 1670, but that indeed his views seem to have had some influence on Charles II's own thinking on the subject. In fact, however, far from going on to

---

[8]   Bibliothèque Nationale, Paris, Fr. MS 23254 p. 101; *Maxims* pp. 100–1.
[9]   Memoirs pp. 39–40 in Sidney A., *Works* (1772).
[10] The evidence was first published by Dalrymple, *Memoirs of Great Britain and Ireland* (London 1773) vol. II Appendix, esp. pp. 198, 261–2, 285, 287, 311–13, 317.

examine the real Sidney, the Dalrymple evidence itself was hotly denied by Sidney partisans and scholars for a hundred years, up to and including his last major biographer, Alexander Ewald. As the Sidney myth showed itself too rigid to accommodate new truths, it also came to look increasingly sterile and empty. In the end Ewald's stiff, hollow, plaster cast of a Sidney, dressed in high-Victorian clothes, strutted off the precipice of public notice and into oblivion. It wasn't just that Ewald's wrong-headed and anachronistic Sidney no longer had anything left to offer the revolutionaries of the nineteenth century; it was that it no longer had anything to do with Sidney himself. The Sidney myth, having lost touch with both subject and audience, fell through the gap between the two.[11]

Today, in the aftermath, it is more than a hundred years since the last book was written on Sidney, so that we still await a full account of the real person to put in its place.

Despite this fact, increasing recent attention has been paid to Sidney's historical importance. His political thought in particular is now acknowledged to have been one of the most important English sources for the ideology of the American Revolution; and the most quoted of them all. During the American Civil War his posthumous allegiance remained a matter for hot dispute, the Unionists invoking his authority on behalf of the 'liberty', the Confederacy on behalf of the 'property' for which they fought.[12]

He was almost equally important in eighteenth-century France where he was taken up by Montesquieu, Rousseau, and Condorcet. In the year of the French Revolution, when his name was a 'household word' among French radicals and 'constantly quoted among the heroes of antiquity', a Letter of Congratulation appeared in Paris entitled 'Sidney's Resurrection', offering revolutionary advice in his name from between the parted clouds of French republican heaven. In these years, with familiar irony, his name was invoked in self-justification by both Robespierre on the one hand and a procession of guillotine-bound French aristocrats on the other. In the aftermath of the Revolution Sidney's works were republished in a second French edition in Paris.[13]

---

[11] Ewald A. C., *The Life and Times of Algernon Sidney* (London 1873), see vol. II pp. 131–76. The collapse of the Sidney myth was assisted by the belated acceptance by whig historians like Hallam and Macaulay of Dalrymple's evidence about Sidney's French intrigues. They wrote, as Dalrymple had, of their deep sense of the Patriot's 'betrayal'; betrayal of principles which, they neglected to consider, were their own and not his. Karsten, *Patriot-Heroes* pp. 44, 138.

[12] Robbins C., 'Textbook'; Bailyn B., *The Ideological Origins of the American Revolution* (1971) pp. 34–5, 40, 45, 132; Maier P., *From Resistance to Revolution* (London 1973), ch. II (pp. 27–42); Karsten, *Patriot-Heroes* pp. 62, 70, 72.

[13] Aulard A., *The French Revolution 1789–1804* (London 1910), vol. I p. 111. The *Discourses* were republished in Paris in 1794; B. Museum F.R. 136 (20) 'Lettre de felicitation de Milord Sidney aux Parisiens et a la Nation Francoise, ou resurrection de Milord Sidney' (Paris 1789); Montesquieu and Rousseau both owned Sidney's works by 1734 (see Karsten, *Patriot-*

In eighteenth-century England Sidney's Machiavellian polemic against corruption, and his classical and Grotian ideology of liberty and property became a basic source for a developing political culture; a culture whose literature became 'soaked with the putative relevance of old Roman example ... of Spartan virtue ... of Tacitean imagery'. From the politicians to the 'Sidney Societies', his *Discourses* remained more influential in England, in the first half of the century at least, than Locke's (less classical but equally Grotian) *Two Treatises* (1689).[14] In the Netherlands, too, and elsewhere in Europe, Sidney's name remained revered until well into the nineteenth century, as we are reminded by the great German classicist Bertoldt Georg Niebuhr who celebrated Sidney's birthday in 1815: 'In my eyes it is a consecrated day, especially as I have just been studying his noble life again ... even with such a death the virtue and holiness of his life would not be dearly purchased.'[15] In the first century after its publication Sidney's *Discourses*, a substantial work of 500,000 words, was produced in thirteen editions, in three languages (English, French, and German) and six countries (England, Scotland, France, the Netherlands, Germany, and America).[16] We still await the first book to be written on Sidney's political thought. He is one of England's most influential, and most neglected, political writers. This is especially remarkable given that Sidney was, unlike Locke, Hobbes, Harrington, or any other major seventeenth-century English political theorist, one of the century's more important politicians as well.

The task of reinjecting Sidney into the modern historical picture was begun with articles by Robbins (1945), and Haydon (1961), and has culminated in those of Worden (1981 and 1984).[17] Sidney is gaining, too, increasing mentions in other works. The amount of new manuscript material which exists to be taken into account in a full-scale study remains, however, substantial. The amount of available material written by Sidney himself alone

Heroes pp. 215–16); Rousseau and Condorcet both spoke of him with great admiration. For Sidney and Montesquieu see Shackleton R., 'Montesquieu and Machiavelli; a reappraisal' in *Comparative Literature Studies I* (1964) pp. 8–10; For Condorcet see Russell B., *History of Western Philosophy* (1946) p. 749; For Rousseau see *The Social Contract and Discourses* trans. and ed. Cole G. D. H. (1973) pp. 93, 120; and Rousseau, *Political Writings* ed. Vaughan C. E. (Oxford 1962) I p. 240, II pp. 205–6; For memories of Sidney among both republicans and aristocrats see Parker H. T., *The Cult of Antiquity and The French Revolutionaries* (Chicago 1937) pp. 172–3, 175–7.

[14] Kenyon, *Revolution* pp. 51–3; Goldie M., review of Gunn J. A. W., *Beyond Liberty and Property* in *Economic History Review* vol. C no. 394 Jan. 1985 pp. 134–6; Robbins C., *Commonwealthsman* pp. 46–7; Ashcraft R. and Pocock J. G. A., *John Locke* (Los Angeles 1980) p. 35.

[15] Gooch G. P., *Germany and the French Revolution* (London 1920) p. 62 (cf. p. 117).

[16] Robbins, 'Textbook', p. 281; cf. Robbins, *Two Republican Tracts* (1969) pp. 56–8.

[17] Robbins, *Two Republican Tracts*; Haydon B., 'Algernon Sidney 1623–83' in *Archaeologia Cantiana* vol. LXXVI (1961) pp. 110–33; Worden, 'Classical republicanism and the puritan revolution' in Worden ed., *History and Imagination* (1981); Worden, 'The commonwealth kidney of Algernon Sidney' in *Journal of British Studies* 24 (1985).

has at least doubled since the time of the last biography; and he must now be at the centre of one of the most amply and graphically recorded political lives, and experiences of political revolution, triumph, and defeat, that the seventeenth century has to offer.

Much of the new material will be used here, or used here comprehensively, for the first time; and there are far too many separate items to be listed. The importance of some particular finds, however, stands out, and they deserve mention here.

The first is the discovery recently, by Blair Worden, of the manuscript of a second major political treatise by Sidney: the *Court Maxims*.[18] This has yet, beyond Worden's own important but necessarily brief comments,[19] to be introduced to modern scholars. It was written in Holland in 1665, and is the only political tract known to have survived from the Swiss/Dutch community of the seventeenth-century Restoration English exiles. It uses, against the religious persecutions under Charles II, the ideas of that community's predecessors, the sixteenth-century Marian exiles, and of their continental contemporaries the huguenot monarchomachs in France. It also draws not only on English republican ideas from the period 1649–60, but on the ideology of Sidney's hosts, the republican Dutch. This is of general interest for our understanding of the influence of Dutch concepts of 'liberty' (religious, economic, and political) on late seventeenth-century English political thought. In general the *Maxims*, since its tone is less restrained and it was not, like the *Discourses*, written to answer the work of someone else, is a more complete exposure of the assumptions behind, and the tensions within, Sidney's thought as a whole.

A number of new Sidney letters, too, have been recently located, again almost doubling the number previously known. In addition to the well-known letters by Sidney written in the years 1659–61, 1663, and 1677–9, we now have many new letters covering the years 1659–60, 1677, 1679–81, and 1683 – in the latter case ten letters written in prison in the months before he died. With Dr Worden's discovery of the true manuscript of part of Ludlow's memoirs, we now also have Ludlow's transcriptions of some marvellous Sidney diatribes from the years 1664–5.

Among the Sidney family papers in Maidstone there has been much material falsely attributed to Sidney, and some important new discoveries actually relating to him. These include a manuscript Chancery plea written in Algernon's hand (1681) which has led in turn to a whole new area of Sidney manuscript evidence. Among Chancery papers at the Public Record Office

---

[18] Algernon Sidney, 'Court maxims refuted and refelled', MS now in Warwickshire Record Office.

[19] Cf. Worden, 'Classical republicanism'; and ed. Edmund Ludlow's *A Voyce From the Watchtower* (1979), Introduction.

there are preserved the full records of six separate Chancery cases initiated by Sidney, with a mass of related legal documentation in Maidstone and the British Museum, including three new manuscripts written in Sidney's hand, and a great body of new biographical information relating to every period of his life. As a whole the legal manuscripts provide a picture of a new dimension of Sidney's life and political thought: his private, professional, legal, and family life and relationships: the personal struggle for liberty which underlay the political.[20]

Newly located documents, too, from the Archives Nationales, the Bibliothèque Nationale and Ministère des Affaires Etrangères in Paris, and a number of other archives in England, all contribute to the new picture of Sidney's political activities, at home and abroad, which has emerged. Included among this material are records of Sidney's conversation in exile with two French contacts (Turenne in 1670, and Lantin in 1677) giving details of Sidney's schemes to regain English government favour from Paris in 1670; his memoirs of the days of the English Republic; and even the names of his favourite political theorists. Other Sidney material not previously used by biographers includes another tract, *The Character of Henry Vane jnr*, and new information about his education in France, time in Ireland, his governorship of Dover, his activities under the Protectorate, his embassy to Scandinavia, and every aspect of his life after the Restoration. All in all well over 50 per cent of the source material used for this book was not known to his last major biographer, Ewald.

I.I THE MYTH REVISITED

Distorted though the Sidney myth has been historiographically, it did nevertheless contain an important core of truth about the man, and it derived in part from a significant, and paradoxical, triumph of the manner of his death over the manner of his life.

Sidney was indeed a dominating and indomitable personality. He was also, like his granduncle Sir Philip, a gifted writer, widely admired by Keats, Shelley, Byron, and Coleridge among others.[21] In addition he was equipped, like his father and other family members before him, with a formidable contemporary humanist education, which left him with a wide range of historical and political knowledge. This left its mark in his political thought,

---

[20] The three Sidney legal manuscripts are: Kent R.O. (Maidstone) De Lisle MSS U1475 L5; U1475 E28/5; and Brit. Museum Eg. 1049.

[21] This opinion of Sidney's writing style has survived; see Sutherland James, *English Literature of The Late Seventeenth Century* (Oxford 1969) p. 360. 'Read Algernon Sidney!' said Coleridge, 'his style reminds you as little of books as of blackguards. What a gentleman he was!' See also E. L. Criggs ed., *The Collected Letters of Samuel Taylor Coleridge* (1959) vol. III p. 137; J. A. Wittreich jun., *The Romantics on Milton* (1970) pp. 552–3.

but was frustrated in practice by his chronic inability to co-operate with or defer to the judgement of others. It is not that Sidney didn't suffer fools gladly; he would not suffer them at all. Both sides of this combination were well illustrated by Burnet, who said that: '[on the one hand] he had studied the history of government in all its branches beyond any man I ever knew' [and on the other, that he was] 'a man of most extraordinary courage ... even to obstinacy ... but of a rough and boisterous temper, that could not bear contradiction, but would give foul language upon it'. All contemporaries agreed about Sidney's dictatorial temper; all agreed, too, concerning the 'greate courage, greate sense, greate parts' that gave it force.[22]

A consequence of these characteristics, and the continual personal tension they generated, was that Sidney did indeed lead a life so conflict-strewn, dramatic, and passionate that it lent itself naturally to some sort of historical myth-making, even if the precise political lines required some amendment. Moreover, the myth grew significantly from the real and self-conscious element of theatre in Sidney's own behaviour: as he once announced his return to political activity to a friend: 'I am once more comme upon the stage.'[23] Sidney's need to justify everything he did to an audience of self, friends, family, and the world, derived from his sharp sense of his place in history; of the way in which he was following his ancestors; and of the way in which he could serve as an example to those who followed him. Sidney lived his whole life under a preoccupation with 'the reputation of the most excellent men in their several ages'.[24]

It was thus no accident that when the time came to climb onto the scaffold, at the end of a long and turbulent career, Sidney was able to muster the consummate piece of political theatre which made his martyrdom and became the starting point for the mythology to come. In the newly available Hampden letters, written from prison during the last six months of his life, we can see clearly how carefully Sidney prepared his mind (along with his legal defence, and two public vindications of his life and conduct) for the ordeal ahead. Consequently there was a genuine nobility and dignity about the manner of his death; the event and the weeks leading up to it were marked, most strikingly, by a saintly calm and complete absence of the histrionics, loss of self-control, and general straining at the leash of fortune which had marked his whole life. As Burnet observed: 'the change that was now in his temper amazed all that went to him'. The power of the Sidney myth derives in part from this paradox; that Sidney used a time of preparation for the manner of his death, to resign himself from the frustrations of a mutable world, to the

---

[22] Burnet G., *History of My Own Time* (1823) vol. II p. 341; John Evelyn, *Diary* ed. de Beer E. S. (1955) *vol.* IV p. 353.
[23] Blencowe, *Sidney Papers* (1825) p. 260.
[24] *Discourses* p. 204 in *Works* (1772).

will of an immutable God, and so to triumph over the defects of his own life; defects that had made it, in his own terms, a chronicle of achievements lost, chances bungled, and a friendless trip to the political grave.[25]

By thus achieving martyrdom, Sidney also achieved a personal release and vindication, and manufactured in the process a public persona which has until recently quite obscured the life and personality which preceded it. It is time now to recover the full picture. In doing so we will find that none of the adjustments necessary to bring the one-time clockwork Sidney hero back from the eighteenth and nineteenth centuries to the seventeenth, and to replace his two dimensions with the complexities, frailties, and contradictions of three, will lessen the interest of the real person, with his dim view of the passion and unpredictability of the world fixed in his own acute self-knowledge, with his self-conscious need for attention and his love of the dramatic gesture, and with his extraordinary capacity for the crystallisation of general political values around himself and his personal concerns. This book will begin the history of Sidney's struggle to win, and thereafter—having lost — to regain, a 'liberty' which was personal before it became political, and which motivated every stage of his life. From the conflict-strewn career which resulted, lived across half a dozen countries, came a powerful and relativistic system of political thought focused on the facts of variability and change; and a dynamic revolution ideology which was to make its mark on three cultures in the century of revolutions that followed.

[25] Burnet, *History of My Own Time* (1823) p. 398; Sidney's letters to Hampden are in the East Sussex Record Office at Lewes, Glynde Place papers no. 794. Sidney had appealed to the fact of his known unpopularity as a line of defence at his trial: 'he sayed he was no popular man and consequently unfit to be concerned in such an Affaire, where it was fit the people concerned should be Darlings of the Mobile', Bodleian Ash. F.6.30; One of Sidney's own relations exclaimed shortly before his arrest that it was 'a wonder nobody shoots him', Blencowe ed., *Diary of the Times of Charles II* (1843) v I p. 239.

Part One

FAMILY AND IDEAS

2

Political and religious thought

The unfortunate Sidney thought like me, but he also acted. It is for his actions, and not his book, that he had the honour of shedding his blood.

Rousseau

And as our author [Filmer] ... thinks learning makes men seditious, Aristotle also acknowledges, that those who have understanding and courage ... will never endure the government of one, or a few that do not excel them in virtue.

Sidney[1]

2.1 PREFACE

Both of the quotes above illustrate simple characteristics of Sidney's thought, a grasp of which should precede any discussion in terms of general intellectual categories. The first is that all Sidney's political writings were written in the heat of the political moment employing any material which came to hand in prosecution of a specific practical design. We should consequently face the essential indignity of the academic attempting to fit the broad conventions and themes of intellectual history to the simple flight of a hand grenade. Sidney's writings were not only highly eclectic, in style as well as content, they are also the work of someone with a severely moral and religious aristocratic background thrown first into revolutionary politics and then into penniless, hunted, and revengeful exile. The result is not always plain sailing, as the clear tension between conventional humanist and Christian morality and Machiavellian resistance politics in the *Court Maxims* shows. Yet, of course, this is precisely the interest and force of Sidney's writing; it was his eventual mature combination of a high moral tone with the most ruthless and militaristic Machiavellianism of the century that made him so powerful.

The second point is that Sidney's thought was, and was expressed as being, fundamentally personal. For all its philosophical and historical justification, it remained at one level a simple expression of Sidney's own personality: of someone who combined a high opinion of his own abilities (in political terms,

[1] Rousseau J. J., *Political Writings* (Oxford 1962) ed. C. E. Vaughan, vol. I p. 240, vol. II pp. 205–6; Sidney, *Discourses* pp. 109ff; cf. Aristotle, *Politics* bk 4 ch. 10.

13

virtue) with a temperamental and aristocratic refusal to be ruled. Sidney's reply to Filmer is an attack on the political system of inheritance, and its substitution with a politics of virtue – a fundamental tenet of Sidney's thought which has, as we will see, its origins deep in his own personal and family life before the political experience which helped to give it political expression. In my citation of particular theorists of whose ideas Sidney may have made use therefore, I do not, despite the inevitable crudeness of the technique, wish to lend encouragement to the fiction that political ideas are autonomous microbes which leap through history from decade to decade and continent to continent as one theorist catches them from another. Sidney did not 'learn' his political ideas in a vacuum from works of political theory: he used theorists with whom his life brought him into contact to arm himself with arguments to support deeper emanations from his personality and situation which were often much simpler, more arbitrary, and less reasoning.

2.2 CLASSICAL REPUBLICANISM, NATURAL-LAW THEORY, STOICISM, PLATONISM

Three historians (Fink, Robbins, and Worden) have dealt importantly with Sidney's political thought, in the process of describing wider movements of which he is held to have been a part. Fink and Worden in particular have associated him with 'classical republicanism', a theme which has been further explored by Raab's work on Machiavelli in England and Pocock's work on Harrington. In the process of this discussion it has become clear that the development of classical republican ideas has a precise political context beginning with the need to legitimate the foundation of a republic in England in 1649 (Milton, Neville, Nedham, Sidney), and continuing through republican opposition to the Protectorate (Harrington, Neville, Nedham, Sidney) to the brief revival of the republic in 1659.[2] In Worden's words the foundation of the Rump 'is often seen as the first of the great national revolutions of the western world; but in terms of ideological precision it fell far short of its successors'. This is in part because, in being forced to arrive at some post-event ideological stance, amid dark times, on the edge of an axe, the English republicans did some of the work of their successors, as Sidney's influence amid the later American and French revolutions shows.

[2] Although Sidney and Neville did not write until after the Restoration, it is clear that it is in this earlier period that their classical republican ideas had their genesis. See Fink Zera, *The Classical Republicans* (1945); Raab Felix, *The English Face of Machiavelli* (1964); Pocock J.G.A., 'The onely politician' in *Historical Studies: Australia and New Zealand* (1965–7) vol. XII pp. 265–96; *The Machiavellian Moment* (1975); Pocock ed., *The Political Works of James Harrington* (1977), Introduction; Worden A.B., 'Classical republicanism and the Puritan revolution' in Worden ed., *History and Imagination* (1981); and Davis J.C., 'Pocock's Harrington; grace, nature and art in the classical republicanism of James Harrington' in *The Historical Journal* 24 no. 3 pp. 683–97.

Classical republicanism describes a paradigm of thought which drew principally on classical Greek and Roman, and Italian Renaissance sources, combining Aristotelian political forms with the Polybian idea of balance between them, and the republicanism of Machiavelli's *Discourses*. Sidney stated his particular regard for 'Aristotle ... Plato, Plutarch, Thucydides, Xenophon, Polybius, and all the ancient Grecians, Italians, and others who asserted the natural freedom of mankind'.[3] Attached to the tradition were a selection of particular republics, each a model for different values: Israel (divine institution); Sparta (discipline and longevity); Rome (vigour and conquest); Venice (stability and longevity). Sidney was to reminisce to Lantin in Paris: 'the design of the English [republicans] had been, to make a Republic on the model of that of the Hebrews, before they had their Kings, and on that of Sparta, of Rome, and of Venise, taking from each what was best, to make a perfect composition.' This is the clearest association of classical republican theory with English republican practice that we have on record.[4]

Classical republicanism is, however, neither a sufficient nor a very precise category for describing Sidney's thought as a whole. There were within the tradition a wide variation of emphases in the use of sources and models and in the type of theory which emerged. Sidney and Milton laid particular emphasis upon Livy and Tacitus for their interest in Rome; Sidney and Nedham added to this an undiluted Roman Machiavellianism but Milton remained chary of Machiavelli; Neville and Harrington used Machiavelli as centrally as Sidney but used him in a completely different way, and linked him to a constitution-alist fascination with Venice which both Nedham and Sidney repudiated (as Machiavelli himself had). Fink's work has tended to distort the disparate shape of the whole tradition around his particular interest, the cult of Venice, and Pocock again around the distinctly idiosyncratic figure of Harrington, whose materialism situates him intellectually closer to Hobbes than to the moral humanists Sidney and Milton. They in turn share the spirit of both their politics and religion rather with another (not classical, but religious) republican, Henry Vane. In this, as in his use of Machiavelli, Sidney is much closer to the mainstream of the classical republican tradition, an essentially moral tradition, than Harrington, the price of whose originality it will be suggested is to call into question his status as England's 'premier civic humanist' altogether.[5]

[3] *Discourses* p. 11.
[4] Bibliothèque Nationale, Paris, Fr. MS 23254 'Lantiniana', fols. 99–101.
[5] This description of Harrington is Pocock's: Pocock ed., *Harrington* p. 15; For Harrington and Hobbes see Zagorin, *A History of Political Thought in the English Revolution* (1964) p. 135; and Raab, *Machiavelli* pp. 180–210. Machiavelli is, for all the fame of his amorality or immorality, a supremely moral theorist. He sought not to remove morality from politics but to save its place by redefining it. Sidney used him for his essentially moral concepts of virtue and corruption, redefined for use in a dangerous and disintegrating political world. Harrington

Those of the English theorists (like Harrington) who sought, above all, stability in politics, combined a fascination with the constitutional orders of Venice, with an emphasis on the Polybian notion of 'balance' within the classical three-part constitutional model by which change could be resisted. Harrington was to take this central concept of balance and change its meaning; to make it a balance between the constitutional 'superstructure' as a whole and the base of ownership in land. Sidney, on the other hand, not only rejected Venice but downgraded Polybius; his point about all the best governments being not one only of the classical types (monarchy, aristocracy, democracy) but a combination of all three, was not to say that the three had to be exactly balanced, to prevent change, but to make the very different relativist point against Filmer that as political conditions varied all over the world, to speak of only one legitimate form of government was ludicrous, and that the various ways of combining the three forms made an 'infinite variety' of constitutions possible. For Sidney there 'never was a good government ... that did not consist of the three simple species' because 'the variety of forms between mere democracy and absolute monarchy is almost infinite'. Accordingly he lambasted in Filmer the 'stupidity and ignorance [of] ... they who neither understand the several species of government, nor the various tempers of nations'.[6]

Caroline Robbins divided the seventeenth century 'commonwealthsmen' into Puritan (Vane and Milton) and others, less religious (Sidney, Neville, and Harrington). In fact if any such division is to be made Sidney belongs on the other side of it, with Milton and Vane. Sidney's political association with Vane will be described at length; his writing is more like Milton's than any other theorist; and both Milton and Sidney wrote formal literary pieces in praise of Vane as the patron of their religious/political cause.[7] Sidney's writings are not only as concerned with religion as Milton's but, since the discovery of the Vanist *Court Maxims*, arguably more so. The political language and tradition which unites Sidney, Milton, and Vane is natural-law theory.

This was the more religiously orientated language of independency in the civil war (the law of nature was the general law of God). Before then it had

---

believed that by creating perfect institutional orders he had transcended the need for essential moral qualities in politics altogether. His citizens, provided they went through the mechanical exercise of voting, were not even required to understand what they were doing: 'it is not possible for the people, if they can but draw the balls, though they understand nothing at all of the ballot, to be out'; Pocock ed., *Harrington* p. 222. Harrington's view of his citizens and their role is made clear by his language: 'the materials [*sic*] of a commonwealth are the people' (p. 212); 'the being of a commonwealth consisteth in the methodical collection of the people' (p. 214). This is not a very humanist, let alone civic humanist, way of speaking.
[6] *Discourses* pp. 107, 138–9.
[7] Robbins, *Commonwealthsman* pp. 4–5; Milton's sonnet and Sidney's 'Character' will be discussed in their place.

been the language of the counter-Reformation catholicism of theorists like Suarez and Bellarmine, the Calvinist resistance theory of huguenots like du Plessis Mornay, Hotman and Beza, and others like Buchanan and (just to round off the picture) the tolerant Arminianism of Hugo Grotius.[8] Like Milton, Sidney used its ideas and most of these sources (the protestants' openly; the catholics' not so) as the basis for much of his theory.

From the range of Sidney's sources as a whole, it is possible to select six writers of outstanding importance. They are two Greek philosophers, Plato and Aristotle; two Roman historians, Livy and Tacitus; and two relative moderns, Machiavelli and Grotius. These could be divided again, according to the previous discussion: behind Sidney's classical republicanism lie Aristotle, Livy, and Machiavelli; behind his Christian natural-law theory Plato, Aristotle, and Grotius. However, the distinction is quite artificial and I wish to remove it, by going behind it, for there is at the heart of Sidney's thought an intellectual framework which unites it and all the sources he uses as a whole.

Sidney's thought is characterised in general by a combination of extreme relativism and scepticism about the variety and mutability of particular worldly things, with an emphasis on a small core of immutable moral values standing outside this changeability, represented by the law of nature, discernible by reason, and anchored finally in the only perfect and unchanging being: God. This dualism is common to the whole Platonist/Christian/natural-law tradition; in Sidney's case the scepticism about particularity which it incorporates leads to what is most interesting about his theory: the *Discourses*'s politics of change. Indeed Sidney's sense of the variety, changeability, and imperfection of the world (variety and change he says *are* imperfection, and 'perfection is in God only, not in the things he has created') is the key to his theory. His favourite theologian, the huguenot sceptic Jean Daillé, asked 'what a man should do amidst these [resulting] diversities of Judgement?'[9] Sidney replied: 'accept them, they are part of the nature of God's creation; harmonise this variety with liberty so that each man may seek the Truth, centred in God, in his own way.' In religion as (with Filmer) in politics, Sidney's lifelong enemy was the imposition of an 'ignorant uniformity'[10] of one (necessarily imperfect) external humane particular, denying the variety of

---

[8] All republicans (including classical republicans) and indeed most other radicals in the mid seventeenth century used natural-law theory to some degree. See Sommerville M. R., 'Independent thought 1603–49' Cambridge Ph.D. thesis 1982; Erskine-Hill H. and Storey G., *Revolutionary Prose of the English Civil War* (1983) intro. pp. 26–7; Tuck Richard, *Natural Rights Theories* (1979); Skinner Quentin, *The Foundations of Modern Political Thought* (1978) vol. II (esp. pp. 148–347); Sommerville J., 'From Suarez to Filmer: a reappraisal' in *Historical Journal* 25 (1982), and *Politics and Ideology in England 1603–1640* (1986); Franklin J. H., *Constitutionalism and Resistance* (1969).
[9] Daillé J., *A Treatise Concerning the Right Use of the Fathers* (1651) p. 28.
[10] *Maxims* p. 84.

judgements among men and nations the liberty to express themselves, and to choose their own path.

For this, and his outlook in general Sidney was clearly indebted to two intellectual traditions: neo-Stoicism and Platonism. Both combined a sharp sense of the mutability and variety of particular (for instance, political) affairs with the search for a higher normative standard by which to transcend and evaluate this state. Both looked for this goal to 'reason' (in Platonism alongside the 'spirit'). Indeed the dualism of both Stoicism and Christianity have their origins in Platonism, and the two classical philosophies themselves could combine in someone like the Roman Stoic hero Cato, who spent the evening before his suicide reading Plato's *Phaedo*.[11]

Sidney's family were personally linked to neo-Stoicism through the friendship of the Dutchman Justus Lipsius, the most important early modern neo-Stoic, with Sidney's grandfather the first Earl of Leicester.[12] Lipsian philosophy, influenced by the upheavals of the French wars of religion and the Dutch war of independence, emphasised the prime concept of constancy in a world where 'all things human are subject to change and decay'. Unreliability, inconstancy, 'the mother of all ills', was to be countered by the exercise of reason, extolled by Lipsius's Stoic model Seneca as 'a part of the divine spirit implanted in man'. 'To obey her is to rule, to submit to her is to be lord of all earthly things.'[13] The scepticism which underlay Stoicism, concerning the unsteadiness and changeability of the world (illustrated by the use made of Lipsius by Montaigne and Charron), led Lipsius to take a close interest in both Tacitus and Machiavelli, writers who had described conditions of moral and political anarchy, and suggested solutions accordingly. Lipsius became Europe's foremost Tacitean scholar, and took a particular interest in Machiavelli's emphasis on military discipline and strength. These are all preoccupations and sources which we will see reappear in an equally central role in Algernon's thought. It was from this period of the French and Dutch civil wars, and from this synthesis, building upon the works of Tacitus and of Machiavelli in particular, that there emerged the sceptical language of 'interest' and reason of state, a tradition to which Sidney himself contributed in Holland nearly a century later with his *Court Maxims*. This was written after England's own civil war, and drew upon all the tradition's Dutch, French, and English branches.[14]

[11] Robinson F. G., *The Shape of Things Known* (Cam., Mass. 1922) p. 25; Bevan E., *Stoics and Sceptics* (Oxford 1913) p. 94.

[12] Worden, 'Republicanism' p. 183; HMC De Lisle p. 371.

[13] Oestreich G., *Neostoicism and the Early Modern State* (Cambridge 1982) pp. 19, 22–3.

[14] Church, *Richelieu and Reason of State* (1972) p. 75; Skinner Q., *The Foundations of Modern Political Thought* (1978) II pp. 253–4; Keohane, *Philosophy and the State in France* (1980) pp. 131–3 (cf. pp. 151–6); Burke P., 'Tacitism' in T. A. Dorey ed., *Tacitus* (London 1969) pp. 162–5; Trevor-Roper, *Princes and Artists* (1976) pp. 131–2.

Even more important for Sidney's theory, and his use of natural-law theory in particular, was a second and closer family connection: his father's friendship with a second Dutch theorist, Hugo Grotius (himself a friend of Lipsius) whom he met while a diplomat in Paris from 1635 to 1641.[15] Later Sidney himself was to name as the most important of all books of political theory Grotius's *De Jure Belli ac Pacis* (1625).[16]

Grotius's object in that work, written, again, against a chaotic background of military conflict (in this case international – the Thirty Years War), was to define beyond the limited confines of 'positive law', 'the laws of particular states', which 'undergo change and are different in different places', a universal law of 'perpetual validity and suited to all times'. This would be applicable both inside and outside society, and serve to govern relations between men both inside and outside particular states, and between states in peace and in war. Grotius accepted, like Sidney, the relativist view that 'laws ... vary according to customs, and among the same peoples often undergo... change as times change', but sought a way beyond the completely sceptical conclusion 'that there is [therefore] no law of nature ... or [universal standard of] justice ... [but] all creatures are impelled by nature towards [self interest]'. Grotius did so by defining a law of nature, principally from Stoic sources (Chrysippus, Seneca, Cicero, and Tacitus especially), and also from some Platonic sources (Plato, Xenophon, Plutarch, Tertullian). By thus, as Grotius put it, 'following Stoic writings learnedly', he became, as Richard Tuck has put it, 'the first modern writer to see that moral scepticism could be countered by stoicism'.[17]

In the general shape of this enterprise Grotius's obvious (and acknowledged) predecessor was his fellow jurist Bodin. Bodin's response to his own (this time French religious) wars had been to attempt, from similar relativist premises, by a similar comparative and historical method, and in similar anecdotal humanist style, to arrive at his own minimalist universal core. Sidney himself not only accepted – though like Grotius he reapplied – the resulting Bodinian concept of indivisible sovereignty; his (and later Montesquieu's) general combination of climatic/geographic/historical relativism with a natural-law core was very much in the early modern humanist style of which Bodin and then Grotius became exemplars. As we will see in *Algernon Sidney and the Restoration Crisis*, Sidney's reply to Filmer was in both content and structure a far more orthodox work of Bodinian theory than Filmer's *Patriarcha* itself.[18]

[15] For Lipsius and Grotius see Somersen L. van, *Umpire to the Nations* (1965) pp. 27–8, 59.
[16] 'Lantiniana', Bib. Nat. Fr. MS 23254 fol. 100.
[17] Grotius, *De Jure Belli ac Pacis Libri Tres* (Oxford 1925) trans. Kelsey F. W., bk I pp. 10, 19, 21, 51; this statement comes from one of Richard Tuck's lectures, not one of his publications.
[18] Bodin, *The Six Bookes of a Commonweale* (1606) ed. McRae K. D. (Cam., Mass. 1962) pp. 4–5: 'we have alwaies had varieties of laws, customs, and decrees, according to the divers

The extent to which Sidney imported into his own work Grotius's political view in particular would be difficult to overstate. Sidney's works are based on the same concepts of particular 'municipal' law and the general law of nature, of the origins of particular societies in consent and of the factors governing relations between them. Most importantly Sidney reapplied the key Grotian concept of just war, from its intended principal application to the troubled state of contemporary relations *between* states, to the question of relations within them, between a king and his subjects, the issue in the troubles with which Sidney himself became involved, the English Civil War. For Grotius war was just only where peaceful settlement of a matter of right was impossible; that is, as the only means of securing justice against those whose position or power placed them outside the jurisdiction of particular codes of positive law (as was the case in international disputes between nations). '[Just] war is directed against those who cannot be held in check by judicial processes.' Sidney, responding to the perceived growth of absolutism in his own country, applied this concept to the case of a monarch who attempted to put his will above the jurisdiction of the positive law of his own country. By doing so he made his transgressions the legitimate target of the just war of his own people, the only way they had of bringing him to justice. Without such a willingness to rebel on the part of the people, explained Sidney, justice could not be protected 'nor innocency maintained'. As Grotius had quoted from Tacitus: 'it is in the love of innocent men that just wars have their origin', and again later: 'the duty of the Christian soldier', is to fight 'on behalf of justice ... on behalf of the safety of the innocent'. It was to these concepts that Sidney returned again and again in the *Court Maxims* and the *Discourses*, those calls to arms by the Christian soldier, on behalf of the persecuted and oppressed under Charles II.[19]

Sidney's second great accompaniment to his scepticism, once again strongly linked to him through his family, and this time the key to his religion as well as his politics, was Platonism. Plato again had written with a similar object to Grotius, to chart a way beyond scepticism, in this case that of the Athenian sophists, whose teachings 'tended to produce relativism and scepticism about questions of value'. Once again, the background to this scepticism was one of political/military crisis; in this case that of Athens, defeated in the Peloponnesian war. In this respect it is no coincidence that Hobbes, for all his later anti-humanism, admired Plato of all classical philosophers, and had

humors and passions of men ... beholdeth the chaunges and chances of the world, the unstaidiness of mens maners, their divers ages, and conditions'. (And see esp. bks IV–V in general.) For Grotius's acknowledgement of Bodin see Julian Franklin, *Jean Bodin and the Rise of Absolutist Theory* (Cambridge 1973) p. 108.

[19] Grotius, *De Jure Belli* pp. 18, 55–6, 75, 90.

himself translated Thucydides's *The Peloponnesian War*.[20] Plato countered with his metaphysics of 'forms' or 'ideas', general moral truths (qualities like beauty and virtues like justice) standing outside the fluctuating world of particularity, and culminating in the ultimate ruling form of 'the Good' (converted, in Platonic Christianity, to 'God'). Thus Plato remained (like Sidney, and like Lipsius and Grotius) 'at once idealist and sceptic'; an idealist about the world of the forms, the only objects of true knowledge, characterised by their unity and permanence (they are 'the essence of the invariable');[21] sceptic about the physical world of particulars, a sea of variety and change in which there was no stability, indeed no reality beyond the imperfect and fleeting likeness of forms which particulars reflected. For Plato, amid the indiscipline and moral chaos of defeated Athens, as for Sidney and Hobbes after the civil war in England, political life at its worst was a chaos in which every man strove for self, in ignorance of the unifying principles which dwelt behind the variety of the visible world.

Plato's forms were to be perceived only by the lonely exercise of the intellect, and then only by a few. 'Philosophers only are able to grasp the eternal and unchangeable and those who wander in the region of the many and variable, are not philosophers.'[22] Like Sidney, Plato was an aristocrat who produced a philosophic justification for the aristocratic prejudices he inherited, not in favour of birth but in favour of wisdom and virtue. This was one reason for the appeal of Platonism to the Puritan/aristocratic circle we will examine shortly. Applied politically Platonism always consequently boiled down to the belief that knowledge, and liberty (the self-rule that knowledge made possible) were the property of those capable of achieving them, and not to be jeopardised by the ignorance and incapacity of those who were not. Those incapable of liberty, that is of ruling themselves, would have to be ruled by those capable of it. The thought of all the mid-seventeenth-century radicals strongly influenced by Platonism, prominently among them Milton, Sidney, Nedham, Stubbe, and Vane, always, despite the populism of their ideas in theory, pulled back to this position when the disappointing political behaviour of the liberated people pushed them to it in practice.

For the Christian Platonist the ultimate goal of the journey through the hierarchy of the forms in search of truth was, of course, to arrive as close as possible to their source, God. As Sidney said in the *Maxims*:

[20] Watkins J. W. N., *Hobbes' System of Ideas* (London 1965) p. 80; Annas J., *Plato's Republic* (Oxford 1981) p. 8. The sophist's spokesman in Plato's *Republic* is Thrasymachus, who puts forward in Book One the same sceptical politics of self-interest as that repudiated (above) by Grotius. Sidney's Platonist *Court Maxims* in its turn seeks to overturn (in favour of the 'public interest') exactly the same sort of subjective, private interest, political principle.
[21] Plato, *Republic* IX p. 647 in Buchanan ed., *The Portable Plato* (1984); Morrall J. B., *Aristotle* (London 1977) p. 111.
[22] Plato, *Republic* VI p. 504.

It is from God not the prince or hangman that we must learn religion. His spiritt discovers truth unto us by the wings of love and faith ... both grounded on the knowledge of his being good and good to us [Sidney's God is Plato's 'Good'] wee rise unto that spiritual height as makes all worldly things appear dung and dross unto us.[23]

Plato's ideas, having been strongly influential in the conception of early Christianity, enjoyed an important renaissance within some circles of English Puritanism, in tune with the desire to rediscover the spiritual purity of the early church. Prominent among them was that of Sidney's Elizabethan great-uncle Sir Philip Sidney. It was, said Sir Philip, 'Plato ... whom I must confess of all philosophers I have ever esteemed most worthie of reverence.' Like Algernon, Sir Philip supplemented his heavy use of Plato with that of Greek Platonists in general, particularly Plutarch and Xenephon. As Sir Philip borrowed, in both his *Apology* and *Astrophel and Stella*, from Plato's *Phaedrus* to describe love of beauty, so, as we will see, Algernon returned to the same Platonic theme in his own *Of Love*.[24] Like Algernon, too (and his father the 2nd Earl, whom Clarendon described as 'much addicted to the mathematics'), Sir Philip showed particular interest in the mathematical side of Platonism,[25] praising 'farre set Maximes of Philosophie, which especially if they were Platonike, they must have learned Geometrie, before they could well have conceived'.[26]

For this Sidney was largely indebted to his mathematics teacher John Dee, translator of Euclid's *Elements* (1570), whose systems, profoundly influenced by neo-Platonism,[27] he 'pursued with some enthusiasm'. This Platonic and Euclidean mathematical tradition was passed on strongly through the family, and Algernon made repeated use of Platonic mathematical imagery and Euclidean examples in all his writing. Finally Sir Philip linked the mathematics of Dee with the logical system of Ramus, again based

[23] Barker E., *The Political Thought of Plato and Aristotle* (1959) p. 61; *Court Maxims* p. 84.

[24] Sidney Sir Philip, *Defence of Poesie* in Feiullerat ed., *Works* III p. 37; Young R. B., 'English Petrarke: a study of Sidney's Astrophel and Stella' in *Three Studies in the Renaissance: Sidney, Jonson, Milton* (1958) (see sonnet 5) p. 36; Rowe K. T., 'Romantic love and parental authority in Sidney's Arcadia' in *Contributions in Modern Philology* no. 4 April 1947 (Michigan) p. 43.

[25] Plato was particularly interested in mathematics and geometry as providing an intermediate level of truth between the variety of particulars and the unity of the higher forms. In this he adopted a great deal of the thought of Pythagoras, and came, like him, to see order amid the particular variety of the world in terms of mathematically ordered harmonies. We will see the influence of these themes in Algernon's thought, particularly the *Court Maxims*. See, for instance, Plato, *Republic* VII (e.g. p. 569); *Court Maxims* pp. 83–4.

[26] *Defence* in *Works* III p. 21.

[27] Dee divided the world into the three Platonic categories: the eternal indivisible 'general Formes', accessible to mind alone; the material divisible corruptible objects of sense perception; and between and linking the two 'Thynges mathematicall', 'perfect geometrical images' linked to the forms, which Dee perceived as 'first mathematical causes linked to the plan of a numerically minded God'. Robinson, *The Shape of Things Known* pp. 15–35, 77–8.

on a Platonic conception of the relationship between general and particular, and seeking a way to bridge 'the chasm that divides the mutable from the unchanging, the temporal from the eternal'. He became a devotee of the Ramian method of subdivision and categorisation, recommending it in a letter to his brother Robert (Algernon's grandfather) in 1580 as the way to organise his notes on his reading: 'so as in a table be it wittie word of which Tacitus is full, sentences, of which Livy, or similitudes wherof Plutarch'. As the Sidney family commonplace books will demonstrate, this method, as well as these sources, found their way into Algernon's lifetime intact.[28]

Sir Philip's interest in Ramus, and as with Algernon his Platonism generally, was vitally connected to his religion. Ramus was a huguenot, and it was while Sir Philip was staying in Paris with his closest huguenot friend Languet that there took place the infamous Massacre of St Bartholemew's Eve (1572). Sidney saved himself by taking shelter in the English embassy but Ramus was among the thousands who died. Prominent among Sidney's close subsequent links with the huguenot resistance in France was Philippe du Plessis Mornay, whose name will recur in future chapters. Sir Philip became godfather to Mornay's child and began the work of translating his *The Trewnesse of the Christian Religion* into English. Mornay's theology was Platonic, 'suffused with platonic epistemology', and Sir Philip's translation consistently heightened the Platonism of its terms.[29]

The attraction of Platonic metaphysics to Puritanism lay in its emphasis on the purity, internality, and so directness, of the individual's path to God's truth; the way, as Mornay put it, to 'be lincked most straightly to Him'. External clerical and state interference in this represented, in Platonic terms, the intrusion of obstacles from the fallible world of particulars onto the path to the forms; in radical Puritan terms an obstacle to truth and salvation and the idolatrous substitution of an external humane particular as the object for reverence in the place of the only real source of truth: God. This conception easily extended itself when impelled by political developments to the question of 'divine right' monarchy in politics as well.[30] Both Sidney and Milton looked back to the purity of the ancient world, to the 'Greeks and Romans, under whom tyrants were not beheld with a superstitious regard ... [nor made] by the subtle casuistry of the priest ... objects of their religious

---

[28] Robinson, *Things Known* pp. 88–92, 112–13.

[29] In Mornay's religion God is the light of the intellect as the sun is the light of the world (cf. Plato's *Republic* bk VII). 'The essence of God is inconceivable to man, but the eye of the mind has the natural power to see God indirectly reflected in the external universe and within the intellect itself.' Robinson, *Things Known* pp. 102–3.

[30] Sidney was fond of linking the struggles for religious and political liberty (in both cases, again, the critical conception was self-rule); as when he declared in the *Discourses* that the absurdity and superstition of Filmer's notion of the divine right of Kings was unparalleled, 'unless by the popish opinion of transubstantiation' (p. 483).

adoration'. For Sidney there was no irony involved in thus looking to pagan sources for spiritual refreshment for Christianity: as he observed in the _Discourses_, after comparing a passage of Plato with a passage from scripture (Eccl. 10.6), it showed how 'true Philosophy is perfectly conformable, with what is taught us by those who were divinely inspired'.[31] This Christian humanism, and its use of Plato in particular, is, of course, both wider and older than 'Puritanism', as the case of Thomas More suggests.

Platonic and Puritan political morality, too, were fundamentally the same. Like Sidney, Milton, and Vane later, Plato looked to state-imposed education and (literally) Spartan discipline, particularly military discipline, to redeem mankind from their 'lawless wild-beast nature'; to set them on the wheel of progress through the restraint of the sensual 'appetitive' part of their soul by the rule of spirit and reason.[32] For Sidney, as for Milton, 'the bestiality and barbarity in which many nations, especially of Africa, America, and Asia now live, shews what human nature is if it be not improved by discipline'. Both were to put particular emphasis on 'the vigour or slackness of discipline' as a moving principle in politics; as Sidney later put it: 'people that want sobriety, usually want diligence, valor...'. Both were to bitterly castigate the indolence, docility, and 'effeminacy' which put their hard-won liberty at risk.[33] During his exile, Sidney boasted of the size and eagerness of 'the army of parliament' and said that 'when [this army] had been on foot one had never seen a soldier abjure God; that they had never suffered cards, dice or women, that each soldier had carried in his pocket a bible in English, and that all had constantly exercised themselves at war [-games] or other sports useful and proper to strengthen the body'.[34] The Spartan flavour is as unmistakable here as it is in Plato's _Republic_.

Like Milton and Sidney, too, Plato condemned the servility, adulation, and flattery of 'slaves' and 'the vilest of mankind', in favour of the virtue and valour of the high-minded.[35] Like them Plato opposed temperance and self-discipline to luxury and vice, to 'lust ... clouds of incense and perfumes and garlands and wines'.[36] Most importantly Plato asserted the values of direct-ness and simplicity against a world of complexity and craft: this was the basis of Platonism (both politics and metaphysics) and both the basis and meaning of 'Puritanism'. As Sidney put it, 'Truth is best discovered by plain words;

---

[31] _Discourses_ p. 65 (and p. 53); Milton, _Second Defence_ Intro. The Ecclesiastes text is Solomon's castigation of a world turned upside down, with princes walking as servants upon the earth and vice versa. The text, interpreted thus as a parable of unrewarded virtue, was a favourite of Harrington's also.

[32] Plato, _Republic_ IX p. 626.

[33] Hill C., _Milton and the English Revolution_ (1977) p. 253.

[34] 'Lantiniana', Bib. Nat. Fr. MS 23254 (my translation).

[35] Plato, _Republic_ IX 637.

[36] Plato, _Republic_ IX p. 627.

[and] nothing is more usual with ill men than to cover their mischievous designs ... by fraud ... [and] figurative phrases.'[37]

A great deal of Plato remained in Aristotle (the elitism, the emphasis on virtue, much of the morality and, above all, 'the combination of relativism with a normative standard', the key to Sidney's philosophy).[38] Both Sidney and Milton used Aristotle accordingly as much as Plato himself (in many respects his pragmatic application of his ideas made him more useful) and both (like Grotius before them) made a point of getting their Aristotle directly, not from the discredited 'schoolmen'. But Sidney made the antecedents for his use of Aristotle very clear, by using him generally in conjunction with Plato, and by referring to him repeatedly in both the *Maxims* and the *Discourses* as Aristotle 'following his master Plato' or Plato 'and his scholar Aristotle'. He used them together most often on the central question of virtue in politics, on which he found them to agree perfectly. He valued Plato and Aristotle to an exceptional degree, said Sidney, as 'having comprehended in their writings the wisdom of the Grecians, with all they had learned from the Phoenicians, Egyptians, and Hebrews, which may lead us to the discovery of the truth we seek'.[39]

For Sidney, in religion as in politics, Plato had charted the direct way by which mankind could, as far as his imperfect condition allowed, recover from the consequences of his fall and seek by knowledge to reunite himself with God. 'As no man' he said in the *Discourses*

can be just or good ... unless he know that original justice and goodness, through which all that is just is just, and all that is good is good, it is impossible for any man to perform the part of the good magistrate, unless he have the knowledge of God, who is the only root of justice and goodness. If Plato therefore deserve credit, he only can perform the part of a good magistrate, whose moral virtues are ripened and heightened by a superinduction of divine knowledge. The misery of man proceeds from his being separated from God; this separation is wrought by corruption: his restitution therefore to felicity and integrity can only be brought about by his reunion to the good from which he is fallen ... In all his laws and politics ... Plato looks upon this as the only worthy object of man's desire.[40]

Most writing on seventeenth-century Platonism has focused upon the Cambridge Platonists. But the influence of Plato in seventeenth-century Puritan religion and politics is a much wider phenomenon, and it covers closely both

---

[37] *Discourses* p. 471.
[38] The central idea in Aristotle of the 'nature' of something (the peg by which it is classed with other particulars as part of a species), is a remainder from Plato's forms, lending the purpose and reality to the particulars that partake of it. In this way the line from Plato through Aristotle to the natural-law tradition in general is direct. Morrall J., *Aristotle* p. 83; see, for instance, Aristotle, *Ethics* bk v ch. vii for the relationship between the unchanging 'natural law of the Gods' and the law of 'our world' 'where everything is subject to change'.
[39] *Discourses* p. 59 (cf. 60–4).
[40] *Discourses* pp. 63–4.

the aristocratic and the later radical circles with which Sidney himself became associated. Mid-century writers who can be shown to have been strongly influenced by Plato include Vane, Milton, Marvell, Hall, Nedham, Stubbe, Sprigge, Neville, and Harrington.[41] Many of these men had clear literary and intellectual links with the Elizabethan Platonist Sidney/Spenser circle itself: Milton, Marvell, and Neville, for instance, as well as Sidney himself. The way in which Platonism found its way within particular aristocratic circles like the Sidneys' from the Elizabethan period to the radicals of the mid-seventeenth century is nicely illustrated by the career of the Cambridge Platonist Peter Sterry. Sterry was a chaplain on the eve of the civil war to Robert Lord Brooke (himself a Platonist writer), nephew and adopted son of Fulke Greville Lord Brooke, who had been Sir Philip Sidney's closest friend and his biographer. From there Sterry became closely associated with Henry Vane jun. (Sidney's later closest political colleague) so that Baxter commented, 'I find in him [Sterry] the same notions ... as in Sir H Vane', and quipped that never had 'Vanity and Sterility' been more successfully combined. By the middle of the 1650s Sterry had become chaplain to Algernon's own brother Philip Sidney Lord Lisle.[42]

What has been written about the Cambridge Platonists certainly fits Sidney's (and Vane's) religion exactly, embracing the range from the stress on reason, the 'candle of the lord' of someone like More (and Sidney's *Discourses*), to the mysticism and spirituality of Sterry and Vane (and Sidney's *Court Maxims*). At this end of the spectrum Platonism readily established links with quakerism, as the careers of both Vane and Sidney illustrate.[43] Platonism combined the centrality of reason with the spirit, the claim that 'Spiritual things are spiritually discerned; and the whole world to him who can see it, is irradiated by spirit' (compare Sidney's *Court Maxims* commending the 'pure spiritual christians, they see things that to other eyes

[41] On Milton's Platonism see Zagorin, *Political Thought* pp. 111–12; and Madson W. G., 'The idea of nature in Milton's poetry' in *Three Studies In the Renaissance: Sidney Jonson Milton* (Yale 1958) pp. 183, 198. Marvell's 'Upon Appleton House' is Platonic, and also influenced by Lipsian ideas, as his thought in general was preoccupied with the insubstantiality of earthly things: see Wallace J. M., *Destiny His Choice* (Cambridge 1968) p. 236 (for his use of Charron see p. 253, and Lipsius p. 256). Most of the others will be discussed in future chapters.

[42] Lichtenstein A., *Henry More* (Cambridge 1962) p. 17; De Sola Pinto, *Peter Sterry Platonist and Puritan* (1934) pp. 3, 11; Powicke, *The Cambridge Platonists* (London 1926) 175–6.

[43] Sidney may indeed have been living with his quaker friend Furly (whose library contained a copy of Sir Philip Sidney's translation of Mornay) as he wrote the *Maxims*. See Hull William, *Benjamin Furly and Quakerism in Rotterdam* (1941) p. 38. For Vane see Reay Barry, 'The quakers, 1659, and the restoration of monarchy' in *History* vol. 63 (1978) p. 197. I am well aware that quakerism and Platonism nevertheless remained theologically distinct, particularly around the question of the subjectivity (quakerism) versus the universality (Platonism) of the inner light.

are invisible').[44] While seeking a path to the knowledge of God's truth, it acknowledged with Platonic scepticism the inherent difficulty of the enterprise for flawed mankind: 'it is better to confess ignorance than rashly to claim that we comprehend him' (compare Sidney in *Of Love*: 'it is better to speak passionately, and perhaps unadvisedly [of what we know], than universally darkly and ignorantly of thoes [things] that we feele nothing of').[45] Above all the Cambridge Platonists placed central emphasis on simplicity and 'practical morality' as the key to the inward religion they wished to substitute for obedience to 'mere outward forms'. For Benjamin Whichcote morality was 'the proper science and busines of mankind in general'.[46] This made men like Whichcote, Sidney, Vane, Milton, and John Locke (also a religious Platonist, naming Whichcote his favourite preacher) advocates alike of an individualistic creed of personal religion and toleration, against the imposition of any particular external dogma, whether by Church or State. This emphasis on morality allowed Sidney to praise the moral gravity of counter-Reformation French and Spanish catholicism while simultaneously organising armed resistance to its attempts to oppose its external dogma.[47] For Sidney, as for Milton and Vane, the 'Puritan Revolution' was a moral revolution, a question of the rectitude or corruption of manners (and so of will). For Sidney good government depended upon 'vigour of spirit, integrity of manners, and wisdom'.[48] Sidney left us no record of his beliefs on doctrine (for instance, predestination) or church government, because they were not for him the crucial matters of religion, they were members, in Platonic terms, of the world of opinion, not of the world of knowledge. Burnet described Sidney's religion at the end of his life:

he was a Christian ... as he said himself, but he hated all sorts of church-men, and so he never joyn'd himself to any, but to ye Independents; he kept up very little of an outward profession of Religion, even in ye late times when Hypocrasy was in fashion; he seem'd in discourse with me to beleive ye truth of Christianity very firmly, yet he thought devotions ... were but slight things, and yt good Morality was all yt was necessary.

What escaped Burnet, but cannot escape the reader of Sidney's writings, in the absence of 'outward devotions', was the passion of Sidney's inward devotions.[49]

The Sidney family's own chaplain up to the civil war was Henry Hammond, recruited for Penshurst by Algernon's father in 1633. It is no surprise then to discover that Hammond's speciality of scholarship was Greek, that

---

[44] Powicke, *The Cambridge Platonists* p. 19; *Court Maxims* p. 78.
[45] Powicke, *Platonists* p. 20: Sidney, *Of Love*, add. MS 34,100 p. 1.
[46] Lichtenstein A., *Henry More* (Cambridge 1962) p. 78.
[47] Lichtenstein p. 28; *Discourses* pp. 183, 481 (see ch. 11 below, n. 4).
[48] *Discourses* p. 461.
[49] Burnet, add. MS 63,057 pp. 137–8.

his theology was Platonic, and that the New Testament and patristic sources he used most of all (St Paul, Tertullian) were those Algernon used most of all. We can hear Platonism and Algernon's *Discourses* speaking in Hammond's *Of The Reasonableness of Christianity* where he stressed that moral right can

be determined by the dictates of nature, in the Heart of every Man which hath the use of Reason . . . for a thing to be good morally . . . depends, by sure connection from that eternal Justice which is primarily in God . . . every thing being good, more or less, as it more or less partakes of that Justice which is in God.

We will see other echoes of Hammond in the *Court Maxims*. The relationship of Hammond's thought to the Sidney family tradition as a whole becomes clearer when we see the names of the two modern authors whom he acknowledges as the principal sources for his theology and methods of biblical exegesis. They are Philippe du Plessis Mornay, and Hugo Grotius respectively. Hammond summed up his favoured ancient and modern sources in an instruction for pupils beginning study: begin with 'the Moralists, Greek (if the disciple be capable of them) or els Latine . . . Tully . . . Seneca . . . Pettrarch . . . And from thence ascending to divinity, beginning with Grotius de Veritate, or [du Plessis] Morney or falling on the Gospels with Grotius Annotations.' During the 1650s Hammond entered the lists of pamphlet warfare on two principal accounts: the first to defend the religion of Grotius; and the second to defend the use by Lucius Cary and the Tew Circle, against Thomas White, of the huguenot sceptic Jean Daillé, Algernon's own favourite already mentioned. It is interesting to discover then firstly that Daillé had begun his career as chaplain at Saumur to none other than du Plessis Mornay, to whom his *Of The Right Use of The Fathers* (1651) is dedicated; and that secondly White dedicated his *The Grounds of Obedience* (1655) to Sir Kenhelme Digby, the bitter (and papist) court rival of Sidney's father, against whose accusation of 'Puritanism' Leicester had been forced to defend himself by letter to Charles I.[50] On the eve of his execution, Sidney himself was to complain in his *Apology* that writing against Filmer, far from being criminal, had simply been common sense; his principles were the same as those of 'one White a priest', who had written a book under Cromwell, though then even 'he, though a tyrant, abominated it'.[51]

In his 'Classical Republicanism and the Puritan Revolution' Dr Worden

[50] Hammond, *Workes* ed. Fell (1674) vol. I pp. 3–4, 191–2. Hammond's central use of Mornay and Grotius is described by J. W. Packer, *The Transformation of Anglicanism* (1969) pp. 64–70, 89–94, 189 (and is evident enough from the marginal notes of his works, see *Reasonableness*, for instance). For Leicester's letter to the King and more on the Mornay/Sidney/Daillé connection see the next chapter. Falkland (Lucius Cary), *Of The Infallibility of the Church of Rome, With Answer, and Reply* (1651); White T., *Daillés Arts Discover'd* (2nd edn Paris 1654); and *The Grounds of Obedience and Government* (1655); Hammond, *A Defence of the Learned Hugo Grotius From The Accusations of Inward Socinianism and Outward Popery* [by T. White?] (1655).

[51] *Apology* p. 12.

was forced, in order to redress the traditional imbalance of attention between Puritan/religious and classical sources respectively, to speak of these modes of thought as different and indeed opposed categories, so that men fell predominantly into one camp or the other, and foreign policy (for instance) took shape according to one view or the other. From the foregoing discussion I wish to suggest that in the case of Sidney (and Milton) at least, such a division did not exist, and that in their thought classical (e.g. Platonic) and 'puritan' Christian ideas combined to reinforce one another. Dr Worden associates Sidney primarily with the ('as far from puritan as east from west') 'Marten–Neville–Morley' grouping in the Rump; whereas I will show that Sidney's friendship with Neville (who was his second cousin) did not extend to the whole of the rest of the group; indeed in divisions of the House Marten was his most consistent opponent. Rather his closest political relationship was with his fellow religious and Platonist natural-law theorist Henry Vane. Sidney's relationships, like his thought, in fact bridged the division between 'classical' Neville and 'religious' Vane, as did Milton's. His (and their) Platonism, and concomitant Platonist/Aristotelian natural-law theory, are that bridge. For Sidney, as for Milton, classical republicanism and the Puritan revolution were the same thing: the combination of pure original Christianity with its pure classical antecedents to bring the truth of God out from the medieval bondage of man.

It was from Aristotle's *Politics* that Sidney, like Milton, took his basic political categories: the 'three simple species', monarchy, aristocracy, and democracy (in Aristotle 'polity'), the one, the few, and the many; with their respective corruptions, tyranny, oligarchy, and anarchy. Both Sidney and Milton devoted one major work each to rehearsing Aristotelian natural-law arguments against tyranny (Sidney's *Court Maxims*; Milton's *The Tenure of Kings and Magistrates*), as the huguenots had the century before. 'He is a tyrant who regards his own welfare and profit only, and not that of the people' (Milton). 'Plato and Aristotle find no more certain way of distinguishing between a lawful king and a tyrant, than that the first seeks to procure the common, and the other his own pleasure and profit' (Sidney).[52]

The English classical republicans adopted Aristotle's political concepts and analysis not simply because they were familiar, but because they, and the Greek historical background which gave rise to them, seemed to describe what was happening in England in particular, and Europe in general, in the middle of the seventeenth century. In Book Three of the *Politics*, Milton observed with satisfaction in 1659, Aristotle had shown how the early Greek kings, degenerating through their obsolescence into tyrants, had been

[52] Milton, *A Defence of the People of England* in St John J. A. ed., *The Prose Works of John Milton* (1848) p. 200; Sidney, *Discourses* p. 71.

deposed by a growing and more populous people.[53] Harrington's use of Aristotelian political concepts to represent the new economic realities of his time is well known. Both Sidney and Milton emphasised the association of political progress – the advance of liberty at the expense of tyranny – with the advance of knowledge, wealth, technology, and population which they saw around them. Both Milton and Sidney emphasised that trade flourished in commonwealths; both served a republic as centred in its trading capital of London as republican Amsterdam or Venice. Both spent their political lives in the most populous city in Europe, the growing trade and colonial activities of which were very like those which had accompanied similar political changes (monarchy to tyranny to liberty) in the most populous city in the Greek world (Athens) and the master of its colonies and trade. Sidney was later to state in the *Court Maxims*, written in the Netherlands, that it was the growth in the wealth of London that had caused the English Civil War.[54]

2.3 MACHIAVELLI AND CHANGE

For Sidney's use of Machiavelli the sceptical intellectual antecedents have already been described. In the mutable political world, when 'political science' was accordingly of all sciences 'the most abstruse and variable according to accidents and circumstances', Machiavelli had something to offer Sidney could not ignore.[55] This was particularly so amid the political rubble of the Restoration, as Sidney wrote home from Italy of the perverse role 'Fortune' had played in taking from him everything he had built, and all means to live. Against political corruption, chaos, and tyranny Machiavelli offered not just virtue (which had proved insufficient) but virtu, realistic, relativistic and, above all, armed to the teeth. This combination of scepticism and ruthlessness proved irresistible. Sidney thus used Machiavelli as he used his other most important 'modern', Grotius (using the former, indeed, to effectively arm the 'Christian soldier' for the 'just war' of the latter), as someone who had written to chart a way through scepticism and political chaos. Indeed what linked Machiavelli, Grotius, and Sidney together was that they were all not just political writers, they had all been political actors, too, driven to become writers when the regimes they served had toppled. Moreover, they had all served republics: Florence, the Netherlands under Oldenbarneveldt, and England. Sidney chose theorists with experience of republicanism, and of exile; and with an understanding of the bruising world of political practice.

---

[53] Milton, *The Readie and Easye Way* (2nd edn 1659) ed. Erskine-Hill and Storey G. (1983) p. 221.

[54] This belief was attributed to the King by Marchamont Nedham in *Interest Will Not Lie* (1659), a tract of interest for Sidney's *Maxims* in other connections (see ch. 12 below).

[55] Sidney, *Discourses* p. 98.

We can compare Sidney and Machiavelli rather more exactly. Within his republic Sidney, like Machiavelli, took a particular interest in military, and foreign affairs, eventually serving as an envoy abroad. Like Machiavelli, he was ejected from a position of some seniority when the government was disbanded by force (twice), and handed over to a tyranny. He then became a political writer, his first piece based (negatively) on Machiavelli's first piece (The Prince), his second and greater work based (positively) on Machiavelli's later and greater work the *Discourses on ... Livy* (and, as much as Machiavelli's own, on Livy as well). The parallel in their lives matches that in their thought. Machiavelli wrote to contrast the vigour and power of the ancient Roman republic with the 'extreme misery, infamy and degredation' of modern Italy, devoid of the 'observance either of religion or of the laws, or of military traditions'.[56] Sidney wrote to contrast the vigour and power of the ancient Roman and modern English republics with the extreme misery, infamy, and degradation of English weakness under the Stuarts, who had undermined religion, the laws, and military traditions.

The particular importance of Sidney's use of Machiavelli stems from the fact that he became the most important English representative of a crucial side of Machiavelli's theory which had marked the Florentine out from Guicciardini and Gianotti as clearly as its acceptance marked Sidney out from Harrington and Neville. This was Machiavelli's preference for the dynamism and expansionist military vigour of Rome, over the example of stability and permanence provided by Venice. Among his contemporaries, heavily influenced by Contarini's cult of Venice, Machiavelli alone 'wished to transcend the search for stability altogether'.[57] His emphasis on Rome reflected the importance of vigorous popular political participation to his civic humanism, and of the military and imperialistic vigour demonstrated by Rome to his concept of 'virtu'. It rested ultimately on his sceptical belief that Fortuna could be channelled by 'virtu' to a certain extent but never finally eradicated from the political world. In the consequent world of flux vigour was more important than whatever static 'stability' Venice was able to lay claim to.

Confused assumptions about Sidney's 'aristocratic republicanism' have tempted commentators like Fink to portray him as an admirer of Venice, like

[56] Machiavelli, *Discourses* bk II Preface (Penguin p. 267); Fink, *The Classical Republicans* (1945) p. 11.

[57] Pocock, 'Only politician' p. 277: 'Throughout the introductory chapters of the *Discourses*, we find a series of decisions against studying the closed, aristocratic, defensive state – Sparta or Venice – which makes stability its only goal, and in favour of studying the dynamic, popular, warlike state – Livian Rome – which opts for liberty, expansion and dominion, even if this choice condemns it to ultimate decline ... Since Machiavelli did not believe that the world of cities could be rendered finally proof against Fortune, he chose to embrace the goddess rather than wall himself off from her.'

Harrington. But Sidney had no more time than Machiavelli for stability at the expense of vigour, and he named Machiavelli as the source for his picture of a modern Italy where 'the thin half-starved inhabitants of walls supported by ivy fear neither popular tumults nor foreign alarms; and their sleep is only interrupted by hunger ... or the howling of wolves.' 'Such a peace is no more to be commended, than that which men have in the grave.'

It is ill, that men should kill one another in seditions, tumults and wars; but it is worse, to bring nations to such misery, weakness and baseness, as to have neither strength nor courage to contend for anything; to have left nothing worth defending, and to give the name of peace to desolation.[58]

Consequently, for Sidney, as for Machiavelli, a republic for warfare and expansion was the best constitution of all, and the example of Rome was pre-eminent; on Venice Sidney stated that 'the too great inclinations of the Venetians to peace is ... a mortal error in their constitution'.[59] Peace and defence would be fine, said Sidney,

if mankind were so framed, that a people intending hurt to none could preserve themselves. But the world being so far of another temper, that no nation can be safe without valour and strength, those governments only deserve to be commended, which by discipline and exercise increase both, and the Roman above all, that excelled in both.

For Sidney the political world was not static; only the active survived; and the struggle for liberty between nations as well as within them, had no static middle ground, only two choices: increase or decrease; liberty or slavery; rule or be ruled.[60]

Unlike Sidney and Machiavelli, Harrington had not been an active politician, and he was not a civic humanist, an enthusiast for the *vita activa*, in his theory any more than in practice. The irony in English classical republicanism was (as Pocock pointed out) that English theorists like Harrington used Machiavelli as the transmitter of the one element of classical republicanism that he had chosen to turn away from: the Polybian formula of balance, and stability. Harrington castrated Machiavelli's stress on popular vigour (he called this 'perfecting' Machiavelli), while formalising its outward appearance, by controlling the participation and activities of Oceana's citizens within an overwhelming and meticulous system of Venetian-style rules and orders designed to remove the possibility of change and uncertainty from political life altogether. He consequently believed he had made constitutional immortality possible for the first time.[61] Sidney, on the other hand, not

---

[58] Sidney, *Works Discourses* pp. 132, 224.
[59] *Ibid.* p. 175.
[60] *Discourses* p. 131.
[61] Pocock ed., 'Onely politician' p. 278; Davis, 'Pocock's Harrington' and *Utopia and the Ideal Society* (1981) pp. 205–42.

only accepted, like Machiavelli and unlike Harrington, the inescapability of political uncertainty and change; he went further than Machiavelli and made the fact of change the ruling principle of his political theory.

Some degree of turbulence, Machiavelli had argued, was not only inevitable in republics, it was even beneficial: it helped them maintain their vitality and vigour. In Sidney's words, it 'sharpened their courage'. A republic could never be immortal, Machiavelli had added, unless it had the good fortune to produce a continual supply of good men, to reduce the constitution, when it erred, to its first principles. Harrington protested against this statement:

If a commonwealth, saith he [Machiavelli] were so happy as to be provided often with men that when she is swerving from her principles should reduce her unto her institution, she would be immortal. But a commonwealth, as we have demonstrated, swerveth not from her principles but by and through her institution.

Get the institution right in other words, as Harrington believed he had in *Oceana*, and the state would be immortal.[62]

Sidney, however, after congratulating Machiavelli for his activism – 'Civil war, in Machiavel's account is a Disease; but tyranny is the death of a state'[63] – went on to question Machiavelli's dictum on the precise reverse grounds; that it did not take *enough* account of change. Said Sidney:

nothing can or ought to be permanent but that which is perfect, and perfection is in God only, not in the things he has created . . . Some men observing this, have proposed a necessity of reducing every state, once in an age or two, to the integrity of its first principle; but they ought to have examined, whether that principle be good or evil, or so good that nothing can be added to it, which none ever was; and this being so, those who will admit of no change would render errors perpetual, and deprive . . . mankind of the benefits of wisdom, industry, experience, and the right use of reason.[64]

In this way Sidney took one step beyond Machiavelli's (classical) cyclical view of change: that the best that could be hoped for was a return to the finest moments of the past; and on to the linear possibility of perpetual advance by the 'benefits of wisdom, industry, experience'. Yet Sidney's is not the eighteenth-century idea of unstoppable progress, for Sidney's linear idea of change could work in either direction. The picture of modern Europe showed the negative road – of corruption and decline through the folly, stupidity, cowardice, and baseness of mankind – to be just as likely.[65]

The importance of politics for Sidney lay in the fact that the type of a state's

[62] Pocock J. G. A. ed., *The Political Works of James Harrington* (1977) p. 321.

[63] Sidney, *Discourses* p. 479.

[64] *Discourses* p. 406. This is also noted by Raab, *Machiavelli* p. 222.

[65] Thus Conniff has concluded that Sidney's theory contained an interesting contradiction between the backward-looking notion of decline from a better 'ancient constitution', and forward-looking 'whig' notion of progress. There is no contradiction; the possibility of either and the necessity of one or the other is the whole point of Sidney's thought. Coniff J., 'Reason and history in early whig thought; the case of Algernon Sidney' in *Journal of the History of Ideas* 43:3 (July 1982).

own government provided the deciding variable. If it provided for 'liberty', progress would be the consequence; if for 'slavery', then degeneration would result (the contrast in power, in military and foreign affairs, between the English Commonwealth and the Stuart monarchy illustrated this point to Sidney's satisfaction). For Sidney the connection between liberty and progress was 'so certain, that whatever we enjoy, beyond the misery in which our barbarous ancestors lived, is due only to the liberty of correcting what was amiss in their practice, or inventing that which they did not know'. Again, the only alternative which was impossible was the static absence of change of either sort:

that government is evidently the best, which, not relying upon what it does at first enjoy, seeks to increase the number, strength, and Riches of the people ... If it do not grow, it must pine and perish; for in this world nothing is permanent: that which does not grow better will grow worse.[66]

Consequently states, to survive in an uncertain world of flux had not, like Harrington, to attempt to resist change, but to embrace it; to become progressive and aggressive accordingly. They had to become competitive. All of these ideas are, of course, alive and central in the world today, particularly in the ideology of that superpower where Sidney himself was to have greatest influence, the United States. The seventeenth century had been England's century of political disruption and change. Much of Sidney's importance lies in his having transmitted, with the *Discourses*, a corresponding set of political ideas to the emergent American nation of the eighteenth.

Sidney's scepticism, his emphasis on variety and change, extended not just to things themselves but to their appearances:

Changes therefore are unavoidable; and the wit of man can go no further than to institute such as in relation to the forces, manners, nature, religion or interests of a people, and their neighbours, are suitable and adequate to what is seen, or apprehended to be seen.[67]

His scepticism about particular political forms was grounded directly in his scepticism about the people that made them: 'such is the imperfection of all human constitutions, that they are subject to perpetual fluctuation, which never permits them to continue long in the same condition'; 'such is the condition of mankind, that nothing can be so perfectly framed as not to give some testimony of human imbecility, and frequently to stand in need of reparations and amendments'. This sense of the imperfection of man Sidney expressed in straightforwardly religious terms: it was the fruit of man's separation from the perfection of God: 'man, by sin is fallen from the law of his

---

[66] *Discourses* p. 178; Again this is Machiavellian: as Machiavelli said in his *Discourses*: 'Since ... all human affairs are ever in a state of flux and cannot stand still, either there will be improvement or decline.' Bk I ch. 6 (Penguin p. 123).

[67] *Discourses* pp. 144–5.

creation'.[68] Sidney's solution, politically, as we have seen, was not to remove this human fallibility from affairs by substituting an infallible utopian constitutional logic; he did not believe this possible (imperfection was the condition of God's creation). Rather he sought to cater for it by calling for frequent change and amendment; change which, in a state run in accordance with correct principles, would be improvement and progress rather than decline.

Finally, then, linked to Sidney's scepticism was a relativism of two dimensions: historical and geographical. He insisted that particular political remedies for particular peoples would vary both from time to time, and place to place. 'No right judgement can be given of human things, without a particular regard to the time in which they passed.' And

if we ought not [therefore] too strictly to adhere to our own constitutions,[69] those of other nations are less to be regarded by us: For the laws that may be good for one people are not for all, and that which agrees with the manners of one age is utterly abhorrent from those of another.[70]

2.4 LIBERTY, REASON, AND VIRTUE

Henry Stubbe summed it up in 1659: 'Truth to say that Liberty, civill, and spirituall, were the Good old Cause'.[71] His own political ideas were based, explained Sidney, on

the principle of liberty in which God created us, and which includes the chief advantages of the life we enjoy, as well as the greatest helps towards ... our hopes in the other [life] ... And ... the liberty asserted is not a licentiousness of doing what is plesing [sic] to every one against the command of God, but an exemption from all human laws, to which they have not given their assent.

Sidney's idea of liberty then was, positively, the classical one of self-government; negatively, it meant not the absence of constraints upon action, but the absence of dependence upon – independence of – the 'will' of another.

---

[68] *Discourses* pp. 404–5; p. 100: 'I believe ... since the sin of our first parents, the earth hath brought forth briars and brambles, and the nature of man hath been fruitful only in vice and wickedness.'

[69] This is, of course, a radical position and a straightforward repudiation of the ancient constitutionalism of Coke. Sidney has been associated with the latter (for instance by Pocock and Conniff) through his attempt to prove not just that men had the liberty to change constitutions but that that liberty was as ancient as the Anglo-Saxons! – a very typically Sidneian attempt to have it both ways. It was the true sceptical radicalism of Sidney's theory which the nineteenth-century Chartists understood correctly; and which Karsten has mistakenly dismissed as a misunderstanding of Sidney's theory. Karsten, *Patriot-Heroes* p. 132.

[70] *Discourses* p. 41. Again Sidney is building here on the foundation laid by Bodin, for whom 'the principal foundation of a commonwealth is the suitability of its government to the nature of the people, and of its laws and ordinances to the requirements of time, place, and persons'. Bodin, *Six Books*, abridged and translated by Tooley M. J. (Oxford 1955) p. 146.

[71] Stubbe, *An Essay in Defence of The Good Old Cause* (1659) Preface p. 2.

Such independence usually had, in seventeenth-century theory, a religious, an economic, and a moral dimension; its republican political application tended to assume all three. Sidney's concept of liberty was, like that of others in the classical republican tradition from Aristotle to Milton and Harrington, morally twofold; freedom not just from the will of others but from will generally – including that of the self where will ran contrary to 'reason', as in seventeenth-century republican morality it was habitually suspected of doing. For Sidney, as for Milton, no discipline was more basic to political liberty than self-discipline.[72]

Correspondingly, Sidney's positive political theory was about the values of self-government; and a favourite political aphorism was that of the monarch-omachs, that magistrates were made for the people, not people for their magistrates. For Sidney 'God [had given] to every nation ... [a] universal right ... the liberty to govern themselves.' Accordingly they could choose their government, from among

the infinite variety which is observed in the constitution, mixture, and regulation of governments ... one nation may justly choose the government that seems best to them, and continue or alter it according to the changes of time or things ... The great variety of laws that are or have been in the world proceed from this.[73]

Sidney's own life, and all of his struggles within himself were about the same principle of self-government, in its personal rather than political dimension. From them the Stoic ideal of constancy, to political principles and to self, emerged as the anchor for a man not only surrounded by a world of uncertainty, temporariness, and loss, but whose own inability to control himself continually added to his political losses and defeats. The constant accompaniment to Sidney's external political struggle for self-government, was the internal object of Isaac, whom he described in the *Discourses* as 'like a stoical king reigning in and over himself'.[74] Accordingly the political tyranny which Sidney castigated as letting will rule for reason, was at least in part a projection of the lifelong tyranny of his own famous and destructive temper. The slaves to passion he denounced in monarchies were projections

---

[72] Hill, *Milton* p. 255. For Harrington in this connection see Pocock ed., *Harrington* p. 170. Liberty, in its political as well as its personal sense, was secured by that recourse to reason, in practice or in law, that liberated men from the consequences of their sinful condition, expressed in passion and will. To be forced, as in absolute monarchy, into dependence upon the will of another, was to be forced to partake of another man's sin, which is why for Sidney, as for Milton and Vane, such monarchs or tyrants were servants of 'the Devill', who did the Devil's corrupting work.

[73] *Discourses* pp. 79, 89. Hotman said 'a people can exist without a king ... wheras a king without a people cannot even be imagined'. Franklin, *Constitutionalism* p. 33; The more militant du Plessis Mornay said 'a king cannot rule without a people, while a people can rule itself without a king'. *Ibid.* pp. 160–1; As Sidney put it: 'Magistrates were set up for the good of nations, not nations for the honour or glory of magistrates.' *Works* Memoirs p. 38.

[74] *Discourses* p. 19.

of his own slavery to a passion which infected every initially 'calm and reasoned' political treatise he ever wrote, and wrecked every co-operative political enterprise he ever undertook. Sidney could not bear to be dependent upon the 'will' of another, partly through his experience of the will in himself; and he was as notable for tyrannising over others in practice as he was for opposing the tyranny of others in theory. Burnet observed this paradox with interest: '[Sidney] was as to Civill Government, a great Asserter of a Commonwealth, and tho he had all ye dispositions to Tyranny in his own Nature, yet he seem'd to abhorr single power.'[75]

In Sidney's sceptical mental framework, then, 'will' and 'passion' were synonymous with fickleness, transitoriness, and 'levity'; and reason on the other hand with solidity and reliability. Truth, Justice, the Public Interest, Sidney's stable of immovable values, could thus only be secured in politics through the mask of unreliable particulars if the most unreliable particular of all, man, were disciplined, made reasonable, fit for liberty. The mechanism to which Sidney looked, in common with other republicans, to secure this rule of reason against the fickleness of human nature, was the law. The law was the fixed standard by which the natural 'infinite variety' among a society's members was to be regulated.

[T]he fancy of ... man ... always fluctuates, and every passion that arises in his mind, or is infused by others, disorders him. The good of a people ought to be established upon a surer basis. For this reason, the law is established, which no passion can disturb. It is void of desire and fear, lust and anger. It is *mens sine affectu*, written reason, retaining some measure of the divine perfection. It does not enjoin that which pleases a weak, frail man; but ... commands that which is good, and punishes evil in all, whether rich or poor, high or low. It is deaf, inexorable, inflexible.

The ancients, said Sidney, recognised that government was a

work [to] ... be performed only by such as excelled in virtue: but lest they should deflect from it, no government was thought to be well constituted, unless the laws prevailed above the commands of men; and they were accounted the worst of beasts, who did not prefer such a condition before a subjection to the fluctuating and irregular will of man.[76]

In this connection the key objection to monarchy was that it placed the fluctuating and irregular will of a man (and one subjected to more temptation than most to indulge himself and become 'the worst of beasts') above the 'inexorable' rule of law. Government by law, on the other hand, if the law embodied reason and so retained 'some measure of the divine perfection', was the closest indeed that mankind could come to the rule of God on earth. In the *Court Maxims* Sidney described, in strongly Platonic (and through Plato,

[75] Add MS 63,057 vol. II fols. 137–8.
[76] *Discourses* pp. 1–2, 346.

Pythagorean harmonic) imagery, how God created the world from Chaos by the ordering principle of reason:

I confess the disorderly fury of a Rude Multitude may well resemble the dark and barbarous confusion of the Chaos. But as God by his word gave order and form to that indigested heap and by various mixtures produced that variety of forms by which the world is made beautifull and fruitfull, he hath left a pattern unto us by the power of reason the reliques of his Image in us ... to produce a civil Society beautifull in perfection of order, regulateing by prudent laws the mad and blind fury by which they were formerly agitated and reducing the barren darkness of confusion into such a state as renders it fruitfull in all things conduceing to a Civil and happy Life. Hereby that variety of nature, in the individuals is renderd usefull to the beauty of the whole as the variety of Elements and humors makes up that temper by which our persons do subsist: he that would have a State composed of one sort of persons only will appear little wiser than he that wold have a body composd of one element or Musick of one Note.[77]

Like Plato, then, Sidney rejected 'constitutionalism, and thinks but little of equality. To equality he opposed harmony, to constitutionalism flexibility.'[78] The *Court Maxims*'s preoccupation with harmony amid variety, shared by all other Platonist republicans, is a theme to which we will return. In general, then, reason in man and politics derived its stabilising, harmonising, and civilising force from its status as the umbilical cord from God. Even blessed with its potential: 'man is not able to stand in his own strength. If he leave dependence on God, he must become the servant of the devil.'[79] Again there is no middle ground; like the dialectic between liberty and slavery, progress and decline, this dichotomy between God and the Devil, good and evil, forms part of a general vision in terms of opposites, or 'contraries', which underlies all of Sidney's thought.

Accordingly Sidney's ultimate political appeal was not to immemorialism or to any particular code of positive law, but to the general law of nature: reason, truth, and justice written by God in the heart of every man. Moreover, where civil law did not accord with these general principles, it was not true law. As the alarmed William Gladstone recorded from Sidney's *Discourses* in the nineteenth century: [Gladstone's emphasis] '*That which is not just is not law: + that wh is not law ought not to be obeyed!*'.[80] Sidney himself elaborated: 'Axioms in law are, as in mathematics, evident to common sense ... the axioms of our law do not receive their authority from Coke or Hales, but Coke and Hales deserve praise for giving judgement according to such as are undeniably true.' Or as he put it earlier in the Platonic *Maxims*: the 'Essence of the Law ... consists solely in the justice of it ... For the understanding of this Law we should not need to study Littleton and Coke

[77] *Court Maxims* p. 19.
[78] Barker E., *The Political Thought of Plato and Aristotle* (NY 1959) p. 119.
[79] *Maxims* p. 102.
[80] Gladstone's notes on the *Discourses* are in the British Museum, add MS 44729 fols. 19–20.

but Plato, Aristotle and other[s and] ... above all the Scripture ... being the dictates of God's own spirit.'[81]

It was human action in conformity with reason that Sidney gave the name of virtue. 'Virtue is the dictate of reason, or the remains of divine light, by which men are made benevolent and beneficial to each other.'[82] Sidney repeatedly invoked Plato and Aristotle to show that amongst the ancients 'who followed the light of reason' the essential quality of virtue, rather than the accidental characteristic of birth, were what qualified a man to rule. And if it was upon virtue that the right and capacity to govern depended, then those incapable of it were incapable of self-government, and so of liberty. Such men were thus not, for Sidney, again following Aristotle, properly political beings at all; they were 'slaves by nature'. They had to be ruled by others and so monarchy – in the hands of the most virtuous individual – was as fit a form of government for them as any.[83] It is difficult to avoid the conclusion that Sidney's sister Isabella fell into this category, with her husband Strangford, in the 1650s, when their lands, by the excess of debt incurred by them, came to be managed solely 'in trust' by Algernon. He recorded that 'The inconvenience and danger of being engaged ... with persons ... soe unsteady every day appearing more and more ... [they] runn[ing] about from one place to another seeking [the] company ... of vild [*sic*] and lewd persons', the situation reached a peak when 'the dislike, that Alg: Sidney expressed of their courses, gave ocasion of new discontents, which servants dayly increased, suggesting he endeavourd to governe them: That he was too severe, for their age, that requird iollity, and the like...'[84]

Hereditary monarchy, however, over a people who were capable of virtue, and therefore of liberty, was objectionable to Sidney not simply for denying men the God-given liberty to rule themselves, but as, to quote the *Court Maxims*, 'irrational in itself'. For it was not based on a mechanism (meritocracy) which could produce the essential quality of virtue, or maintain it if (accidentally) it did. What sane seamen, asked Sidney, would give the direction of their vessel to the son of the best pilot in the world?[85]

Finally, Sidney attached to this political picture a version of English history which depicted the relative liberty, vigour, and military prowess of a previous state. The function of this history was to represent the same values of liberty, conquest, and expansion which he admired in the Roman republic, on the domestic English map. The historical details underwent a complete revision between the *Court Maxims* and the *Discourses*; the former describing the

---

[81] *Works* (1772) 'Discourses' p. 410; *Maxims* pp. 111–12.

[82] *Discourses* p. 229.

[83] *Discourses* p. 4; See Aristotle, *Politics* I ch. 5. For a full discussion by Sidney of the categories of slavery see the *Court Maxims* pp. 205–6.

[84] Kent Record Office, De Lisle MSS U1475 E28/5.

[85] *Discourses* p. 61; The analogy of the pilot was Plato's own favourite.

'Plantagenet Age' and the latter the history of the Anglo-Saxons. In both, the crucial group were the 'nobility', and in both the critical and only criteria for 'nobility' was military service. Sidney's history of the nobility has been traditionally misunderstood; the *Discourses* section on the 'noble nation' of the Anglo-Saxons is not an argument in *favour* of nobility or the traditional political role of the peerage; rather the specifically military values it advances are used as a devastating critique of modern aristocracy itself on behalf of the superior claims to political honour by military service of many among the modern 'commonalty'.[86]

According to the *Court Maxims*'s version the bold fighting Plantagenet kings, heads of expansionist states for overseas conquest and scourges of France, had been surrounded by a valiant, proudly independent, militarily vigorous nobility who eschewed luxury and effeminacy and preferred the camp to the court. In Sidney's theory they served as the middle point, balance and buffer in a (proto-Polybian) three-part Gothic constitution by protecting the people from the excesses of the monarch and the monarch from the excesses of the people. This heroic and militaristic age provided a striking contrast to the corrupt, indolent absolute monarchies of the seventeenth century, with their ludicrous 'effeminate' 'titular nobility', decked out with 'blue ribands', who gained their titles not by service in battle but by private services to the monarch which were 'not to be mentioned without blushing'. These seventeenth-century monarchs, Sidney argued, had gained absolute power from the previously balanced constitutions by breaking the independent power and 'interest' of the nobility in the state. In so doing they had broken the backbone of the state as a whole and in particular its capacity for foreign conquest; absolute power at home was purchased at the expense of dominion abroad. Whereas the ancient nobility had received political honour for 'the number of men they could bring into the field', for voluntarily putting their private 'interest' at the service of the public, the modern 'titular nobility ... have neither the interest nor the estates required for such a work ... Those who have estates at a rack-rent have [money but] no dependants.'[87] They spend the money on idle pleasures at court. They have substituted the real honour which resulted from independent public service, for empty titles of honour earned by private servitude; by dependence upon the will of another.[88]

Sidney probably borrowed part of this picture from Harrington; certainly the chapter in which it is most succinctly set out houses a sudden profusion of Harringtonian terms like 'superstructure' and 'balance', within a historical framework similar to Harrington's own. Yet Sidney's picture of a balanced

---

[86] Sidney, *Discourses* pp. 421–37; *Court Maxims* pp. 55–9.
[87] *Discourses* p. 464.
[88] Cf. *Discourses* pp. 425–7.

Gothic constitution, and so of a golden age of noble power, is at complete odds with Harrington's own picture of the Gothic polity as an imperfect and unstable embodiment of 'modern prudence', not balanced but unbalanced by the preponderance of power in one group (the nobility). Moreover, Sidney's use of 'balance' here is Polybian, not Harringtonian, and his conclusion is, as we might expect, crucially different; the balance cannot be recreated, it is gone for ever.

The balance by which it [the ancient state] subsisted was broken; and it is as impossible to restore it, as for most of those who at this day go under the name of noblemen, to perform the duties required from the antient nobility of England.[89]

Change in politics was inevitable, and Sidney believed this phenomenon – the breaking of the balance – had happened right across Europe by the seventeenth century. Everywhere as a result the two extreme ends of the old constitution – the people and the monarchs – were left facing each other directly without the buffer, the nobility, in between. Consequently Europe was now divided between states ruled by one or the other; backward and poverty-stricken absolute monarchies (Hapsburg dominions, Spain, France) and rich and flourishing free commonwealths (Venice, Holland, Switzerland). The political question now was to choose the correct side. Again typically there was no third or static alternative in between: tyranny, and so slavery, resulted in degeneration and decline; self-government, and so liberty, resulted in prosperity, power, and progress. The importance of England in Sidney's view and lifetime was that it had experienced both; attempted absolutism or tyranny (Charles I) and attempted liberty (the Commonwealth). Under the Restoration, for Sidney, it seemed to still hang in the balance. It is against the background of this historical perception that all Sidney's political activities and writings are to be seen.

Sidney's theory is clearly an interesting aristocratic response to the Europe-wide early modern decline of independent aristocratic power in the face of the centralisation of the power of the state. As his comments on the 'rack-rents' of the nobility showed, he recognised that the decline of the great independent nobility formed only part of a new era where feudal concepts of dependence had become obsolete. The struggle for liberty and independence as political values acquired new urgency in a world where the only alternative now was slavery. As he said: 'This [feudal] dependence being lost, the lords have only more money ... but no command of men; and can therefore neither protect the weak, nor curb the insolent. By this means, all things have been brought into the hands of the king, and the commoners.'[90]

Sidney's consciousness of these changes, of course, no more proves that he

[89] *Discourses* p. 464.
[90] *Ibid.*

read Harrington, than it proves that he read Lawrence Stone's *Crisis of The Aristocracy*; the decline of the independent aristocracy was a historical fact observed by many seventeenth-century contemporaries.[91] Sidney had plenty of opportunity to view the wider changes in economic relations that accompanied it, and made new political relations – the substitution of 'liberty' for dependence – necessary. As we will see, Sidney spent many years managing his father's and his brother-in-law's landed estates and business affairs; and he worked, during his membership of the Commonwealth government, with the London merchant community for the aggressive advancement of English trade. After the Restoration, in exile in the Netherlands and in co-operation with his merchant friend Benjamin Furly, he produced the *Court Maxims*, which drew on Dutch republican ideas of mercantilism and liberty. Accordingly, Sidney was to help transfer to England (and later to America) concepts of liberty – of trade, of religion, and of self-government – further developed under the first fully formed capitalist economy in early modern Europe.

In the eighteenth century Sidney's political ideas were influential, as I have said, in both England and France. But the reason they had the most impact of all in a third country, America, is simple. Sidney's historical theory failed to predict the revival of the English aristocracy and the deferential social and political relations which dominated the eighteenth century in England. It had more to offer, temporarily, when the old order collapsed in France in 1789. But it had most of all to offer – and was ideal for – the youthful social structure of America, where liberty and slavery were indeed the only two relations with which politics had to contend.

---

[91] See, for instance, Hutchinson Lucy, *Memoirs of Colonel Hutchinson* (1965) pp. 59–60. The Earl of Peterborough wrote to Joseph Williamson in 1663: 'These old notions, of mix'd Governments, priviledges, and conditions, have ... beene put out of the essence of things ... and the consequence of all undertakings, can noe more bee, but monarky, or a commonwealth'. PRO SP29/81/94. (My thanks to Paul Seaward for this reference.) See, too, Tawney's speculations on his question, though he overestimates the extent to which Sidney and Harrington were part of separate political movements. Tawney R. H., 'Harrington's interpretation of his age' in *Proceedings of The British Academy* XXVII (1941) p. 222.

3

Family background

I ... esteem myself free, because I depend upon the will of no man, and hope to
die in the liberty I inherit from my ancestors.

Discourses p. 387

3.1 THE PERCYS

Algernon Sidney was born in 1623, from the union of two families: the
Sidneys and the Percys. His father, Robert Sidney, was the second Earl of
Leicester; his mother, Dorothy, was sister to the man he was named after,
Algernon Percy, the tenth Earl of Northumberland. Algernon was their third
child, and second son.

Sidney's relationship with the Percys, and with Algernon Percy in particular, owed its origin to the close lifelong friendship (and, under Charles I,
political alliance) between his father and his Percy uncle. As he often told him,
Leicester valued Northumberland's friendship above any other he had.[1]

In 1640 Northumberland tried to procure military employment for
Algernon Sidney under the Prince of Orange.[2] Three years later Sidney took
the Parliamentary side in the civil war; something his father had been unable
to bring himself to do. His uncle Northumberland, however, had done so,
and signs of his political patronage thereafter punctuate Algernon's 1640s'
parliamentary career.

In 1645 Algernon was made Governor of Chichester, the town for which
Northumberland had served as an MP in the 1620s, and which lay close to his
Sussex country house of Petworth. Northumberland was Lord Lieutenant of
the county; he sat on the Committee of Both Kingdoms which directed
Sidney's governorship; and his signature headed the Committee's letter of
appointment. Northumberland had been involved, throughout 1645, in a

---

[1] Collins A., *Letters and Memorials of State* (1742) vol. II p. 682; cf. Hibbard C., *Charles I and The Popish Plot* (1983) p. 33.
[2] Kent R.O. De Lisle MSS U1475 C85/7, C85/9; HMC Third Report Northumberland MSS fol. 81.

conflict with the Sussex County Committee over their employment of 'men of base condition . . . unnecessary oppression and insolent behaviour towards men of property'. The appointment of his own nephew to govern Chichester must have been a satisfying step in the right direction.[3]

During the civil war Northumberland referred political clients to

> my nephew Coll Sydney . . . and [I] do not doubt but I shall receive thanks from him for recommending you to his acquaintance; [he] is a person that understands very well how to value such as are de[s]erving, and I am confident you [w]ill give him cause to esteeme you [o]f that number.[4]

Sidney's votes and activities in the House throughout the period 1647–8 in particular are consistent with the patronage of his Northumberland uncle in the Lords, and with membership of the group (including Lords Saye and Northumberland, Sir John Evelyn, Pierrepoint, and others) who sought to shape a 'safe' settlement with the King that would protect the nation in general, and the aristocracy in particular, from further royal encroachments. In December 1648 following the Army's decision to try the King, Sidney wrote to his father communicating Northumberland's movements, and questioning the legitimacy of the decision on the grounds that it lacked, and might with a little patience have gained, the concurrence of the Upper House. In the same year the Northumberland accounts recorded the receipt of a gift: 'Mr Algernon Sidney's groome presenting a horse.'[5]

Throughout the 1640s Sidney's young sister Diana had lived permanently among the Percy family at Petworth. By the early 1650s Algernon had moved from London to live with them too. He moved from Petworth in late 1655, and returned thereafter for regular visits.

After 1659, as an ambassador and then an exile, Algernon wrote to Northumberland regularly; and he entrusted to his uncle (rather than his father) a last and delicate piece of political patronage: the presentation of his (less than abject) letter to the King, following the Restoration. Sidney's reconciliation with the monarchy had been made almost impossible by news of his strident defence while abroad of the execution of Charles I. According to Ludlow, Northumberland himself had, in the same year (1660), been 'heard to say, that though [like Sidney] he had no part in the death of the king, he was against questioning those who had been concerned in that affair: that the example might be more useful and profitable to kings, by deterring them from such exorbitances'. The Earl's continued identification with the 'cause' had led Sir Arthur Haselrig to exclaim in Parliament in 1659, 'I from my soul honour the Old Lords. I exceedingly honour Lord Northumberland.' One of

---

[3] British Museum add MS 33058 fol. 71; Underdown D., *Pride's Purge* (1971) p. 34; Morrill J. S., *The Revolt of the Provinces* (1980) p. 180; Kent R.O. U1475 O101/2.

[4] North MSS Alnwick Letters and Papers vol. 16 1641–56 23/5 B.M. reel 286 fol. 59.

[5] B.M. add. MS 21,506 fol. 55; B.M. North MSS micro reel 291 Syon House U.1.6.

the only two letters back to England of which we have record from Algernon after 1663 was to his uncle at Petworth (1668). Later in that year the Earl died.[6]

The distinguishing features of Northumberland's character are clear. He was, said Clarendon, 'the proudest man alive' and 'if he had thought the King as much above him as he thought himself above other[s], he would have been a good subject ... He was in all his deportment a very great man' and behaved 'with a dignity and independence more characteristic of a feudal potentate than a seventeenth century nobleman'. Nowhere was this more evident than in the 'government of his family, where no man was more absolutely obeyed'. Burnet commented too: '[Northumberland] was a man of great spiritt, of a high sence o[f] honour, that lived with all the greatness of the Antient Nobility and under much Forme and high civilities ... he had a high sence both of Publick Liberty and of the Dignity of Peers.' Northumberland was, in short, the prototype, in character and aspirations if not in fact, of the ancient independent noblemen Algernon lionised in his version of English history. He not only continued to express, after the Restoration, anti-monarchist political sentiments very like Algernon's own; he had even written, anticipating Sidney's *Discourses*, a Tacitean political treatise on the Roman emperors.[7]

Algernon's own personality was crucially characterised by this Percy-style imperiousness and pride. What is most important, however, to an understanding of Sidney's political thought and self-image, is not the pride itself, but where it came from. Percy family history was a special phenomenon, and its more spectacular characters and episodes were as much public knowledge in the seventeenth century as they still are today to audiences of Shakespeare's *Henry IV*, parts I and II. The Northumberlands were probably the oldest, and certainly historically the best known, noble family in seventeenth-century England. Moreover, these survivors of a previous age had been the most powerful. Algernon Sidney was certainly aware of the dramatic turnaround in the family's historical fortunes which lay behind Northumberland's allegiance in the civil war.

In 1066 William de Perci (surnamed 'of the moustaches'; 'als gernons') arrived in England from Normandy with William the Conqueror. Speaking later in the *Discourses* of the heroic 'actions of our ancestors' in that time, Sidney was to claim:

---

[6] B.M. micro reel 291; PRO Chancery MSS C7 327/50; Blencowe, *Sidney Papers* p. 187; PRO State Papers Flanders 36 fol. 208; Ludlow iii, 10 quoted in *Burton's Diary* ed. Rutt J. T., III p. 78 and note.

[7] DNB vol. XLIV pp. 385, 389; Burnet, add MS 63,057 vol. 1 174–5; HMC 3rd Rep. North MSS fol. 109. Interestingly, a French language edition of Sidney's *Discourses* (1702 La Haye trans. Samson) in the Bibliothèque Nationale contains some manuscript notes (*c.* eighteenth century) which point out that Sidney was the nephew of Northumberland and that 'il inspira probablement sa sentiments a sa neveu'. BBN *E.994.H.a.

There was then neither conquering Norman, nor conquered Saxon, but a great and brave people composed of both, united in blood and interest in defence of their common rights, which they so well maintained, that no prince since that time has too violently encroached upon them, who, as the reward of his folly, has not lived miserably, and died shamefully.[8]

The Percy family, centred in their northern fortress of Alnwick castle, made themselves, by ruthlessly effective military service and often-displayed valour, undisputed 'Kings of the North'; 'the hereditary guardians of the north and scourge of Scotland'. This was Sidney's expansionist 'Plantagenet Age'; the Percys rendered repeated service as military leaders in France; Hotspur served from 1393 to 1395 as Governor of the conquered province of Bordeaux. Sidney was later to glorify the government of the English Commonwealth on the grounds that its military conquests and consequent foreign prestige had restored to the nation the glory of that age when 'we possessed the better half of France, and the Kings of France and Scotland were our prisoners'.[9]

Such was the independent power of the Percy 'kings of the North' that when Richard II assumed 'tyrannical' new powers in the south it was Hotspur and his father Henry Percy, first Earl of Northumberland, who handed him over to Henry IV at Flint on 19 August 1399. Their subsequent boast to have placed Henry of Lancaster on the throne was acknowledged to be 'not without foundation'. When the new King's military ineptitude began to contrast glaringly with the Percys' continued success, the latter rebelled. In a famous interview the King drew his dagger, and Hotspur withdrew crying 'Not here, but in the field!'[10] Hotspur raised an army, publicly accused Henry of 'tyrannical government', and issued in 1403 a proclamation labelling himself and his noble followers 'Protectors of the Commonwealth'. He was defeated and killed at Shrewsbury in July 1403.

Under tyrants or absolute monarchies, said Sidney in the *Discourses*,

The most eminent [subjects] are always most feared, as the readiest to undertake, and most able to accomplish, great designs. This eminence proceeds from birth, riches, virtue, or reputation, and . . . I know not where to find an example of such a man who could long subsist under absolute monarchy . . . he must, like Brutus conceal his virtue, and gain no reputation, or resolve to perish, if he do not prevent his own death by that of the tyrant. All other ways are ineffectual: the suspicions, fears, and hatred, thereupon arising, are not to be removed; personal respects are forgotten; and such services, as cannot be sufficiently valued, must be blotted out by the death of those that did them . . . Henry the fourth was made king by the earl of Northumberland, and his

---

[8] *Discourses* pp. 85, 452.
[9] *Works* (1772) *Discourses* pp. 240–1.
[10] A scene to be repeated in Sidney's own career in Sweden in 1659. Following this incident Sidney wrote his famous motto: 'Manus haec inimica tyrannis' ('this hand always an enemy to tyrants').

brave son Hotspur; [but that king] ... could not think himself safe, till his benefactor was dead.

This was written one year before Sidney's own execution by Charles II, on the eve of which he claimed, somewhat obscurely, to have 'done many personall and most important services, as well to the royall family, as unto such as depended upon it'.[11]

The relevance of all this to Algernon's picture of the great and militarily independent 'Plantagenet Age' nobility should be clear: they assisted the kings in their conquests, and defended the people against their tyranny. So, too, should the relevance of Hotspur's example be to the self-image adopted by Algernon in the subsequent course of his own life and martyrdom. What Algernon's thought shows, however, is a consciousness of something more general; the fate of the Percys between the 'Plantagenet Age' and his own time. They were broken, as an independent political force, by the encroaching monarchy.[12]

The turning point for the Percys came with the early Tudors. Northumberland history between Henry VIII and the English Civil War is an unbroken succession of prisons, scaffolds, and graveyards. It is the road which Algernon Sidney continued to take with his own rebellion and execution in 1683, after declaring that all hope of liberty was not lost 'if we have the spirit of our ancestors'; he was in an important sense the last seventeenth-century Northumberland.[13] Under Henry VIII the fifth Earl of Northumberland was imprisoned by Wolsey, the sixth Earl treated by him 'like a child', and both the sixth Earl's brothers executed after the Pilgrimage of Grace. The sixth Earl was forced to surrender his title by Henry; it was revived for his nephew Thomas Percy, who as the seventh Earl led the Northern Rebellion in 1569. He was executed and the title passed to his previously scrupulously loyal brother, for whom the adoption of the family mantle seems to have acted as a treason-inducing agent in his blood. He was tried for treason in 1572 and in a momentous and decisive development the monarchy forbade the Percys the use of Alnwick or the right to venture north of the Trent. From then to Algernon's time their seat remained Petworth in Sussex. Treasonable intrigues with France landed the eighth Earl back in the Tower where he was found shot under mysterious circumstances in 1585.[14] The ninth Earl was imprisoned for fifteen years in the Tower following the Gunpowder Plot in

---

[11] *Discourses* p. 205; Sidney's *Apology* p. 1; DNB XLIV pp. 392–8; *Discourses* pp. 240–1.

[12] See Sidney's *Discourses* p. 213 in conjunction with the following three paragraphs below.

[13] Jocelyn Percy, the 11th Earl, last of the seventeenth-century line, had died young in 1670. The title was revived in the eighteenth century, maintaining its blood link through the descendants of Jocelyn's sister Elizabeth.

[14] As the next book will show, almost a century later his death would serve as the model for the suicide in the Tower of Essex, Sidney's friend and colleague, and the husband of Elizabeth Percy.

1605. Ten years after his release he handed the title on to Algernon, the tenth Earl, who explained privately to Sidney's father Leicester on the eve of the war: 'the king ... [sh]ould not expect [more] from me (whos house hath in these latter ages received little or no advantage from the Crowne)'.[15]

Sidney's own anti-tyrant political writing is peppered with references to Edward II and Richard II, 'they who had murdered the best of the nobility', and the heroic actions of 'our ancestors' in bringing them to account. It reserves particular abuse, too, for Henry VIII and Wolsey. The subsequent dynasty of the Stuarts, beginning with the elevation of Buckingham under James I, 'that Scotch solomon with a padlock on his sword', showed that the rot continued in the new line more than ever. During the 1620s the Earl of Northumberland had been particularly 'offended by Buckingham's ostentatious coach with its six horses', and Lord Percy had referred to him as 'the great usurper'. Everything had changed, and the only solution now acceptable to Sidney to the problems of government with independence and armed vigour, lay in liberty from monarchy altogether.[16]

3.2 THE SIDNEYS

The other, and even more important side of Algernon's weighty ancestral heritage came, as the previous chapter has suggested, from the Sidneys; and particularly Sir Philip, Algernon's great-uncle. Here two factors remain constant; the example of knightly valour in arms in defence of the oppressed, and the idea of empire and involvement abroad; but for its setting we exchange the late medieval for the Elizabethan era, to its background we add an internationalist political and intellectual culture, and to its motives we add that of religion; the defence of international protestantism against persecution, at home and abroad. The legend of Sir Philip's martyrdom fighting at Zutphen against the papist Spanish armies was already well established in England during Algernon's lifetime. The work which did so much to establish it, Fulke Greville's *Life of Sir Philip Sidney*, was first published under the Commonwealth government in which Algernon served, in 1652. The examples it held out of Elizabethan military virtue employed abroad and the spirited defence of protestantism (though not, as the Commonwealth found, necessarily both at once) were of great relevance to the Puritan culture which had grown up to opposition under the early Stuarts, and then to government

---

[15] DNB XLIV 385–441; North Alnwick MSS B.M. micro reel 286 9 January 1639.

[16] See *Discourses* pp. 205, 461, 465, 484 (and pp. 425–7 on nobility generally); *Apology* pp. 17, 30; *Maxims* p. 50. For an attempt to *refute* the legitimacy of applying the precedents of either Richard II or Edward II to Charles I's case see William Prynne, *A Briefe* [sic] *Momento To The Present Unparliamentary Junto* (1 January 1649) pp. 9, 12–24. Sharpe K. ed., *Faction and Parliament* (1978) p. 242; cf. Stone L., *The Causes of the English Revolution 1529–1642* (London 1972) p. 49.

after their demise. Of equal interest was the contrast it drew between 'those active times . . . and this effeminate age'.[17] The point about Sir Philip's legend, was

That he dyed not languishing in ydleness ryot and excesse, nor as overcome with nyce pleasures and fond vanities; but of manly wounds received in defence of persons oppressed, in maintenance of the only true . . . Christian Religion . . . in the open fielde, in Martiall maner, the honorablest death that could be desired, and best beseeming a Christian Knight, whereby he hath worthely wonne to himselfe immortall fame among the godly, and left example worthie of imitation of others of his calling.[18]

Moreover, Greville's *Life*, dedicated to Algernon's sister Dorothy, was at pains to stress that such exceptional virtue could be, and had been, inherited through the Sidney family.[19] The Sidneys themselves needed no instruction on this point; they had been raised in Sir Philip's image from the very beginning, even during his own lifetime. Algernon's grandfather, the first Earl of Leicester (Sir Philip's younger brother), was admonished from the outset by his father:

Imitate his [Sir Philip's] virtues, exercises, studies and actions. He is the rare ornament of his age; the very formula that all well-disposed young gentlemen of our Court do form also their manners and life by. In truth I speak it without flattery of him or myself; he hath the most rare virtues that ever I found in any way. Once again I say, imitate him.

Sir Philip himself was the product of a prestigious marriage alliance between his father Henry Sidney and the Dudleys, which allied Henry with Warwick under the Edwardian Protectorate, and made Sir Philip nephew of Elizabeth's favourite, the Earl of Leicester. Sir Philip was accordingly told by his father, as Algernon might well have been: 'Remember my son, the noble blood you are descended of by your mother's side; and think that only by virtuous life and good action you may be an ornament to that illustrious family.' Sir Philip was to take this advice to heart, and say: 'my cheefest honour is to be a Dudlei'.[20]

Algernon Sidney was to inherit, through the upbringing and education he received under the personal direction of his father, a host of aspects of the intellectual culture founded by Sir Philip, and for reasons which will be explained, the burden of that Sidney heritage was to fall squarely, in his own generation, onto Algernon's shoulders. Consequently Algernon was to share

[17] Worden, 'Classical republicanism' pp. 185–6; Greville Sir Fulke, *Life of Sir Philip Sidney* (first pub. 1652 Oxford 1907); cf. Hill C., *The Intellectual Origins of the English Revolution* (1965) pp. 131–5; Trevor-Roper, 'Cromwell and his Parliaments' in *Religion, The Reformation, and Social Change* (1967) pp. 359–63.

[18] Du Plessis Mornay, *A Woorke Concerning the Trewnesse of the Christian Religion* (1587) translated by Sir Philip Sidney, Dedicatory Epistle.

[19] Greville, *Sir Philip Sidney*, Dedicatory Epistle.

[20] Cartwright J., *Sacharissa* (1901) pp. 4, 6, 7; Sidney Sir Philip, *Works* III pp. 65–6; Worden, 'Republicanism' pp. 185–6.

with Sir Philip characteristics crucial to the future lives, martyrdoms, and political legends of both. Both men laboured under the same heavy sense of family expectation and public observation, and both men found that their Platonic idealism and obsession with honour, propriety, and the watchful eye of history, led much more often in the fallible real world to frustration, outbursts of temper, and missed political opportunities than to the political advancement that both really deeply desired. Both lives led accordingly to the violent and heroic death of a single individual pitted over a point of political and religious principle against overwhelming odds; and thus each Sidney founded the legend of his own martyrdom with an effectiveness which borders upon historic rivalry.[21]

In the Elizabethan political arena the Sidney family's fortunes were bound up, from the outset, with empire, and the advocacy of an active interventionist foreign policy. Sir Philip's father, Henry, had served Elizabeth as the leading figure in her conquest of Ireland. When the huguenots requested English aid in 1574 they did so through Sir Henry, and consequently it 'was Sir Henry who made the military arrangements for English intervention in the first of the [French] Religious Wars'.[22] Sir Philip himself looked keenly to that 'heroical design of invading and possessing America'; he believed that the Spaniards had, by their cruelty, doomed their world empire, and that England should be moving into the gap.[23] He had close contacts with Drake, and unsuccessfully attempted to accompany him on one of his voyages. He encouraged untiringly Elizabeth's active continental intervention on behalf of the protestant Dutch against Spain, the cause in which he died, and a family involvement with the Netherlands which his brother, the first Earl of Leicester, continued as governor of the cautionary towns (Flushing and The Brill) under James I. These family outlooks, and the traditions of involvement in Holland and Ireland in particular, survived unbroken through to Algernon's day. Political and military involvement with Ireland and Holland were to become the most important features of Algernon's own career. The active expansionist foreign view behind them is what drove his own political activities in the English Commonwealth government, and provided the Elizabethan background to his own slashing attacks on the toothlessness of English foreign policy under the Stuart monarchs. On the Rump Council of State he worked with Vane, Scot, and Challoner to revive the naval glory of the days of 'worthy Hawkins and famous Drake'.[24] Algernon's involvement with the conquest of Scotland and Ireland, with the East India Company,

---

[21] Cf. Hamilton A. C., *Sir Philip Sidney* (1977) pp. 1–4, for a description of Philip and his life which would apply equally well to Algernon.

[22] Salmon J. H. M., *The French Religious Wars in English Political Thought* (Oxford 1959) pp. 154–5.

[23] Hill C., *Intellectual Origins* p. 135.

[24] Worden, 'Republicanism' p. 189.

with the aggressive advancement of trade, and with Furly, Penn, and the drawing up of the Pennsylvanian constitution, are all of a piece with this tradition and outlook.

In line with this internationalist context, both Algernon and Sir Philip were to spend much of their time and political careers outside England, as travellers and diplomats all over continental Europe; in Scandinavia, the German cities, Holland and Flanders, the Italian cities, Paris and the south of France. Both Sir Philip and Algernon spent much of their lives engaged in diplomatic, and trying to organise military, action on the European continent on behalf of their respective religious and political causes. Both saw Europe as an interdependent whole; and even Algernon's enemies were to describe him during his exile as 'a man of excellent parts and knowledg in the affaires of Europe'.[25] Both Sir Philip and Algernon shared the same deep commitment to the European-wide struggle against intolerance and persecution in general, and intolerant papism in particular. Neither needed any book-learning on this subject. As already mentioned, Sir Philip had been witness in Paris to the horrific massacre of protestants on St Bartholemew's Eve 1572, and narrowly escaped with his own life. Algernon was sent in 1641 by his father, the newly appointed Lord Lieutenant of Ireland, to fight against the 'rebels' there responsible for the massacre of protestants in the same year. Algernon served there with his lifelong friend to be, Sir John Temple, son of Sir Philip's secretary (and England's foremost Ramist scholar) Sir William Temple, still a Sidney family client, and the author-to-be of the standard and grossly exaggerated account of the 1641 massacre, in which he claimed that 'there were above 300,000 protestants murdered in cold blood'.[26] From Sir Philip, Ramus, and Sir William Temple in 1572, to Philip, Algernon, and Sir John Temple in 1642, the cause had changed very little.

I have already mentioned that, among Sir Philip's close subsequent contacts with huguenot leaders, were Hubert Languet and Philippe du Plessis Mornay. John Temple's *Irish Rebellion* (1646) similarly prefaced its account of the horrors of the Irish massacre by a reference to the times of 'Monsieur du Plessis, a person of extraordinary abilities and learning ... as it appears by a letter of his to Monsieur Languet'.[27]

It is perhaps no surprise, then, that Mornay's monarchomach classic *Vindiciae Contra Tyrannos* (1579) anticipates the whole range of the anti-

---

[25] Unknown corresp. to Charles II 26 April 1667 PRO State Papers Flanders 36 fol. 205.

[26] The true figure was closer to three thousand, but Temple's claim was widely accepted by English protestants. Temple Sir John, *History of the Irish Rebellion* (1646); Prendergast J. P., *The Cromwellian Settlement of Ireland* (1922) p. 66.

[27] Temple, *Rebellion* Preface pp. 2–3. See also p. 14 where Temple introduces Algernon's father Leicester as 'heir to Sir Philip Sidney his uncle, aas well as Sir Hen. Sidney his grandfather, who with great honour ... long continued Chief Gouvernour of Ireland during the Raign of Queen Elizabeth'.

tyranny arguments of Milton's *Tenure* and Sidney's *Maxims* as strongly as his *Trewnesse* anticipates their Platonic/protestant religion. Indeed Sidney was to make extensive use, in both the *Maxims* and the *Discourses*, of all the French monarchomach writers, particularly Mornay, Hotman, and Beza, as well as all the other French literature connected to their cause, including Davila, de Thou, Mezeray's *History*, and Philip de Comines's *Life of Louis XI*.[28]

The *Court Maxims* in particular is a work written in a place (the Netherlands) and in pursuit of a design, which most overtly joins the themes of Sir Philip's and Algernon's lives together. The *Maxims* is an internationalist defence of religious and political liberty in the 1660s against papism, persecution, and tyranny in general, and Stuart papism, persecution, and tyranny in particular. To make its point it employs monarchomach political arguments against the historical background of the sixteenth-century French wars of religion and the popish massacres in Paris (1572) and Ireland (1641). Sidney depicts the seventeenth-century English Civil War as a continuation of the sixteenth-century French struggle, with all the same issues at stake; and he links his accusations of Stuart involvement with the 1641 massacre, with the statecraft of Catherine de Medici in France in 1572. He was to make the same connections again in the *Discourses*, with the 1678 popish plot as new evidence of the continuing problem. In the *Maxims* Sidney argues that not only are the political and religious fortunes of England and Holland in the 1660s interdependent, as they had been in Elizabethan times, but the fate of the French huguenots, too, hinges upon the success of himself and his colleagues, in their republican designs with the Dutch. This republican design for Dutch–English co-operation Sidney had first represented as the English Republic's ambassador in 1659, when it was specifically described as an attempt to revive the Anglo–Dutch policies of Elizabeth I. During the embassy itself Algernon publicly signed himself, in the presence of the Dutch envoys, 'Philippus Sidney'. Following the failure of the *Court Maxims*'s design Algernon retired to the huguenot south of France where, again, he was referred to by the French as 'Philippe'. Time and again on his peripatetic European travels and discussions with European leaders Algernon reminds us of Sir Philip; not least in Rome, ordering from Frankfurt a copy of his great-uncle's portrait.[29]

---

[28] For instance, *Discourses* p. 253; For Sir Philip's and Algernon's links with the huguenots and use of huguenot ideas see Salmon, *French Religious Wars* pp. 134–7, 184–5.

[29] Du Mornay, *Trewnesse*, Dedicatory Epistle [to Henry of Navarre] p. 1; cf. *Court Maxims*, esp. pp. 65–7, 107, 181–94 for the Philip Sidney perspective. BBN 'Lantiniana' p. 101; Algernon was referred to by Turenne, the French King (Louis XIV), and the French ambassador (Colbert de Croissy) as 'Philippe' Sidney; Ministère des Relations Exterieures, Corresp. Politique, sous-serie Angleterre, vol. 99 'tome XV de la negociation de Mr Colbert' 30 Juillet 1670 and 102 fols. 163–7.

The role of Algernon's father, the Earl of Leicester, in passing on these traditions was crucial. When posted as ambassador to Paris in 1636 he took his two eldest sons with him (Algernon then aged 13) and in France they stayed for the next six years. Consequently Algernon and (eventually) all his brothers were educated in France. Either Algernon or Philip or both were accordingly enrolled at the huguenot academy at Saumur, founded by none other than du Plessis Mornay in 1602. In the same period Algernon, at least, spent much of his time in Paris with his father, who was observed from England to be attending services at the huguenot church at Charenton, a practice which earned him the label from Laud of 'a most dangerous practising Puritan'. The minister at Charenton in this period (and a visitor to Saumur in 1638) was none other than Jean Daillé. In the *Court Maxims*, following a sceptical refutation of the English bishops' use of the Church Fathers to bolster their own authority, Sidney said: 'I learnt these cautions in reading of them from Monsieur Daillé, that excellent and learnd preacher of the Gospell in Charenton.' The birth of Daillé's theology under du Plessis Mornay's patronage has already been mentioned.[30]

Clarendon reported Leicester to be 'generally understood to be a Puritan abroad; at least [the French] knew him more than ordinarily averse to their religion'. Leicester retorted that he had never been called a Puritan 'by any Body, that was not a Papist', though when later required to defend himself by letter to the King himself he was forced to take a less abrasive line. In this letter to Charles I he stated, unfortunately, that if Puritans were thought to be politically dangerous because they might read Buchanan, papists were just as dangerous because they could read Bellarmine, thus demonstrating his own familiarity with both.[31]

Indeed, during this period in Paris, Leicester maintained the family tradition of high-level huguenot contacts in general. Another was the Duc du Rohan, who had led the huguenot rebellion at La Rochelle in 1627, and whose writing did so much to introduce to English political theory the French language of 'interest', later used by Algernon. As both a great noble, and a huguenot leader, du Rohan embodied in his person the two greatest obstacles to the centralisation of French state power in progress under Richelieu's management during the time of the Sidney's residence in France. Later in the

---

[30] De Lisle MSS U1475 C97/1, C124/2; HMC De Lisle VI 554, xxii; *Court Maxims* p. 96. Sidney's French education (and later exile) provide one obvious context for understanding his own links with French thought (e.g. Bodin, de Rohan) as well as his later appeal to French thinkers of the eighteenth century (Montesquieu, Rousseau, Condorcet). His connections with the French nobility will be described in ch. 14 below. On the role of Saumur vis-à-vis the Enlightenment see Trevor-Roper, *The Reformation* p. 209; Packer J. W., *Anglicanism* p. 66 (and n. 3).

[31] De Lisle U1475 C124/2; Butler M., 'Mercurius Brittanicus: a case study in Caroline political theatre' in *Historical Journal* 27, 4 (1984) p. 951.

Discourses Algernon, intensely sensitive, as we have seen, to the fate of both protestantism and the nobility in his own country, typically internationalised his discussion of the threat to both by linking his treatment of the English aristocracy with a survey of noble status in France. He dated the growth of French absolutism from Richelieu and the failure of the Caroline monarchy to effectively intervene on behalf of the huguenots under du Rohan at La Rochelle.[32] Against this background Algernon's subsequent eleven-year exile in the huguenot south of France, and his contact during that time with huguenot aristocrats and military leaders like Turenne, comes to look less irrelevant to the rest of his life than it has hitherto seemed.[33]

Most important, however, among Leicester's protestant contacts in Paris for Sidney's own political theory was, as already mentioned, the ambassador for Sweden, Hugo Grotius. The Earl's surviving notes are full of Grotius's social chatter and reflection upon his political ideas; interspersed with notes on his other favourite authors (all later used in the same proportion by Algernon): in particular Livy, also Cicero, Suetonius, Coke, Littleton, Selden, Buchanan, Hooker, and Suarez. The Earl shared with Grotius the political enterprise of selling to France in the Thirty Years War the cause of Europe's two principal protestant powers, and the two men discussed together their religious aspiration of establishing a structure for the promotion of protestant unity in Europe.[34] It seems most likely that Sidney himself met Grotius in this period; but the point is not crucial. For the general way in which Sidney inherited through his family both his broad intellectual outlook, and his reliance on particular theorists like Grotius, can be specifically demonstrated by the Sidney family commonplace books still surviving at Maidstone.[35]

In these books Algernon's grandfather the first Earl made notes on the

---

[32] *Discourses* pp. 237–8; Worden, 'Republicanism' p. 186. For Rohan and interest theory see ch. 12 below.

[33] The most often quoted name (apart from Grotius) in the commonplace-book notes of the second Earl of Leicester is 'd'Ossat' – Cardinal d'Ossat, the head of Henry IV's church, to whose accounts of Machiavellian intrigue at the papacy Leicester was addicted. There exist, in the Bibliothèque de Lille in France, a seventeenth-century collection of handwritten biographical 'portraits' of 'Hommes Illustres' in huguenot history: they include Mornay, d'Ossat, d'Hopital, Turenne, Henry Sidney, and 'Philippe' Sidney. Bibliothèque de Lille MS 692, Bullart MSS, no. 482 fols. 237, 239–41, 283, 315–17, 319–21, 323, 325.

[34] Never one to confine himself to a single point of view the relativist Leicester ordered from England in 1638 a copy of Selden's *Mare Clausum*.

[35] Grotius H., *Of The Law of Warre and Peace* (London 1655) trans. Clement Barksdale: see letter Grotius to Joannes Duraeus 21 November 1637 in 'Memorials of the Author'. For the second Earl see De Lisle MSS U1475 Z1/9 loose pages fols. 1–3 (Grotius), 6 (Livy), 7–8 (Cicero, Suetonius), fourth loose item fol. 2 (Livy), main volume fols. 68 (Grotius), 84–5 (Coke, Littleton), 101 (Suarez, Hooker), 317 (Buchanan), 353 (Livy), 328–9, 344–5, 348–9 (Grotius); Z9 pp. 11 (Grotius), 21ff, 263, 402 (Coke). Readers of Blair Worden's article 'Classical republicanism' will know how indebted I am to him for the initial discovery of the importance of these sources.

nature of political sovereignty. He noted that it could be located in 'Monarchy, Aristocracy, or Democracy', or some sort of 'mixed estats according as the authority is establishd' between the three. The point about this authority, the Earl noted, was that it ought to be exercised according to 'what is necessary or convenient for the whole body' rather than 'the privat use of the member governing'; any such misuse of sovereignty resulted in 'Tyranny or Anarchy'. Moreover, he went on, it was natural for the king to attempt to stretch his prerogative, and the people their power, 'every creature delighting in liberty, and no man holding his estate or person secure while he knows himself subject to the pleasure of another', from which fact arose the 'uncertainty of prerogative and the need to fix it in law'. The Earl then went on to discuss the Roman emperors as examples of absolutism and to ask '[What is] the difference between subjection and slavery?' and 'How greate men are to carry themselves under tyrants?' The centrality of these concerns to Algernon Sidney's own political thought should require no elaboration. Their flavour of Aristotle, Bodin, and Tacitus is a good indication of the sixteenth-century background to Sidney's own theory.[36]

The second Earl's notes are even more relevant. Their most pervasive overall feature is their scepticism and relativism, their preoccupation with the many variations among 'the opinions and fancyes of men'. 'How much wise men', sighed Leicester, 'trouble themselves sometimes about external ceremonyes.'[37] Like the European diplomat he was, the Earl wrote interchangeably in his commonplace books in five languages (English, Latin, French, Spanish, and Italian) and his vast reading centred on the politics, religion, history, and customs of the various nations of the world, protestant and catholic, Christian and Islamic, ancient and modern; to quote from one of his own letters to [the no doubt rather confused] Charles I: 'the Jews, Rechabites, Pharises ... antient Greekes, Pythagorians, Peripateticks, Cynicks, Stoicks ... Christians ... Mahometans ... Arians, Eutychians ... Acephali, Monothelites and too many more'. His extraordinary library, a mid-seventeenth-century catalogue for which survives, listed its contents alphabetically; under the first letter, 'A', alone, there are 481 titles.[38]

Leicester's notes indeed display specifically the scepticism and relativism

---

[36] De Lisle U1475 Z1/10 fols. 19, 477; Z1/1 fols. 711–12.

[37] U1475 C124/2; Z1/8 fol. 290.

[38] U1475 C124/2; Z45/2. The library included, for example, eighteen volumes of Aristotle, eight of Hooker, twelve of Bacon, seven of Bellarmine, three of Buchanan, fifteen of Grotius, ten of Machiavelli, six of Tacitus, twelve of Selden, and many others by Plato, Suetonius, Seneca, Thucydides, Gerson, Coke, Guicciardini, and Richelieu. Recent English works included Henry Vane jun.'s *Retyred Mans Meditations* (1655) and *A Healing Question*, Harrington's *Oceana*, Hobbes's *De Cive* and *Leviathan*, 'Thucidides in English by Hobbs', and Sir Robert Filmer's *The Freeholders Grand Inquest* (1648). These purchases of recent works show Leicester's interest in keeping tabs on the output of his Kentish next-door

which were later to characterise Algernon's *Discourses*. He anticipated the *Discourses* with his notes on the variety of different customs of monarchical inheritance in the world,[39] different forms of nobility, title, diplomatic custom and address,[40] different national codes of positive law and, most specifically, the different, and changing, meaning of words themselves, the particular labels for things. In this he recalled Algernon in the *Discourses*: 'except there be a charm belonging to the name, or the letters that comprise it, which cannot belong to all nations, for they are different in every one according to their several languages'; 'the name given is no way essential to the thing'.[41] In the *Discourses*, Algernon had paused to consider the crucial word 'rebellion'. The word itself, he argued, was nothing to be superstitious about; it was simply 'taken from the Latin "rebellare" which signifies no more than to renew a war'. Sidney illustrated this point from Livy before concluding that therefore 'Rebellion being nothing but a renewed war ... of itself is neither good nor evil, more than any other war, but is just or unjust according to the cause or manner of it' [at which point, of course, Grotian theory comes in].[42] In notes made in his commonplace book Sidney's father had observed:

And though Livy use the word Rebellare, that seems to be the makin warr again; rather than to imply subjection ... Rebellare is frequently used in Livy, as Lib :35 p651 ... yet neither Philip, nor Habis were subjects to the Romans, but the meaning was, that ... [they] would make warr again upon the Romans ...[43]

Sidney later said at his trial that his unpublished *Discourses* were simply a heap of private political reflections and notes after the manner of those of his father: 'I believe there is a brother of mine here has forty quires of paper written by my father, and never one sheet of them was published: but he writ his own mind to see what he could think of it another time, and blot it out again may be.'

In *Of Love* Sidney explained: 'I write only today, that which I shall read the next week or month, and then burn, having no other intention but to ease my troubled thoughts, and to attain to the knowledge of myself ... I little care for those rules which are necessary to those who are to depend upon others judgements; I content myself with setting down my thoughts without caring

---

neighbours – Vane and Filmer – a point of interest since the relevance of the ideas of both to the thought of Algernon needs no emphasis. Cf. U1475 Z45/1.

[39] Z1/9 fols. 83–93.

[40] Z9 fol. 1; Z1/9 fol. 147.

[41] *Discourses* pp. 297, 333; For the different and changing meanings of words and names see Daillé, *A Treatise* p. 98.

[42] *Discourses* pp. 457–8, 460.

[43] Z1/9 loose pages, fourth item fol. 2.

for rule or order...', a claim any reader of the *Discourses* will unhappily confirm. It is, indeed, probably only through the historical accident of his arrest and execution that the *Discourses*, a jumble of half a million words written at the age of 60, is the major political writing of Sidney's to survive.[44]

The best specific example of all in the Earl's papers of the way in which his own inquiries influenced the initial orientation of Algernon's own, is provided by a series of reflections he made on the theories of Grotius. In a few pages the Earl worked through a series of connected questions which lay at the heart of English political thinking during the civil war years and after (and at the heart of the later theories of Sidney and Locke); namely, how were civil societies initially set up?; why?; in accordance with what specified needs?' and, accordingly, what (if any) were the limits of individual obedience, and of the State's powers over individuals or families, in accordance with these needs? 'That wch I seeke', wrote Leicester, 'is this, whether or no in some cases, not only Princes and other superior magistrats, but even the whole society from wch the power of princes and magistrates is derived be restrained in some cases; and cannot do every act upon ever [sic] particular person.' His conclusion was the same as Algernon's, expressed in the same form as was Algernon's later. 'I conceive they are restrained,' said Leicester, 'though that resttriction [sic] may produce some inconveniencies for in civille matters there is nothing that on all sydes is [free] of inconveniences, and right is measured by that which seems best to this or that man ... [and] by his or theyr will, from whence that right or power proceeded.'

The Earl took this from Grotius's *De Jure Belli*, Book I: 'in matters of government there is nothing which from every point of view is quite free from disadvantages; and a legal provision is to be judged not by what this or that man considers best, but by what accords with the will of him with whom the provision originated'.[45]

Algernon later echoed this conclusion in the *Discourses*: 'If it be said, that this may sometimes cause disorders, I acknowledge it; but no human condition being perfect; such a one is to be chosen which carries with it the most tolerable inconveniencies.' Yet with little shift of meaning, Sidney's quote represents his progression from one sceptical source to another, for it comes not from Grotius but from Machiavelli, whose own *Discourses* said: 'So in all human affairs one notices ... that it is impossible to remove one inconvenience without another emerging ... Hence in all discussions one

---

[44] State Trials 35 Charles II, 1683, p. 878. The Earl took great care that his political notes, added onto those of his father, would be passed on, with his library, to his sons, as a growing repository of political and historical wisdom. He took particular care over specifying the inheritance of the library. Cf. U1475 F32/4, Codicil 4 April 1671; 'Of Love', add. MS 34,100 pp. 1, 6–7.

[45] Grotius, *De Jure Belli* trans. F. W. Kelsey (1925) vol. II (bk I) p. 124.

should consider [only] which alternative involves fewer inconveniences ...
for one never finds any issue that is clear cut and not open to question.'[46]

Leicester recorded four more linked conclusions: 'I [conclude] ... as
Grotius sayeth, that men, not by the commandment of God, but of their own
[mind] ... did gather themselves together into civile societyes from whence
the civile power hath beginning, and is therefore called a humane ordinance.'
Secondly, therefore, 'Kings made not themselves by force, but were created in
all nations by the people for the public good.' 'I thinke', said Leicester, 'this is
cleare enough in ye mindes of all men, unless it be of such as for their own
interests flatter princes in the ruine of theyr country and of all honest men.'

Finally, then, forms of government being not absolute nor divinely created,
but merely particular and fallible human creations, regard needed to be had
to the fact that 'men were we[ak] and ought to make Laws with consideration
of humane infirmity, and for the benefit of the whole'.[47]

Sidney not only echoed all of these claims, they together form very much
the heart of his theory, and his answer to Filmer. As Leicester's own
tortuously conservative reaction to the civil war was to show, there was
nothing about these ideas themselves, or the reading from which they were
developed, to make a person who held them an actual, as opposed to
potential, rebel. But once the impetus for that had come from elsewhere, they
could provide, as Sidney was to show, the basis for a formidable resistance
ideology.

To pursue this line of inquiry, and before turning to his public career, it is
necessary to examine the nature of Sidney's private and family relationships.
Apart from providing a range of new details about his life, this account will
begin to address two questions begged by the previous section. Firstly, why
did Algernon – and only Algernon – so self-consciously take up the Sidney
family mantle and tradition, initiated by Sir Philip, and represented in his own
lifetime by his father? Secondly, why did Algernon's personal crusade take
the political form it did? The answers centre not simply on his political career
but on his relationship with his father itself; and we may indeed be led to the
disconcerting conclusion that republicans of Sidney's order are not only made
but also born. To borrow Machiavelli's language, behind the republican
ideology of virtu, there may lurk the full destabilising force of virtu's enemy:
fortuna, in this case the arbitrary fortune of birth, in relative order to the birth
of one's siblings. It is along the direct road from Sidney's paternal relationship
to his refutation of Filmer's *Patriarcha* that we must now travel.

---

[46] Machiavelli, *Discourses* trans. Bernard Crick (Penguin 1985) p. 121; Z1/9 loose pages fols.
    1–3, 3; Sidney, *Discourses* p. 461.
[47] Z1/9 loose pages fols. 1, 3; Z9 p. 251.

4

Family politics

[T]hough the law of England may make one man to be sole heir of his father, yet the laws of God and nature do not so.

Discourses p. 73

virtue only can give a just and natural preference

Discourses p. 62

His relationship with his father overshadowed Sidney's life as much as it did partly because the Earl, who announced the imminent approach of death in 1659, lived until late 1677, with Algernon himself to die only six years later, at the age of 61. The relationship was automatically important to Algernon because he was the second son in an aristocratic family whose wealth and title stood to be inherited, should the father will it, solely by the first. Moreover, both previous Earls of Leicester had inherited the estate and title themselves as second sons; first Sidney sons had a poor record of life expectancy.

The stakes, and the tension surrounding Algernon's prospects were considerably raised by his emergence, from an early age, as precociously able, and the only intellectual heir to his father and the Sidney heritage, in contrast to his dull and lazy elder brother Philip. This was the beginning of a turbulent family history in the long course of which Philip became disowned by the Earl and eventually substantially disinherited. Algernon's personality and intellect took shape as he moved, in pursuit of his father's approval, into the gap. This is the personal and family background to Sidney's political insistence that ability and virtue [republicanism], rather than primogeniture inheritance [monarchy], constitute the only just claim to title and power.

It would be unwise to accept without scepticism Algernon's retrospective sneer during the first of his chancery suits against his brother Philip over the inheritance (1677–81), that the Earl's 'eldest son [Philip was someone] of whome from his childhood [he] . . . had ever expressed a sinister opinion', and that in later life the Earl could only fruitlessly demand that Philip 'should leave the lewd, infamous, and Atheisticall life that he led'. Yet Philip's fall from grace, and indeed the Earl's changes in attitude through his life to all of

59

his children, are abundantly documented elsewhere, particularly in the dozen or so codicils to his will made by the Earl between 1660 and his death in 1677. Many other legal and family sources confirm the overall picture. Even Algernon's sanctimonious testimony on Philip receives support from modern political historians, who have found him 'distinctly lightweight', 'arrogant, quarrelsome and loose in his morals', and 'a lazy councillor ... [who] ... avoided parliamentary committees like the plague'.[1]

There are also independent signs that although the Earl's principal break with Philip did not come until 1652, Algernon began to shoulder him out of the limelight well before that. Although the Earl took both his eldest sons with him to France, Algernon seems to have spent much more time in Paris, and so in the Earl's own household, than Philip. We know from correspondence, and other sources, that Algernon was in Paris with his father on a number of occasions in 1636, 1637, 1638, and early 1640. We know of only one visit Philip made before 1640. The contrast is certainly clear enough in the following two comments written to the Earl by the Countess of Leicester, the first relating to Algernon in late 1636; the second to Philip in late 1638:

To Allgernoone I do send a blessing whom I hear much comended by all that comes from you, and Nic who spoke well of verie few, saide he had a huge deall of witt and much sweetness of nature.

I will not presse Phillop's comeing to me contrarie to your inclination, though I am desirous to see him but I confes it troubles me that he lives so long in a countrie towne, whear nothing can be learned, If you will neather suffer him at Paris nor send him in to England I wische he might go to Ittalio [sic] that his time maie not be is [sic] losse as I fear it is in that obscure place.[2]

In 1645 Philip was married.[3] As part of the matrimonial agreement the Earl settled the inheritance of the estate upon him, but retained to himself the right to charge the estate with up to £29,000, to be paid before it could be inherited, £21,000 nominally for marriage portions of £3,000 each for his seven daughters, and the other £8,000 for other debts and legacies. In effect this massive proviso, which Leicester was free to maintain, reapportion, or expunge as he saw fit, was simply a way of maintaining financial autonomy for himself, and effective control over what each of his sons would inherit, for

[1] B.M. Egerton 1049 fols. 5, 8; Woolrych A., *Commonwealth to Protectorate* (1982) pp. 167, 198, 313–14.
[2] HMC De Lisle vol. vi pp. 64, 554; De Lisle MSS U1475 C97/1; U1475 O89/11; Collins, *Letters and Memorials* p. 709; U1475 C82/34.
[3] To Lady Catherine Cecil, the daughter of Northumberland's brother-in-law the Earl of Salisbury.

the course of his lifetime. On account of its size the troubled Philip 'often confessed unto Algernone Sydney ... that ... he esteemed as nothing all he expected from the Earle his father'.[4]

In the years following, in the words of David Underdown, 'Lord Lisle quarrelled with his father, the Earl of Leicester, almost incessantly ... obviously jealous of the parental preference for his younger brother Algernon.' The row which finally led to a permanent estrangement between the two men came in December 1652.[5] In consequence Philip 'sent [his father] word by the Countesse of Leicester his mother, that he esteemed himself discharged of all duty and obedience towards him, which did produce such effects, as are not fit to be related, and might have had worse, if the sayd Countesse and Robert Sydney, had not parted them'. In the course of the argument Philip had struck the Earl's face, a blow from which, in terms of the inheritance, its giver was never to recover, despite a partial and temporary reconciliation with the Earl after Algernon's departure for Sweden in 1659.[6]

Meanwhile, in the years since 1645, Algernon had combined the advancement of his military and political career (assisted by Northumberland) with the advancement of his own independent financial prospects, by cultivation of his father. He began to devote himself increasingly to the management of his father's onerous legal and estate affairs, lending them his influence when he was in government and his time – eventually all of his time – when he wasn't.

In 1652 both Philip and Algernon were members of the Republican government. While Philip was fighting with his father, Algernon was relating to him harrowing stories of slavery in the English colonies. Leicester recorded:[7]

In the Islands of the West Indyes the English keepe the Negros theyr slaves in such servitude and misery that they being weary of theyr Lives have found a way to ... kill themselves, and nobody can yet discover by what meanes they do it, but they keepe it secret among them-selves ... This I heard by relation from Aulgernon Sydney 17 Feb 1652. He told me also (as I remember from the relation of one Liygen, who hath lived much in these islands) that the masters of these Negros, keepe from them all knives or other weapons, [but] so miserable is theyr servitude that they make themselves away whensoever they can ... theyr masters for theyr sustenance give them only a portion of Gruile of bread ... as men use to give to theyr beastes, oates, barley ... and water is all

---

[4] B.M. Eg. 1049 pp. 1–4; PRO Chancery C5 515/25; C10 195/28; C38 201; B.M. add MSS 32,680 fol. 17; De Lisle MSS U1475 F32/4.

[5] Underdown, *Pride's Purge* p. 221; Eg. 1049 p. 4; The argument came only four months after the death of Philip's wife Catherine in childbirth. Its occasion was the Earl's putting into execution the terms of the marriage settlement under which the £800 a year maintenance allowed the couple would be reduced to £600 upon the death of either one of them.

[6] B.M. Eg. 1049, esp. fol. 4.

[7] De Lisle MS U1475 Z1/9 loose pages, fifth item, fols. 2–3.

they drinke. They are servants to every nation, to the Spanyards, and Portugheses [*sic*] who employ them in theyr ... sugarworkes, so the English do, and the Hollanders ...[8]

Both Algernon and Philip had, under their father's eye, absented themselves from the King's trial and execution. But whereas Algernon's tenure of power ended with the dissolution of the Republic by Cromwell, Philip had gone on to cultivate his career under the patronage of the Protector. Sidney's later emphasis on the (relative) legitimacy of his 'entirely parliamentary' political cause, as distinct from the usurped (and regicide) tyranny of Cromwell, chimed in as far as possible with the Earl's own feelings. As we will see, when Sidney was less careful about his views of the regicide later he was to pay the price in paternal favour. In 1656, however, his ruling the roost at Penshurst provoked an outraged letter from Philip:[9]

[it is] my constant sorrow, to see that your Lordship never omits an oportunity of reproach to me; and in ernest I thinke, laying all other matters asyde ... [it] is very extraordenary, that the younger sonne sould so dominere in your house that ... it is not only his chamber but the greate roomes of the house, and perhaps the whole, he commands. And ... I thinke I may most properly say it, that his extreamest vanity and want of judgment are so knowne that there will be some wonder at it.[10]

Indeed for ten years, from 1648 until his departure from England in 1659, Algernon worked, often full-time, to assist the Earl with the management of his business affairs and estate, and most particularly to help him with 'several great suites at lawe' with which Leicester became involved, principally in chancery, between 1648 and 1655. In recognition of these services he was given £500 by the Earl in 1654, but in general told 'that [because of] the many charges ... fallen upon him, he could not well give him any thing for the present, but would consider it for the future'. These activities taught Sidney how to use the language and manipulate the procedures of law with an effectiveness which was to be seen in his later political writing and in his own six chancery cases following his return to England in 1677.[11]

In the course of the Earl's disputes with his own secretaries, employees, and tenants, Algernon served as an estate manager and policeman, being personally responsible for the arrest and imprisonment of at least one litigant against Leicester, Thomas Cowper. His knowledge of his father's affairs, particularly his legal affairs, became so indispensable that in 1672, when Leicester faced two chancery suits relating to building rights on his London

---

[8] From this suffering, which 'grieved' him, the Earl concluded that the Negros were the cursed descendants of Cain, condemned to be 'servants of servants'. From this he drew two lessons: first the power of 'The wrath of God', and second 'The Fulfilling of a divine prophecy made so long ago ...'.

[9] B. M. add MS 32,680 fols. 9–11; Blencowe, *Sidney Papers* pp. 205–27.

[10] Blencowe, *Sidney Papers* pp. 270–1.

[11] One of Sidney's closest republican colleagues and correspondents, Bulstrode Whitelocke, was in political charge of Chancery in the early 1650s. B.M. Eg. 1049 fol. 4; PRO Chancery C6/4/193; C10/22/137; C6/124/78; C10/25/46; C6/128/110; C6/161/65.

property of Leicester Fields, he applied for a pass for Algernon to be permitted to return from exile, 'that he might be assistant unto him in his affaires . . . complaining [that his younger son Henry] would not assist him'.[12]

The most important single consequence of his involvement in his father's affairs in the late 1640s and throughout the 1650s was Algernon's coming into contact, through them, with the affairs of the Strangfords. This was a supreme misfortune for both Algernon and Strangford and the resulting difficulties were to dominate Sidney's life from 1654 to 1659, and again from late 1677 to 1679.

Strangford was the only son of Thomas Smith, first Viscount Strangford, and Leicester's sister Elizabeth Sidney; he was thus Algernon's cousin. Both Strangford's parents had died within a year of his birth, following which he had gone into wardship to the Crown. The administration of his wardship had then been sold by Charles I to Sir Thomas Fotherly for £2,000. Thomas Smith's own sister, also Elizabeth, had married Henry Neville, a marriage which produced Henry Neville jun., Algernon's classical republican parliamentary colleague. Henry Neville (jun.) and Algernon were thus themselves second cousins through the Strangford family, and Sidney was to spend the Protectorate years living on and administering the Strangford estates where Neville's mother had been born and raised. Since the early 1640s Leicester was under pressure to take over the wardship from Fotherly – described darkly by Strangford's relations as 'non of the honestest'.[13]

The Earl, with many other cares, was reluctant to shoulder the trouble and responsibility, though he felt a duty towards the memory of a favourite sister. In mid-1646 a compromise was agreed, and Strangford came to live at Penshurst, with an allowance from Fotherly who continued to manage his estate. In December 1649 Fotherly died and Strangford, still a minor, elected the Earl to be his guardian and assume his wardship. This meant that the Earl also became his legal representative. This was one reason for the sudden group of chancery actions; it was also one reason why the Earl permitted Algernon to persuade him to take the 1650 engagement to the Commonwealth, without which he could assume no identity in law.[14]

In 1650 the picture was complicated by the seventeen-year-old Strangford's ardent courtship of Algernon's sister Isabella, or perhaps more particularly her £3,000 marriage portion. In this he had an ally in the formidable Countess of Leicester, whose principal object in life was to marry off her daughters to noblemen. The marriage was celebrated at Penshurst on 22

[12] PRO C6/128/110; De Lisle U1475 L5 fol. 1.

[13] U1475 E28 fols. 3–7; PRO C6 124/78; Veall D., *The Popular Movement for Law Reform 1640–60* (1970) pp. 54–5.

[14] The Earl agreed with Strangford a system of rent collection through a committee of two of Strangford's servants and one of his own; and this operation proceeded from 1649 to 1653. U1475 C125/2b; HMC De Lisle vol. vi pp. 557, 598; PRO C6/128/110; C6/124/78.

August 1650, 'to which mariage [noted the Earl in his diary] I was pressed by my sayd nephew's desyre and perswasion of my wife and some other friends, and not by any inclination of my own, for I like not mariages of so neare persons'.[15]

Algernon's personal involvement in this situation was automatic; his professional involvement began from the moment of Leicester's assumption of his nephew's legal guardianship, because the Earl was immediately required by Strangford to represent him in a chancery action against Fotherly's heirs, accusing him of pocketing vast proceeds from the estate. Algernon, at the request of his father involved himself deeply in the Fotherly case. It ran from 1651 to 1658, by which time the Strangfords, according to Sidney, 'might have recovered a good summe of money' but settled instead for 'a foolish composition for much lesse'.[16] In mid-1653, however, Strangford continued his reaction against his history of wardship by rebelling against Leicester too. Taking Isabella and his servants, he went to live in his own estate house at Sterry, also in Kent. There, on 28 September, he revoked Leicester's title to his guardianship, and nominated his tutor John Smith in his stead. He then instituted, through Smith, a legal action in chancery against Leicester, repeating the same charges as those levelled earlier against Fotherly. Algernon consequently had the unusual and useful experience of having to construct a defence (for his father) against the devastating line of attack he had himself devised (against Fotherly).

Out of the puritanical clutches of the Sidneys at Sterry, the young Strangford's lifestyle assumed a pleasantly licentious aspect which did not go unnoticed at Penshurst. It was financed by his servants, now collecting rent directly from his estate. Meanwhile, the legal suit against Leicester, which was soon joined by a counter-suit, blossomed to involve the rent collectors, secretaries, and servants of both parties in accusations of fraud, theft, perjury, and vandalism which kept the Earl concerned, Strangford hopeful, and Algernon busy through the rest of 1653 and 1654.[17]

Understandable though Strangford's behaviour was, his legal actions against Fotherly, and then Leicester, were the beginning of a lifetime of blaming others for his chaotic financial situation. In his chancery suit against Algernon twenty-five years later in 1678, Strangford was to represent Leicester's assumption of his guardianship as a kidnapping for gain previously agreed with Fotherly; he claimed to have been tricked and coerced into his marriage by the Earl and Algernon in order that they might continue control over his estate after his minority; and yet his own letters survive wherein 'I humbly beseech . . . your Lordshipp to take upon yow the trouble

15 HMC De Lisle vol. VI pp. 479, 486, 599.
16 PRO C6/4/193; C10/22/137; HMC De Lisle vol. VI p. 522.
17 PRO C6/124/78.

of being my Guardian', and 'I hope your Lordshipp will excuse the impor-
tunity of an impatient lover ... [towards] my lady Isabella.'[18]

By the end of 1654, however, Strangford had come to his senses, or rather
to a more realistic assessment of his legal chances. He had also run out of
money. According to Algernon:

> He confessed unto me that he had bin perpetually drunck or out of his wits, that tutor
> Smyth had principally instigated him, and never gave him a better title than rogue for
> his pains ... I [promised him] ... if he did desist from the foolish courses he had taken,
> shewe him self kind unto his wife, live civilly, leaving the filthy company with which he
> conversed, and made his peace with [the Earl] ... endeavouring to merite [his] ...
> favour ... I would be his sollicitor unto [him] ... and if he liked it not, he might [take
> what course he wished].[19]

On 6 December Strangford wrote to Leicester pleading for the opportunity to
return to 'your lordship's good opinion'. By 1655 he had returned with his
wife to Penshurst. His wretched financial situation now became a family
concern; he had over £4,000 in debts, and was being pursued by his creditors.
Algernon, partly (but not, one feels, entirely) at the instigation of his parents,
agreed to be one of three trustees undertaking to manage a part of Strangford's estates – the manors of Swingfield and Boynton – on behalf of
Strangford and his creditors, with power to sell, lease, or mortgage to raise
the necessary money. The indentures formalising this agreement were signed
between 31 March and 28 May 1655. Almost immediately it became clear
that Strangford had either failed to declare all his debts or had accumulated
new ones, so that the true total of indebtedness was really over £6,000. Under
these circumstances the other two trustees, Sir John Pelham, and Sir James
Harbord, wisely refused to act further in the Trust or in Strangford's affairs,
although he sued them in chancery to try to force them to do so. On 5 July
1655 another indenture was signed, by which Algernon agreed to manage the
Trust on his own. He moved accordingly from Petworth, where he had been
living with Northumberland, to Leicester House in London, where he took
up the management of Strangford's estate full-time, commuting frequently to
Sterry and Ostenhanger in Kent to administer them. This task was to occupy
Sidney's attention for four years, until he left the country in 1659.[20]

In terms of its effect on Algernon's life, at the time and after, this was a
momentous decision. His careful calculations of self-interest within it centred
upon the conditions he was able to impose on Strangford as the price for his
shouldering the administrative nightmare of his bankrupt finances alone. He
demanded a flat fee of £250 a year, and that the Strangfords leave the country
for France, leaving the management of their whole estate in England (not just

---

[18] PRO C7 327/50; C6 82/60; HMC De Lisle vol. vi pp. 520–2.
[19] HMC De Lisle vol. vi pp. 520–2.
[20] PRO C7 327/50; C7 419/39.

the Trust lands) to him until he had restored their liquidity. In 1657, after their departure for Paris, Sidney moved down from London to take up permanent residence in Strangford's principal seat of Sterry. He lived there until his departure from England two years later, and guarded it most jealously as his own home, particularly against the Strangfords themselves. Most importantly, the Trust lands themselves, Swingfield and Boynton, were conveyed entirely to Algernon, and made over to him and his heirs in perpetuity, subject to his performing the terms of the Trust.[21]

The calculation behind the Trust was that the Trust lands, if sold outright, would be sufficient to pay the £6,102 6s. 3d. in debts. But Algernon needn't sell outright if he could meet the debts in other ways; by paying in his own money, and by raising new loans and mortgages from his own friends on his own authority, on the land. If he could thus himself pay the debts and then eventually pay off the mortgages as well, the Trust lands would be his.

From the Strangford Trust, therefore, Sidney stood to gain, or create, the thing which drove him all his life: liberty, in this case economic liberty, 'depend[ance] upon the will of no man', a freehold estate of his own. The Trust became his nest-egg, the nurse of his ingenuity and fledgling fortunes. He put over £3,000 of his own money into meeting the most urgent debts as soon as he took it up, and then began to wheel and deal to pay off the rest.[22]

A short narrative of Sidney's management of the Trust will be included in Chapter 6. Something of its flavour, and of the way in which Sidney took it upon himself to use his full powers over the estate regardless of, and in opposition to, the wishes of its nominal owners, may be gleaned from his later comment in the chancery suit against Strangford, that he

never refused to concurre with him in any reasonable act that was requird of him for his good ... but doth confesse, he should ill have performed the part of a trustee, or the duty he owed to the Earl and Countesse of Leicester, who had commanded him to take care of their daughter, soe unhappily married ... if he had not in somme degree endeavoured to restraine their extravagance, and let them run headlong to ruine; he had reason to believe that the whole estate would have bin dissipated, if they had bin left fully to their liberty.[23]

In short it does not seem too much to say that in the absence of inheritance rights to his own estate Sidney had – in 'duty' to the 'command' of his parents – worked his way into possession of somebody else's.

Up to 1660, then, to summarise, Algernon showed himself to be a precociously able, energetic, and fiercely competitive second son, pursuing his independent fortune and prospects through two decades of national upheaval with the same qualities in his private and business affairs as we will

---

[21] PRO C7 327/50; De Lisle MS E28/5.
[22] PRO C7/327/50.
[23] De Lisle MS U1475 E28/5.

shortly see in his political affairs; throughout Sidney's life we will see the same single-minded and sometimes ruthless pursuit of personal power and autonomy. In this chapter we have seen how he combined the cultivation of primary claim to his father's intellectual esteem, growing indispensability in the affairs of his estate, and the basis for extremely favourable prospects against his elder brother in the final estate settlement, with the simultaneous pursuit of independent wealth and an independent landholding of his own. This independence was part of the 'liberty', the self-government, Sidney spent his life fighting for; he was not prepared, as he later said, to become the victim of a situation whereby Leicester could make 'his other children slaves, unto his eldest son'. Economically, as politically, this 'liberty' was power, wealth, and independence won by energetic merit and ability (virtue) – the sort of qualities which thrived in a republic; not the accident of birth (the quality essential to monarchy).[24]

This story has many fellows during this period in primogeniture England; younger sons were often seen as 'angry young men' lacking security in a world stacked against them, and seizing aggressively upon the opportunity to better themselves amid the disruption of the civil-war and interregnum years. There is a substantial accompanying body of contemporary political literature about the injustices of, and desperation caused by, the custom of primogeniture inheritance, particularly written by other republicans like Sprigge and Harrington. Harrington likened primogeniture to the drowning of younger puppies in a litter, 'nay yet worse, for as much as . . . the children are left perpetually drowning'. As we will see, Sidney's reply to Filmer acquires new light when seen in this context; a context which can now be demonstrated for the first time by using a major legal manuscript written by Sidney at the same time as the *Discourses*, arguing against the primogeniture claims to his father's inheritance of his brother Philip. In the next chapter we will see Sidney trumpeting the greatness of the new (headless, fatherless) Republic at home and abroad. His very stated reason for initial involvement in the civil war was not the matter of selfless political principle he later claimed it to be; but rather 'the fortune of one that hath noe stock to rely upon . . . Nothing but extreame necessity shall make me think of bearing arms in England, and yet it is the only way of living well for thoes that have not estates.'[25]

What distinguished Algernon Sidney from most other second or younger sons in England were two things. The first was that by 1659 he had,

[24] B.M. Eg. 1049 p. 7.
[25] Thirsk, J., 'Younger sons in the seventeenth century' in *History* LIV (1969) (p. 373, for Sprigge) pp. 358–77; Harrington, *Oceana* (1883) p. 112; Zagorin P., *Political Thought* pp. 155–6; The legal tract is 'The Case of Algernone and Henry Sydney referred to Sir William Jones, as it stands in reason and common sense, which is true equity, and the ground of Lawe.' (1681) In the British Museum Eg. 1049; Gilbert J. T., *History of the Irish Confederation and the War in Ireland 1641–43* (1882–7) vol. II pp. xlviii–xxx (18 June 1643).

extraordinarily, actually achieved the fruition of all three roads to power and autonomy he had pursued, personal, political, and economic: the *de facto* position of first son in the family despite the tradition of primogeniture; a position at the apex of political power in a republic, despite the tradition of monarchy; and an independent economic base of his own in which he could invest and build. In all three things he had achieved the security of self-government, made real his passion for 'liberty'. The second thing is that in 1660 he lost all three.

These two facts together form the basis of both Sidney's life, and his legend; the dogged, uncompromising, and bitter fight from 1660 to 1683 to regain lost liberties which put an old man of 61 on the scaffold.

As we will see, Sidney's violent conduct on behalf of English republicanism abroad in 1659 sowed the seeds of a political exile which cost him all he had worked for. It began a breach with his father which never became total like Philip's, but which could not be adequately repaired over the distance and time of his exile (seventeen years) and which opened the way, eventually, for younger brother Henry to succeed to the position of favourite. He lost completely, of course, his political position and power. Then, in 1665, the Cavalier Parliament dissolved his legal powers over the Strangford estate. Sidney was thrown into the nightmare situation he had done everything to avoid: dependence; dependence upon 'the charity of strangers' and upon a now difficult father for money, support, and consideration. Thrown back, in effect, to his situation at the outset of the civil war, he sought military employment abroad, but even here all his attempts, he later complained most bitterly, were destroyed by the long and malicious arm of the English Court.

Sidney returned from exile seventeen years later in 1677, just in time to see his father die. From then until his execution in 1683 he tried to revive his lost personal and political causes for 'liberty' on both fronts: legal action and writing for the former; political action and writing for the latter. He pursued his father's inheritance, his brother Philip, his cousin Strangford, and even his own electors in the borough of Amersham, through the courts with grim determination. He simultaneously began to intrigue politically on four levels: with foreign diplomats; with his nonconformist and merchant friends in London; with Parliament (to which he stood for election five times); and with his aristocratic friends and relations around the Court. Finally, he wrote the political work which remains, historically, his greatest achievement, and which was to cost him his life: the *Discourses Concerning Government*. To illustrate finally the proximity of Sidney's personal and political struggles for liberty we can compare the argument of the *Discourses* with his legal tract 'The Case', written in pursuit of his father's inheritance in the same year (1681).

The *Discourses* was a reply to Sir Robert Filmer's argument in defence of primogeniture monarchy; an argument so pure and extreme as to strike Sidney as intellectually ludicrous. There were many reasons why Sidney felt moved to begin his long work; the fact that the *Discourses* is twelve times the length of *Patriarcha* and was still going when he was arrested is just one of the indications of how strongly moved he felt.

In the context of this chapter, the knife of *Patriarcha* went to the heart of Sidney's lifelong struggle for 'liberty', as the title suggests, not simply by equating legitimate power solely with primogeniture inheritance monarchy, but by equating that monarchy literally with natural fatherhood. The implication was that a denial of political obedience was the same as – and implied – a denial of filial obedience. According to Filmer, said Sidney indignantly, 'they who have hitherto been esteemed the best and wisest of men ... were rebellious and disobedient sons, who rose up against their father'. At a time when Sidney was drawing to the end of the long court battle arguing his hard-earned superior claims to paternal favour over his primo-geniture-supported brother Philip, this was waving a red rag to a bull. Accordingly, in tones of high moral outrage, the *Discourses* argued that there was no divine precept, by God's word or his deed, 'for that continuance of the power in the eldest', but rather that the 'light of reason, which is ... from God' suggested quite otherwise: that government should rather be in the hands of those 'that can best perform the duties of it', not the eldest but the ablest. At the same time in the *Discourses* Sidney repeatedly mentions the duties children owe their real and natural fathers, and defends them vocifer-ously – 'no good man will ever desire to be free from the respect that is due to his father, who did beget and educate him'. In general he arrives at the pointed conclusion that: 'the law of England, which acknowledges one only heir, is not general, but municipal; and is so far from being general, as the precept of God and nature, that I doubt whether it was ever known or used in any nation of the world beyond our island'.[26]

It has sometimes been (falsely) assumed that the many relativist passages in the *Discourses* about the 'infinite variety' of systems of monarchical inheritance in the world,[27] were an attempt to prepare the ground, against the political background of the Exclusion Crisis, for the candidacy of the illegitimate Duke of Monmouth. Yet Sidney, who loudly declared that it made no difference to him whether James Duke of York or James Duke of Monmouth succeeded, had nothing to do with any royal candidacy: his republican political struggle lay elsewhere.[28] The context for these passages is

---

[26] *Discourses* pp. 27–8; 43–4, 49–50, 52–3, 69, 271–3, 275. Worden, 'The commonwealth kidney' p. 22, n. 115; *Discourses* pp. 20–1.

[27] *Discourses* pp. 44–8, 89–98, 282–6, 339–40, 363–78, 390.

[28] Ewald, *Sydney* II pp. 207–8; cf. Salmon J. H. M., 'Algernon Sidney and the Rye House plot' in *History Today* vol. IV n. 10 (1954) 700–1.

to be sought less in the upstart Monmouth's political challenge to the throne against York, than in the upstart Sidney's personal defence of the throne of his father's estate against Philip. For Sidney was, alongside and quite separately from the political struggle going on around him, involved in his own personal Exclusion Crisis: a battle against exclusion from the express provisions of his father's will; provisions which represented for Sidney everything left to him from the effort of his pre-1660 world.

The Earl's will had left control of the estate to the younger sons, Algernon and Henry, as co-executors. It was now under challenge from Philip as a matter of equity, on the sole ground of the custom of primogeniture. It was a clear attempt, as Algernon put it, to 'overthrowe all of his father's designes ... a man of soe much justice, truth, and prudence ... to the ruine of his brothers'. This, he continued, went against all 'the Lawes of God, and the best that have bin in use amongst men, cutting off all such disputes, by subjecting the son unto the father, and enjoyning the most severe punishments for such as weare rebellious'.[29]

The deep irony here should be clear. In the same year that Sidney was writing in politics to defend the right of rebellion against Filmer's absolute patriarchal monarchy, he was writing in law to defend the absolute patriarchal authority of his father against the rebellion of his brother Philip. The connection was that both Filmer's monarchy and Philip's rebellion were founded on the basis of primogeniture. Sidney's response in both cases was founded on virtue and law.

. Burnet summarised Sidney's argument in the *Discourses* as proving that

if primogeniture from Noah was the ground settled by God for monarchy, then all the princes now in the world were usurpers ... [but in fact] since God did not ... by any declaration of his will ... mark out such or such persons for princes, they could have no title but what was founded on law and compact.[30]

It was by means of this law and compact, said the *Discourses* (following Grotius), that men had emerged from their initial primitive condition in forests and woods, and 'by common consent joining in one body' made governments to suit themselves and their own particular situations. The function of these governments, the particular forms of which could be changed by the people at any time, was to frame and enforce laws for the public interest of the whole society, and 'the defence of the liberty, life, and estate of every private man' within them. No one's person or property in such a society could be made a 'slave' to the 'will' of another man, though monarchies habitually tried to turn the laws into a 'snare' for this purpose. In a hereditary monarchy one man's will was set above the law and made all

29 B.M. Egerton 1049 pp. 14–16.
30 Burnet, add MS 63,057 p. 399.

powerful: 'if this were the condition of men living under governments, forests would be more safe than cities; and it were better for every man to stand in his own defence, than to enter into societies. He that lives alone might encounter such as should assault him upon equal terms, and stand or fall according to the measure of his courage or strength; but no valour can defend him, if the malice of his enemy be upheld by a public power.' In a just society, and in accordance with 'the laws of God and nature', the only attribute which should command power was fitness to exercise it on the people's behalf: ability, wisdom, courage, virtue; not the irrelevant accident of birth. In short, 'If the public safety be provided for, liberty and propriety secured, justice administered, virtue encouraged, vice suppressed, and the true interest of the nation advanced, the ends of government are accomplished.'[31]

As his simultaneous legal struggle with Philip reached a climax, Sidney summarised his legal argument in 'The Case'. He argued that the Earl had possessed in law the liberty to dispose of his own freehold property as he wished; and that it was the function of the law to protect this liberty, this property, and the rights attached to them. He contended that his virtue, his voluntary placing of his personal time and abilities at the disposal of his father for many years on end, was the true claim to the Leicester inheritance, not to be overridden by an appeal to the empty custom of primogeniture on the part of an atheistical, licentious, and virtueless elder son, which sought to stand above the letter of the Earl's will and so against the authority of the law. To uphold such a claim would be to destroy liberty, and justice, and 'render himself and all his other children slaves unto his eldest son'. Would the Chancellor, he asked, choose 'reason or justice ... [or] such advantages as may be snapped up by fraud or surprize?'[32]

Sir William Jones [being] Chancellor in this businesse, it is presumed, he will not, by giving successe unto such practices ... deterre fathers, from setling their estates, least the inadvertence of a councellor, the fraud of a servant, or the slip of a clerks pen, should invert all the Lawes of God, and nature, Render them slaves to their ungratefull children, Overthrowe all that they have endeavourd to establish in the[ir] lives, to the ruin of thoes that have best deserved from them, which would be soe derogatory to that justice which is the foundation of Law, and that Lawe, which is only made for the obtaining of justice, that it weare better to live in a wood, wheare every man, owes the defence of his right to his owne hand, then under a Lawe, that is made [such] a snare.[33]

In a resounding disaster for Philip, Jones decided the case for Algernon. Jones was a political opposition leader, a personal friend and ally of Sidney's, and the two men had co-operated to write a political tract in the same year (1681)

---

[31] *Discourses* pp. 22, 194, 389.
[32] Eg. 1049 pp. 7, 20.
[33] Eg. 1049 pp. 20–1.

which Burnet described as the best of the whole period.[34] Jones respected Sidney's struggle for liberty and the political/legal reasoning that he employed to support it.

By the following year, however, new legal complications had arisen: Jones was dead, and the political tide had turned against 'liberty'. By the year after, Sidney had been arrested, amid the rag-tag papier-mâché of a hopeless political design, and the manuscript of his *Discourses* had been used to convict him of treason.

On 7 December 1683 he was beheaded on Tower Hill.

It is to the political career which carried him there, that we must now turn our attention.

---

[34] Burnet, *History* II p. 289; Worden, 'Commonwealth kidney' n. 69; The tract was W. Jones [and Sidney, Titus, and Wildman] *Just and Modest Vindication of The Proceedings of the Last Two Parliaments* (1681). I am grateful to Blair Worden for directing me to Burnet's largely ignored claim about Sidney's co-authorship; I hope to demonstrate its correctness beyond doubt in the volume to follow. Cf. *Discourses* p. 437; *Vindication* in *State Tracts in the Reign of Charles II* (1689) vol. I p. 173.

Part Two

WAR AND POLITICS

❧ 5 ❧

Diplomacy and war 1635–48

On 19 May 1635, France was driven to enter the Thirty Years War against
the successes of Habsburg Spain. In May 1636 the Earl of Leicester arrived in
Paris (bringing Algernon and Philip) as Ambassador Extraordinary from the
English Court.[1]

The Earl was a man of strong French sympathies, very keen on committing
England to some sort of effective intervention on the continent against
Spain.[2] His attitude was the result of religious and political considerations.
France now headed the protestant alliance in Europe against the Habsburgs;
Leicester shared with Sweden's Grotius the object of strengthening this bond.
Secondly, Leicester shared strongly the strategic perception, held in both
England and France, that England's principal foreign policy interest lay in
keeping the balance in Europe even between its two greatest powers, Spain
and France. It was clear in 1635–6 that this balance lay under serious threat
from the Habsburg side, a threat dramatised for Leicester by the Imperial
invasion of France in the first months of his embassy which came within a
whisker of reaching Paris. As the Earl wrote urgently from there in 1640:
'This equiponderance is not to be maintained by neutrality or looking on, but
by interposing and, if need be, by siding with the more reasonable party.'[3]

Unfortunately the Earl served a king attempting to run his foreign policy on
a shoestring, by capricious flirtation with Europe's leading, rather than
secondary, power. This was a standard Stuart technique which was to land
the King's and Leicester's respective sons (Charles II and Algernon) at
loggerheads on the same issue a generation later. Initially sent to France only
in response to a temporary snub received from the Habsburgs, the increasingly frustrated Leicester was the doomed handmaiden of a strategy in which
no serious commitment was ever intended. Instead he was instructed to

---

[1] The substantial correspondence from Leicester's embassy is in PRO State Papers 78 nn.
101–11.
[2] Clarendon, *History* (Oxford edn) vol. II p. 299, quoted in Blencowe, *Sidney Papers* pp. 268–9;
Hibbard C., *Charles I and the Popish Plot* (1983) p. 33.
[3] Church, *Richelieu* p. 285; HMC De Lisle VI p. xxviii.

request, in effect, that France help restore the Prince Palatine to his electorate by surrendering a French conquest, without any concrete compensation from England in terms of either troops or a firm alliance 'defensive and offensive'. This proposition did not accord with Richelieu's finely tuned conception of France's 'reason' or 'interest' of state, a political language which Leicester himself understood well and in terms of which he gamely attempted to argue England's case: 'Our interest in the Prince Elector Palatine is but from affection and nearness in blood, which will necessarily be lessened in time. But yours . . . is from reason of state and nearnesse of situation, which will for ever remain the same.' Leicester was here employing the maxims of his friend Rohan, whose work *Of The Interests of Princes and States* (1638), published in this period, popularised the conception that 'interest alone is forever sure'. This is a context, a language and, by the relativist Earl, a strategy, to which we will return when we find Algernon thirty years later writing the *Court Maxims*, with the same foreign policy perception, in the same interest theory language, and once again employing the language of his host regime (in this case the republican Dutch) to argue the English republican case.[4]

Indeed the footsteps of Leicester's long and humiliating experience are visible throughout Algernon's later thought and actions, most particularly in his emphasis on the military weakness of England under the Stuarts and his conviction that a few short years of republican government had restored to England the glory of real power in Europe. 'Under favour' the ever-polite Earl was driven to write to the King, 'it is not sufficient to propose the End, the Meanes must be assured'. By 1640 the Prince Palatine, far from being restored to his electorate, had been thrown into a Parisian gaol. The latter part of Leicester's embassy was spent ignobly treating for his release – an object eventually achieved for him by the intervention of Grotius. At this point, after a steady five-year diet of empty diplomatic ceremony and delay from both London and Paris, the Earl arrived at the bald conclusion: 'when all comes to all, in my weeke opinion, it is force or the terrour of force and nothing els can do it'. This conclusion, as we will see, was the starting point for Algernon's own embassy on behalf of the Republic in the Baltic in 1659.[5]

In the absence of any political point to his embassy, Leicester fell to quarrelling with his colleague there, the ambassador in ordinary Lord John Scudamore. Scudamore he described as a 'ridiculous Creature', 'a formal Pedante' with 'neither Reason to argue, nor power to conclude'; '[he] speaks French, as if he had learn'd it in Herefordshire, and would shew by that his good breeding'. Not surprisingly Scudamore found Leicester an unbearable snob, apparently suffering from an 'inordinate desier [sic] of glory'. In early

---

[4] HMC De Lisle vi p. xxii 23 August 1636. Hibbard, *Charles I* pp. 73–4.
[5] HMC De Lisle vi pp. xvii, xxii; Collins A., *Letters and Memorials* p. 432.

1640 Philip and Algernon were both involved in a public incident with Scudamore which caused some scandal at the English Court.[6]

Leicester's frustrations with English Court foreign policy were shared by the 'French party' in England, which centred on the Percy family and had cordial links with Strafford. Northumberland (Algernon Percy) in particular complained in letters to Leicester about the 'corruption and hispanophile atmosphere of the court'. It was from Northumberland that Leicester heard (through his wife) that 'it was said [at Court that] Seigneur Condé had persuaded you to be more inclinable to France than is well thought on here, and that you were more earnest to engage the King in a war than the wise here doth think fit'. It was Condé, prince of the blood and archetype of the French nobility of the sword, who was to go on to lead the noble Fronde, and Algernon's relations with the remnants of that adventure from 1666 to 1677 will be discussed in Chapter 14.[7]

In 1640 Algernon's brother Philip returned to England to take up a command in the personal regiment of Northumberland, who had been appointed to lead the campaign against the Scots, a campaign which Leicester had pleaded with the King to reconsider, and about which Northumberland himself harboured visible reservations. It was hard for men who had begged the King for six years to go to war on the continent on behalf of protestantism against the Spaniards (as Elizabeth had done), to see him ready at last to institute military action only against his own protestant subjects. When that campaign, too, ended in utter humiliation, England faced a crisis of confidence in its government. In his recent work on Caroline drama, Martin Butler has found evidence of deep frustrations with royal policy incorporating not only these themes but all the other political, religious, and historical concerns we have traced in earlier chapters on the Percy and Sidney families, and he has found them in works connected with a circle of aristocratic families incorporating the Percys and Sidneys themselves. Indeed there is a clear pre-civil-war context to Algernon's *Court Maxims*, and his *Discourses*, which can be sketched in here.

The plays Butler has studied, from the mid 1630s to 1641, exhibit most strongly two nostalgic themes. The first is a 'quite extraordinary' cult of the policies of Elizabeth, mourning the loss of 'those honest dayes . . . when men

[6] Collins A., *Letters* p. 387; PRO SP78 no. 102 fol. 289; De Lisle MS U1475 C87/4. At some point during the French period Algernon visited Rome; when he lived there later he spoke of the Rome he had known during 'pope Urban his time' [Urban was Pope 1623–44], and of family friends still there, including 'Father Courtenay'. He may have gone there at the same time as Milton, who travelled to Venice, Florence, and Rome via the English embassy in Paris in 1639, where he met Scudamore and Grotius, though not apparently Leicester. Parker W., *John Milton* (1968) pp. 169–70.
[7] Hibbard, *Charles I* p. 33; Butler M., 'Mercurius' p. 951; Cartwright J., *Sacharissa* (London 1901) pp. 43–4.

of honor flourish'd that tam'd the wealth of Spaine, set up the States, and help'd the French King'; a time of 'opposition to Spain and the Pope, support for international Protestantism, aggression abroad, unity at home in a church properly reformed'. The second, closely linked, was the nostalgia of those 'saddened by the decline of the English nobility', lamenting the loss of those times 'when knights were Gentlemen' typified by 'honest plain valour' in prosecution of active policies abroad, and 'nobles and people lived in harmony'. This was before the nation became split into two contrary interests, Court and people, the former dominated by ignoble new courtiers, wise in 'the science of wearing different coloured ribbons', 'caterpillars of the state', and 'realme-sucking slaves', bleeding the state by royal 'patent and monopoly'.[8]

Prominent among the personnel of this mythology were the Elizabethan Earl of Leicester, the gallant rebel Essex, and Sir Walter Raleigh. Sir Philip Sidney's relation to Leicester has been mentioned; Algernon mentions Raleigh in both the *Maxims* and the *Discourses*, and praises 'the brave Earl of Essex' in the latter too; he carried a banner at the grand funeral of Essex's son, the parliamentary general, in 1646. Dr Worden, too, has traced the links of Sidney's family with the 'party of the Elizabethan Earl of Leicester; [and] the party of Essex ... with its self-conciously Tacitean' political values.[9] The play *The Wasp* examines arbitrary government over an enslaved nation, under the King's favourite, 'Varletti ... a courtier of Buckingham's stamp'. The tyrant confesses to 'plucking downe the trew Nobillity and raiseing Boyes and upstarts', one of the play's 'astonishing range of grievances in court and state; the sale of honors ... the system of wardship, the legal profession ... exactions ... monopoly ... extortion, Rack rent ... not an honest British name amongst 'em'. When the hero and opponent of this corruption, Archibald, 'disguises himself as the blunt and discontented northerner Percy', some of the play's topical allegiances become clear. In Braithwaite's *Mercurius Britannicus*, Butler believes he has found, by the play's Parisian antecedents, a likely link in patronage to Leicester himself. *Britannicus* 'depicts the impeachment [in Parliament] of the judges involved in the notorious Ship Money case 1637–8, the show trial of John Hampden'. Since this had not taken place by the play's date (1641) and Parliament was showing itself 'slow to proceed' in it, the play 'is not recounting but anticipating events and urging parliament to pursue a particular course of action'.[10] It is interesting to jump forward forty years to Sidney's *Discourses*,

---

[8] Butler M., *Theatre and Crisis* (Cambridge 1984) pp. 195, 196, 197, 198, 199, 201–2, 204–5.
[9] *Discourses* pp. 80, 440–1, cf. 487; Worden, 'Republicanism' p. 188; Dr Worden finds the Tacitism of Essex's faction expressed in Ungerer's study of the correspondence of the Spaniard Antonio Perez; Sidney uses Perez's writings in the *Discourses*.
[10] I myself believe a direct Leicester connection unlikely. Butler, *Crisis* pp. 207–9; 'Mercurius' pp. 947–8.

written in the course of an insurrectionary partnership with John Hampden's grandson John Hampden jun. In the *Discourses* Sidney relates all the troubles of Charles II's corrupt reign to those of Charles I: foreign (by this time French rather than Spanish) popish influence; corruption at Court; attempts by Danby at financial extortion for the Crown. It is up to Parliament to bring the offenders to account, says Sidney, and to remember how in 1637–43

[Justice] was injured, when the perjured wretches, who gave that accursed judgement in the case of ship-money, were suffered to escape the like punishment by means of the ensuing troubles, which they had chiefly raised. And I leave it to those who are concerned, to consider how many in our days may expect vengeance for the like crimes.[11]

Indeed it is the key to understanding its bellicose tone and intention, to understand the extent to which the *Discourses* imports into the crisis of the reign of Charles II, the concerns of the crisis of the reign of Charles I. It explains not only why Sidney chose to answer, not a contemporary writer, but the pre-civil-war theory of Sir Robert Filmer; but also why Sidney groups Filmer throughout with his 'disciples', 'Heylin, Sibthorpe and Manwaring'.[12]

In the *Maxims*, the 1640–2 context is even clearer. It portrays monarchy, and its instruments the courtiers, lawyers, and bishops, as a parasitic organism with a distinct interest contrary to that of the rest of the nation, which it can only nourish by bleeding them. Under monarchy, then, the Court can only become stronger by making the nation as a whole weaker: effeminating and destroying the nobility, impoverishing the people with taxes and monopolies, and persecuting their religion. Sidney emphasises the contrast between the religious and foreign policies of Elizabeth, and those of the Stuarts, the exchange of protestant conquest of enemies and so empire abroad, for popish conquest of subjects and so absolutism at home. He devotes a chapter to the royal corruption of lawyers, showing how under absolutism those experts who should have been the people's bulwark against tyranny are instead made its principal instruments. It was the (later royalist) moderates Falkland and Hyde who had said at the outset of the 1640–2 crisis, respectively:

But this security [the law] has been almost our ruin, for it hath been turned, or rather turned itself into a battery against us: And those persons who should have been dogs to defend the sheep, have been as wolves to worry them.

[What] greater instance of a sick and languishing Commonwealth . . . when the judges

---

[11] *Discourses* pp. 488–9.
[12] Interestingly, John Locke, too, in his answer to Filmer observed: 'By whom this Doctrine came at first to be broach'd, and brought into fashion amongst us, and what sad Effects it gave rise to, I leave it to Historians to relate, or to the Memory of those who were Contemporaries with Sibthorp and Manwaring to recollect.' ed. Laslett P., *Locke's Two Treatises of Government* (Cambridge 1967) I, 5 (p. 161).

themselves have been delinquents! Tis no marvel that an irregular arbitrary power, like a torrent, hath broke in upon us, when our banks and bulwarks, the Laws, were in the custody of such persons.[13]

The *Maxims*'s companion chapter on kingship's second great wheel to tyranny, the bishops, confirms this setting, and its many other specific grievances in an English context coalesce again and again around the concerns of the City and Parliament as they faced Charles I in 1640–2: monopolies, ship money, popery.

Butler himself comments that 'future royalists such as Edward Hyde and Falkland [were] ... as prominent in [the] attack on Ship Money as future parliamentarians'. It is worth recalling here Sidney's own association, and that of family clients like Hammond, with Grotius, Daillé, and others associated intellectually with the Tew circle. Hammond's Tew links are noticed both by his biographer Packer, and by Tuck.[14] If they are to be seen in the context of the Sidney family's intellectual associations on the eve of the civil war in general, then perhaps this helps to explain, too, Algernon's later sharing of ('middle group') political allegiance from 1646 to 1648 with John Selden, and how later, in Paris, he was able to regale Lantin with stories about Selden's private life.[15] This dovetails exactly with Sidney's wider political associations, during both civil war and Rump periods, with Selden's friends Bulstrode Whitelocke and John Evelyn, and others allied to their and Northumberland's 1647–8 group like Walter Strickland and Henry Vane. It was this group in the Republic: Sidney, Whitelocke, Strickland, and Vane, whom Milton singled out for special praise in his *Second Defence* (1654).[16] Indeed for the true antecedents of the Polybian/Aristotelian classical republican theory with which Sidney and Milton were involved in the Rump period, we should perhaps look towards the civil-war-period writings of the 'Tew circle' elements on each side of the 1641 split within the ranks of opposition

---

13 Harris R. W., *Clarendon and the English Revolution* (1983) p. 67.

14 Packer J. W., *Transformation* 64–70, 89–94; Tuck Richard, 'The ancient law of freedom: John Selden in the civil war' in John Morrill ed., *Reactions to the English Civil War* p. 158, and *Natural Rights Theories* 101–10.

15 Sidney's account on this score provides a charming supplement to the well-known 'Life' of Selden by Aubrey: 'Le Comte de Sidney ... me dit encore que le Scavani Selden estoit fils d'un Excellent joueur de violon; qu'il estoit tres instruit de toutes les Loix d'Angle[terre], et qu'il estoit consulte par les Grands: que le commencement de sa fortune venoit de ce qu'il entra dans la Maison du Comte de Cantorberi, pour avoir soin de ses affaires, parce que le Comte manquir d'Esprit et de conduite; qu'il se maintini dans cet Emploi par le moyen de la Comtesse qui estoit jeune, et qu'il baisoit [illeg]. Leur amite s'acrut meme apres la mort du Comte, et jusques a la mort de Selden. Et que comme ils craignoient qu'ils ne se lassassent l'un de l'autre, Selden avoit pris a son service deux ou trois jeune hommes qui caressoient la Comtesse, et qu'elle de Sa part avoir repondu a la complaisance de Selden, ayant aussi aupres d'elle, 3 ou 4 Demoiselles avec qui Selden se divertissoit et se rejeunissoit. Voila des Amans commodes. Il en est peu de sembla[]e[].' Paris BBN Fr. 23254 101–2.

16 Compare the translation in Milton, *Prose Works* (New York 1933) vol. VIII pp. 234–5, with *Milton's Prose Works* ed. J. St John (1848) vol. I p. 293.

to Charles I that made the civil war possible. On the royalist side, in 1642 Falkland and/or Colepeper produced the *Answer to the Nineteen Propositions*, a classic statement of the Polybian/Aristotelian theory of the need for balance between the one, the few, and the many. On the other side, in 1647, from the ranks of the 'royal independents' (including Northumberland, Evelyn, Pierrepoint, Sidney, Selden, and others) Lord Saye and Sele produced the *Vindiciae Veritatis*, another statement of the same theory, together with a particular emphasis on the importance of the middle point, the nobility, in keeping the balance between the potential extremes at either end: between the anarchy of the multitude and the tyranny of the Crown. This is an earlier statement of the theory I have shown reappearing in Sidney's *Discourses* in 1681–2 (in which period Pocock, observing the same theory in Neville, too, is pleased to label it 'neo-Harringtonianism'). 'As we hate tyranny in one', wrote the *Vindiciae*, 'so we do ... confusion in the many-headed multitude. We resolve therefore to keep the three estates co-ordinate equally to poise and balance each other.' Throughout his life, beneath his increasingly bitter anti-monarchical radicalism, this aristocratic pursuit of order and balance between the two extremes of 'the Chaos ... and disorderly fury of a Rude Multitude' (*Maxims* p. 19) and royal 'Tyranny', remained at the heart of Sidney's theory. It is an echo from this Northumberland/Saye group advocation of a balanced and bounded 'mixed monarchy' in 1647, that we can hear in Sidney's (rightly questioned) later statement in the *Discourses* that it is not monarchy as such, but 'only absolute monarchy ... that I dispute against, professing much veneration for that which is mixed, regulated by law, and directed to the public good'. Sidney continued to make statements in these terms, even when the general development of his own thought had made them obsolete, when he stated, himself, that the balance could no longer be restored, and that monarchy itself was intrinsically irrational and evil.[17]

It is worth remembering, then, that both the *Answer* and the *Vindiciae* were written as attempts by aristocratic groups on either side in the civil war to establish realistic terms for a 'safe well-grounded' peace with the other, before it became too late: before the tyranny and folly of the King pushed the country into something as bad or worse, the anarchy of the multitude. It was following the collapse of Northumberland and Saye's last desperate attempts to bring Charles I round at Newport in 1648 that the Army finally decided to

---

[17] For Whitelocke's views of Caroline government, identical to Sidney's own, and his friendship with Selden see his *Memorials* (1853) vol. I pp. 3, 22–3, 27, 34, 38, 49–52, 137–8, 149, 208; vol. II pp. 181, 248; Underdown, *Pride's Purge* p. 63; Pearl V 'Royal independents in the English Civil War' in *Transactions of The Royal Historical Society* 5th ser., v 18 (1968) pp. 93–6; Sidney, *Discourses* p. 111; For Saye's authorship of the *Vindiciae*, I am indebted to a paper given by John Adamson in Cambridge in 1984: 'The political thought of Lord Saye and Sele'.

impose its own settlement and to do away with the King. Following this shocking act some of the men with proven contacts with the Northumberland/Saye group, like Sidney, Vane, Whitelocke, and Strickland, decided despite their opposition to both the Purge and the execution, to go with the new regime. Other adherents of the same group like Northumberland himself, Evelyn, Pierrepoint, and Browne, decided, equally painfully, to go the other way. In the post-event justification of republicanism which followed, even more necessary for those who had joined the regime with doubts about its legitimacy, it is interesting that Sidney, and friends or relations like Neville, became associated with a classical ideology adapting to the republic the earlier notion of co-ordinate balance between the one, the few, and the many, even if, as Pocock later observed in Harrington, there was no longer 'much role for a one'.

All the anguish which accompanied the split within the Caroline opposition (and a component of it, the 'Tew circle') on the eve of the civil war, is visible in the tortured behaviour of a single figure: Algernon's father. His pleas to the King for an accommodation with his opponents unheeded, Leicester returned to England with his family in 1641. It was symbolic of his whole political career that when his long-awaited ministerial appointment finally came it was to the Lord Lieutenancy of Ireland on 14 June 1641, to replace a friend and predecessor (Strafford) sent to the block, to see the kingdom concerned convulsed by a massacre and rebellion, and to see the authority which employed him in England split into two warring halves. Leicester was appointed by Charles I's personal command, but the army he eventually assembled was under the command of officers nominated by the Commons, and the Earl was to prove miserably unable to extricate himself from the problems posed by the growing antagonism between the two. The army of 3,500 infantry and 600 cavalry, which departed without him in early 1642, contained his two eldest sons; Philip, in overall command of the horse; and Algernon, in his first military post, at the age of nineteen, as a captain of cavalry under him.[18]

The army arrived at Chester by 21 January 1642; Dublin a month later, and was in action by April. Little is known about Algernon's Irish service save customary references to his 'great spirit and resolution', on the strength of Sir John Temple's assurance to Leicester from Dublin of Lisle's 'stronge and . . . zealous affections to this service . . . he caries himself so gallantly . . . thay both deserve very well of the public here'.[19]

---

[18] Meadley G. W., *Memoirs of Algernon Sidney* (1813) pp. 8, 10; Cal. S.P. Dom. 1641–3 p. 164.
[19] Meadley, *Memoirs of Algernon Sidney* p. 11; Ewald, *Sidney* p. 76; De Lisle MS U1475 C114/26; For the progress of Algernon's troop in Ireland see troop lists in HMC Ormonde 14th Rep. vol. I 5.1641/2; 8.42; 13.42; 14.42; 15.42; 17.42; 18.42; 19.42; 21.42/3; 23.43; 34.ii; vol. II 7 October 1643.

In fact, so far as we can know it, the reality was rather different. It was a miserable war, characterised by 'signal acts of cruelty', deficient supplies, indecisive skirmishes, and the tactics of plunder and destruction. Lisle distinguished himself in the slaying of villagers at market; but from a document in the Sidney papers it seems that the one set battle the two brothers are definitely recorded as having fought in, far from being characterised by heroism, landed them both before a court martial in Dublin on charges of cowardice.[20]

The battle was fought near Rosse on 28 March 1643. At a court martial on 5 April the picture was unveiled of 'Lord Lisle, Sir Richard Grenville, Captain Sydney, Captain Treswell, Captain Pate, Captain Pickeringe' routed and retreating in disorder, while the foot stood their ground alone and won the day without them. The particular focus was on the behaviour of Lisle who (his horse having been shot from under him) 'possesst with a pannick feare, ran away from the flying and pursued enemye ... loudly offering ten pounds for a guide to Duncannon'. This accusation was vigorously denied, but it is clear that the cavalry charge had, at the least, been incompetently planned and executed.[21]

The effect of all this on the young Algernon is clear from a letter written to his mother in June (1643). Contrary to Ewald's picture of a heroic, Saxon, Sidney going 'bravely to his work' and 'smiting' the Celtic rebels 'hip and thigh',[22] the letter demonstrates both Sidney's desperation to leave Ireland ('to leave that which is certainly bad for that which may be better, I think not possibly worse') and his equal concern to avoid the war in England.

'Nothing but extreame necessity shall make me thinke of bearing arms in England ... And besides, theare is so few that abstaine from warre for the same reason I doe, that I doe not know wheather in many mens eyes it may not prove dishonorable to me.' Whatever that 'reason' was, and whatever that 'abstention' consequently amounted to, Sidney was soon to find the motivation of 'honour', and his other problem of 'living well for thoes that have not estates', too strong to maintain his scruples.[23]

---

[20] De Lisle MS U1475 C126/1; Clarendon, *History* (1843) I p. 504. 'The Lord Lisle marched to Kells ... there he surprised divers of the Rebels, who then held in that place an open market, spoiled their market, slew many of them, and scattered the rest ... [he then] caused ... all the villages and towns adjoining to be burnt, as also the hay and turf in all that country about them. He still proceeds in burning, wasting, spoiling and destroying all the country about him, and all the Rebels' corn, hay ... turf ... cattle', Gilbert J. T., *History of the Irish Confederation and the Wars in Ireland 1641–43* (7 vols. 1882–7) vol. I p. lviii.

[21] De Lisle MSS U1475 O142; Gardiner S. R., *History of the Great Civil War* (1893) vol. I p. 122; Gilbert, *Irish Confederation* pp. 131–3. The cavalry had charged at a ditch too wide for the horses to jump, and not seen until it was too late.

[22] Ewald, *Sidney* vol. I pp. 76, 104.

[23] Gilbert, *Irish Confederation* pp. xlviii–xlx (18 June 1643).

This letter may display either a premature conversion to pacifism or the dilemma of a young man who was not prepared to fight for the King, and could not fight against him while his father remained awaiting the King's commands at Oxford. Thus Charles I's action in withdrawing from Leicester his Lord Lieutenancy in favour of Ormonde in October may have been the decisive factor in determining the two sons' eventual parliamentary allegiance.

Their last months in Ireland had seen growing unease among some of the English officers about Ormonde's negotiations, on behalf of the King, for a cessation with the rebels. Lisle and Temple – while remaining carefully deferential towards the King's person – had moved to the forefront of this opposition to Ormonde (an opposition which was, as far back as Elizabeth's reign, part of Sidney family history). Charles I's continued detention at Oxford of Leicester himself – whom he still suspected of being a 'puritan' – throughout 1643 had been partly through concern that the Earl's arrival in Dublin would tip the balance towards the pro-parliamentarian and Lisle-supported Chief Justices in Dublin and away from Ormonde. By October the Sidneys had left Ireland, Ormonde had replaced Leicester, and Sir John Temple had been imprisoned by the new Lord Lieutenant in Dublin.[24]

When Sidney first landed in England in August with Lisle and Grenville, he seems to have intended to go straight to Oxford, though there may have been some hesitation, for his mother wrote on 31 August of Lisle: 'I canot inmagine [*sic*] what my sone means to do, for certainlie he canot avoid goeing to the King.' Upon their initial landing, however, the party fell victim to royalist marauders who stole their horses. Algernon wrote an indignant letter to Orlando Bridgeman at Chester stating his intention to go immediately to Oxford, his father, and the King, and have the matter seen to. This letter was intercepted by Parliament, already extremely worried about the problem of uncommitted troops returning from Ireland. The three men were taken into custody by the Committee at Lancaster and sent under guard to London.[25] So far whatever ideology existed had rather fallen prey to events.

From this uncertain beginning Lisle and Sidney were to emerge as parliamentarians; and Grenville royalist (once he had been parliamentarian long enough to collect his pay). We next hear of Algernon on 15 April 1644, with his appointment as a colonel in Manchester's regiment of horse in the Eastern Association. This was followed six weeks later by a Parliamentary order for £400 'Arrears for service done in Ireland'; thus quickly was Sidney's decision to take sides followed by satisfaction on his first point of motivation.

[24] Gardiner, *Civil War* vol. i pp. 116, 122.
[25] *Commons Journal* iii p. 223; De Lisle MS C133/31; C162/1; C132/78; Collins, p. 150; Meadley, p. 15.

Success for the second, pursuit of honour, was just around the corner. At the battle of Marston Moor:[26]

Colonel Sydney, son to the Earl of Leicester, charged with much gallantry at the head of my lord's regiment of horse, and came off with much honour, though with many wounds, to the grief of my lord, and many others, who is since gone to London for the cure of his wounds.[27]

Indeed Sidney's reckless bravery on this occasion was reported by five different parliamentary journals, and the legend soon appeared of his galloping into the very jaws of death, only to be rescued at pike-point by a humble soldier who then refused to name himself to his beneficiary for reward. Some people apparently create such legends; this was the first of many to be accumulated by Algernon. Four years later the parliamentary papers would be translating his name into Hebrew, to say that the Hebrew then turned into English made the phrase: 'He is against strange men that destroy the cause.'[28]

The possibility that the Hebrew, turned back into English, meant exactly what it had meant before it was turned into Hebrew (and the fact that the name given by the journal was spelt wrongly in seven places: 'Col Sydeham, Algenon Sydnham') mattered, of course, not at all, either then or now.

With wounds which were clearly severe, and no doubt profoundly affected by this public baptism of fire, Sidney retired from the public eye – and public records – for another year. Forty years later Burnet reported: 'Sidney … was a man of great Courage, of which as he had given eminent proofs in ye Civill Wars, so he carried ye marks of it in many parts of his body.' Although Marston Moor was at once Sidney's first great battle and his last active service, his militarised political thought shows that 'he carried ye marks of it' elsewhere as well.[29]

A year later, in April 1645, Sidney was appointed to a command in the newly formed New Model Army. Sidney, observes Mark Kishlansky, 'submitted his resignation, suffering from a leg wound that he claimed made him unfit for service. He would soon recover sufficiently to become governor of Chichester. He, too, preferred men of unquestionable zeal.' But I can find no

---

[26] De Lisle MSS O101/1; CJ III p. 507; DNB Grenville, p. 125.
[27] *Ash's Intelligence from the Armies in the North* no. 6; Meadley, *Memoirs* p. 18. Manchester himself reported: 'Divers we have wounded; amongst whom it much troubleth me to tell you is my cousin Sydney; but yet he is very hearty.'
[28] *Perfect Occurrences* n. 94, 13 October 1648; Meadley, *Memoirs*. (More significant in my view is the republican anagram that results from spelling Algernon backwards, leaving the final two letters in their original order.)
[29] Add. MS 63,057 p. 137.

evidence for this assumption about Sidney's preference for 'zeal'. Indeed Sidney's own letter to Fairfax was quite open about the offer of Chichester, which came before, not after, his resignation from the New Model, and about the role it played in his decision. Sidney assured Fairfax, 'I have not left the army without extreame unwillingnesse ... [and only] by reason of my lamenesse'; a statement which, given Burnet's later testimony, it seems reasonable and simpler to accept at face value.[30]

Sidney took over the governorship of the Sussex port from Colonel Stapley on 10 May 1645. The following year Sir John Temple, safely out of Ormonde's clutches in Ireland, entered Parliament as MP for the same town. Both the Sussex Committee, with which Sidney worked, and the Chichester garrison, over which he was commander, were deeply unpopular within the county; the latter was to be finally disbanded under public pressure in March 1647. Indeed Sidney's principal military duties there were to be directed not against royalist troops, but against the Sussex club-men. Their activities reached a peak in October 1645, so that no one in the county dared to collect taxes 'for fear of having his brains dashed out, the servants and women rising together to resist armed with prongs and other weapons'. Sidney published proclamations against them and loaned troops to assist the County Committee in mopping-up operations once they had been routed. In early 1646 he supplied infantry from his garrison to assist with the siege of Corfe Castle.[31]

In December 1645 Algernon was elected to Parliament as a recruiter for Cardiff (close to the Sidney family lands in Glamorganshire). In this year Cardiff, too, had been a centre of club-man activity, resulting in a movement from royalist to parliamentary allegiance in Glamorganshire behind which the Earls of Leicester and Pembroke were held to have been involved.[32] In September 1646 he carried a banner, with his brother, at the funeral of the Earl of Essex.[33] A later remark in the Earl of Leicester's diary suggests that he was 'deprived' by Parliament of his governorship at Chichester, but we do not know why, or when. By the beginning of 1647 Sidney was preparing to accompany his brother on a second military expedition to Ireland. Lisle was

---

[30] B.M. Sloane, MSS 1519 fol. 112; Kishlansky M., *The Rise of The New Model Army* (1979) p. 49; Collins, p. 151.

[31] De Lisle MS U1475 O101/2; Thomas-Stanford, *Sussex in the English Civil War* (1910) p. 164; Cal. S.P. Dom. 1645–7 pp. 132, 148, 151–2, 173, 182, 349, 355; Fletcher A., *Sussex 1600–1660* (1975) pp. 274–6.

[32] Algernon was to serve on the assessment and militia commissions for Glamorganshire every year until 1652/3, and again in 1659. Underdown D., 'Party management in the recruiter elections 1645–8' in *EHR* CCCXXVII April 1968 p. 242; Jenkins P., *The Making of a Ruling Class* (1983) pp. 107–8, 289; ed. Firth and Rait, *Acts and Ordinances of The Interregnum* (1911) vol. I pp. 979, 1097, 1136, 1238, 1254, vol. II pp. 47, 314, 483, 680, 328, 1371. Thanks to Blair Worden for these last references.

[33] PRO SP 16/514 fol. 149.

appointed Lord Lieutenant of Ireland in early 1646, but he did not finally leave for that country, with an army, and accompanied by Algernon, until 19 February 1647, when only two months of his commission remained to run.

Accompanying his brother this time carried far greater benefits for Algernon than formerly: a vote by the House of £2,000, and the posts of Governor of Dublin, and Lieutenant-General of the Horse in Ireland.[34]

Philip and Algernon arrived at Cork on 21 February 1647, with 120 horse, and Sir Hardress Waller in command of 15,000 foot. There they found 'the government and all things in strange disorder, and the abuses very great'. Their expedition was notable for nothing but the public row it produced in Dublin, with Inchiquin, over the military command to be adopted in Ireland after Lisle's commission of Lord Lieutenancy ran out on 15 April.[35]

On 8 April, a successful move had been made in the House of Commons to countermand the initial appointment of Algernon to the governorship of Dublin, and substitute his deputy, Colonel Jones. Leicester noted:

This motion of the Recorder [Glyn] was seconded by old Sir H. Vane, who pretended ... that since the House had thought fitt to recall the Lord Lisle it was not good to let his brother remaine Governor of so important a place as Dublin; which is as much as to say ... that since you have used one brother ill, you ought to do injustice to the other: an excellent maxim, and fitt for such a man's conscience.

At the same time, however, it was resolved 'That, in due Time, this house will take into Consideration the Merit and Services of Colonel Algernon Sydney'.[36]

A week later Lisle called an emergency Council of Officers in Dublin which met on the day his authority was due to expire. There he proclaimed his intention to leave the command of the Army in Munster in the hands of a four-person commission: Algernon, Lord Broghill, Hardress Waller and Inchiquin, to replace Inchiquin's sole authority. Simultaneously, however, in a private interview with a suitably imperious Algernon (who refused to argue the point) Inchiquin refused to accept the extinction of his authority 'under the great seal' to Lisle's 'paper commission'. He then swept into the Council of Officers' meeting and addressed it on the subject of Lisle's shortly expiring powers, warning them that if they obeyed Lisle's order after 'twelve o'clock that day ... they would be guiltie of treason'. Sir John Temple made two

---

[34] Sidney spent half of the £2,000 on East India company shares. British Library ch. 70777 28 March 1648.
[35] Gilbert, *Irish Confederation* vol. IV p. 19.
[36] Blencowe, *Sidney Papers* p. 16; HMC Egmont, vol. VI pp. 376, 389; CJ v p. 136. Whitelocke, *Memorials* II p. 129.

further visits to Inchiquin, but without effect. Eventually Lisle, his powers expired, fell into 'a great rage'. He arrived back in England on 21 April with Algernon, Temple, and Sir Adam Loftus, the latter sending his son Arthur on ahead from Bristol with a letter to Parliament to explain their version of events.[37]

Once back the faction of Irish interests represented by the Sidneys and Temple did their best to defend themselves and hound their opponents through the House. The lines of their struggle acquired shades of the wider division beginning to paralyse Parliamentary politics in general, over the terms for disbandment of the army, an issue within which the relief of Ireland occupied a prominent place. On 7 May Lisle and Temple both reported at length on the state of affairs they had left in Ireland, and they, and Algernon, received the thanks of the House for 'the good Services they have done'. On 25 May Sir Philip Percival, a friend and correspondent of Inchiquin's, 'was admitted into the House of Commons, and twice voted for the disbanding of the army of which notice was taken by divers who were of another mind'. On 2 June, the day Cornet Joyce seized the King at Holmby, Temple and one Alderman Hoyle stood up in the House and denounced Percival as 'a dangerous person, privy to all the designs of the cessation of Ireland' and one who had been seen at Oxford. Lisle seconded Temple, adding that he had always looked upon Percival as a great confidante of Ormonde's, and recommending that a committee be set up to investigate him. 'Col [Algernon] Sidney then declared that [Percival] had sent certificates to the King at Oxford, which occasioned the cessation, and had proposed to the soldiers afterwards to come into England to fight the Parliament, and that it was an abominable thing etc.' The committee on Percival was duly set up, and Lisle, Temple, and Sidney appointed to it. On 5 July a vote was passed that 'no-one who had assisted at, signed, or consented to the cessation, or otherwise assisted the Rebellion, should sit'. On 1 November 1647 Algernon and Temple were both added to the permanent Committee for the Affairs of Ireland. For the rest of his parliamentary career, Irish affairs were to remain Sidney's particular speciality.[38]

Sidney was involved during 1647 in only two divisions in the House: one concerning the House's reply to the Army's petition on 25 May; the other concerning the Lords' four propositions for negotiations with the King on 27 November. On both occasions Sidney voted in partnership with John Evelyn, a Northumberland friend and client, and on both occasions his alliance with the Saye/Northumberland group straddling the Lords and the Commons is

---

[37] Gilbert, *Irish Confederation* pp. 19–26; HMC Egmont, vol. VI pp. 419–20.
[38] CJ v p. 166; Egmont, p. 430; Underdown, *Pride's Purge* p. 82; CJ v pp. 195, 347. Whitelocke, *Memorials* II p. 139.

evident.[39] The nature (and name) of this 'middle' group, incorporating a number of independents, which attempted to reach a settlement with the King in 1647, and then again in 1648, has been variously discussed by Valerie Pearl, David Underdown, F. R. Willey, and John Adamson among others. I have no intention of entering the debate, since available details of Sidney's precise activities in these years are too slim to warrant it. Yet it is worth noting that the general outline of the group's political, religious, and personal make-up fits Sidney's own beliefs and later associations perfectly. Sidney's association in the Rump and afterwards with Vane, Whitelocke, Strickland, and Howard, against men like Marten, was already a feature of this group in this period. Pearl has commented on the 'grand aristocratic style' of both Evelyn and his colleague Pierrepoint, despite the fact that Pierrepoint was 'a puritan' (and, like Vane, a friend of Cromwell). It is no surprise, then, that both men were close friends of Northumberland; indeed it was from Pierrepoint that Burnet said Northumberland 'Imbibed all his political understanding'. As Algernon teamed with Evelyn in the Commons, his brother Philip kept their father informed of the political fortunes of 'Mr Pierrepoint ... [and] Mr Selden' – as we have seen, another associate of the group. And as Sidney's closest associate in the Rump was to be Henry Vane – whom he would praise as the Republic's naval genius and inventor of 'the Frigat' – so in this period Vane was working as a naval administrator under Northumberland, and was to team as often with Evelyn in the Commons as Sidney himself. I have already described the correspondence between Sidney's political thought and that of this group, as represented by the *Vindiciae*. In religion, equally, their concern, like Sidney's own, was less with particular forms than with the internal moral content of the reformed religion. Saye wanted to abolish episcopacy and tolerate both independency and the Book of Common Prayer; he saw no role for the state or clergy in religion save the regulation of basic moral conduct.[40]

---

[39] For Evelyn and Northumberland see Whitelocke *Memorials* I p. 208; Yule, *The Independents in The English Civil War* (Cambridge 1958) p. 44. The first division (for disbandment) on 25 May was opposed by Sidney and Evelyn, but carried by the 'presbyterian' majority in the House. (Re the flight of the 'independents' to the Army Sidney does not appear in the Rushworth or Lord's Journal lists of those who signed the Engagement (although Northumberland and Lisle both do), but he does appear, along with Sir John Temple, in the Egmont MSS list, compiled by none other than Sir Philip Percival.) In his second division, concerning the Lord's four propositions for treating with the King, Sidney and Evelyn this time carried the motion in favour of accepting them. In the latter vote Sidney was pitted against the radical Henry Marten, an opposition which was to become habitual in the Rump. HMC Egmont, p. 440; CJ v p. 371.

[40] Add. MS 63,057 I 175; Pearl, 'Royal independents' pp. 85–7; HMC De Lisle vol. IV p. 486; Adamson, 'Saye and Sele'; Underdown, *Purge* pp. 63, 95, 102; Willey F. R., 'The independent coalition and changing parliamentary alignments December 1646 to January 1648' Cambridge Ph.D. 1971 pp. 101, 118, 242, 327–8, 345–9.

In 1648 Sidney was appointed to a new governorship – Dover.[41] This was clearly in some sense the 'consideration' promised to him in lieu of his lost governorship of Dublin.[42] On 26 May, Sidney had been appointed to liaise with the Derby House Committee to suppress all tumults in his home county of Kent; his appointment to Dover in the same county by the same committee seems to have come in the wake of his resulting activity.[43] He corresponded with the Committees of Both Houses and of Kent concerning the situation in the county in early July, as the royalist military escapade involving Holland and Buckingham was routed by Livesey's troops. This period probably marked the beginning of Sidney's co-operation with Livesey, whose will in 1666 was to name him first among the ex-political colleagues to whom he left most of his estate.[44]

In early October Algernon wrote to William Aylesbury, an old member of his father's household, giving advice on Aylesbury's friend Buckingham's chances of an accommodation with Parliament. 'I should advise that he would take this time for that work; for now that all men are inclined to a peace with the King and his party, much more gentleness is to be expected than at another time.' Later Sidney was to claim at his trial 'that though I had ever opposed the [King's] party, noe man had ever shewed himself to be a fairer enemy, and that I had done many personall and most important services, as well to the royall family, as unto such as depended upon it'.[45] Indeed as Sidney found himself drawn deeper into the radical parliamentary cause, he could not escape his background and connections; connections for which he was to suffer suspicion from army officers and radicals after 1649. They included Aylesbury, Hammond (by 1648 personal chaplain to the King), Northumberland, Temple (to be excluded at Pride's Purge), and his own parents, by 1650 the official hosts at Penshurst to the remainder of the royal family itself. Sidney saw the end of the year out nursing his father's estate through the Committee for Sequestrations.[46]

---

[41] He seems to have taken up his post as early as 13 July, although the two Houses didn't confirm his nomination (which came from the Derby House Committee) until 14 October.

[42] Cal. S.P. Dom. p. 189.

[43] On this same day, 26 May, Sidney was involved in his only division in the House in this year, interesting because it pitted him against Vane. See CJ v p. 574; Underdown, *Purge* pp. 102, 104, 111–12; Judson, *The Political Thought of Henry Vane The Younger* (1969) p. 9.

[44] From December 1648 to 1653 and in 1659 Sidney served on the Kent militia and assessment committees, with Livesey, his brother Lisle, and others. CJ vi pp. 52, 574; Cal. S.P. Dom. 1648–9 pp. 185–6; A copy of Livesey's will survives in the Sidney papers, De Lisle MS U1475 F32/7; Firth and Rait, *Acts and Ordinances* vol. i p. 1238, vol. ii pp. 36, 300, 469, 665, 1326, 1371.

[45] Clarendon State Papers vol. ii p. 421; Works, 'Apology' p. 1.

[46] Toynbee M. R., 'A Sydney lawsuit' in *Archaeologia Cantiana* LXIV (1951); add. MS 21,506 fol. 55; Hammond was Temple's brother-in-law. At the beginning of 1642, on the eve of the civil war, Algernon, Aylesbury, and Hammond had all been at Penshurst together, where they witnessed Sunderland's will: De Lisle MS U1475 C113/1.

For by November the 'inclination to peace' of which Sidney had spoken had begun to collapse into the tide of Army bitterness. The Newport negotiations had failed despite Saye's tearful appeals to the King. On 20 November the Army presented to Parliament its uncompromising *Remonstrance*, condemning Charles I's duplicitous 'Court Maxims' as inconsistent with the welfare of the people. This was the position from which Sidney was to begin his own *Court Maxims* seventeen years later. On 2 December Vane made it clear that his flirtation with the Newport negotiators and the Northumberland/Saye group was over: the treaty, he said, had been a mistake; monarch and monarchy were not to be trusted; the nation must be settled without him, and the instigators of the second civil war punished severely. But it was too late for even this Army-minded compromise and events were moving out of Vane's control as well. By the end of the year all those who had sought continued negotiation with the King had been expelled, and 'that man of blood' himself put on trial for his life. A month later a shocked Europe heard that Charles I had been publicly executed, and England's government settled 'in the way of a republic, without king or House of Peers'.

6

Republic 1649–53

6.1 POLITICS

According to the Earl of Leicester's diary, at the time of the King's execution both his eldest sons were with him at Penshurst; '[and] young Sir Henry Vane . . . [too] had long absented and retyred himself by scruple of conscience'. Philip had at no time been in the High Court, though Algernon had been 'there sometimes, in the Painted Chamber, but never in Westminster Hall'.[1]

If Sidney expressed doubts about the trial itself, on the grounds that the Lords had been given insufficient time to participate, he at no time disputed the justice of the charge. Indeed he described his objections more fully, in 1660, in an attempt to clear himself from the [correct] accusation that he had defended the regicide overseas as 'the justest and bravest acti[o]n that ever was done in England, or anywhere'. We thus need to be suitably wary about this face-saving account to his father:[2]

[in] the directing of that businesse, I did positively oppose Cromwell, Bradshawe, and others, whoe would have the triall to goe on, and drewe my reasons from theis tow points: First, the King could be tried by noe court; secondly, that noe man could be tried by that court. This being alleged in vaine, and Cromwell using these formall words (I tell you, wee will cut off his head with the crowne upon it) I replied: you may take your own course, I cannot stop you, but I will keep myself clean from having any hand in this businesse, immediately went out of the room, and never returned.[3]

Certainly the idea that a king 'could be tried by noe court' will strike any reader of the *Discourses* as quaint; where 'many . . . kings of the greatest nations in the world . . . have been so utterly deprived of power that they have been imprisoned, deposed, confined to monasteries, killed, drawn through the streets, cut in pieces, thrown into rivers, and indeed suffered all that could be suffered by the vilest slaves'. Yet there is little reason to doubt that Sidney objected to the illegal interference by the Army in parliamentary politics as

[1] Blencowe, *Sidney Papers* (1825) p. 54
[2] B.M. add MS 21,506 fol. 55; add MS 32,680 fols. 9–10.
[3] Blencowe, *Sidney Papers* pp. 236–9.

strongly as he had to that earlier by the King.[4] This was to be one of the key threads uniting Sidney's whole career; even in 1678–83, as we will see, the 'good old cause' was the cause of Parliament, the cause for which the civil war had been fought. Both the nature of his objections to the King's trial and his decision to join the Rump are explicable from this standpoint, as is his retrospective description of his cause in 1670 as 'entirely parliamentary'. We must not let the mathematical reality of the Rump blind us to one political reality: that for a core of its members (and others) both from 1649 to 1653, and in 1659, it was this body which was seen to enshrine the 'good old cause', as the last faithful remnant of the Parliament and so the parliamentary cause. It was a remnant which had in the 1650s to defend its existence against the Army as it had in the 1640s against the King.

Accordingly Sidney marked his return to the House by provoking a spectacular row over Ireton's proposed oath of allegiance, opposed likewise by Haselrig and Vane. This would have expressed 'full approval of the judicial proceedings against Charles I and of the abolition of the House of Lords'. 'I chanced to use this expression', recounted Sidney charmingly, 'that such a test would prove a snare to many an honest man, but every knave would slip through it.' The ensuing uproar, with Lord Grey of Groby saying 'I had called all thoes knaves, that had signed the order', was eventually calmed by Marten, but not in time to prevent Sidney's typically piquant phraseology from having 'soe ill effects as to my particular concernments, as to make Cromwell, Bradshawe, Harrison, Lord Grey and others, my enemys, who did from that time continually oppose me'. A milder form of the oath was subsequently passed, requiring only 'the settling of the government of this nation for future in the way of a republic, without King or House of Peers'.[5]

As in his earlier career, Sidney's decision to fall in with the parliamentary power in being in 1649 brought him quick financial reward. In mid-May he reported to the House from the Committee for Irish Affairs on officers' overdue pay. Parliament responded in October by voting him £1,809 13s. 6d. Irish arrears for himself, though the motion was opposed in a division by Marten.[6] In the same year Sidney joined with Marten to support the election of his kinsman Henry Neville to the House. Though Neville maintained

---

[4] *Discourses* p. 330; Worden, *Rump* p. 41; Underdown, *Purge* p. 215.

[5] Worden, *Rump* pp. 180–1; Blencowe, *Sidney Papers* pp. 238–9; Gardiner, *History of the Commonwealth and Protectorate* vol. 1 p. 5. Compare with Ludlow's later argument against the oath to Richard Cromwell in 1659: 'for the most part oaths proved only snares to honest men', *Burton's Diary* ed. Rutt J. III p. 69. Sidney himself said later in the *Discourses* (p. 359; see pp. 355–9 generally): 'A worthy person of our age was accustomed to say, that contracts in writing were invented only to bind villains, who having no law, justice, or truth, within themselves, would not keep their words, unless such testimonies were given as might compell them.'

[6] CJ VI 206–7, 282, 302; *Perfect Occurences* no. 145 Wednesday 5 October; The CJ ordered the money paid in cash; *Perfect Occurences* reported that it was made in [Irish?] land.

connections with both his benefactors, Sidney and Marten themselves sustained a consistent and deepening animosity.

It is perhaps easy enough to understand why. The irreverent, irreligious, and anti-aristocratic Marten cannot have naturally appealed to the moralistic and imperious Sidney, or vice versa. It is interesting to contrast Aubrey's testimony to Marten's ability in the House: 'He alone haz [sic] sometimes turned the whole House'; with Sidney's similar words: 'He often used to bring over the Parliament to his Single Opinion, when their own sentiments and debates, till his were heard, had a different tendency and view.' It is interesting because Sidney is talking not about Marten but about Henry Vane. Marten was 'long an enemy of Vane', and Rump politics was punctuated by the conflict between Vane's religious radicalism and social conservatism, and Marten's irreligious social radicalism. Marten was allied with Neville, Chaloner, and Lord Grey of Groby who had helped preside over Pride's Purge and whose 'continual opposition' to him Sidney has already mentioned. Indeed Dr Worden's association of Sidney with the Neville–Marten–Chaloner group in the House cannot be sustained far beyond the person of Neville himself. All Sidney's work with Chaloner, in 1653 and 1659, took place under Vane's auspices as chief naval administrator, an administration which they (but not Marten, Morley, or Neville) came to share with Vane closely.[7]

Sidney's *Character* of Vane traced Vane's political and military prowess from the period of the civil war through to his 'absolute Master[ship] of the Naval Affairs' under the Rump. We have seen the contacts Sidney and Vane had in common throughout that period; in addition they were family friends and Kentish next-door neighbours, hence Leicester's notice of Vane's absences from the King's trial in his diary. Most importantly, Sidney was not to take up highest office on the Rump Council of State until November 1652, in the same election in which Marten and Neville were both dropped from the Council, and their and Chaloner's power as major influences on policy permanently destroyed. The control of the Navy had been recaptured by Vane and his allies, Sidney among them, a spectacular reversal of the earlier situation in June 1652. Then Vane had suffered a crucial defeat at the hands of Marten over terms for dealing with the Dutch, his desire for peace and alliance with the fellow protestant republic overridden by the Marten-group policy of Anglo–Dutch war. Following this Vane had retired entirely from politics for some months, but now he returned to commit himself, from November 1652 onwards, to the management of the war in progress. It was at this point that Sidney joined him on the Council.[8]

---

[7] Worden, *Rump* pp. 172–3, 187, 221, 218–19, 284; Aubrey, *Brief Lives* (1972) p. 354; Sidney, 'The Character of Henry Vane Jnr' in Rowe, *Vane* Appendix F.

[8] Worden, *Rump* pp. 313–14.

Like Vane, and Whitelocke, Sidney was to take great pride in the consequent naval victories he helped to direct; but like both of them there is no
evidence that he sought the war in the first place, or that the protestant
republic was a comfortable or ideal enemy. Indeed Sidney, as his family
history of Dutch contacts suggests, was a more likely candidate for the Vane-
supported policy in 1651–2 of union with the Dutch rather than war,
inclinations further suggested by Sidney's co-operation in the House with
Strickland, the architect and one of the ambassadors of that mission. This fits,
too, with Sidney's praise of the 'valour' of the Dutch navy in the *Discourses*,
and of Vane in the *Character* as having 'zelously promoted the peace with
Holland, and helpt to carry on vigorously whatever War was begun by any
other Nation'.[9]

Above all, this impression is reinforced by the role Sidney was to play when
Vane re-established control over foreign policy again in 1659. Indeed from
comments in 1659 by members of that Council of State and Committee of
Foreign Affairs who had worked with Sidney and Vane to manage the war
after November 1652, there seem excellent grounds for seeing paramount in
their war policy not commercial rivalry so much as an ideological pursuit of
the protestant/republican union plan by other means. Thomas Scot
explained: 'we intended to have gone off with a good savour . . . but we stayed
to end the Dutch War. We might have brought them to a oneness with us.
Their Ambassadors did desire a coalition. This we might have done in four or
five months.' Vane, too, said bitterly that before Cromwell disbanded the
Rump 'the endeavouring to bring the two nations to a coalition . . . had made
a great progress'. In the Rump under Vane in 1659; in the Netherlands itself
in 1665; and in England again in 1678–9, Sidney was to work for unity
between the two Republics, for the mutual security of their republican and
protestant liberty, in the face of the threat each faced from the united 'interest'
of the Houses of Stuart and Orange.[10]

In his *Character* Sidney praised in Vane his 'valor and wisdom and that
Glory of [his] unblemish'd life'; his being 'not a little conversant in human
Learning, but [especially] . . . vers'd and skill'd in the Sacred Writings', and
for being 'as sollicitous for the public good, as he was negligent of his own
private interest'. He painted in Vane an incorruptible Stoic hero, with a calm
and self-knowledge which kept him securely on the path to truth throughout
two decades of civil war and upheaval. He made Vane the Sir Philip Sidney of
the Puritan revolution; a great military leader and, above all, the great martyr
to the cause, 'who by obeying reason, at once seem'd to renounce all kind of
unbecoming passions and affections: nay such was his Magnanimity, that if

[9] Rowe, *Vane* pp. 145–5, 155; Worden, *Rump* p. 301; Strickland had been proposing various
forms of union to the Dutch on parliament's behalf since 1642.
[10] *Burton's Diary* iii 111–12.

the frame of the whole world had been dissolv'd and gon to rack about his ears, he would have remained undaunted in the midst of its ruins'. Needless to say, Vane's road was Sidney's also, from the civil war, to the Rump, Protectorate, and Rump restored, and finally to the scaffold.[11]

Thus if Sidney's clear association with Neville is not to be overlooked, his association with Vane is a good deal more evident, and it is clear where Sidney stood on the Vane/Marten policy and ideology divide.[12] Where he stood most firmly with Vane, as we will see in the Platonist *Court Maxims*, and where Milton, Nedham, and Stubbe (but not Harrington) stood with him, was in allegiance to Vane's central religious/political principle: that the 'mystery of iniquity' consisted in the mixing of civil with spiritual power. Vane was looked to as the principal patron of the cause of separating the two,[13] of freeing the spirit for worship from any political jurisdiction whatever. This was the cause which Sidney pursued unwaveringly for the rest of his life, which Locke espoused too, and to which Milton paid tribute in his sonnet of 1652, to

> Vane, young in years, but in sage counsel old
> than whom a better senator ne'er held
> The helm of Rome
> ... to know
> Both spiritual power and civil, what each means,
> What severs each, thou hast learned which few have done.
> The bounds of either sword to thee we owe;
> Therefore on thy firm hand Religion leans
> In peace, and reckons thee her eldest son.[14]

Although early on in the Rump Sidney was appointed to many committees (including importantly that on Ireland, another to oversee the Commonwealth's accounts, and Vane's Committee 'to take into Consideration

---

[11] Sidney, 'Character' in Rowe, *Vane* pp. 278–9.

[12] The association of Sidney with the ungodly 'wits' in the Rump – Chaloner, Marten, and Neville – has a historiographical pedigree as old as Toland and Burnet, and its roots firmly in the whig playing-down of Sidney's religion. In Burnet's words: 'Cromwell studied to divide the commonwealth party among themselves, and to set the fifth monarchy men and enthusiasts against those who pretended to little or no religion, and acted only upon the principles of civil liberty, such as Algernon Sidney, Henry Nevill, Marten, Wildman, and Harrington.' Burnet, *Own Time* (1897–1900) I p. 120. Yet as soon as we step beyond these whig historiographical sources (including the now discredited Toland's Ludlow) for 1652–3 and 1659, we find the manuscript evidence for Sidney full of a different picture, associating him primarily with Vane and Whitelocke in the Rump rather than Neville and Marten, and against Marten and his crew of 'little or no religion'. Moreover, this manuscript picture, unlike the other, is consistent with Sidney's career and associations during the civil war as well as the Rump (both from 1649 and in 1659), and with the ideology of his own writings, particularly the Vanist *Court Maxims* (which Burnet's characterisation would make inexplicable).

[13] Worden notes of Ludlow's *Voyce*, too, that it makes clear Vane's 'role as the leading spirit among the Commonwealthsmen after 1653' and Ludlow's 'reverence for him'.

[14] Parker W. R., *Milton* (Oxford 1968) I p. 414.

the Settling of the Succession of future Parliaments')[15] his principal responsibility remained the governorship of Dover Castle, a strategic front-line defence against the exiled King. In the early part of 1649 the Castle was restocked with troops and ammunition, and Sidney's regular pay established, 'from the sequestrations of Kent'.[16] On 4 June he was ordered to repair to the Castle 'in regard of the disorders like to ensue in Kent, and [his fellow Kentishmen] Sir Henry Mildmay and Sir Henry Vane to confer with him about it'. On 6 August he had to be ordered to his charge again.[17]

Between these two dates the Council of State (Fairfax and Cromwell being present), were informed of 'outrages' committed by soldiers in Kent due to the absence of their officers. Particular offenders were 'Captain Swan's company', the contingent which had been transferred to Sidney's command as part of the reinforcement of Dover. The Council expressed sharp concern at 'those inconveniences, whereby the people are much discontented and alienated from the Parliament'. In early August they assured the Kent Committee that all soldiers in Kent were to 'use all civility and pay quarters', and that Sidney had been ordered to repair to Dover Castle. Meanwhile, however, Sidney had written a stiff letter of rebuttal to the Corporation of Sandwich, who requested payment for the quarter of his troops. There would be no payment, said Sidney, until the Committee of the Army furnished adequate supplies: 'unlesse the Comttee for the army be pleased to allow them marching pay . . . I desire you not to take any money from my soldiers . . . if they doe, you shall be fully satisfied . . .' The stage was thus already set for the confrontation between Sidney and the Army Council over his conduct at Dover, which was to disturb the political peace in the following year.[18]

During 1650, Sidney made use of his deepening involvement in the Commonwealth's financial affairs to advance his own. In May he was appointed to the committee to oversee the Impropriations of Deans and Chapters Lands, and 'the Manors . . . belonging to [them]'. Four months later he purchased for himself from the Trustees of Fee-farm Rents 'the 10th of the Mannor of Conisby in . . . Lincolne at £30 p.anno', and a total of seven other fee-farm rents. In July he employed a Mr John Gay to manage these and other business affairs for him. In this same year Sidney began his involvement with diplomatic and foreign negotiations. He was appointed one of a committee to treat with the Spanish ambassador, Don Alonso de Cardenas, negotiations to which he was later to refer when he came across the ambassador's interpreter

[15] CJ vi pp. 118, 132, 134, 307; cf. p. 156.
[16] Sidney received 20s a day. PRO Chancery C7 325/2.
[17] Cal. S.P. Dom 1649–50 pp. 63–4, 67, 75, 130–1, 172, 263; PRO Chancery C7 325/2.
[18] CSPD 1649–50 pp. 174, 264–5 (cf. pp. 348, 412, 439) Kent R.O. Sandwich MSS Sa/ZB2/114. A letter from Sidney at Dover also survives, written on behalf of the 'poore widdowe . . . [of] a gunner of this castle'; it is reproduced in Elizabeth Melling, *Kentish Sources* vol. II (Maidstone 1959) pp. 32–3.

again in Rome in 1661. In his two divisions in the House in 1650 one was over the appointment of a Treasurer for the Navy, in which he teamed with Vane; the other over an issue 'touching the hospitals', in which he opposed Marten.[19]

The storm over Sidney's conduct at Dover began to break in April (1650). The council wrote 'to the Lord General, enclosing the papers against Col. Sydney, and [to] desire him to quicken the business, which is already before the Council of War, and meantime to take care of the place'. In the same month Sidney wrote from Leicester House, to Whitelocke, requesting 'the papers concerning the Dover businesse'. In July, one Capt. Cannon was appointed deputy Governor at Dover, and seems to have taken effective command there, 'observing orders from Parliament, [the] Council of State, the Lord General, and Major General Harrison' – the last two, of course, being the Army leaders who Sidney stated 'did, from [1649] ... continually oppose me'. The dual command structure – Parliament and Army leaders – under which garrisons like Dover operated, was not the original point at issue, nor were these authorities assumed to be in conflict in the command hierarchy. But it soon became the issue, and they soon became locked in conflict, because of the way Sidney chose to play the case.[20]

That the initial charges against Sidney included a 'petition ... from Sandwich', and another from Dover, confirms the impression that an important cause of the dispute lay in Sidney's intransigence about the quartering of his troops, in opposition to the Army Committee's own policy. In late October, however, the Council of State (with a number of Sidney's friends present, including Vane, his brother Lisle, and Ludlow) concluded that since 'the charge formerly exhibited' against Sidney had been dismissed by a Council of War, and Algernon 'adjudged a fit person to be continued in his trust', no further proceedings should be had therein. Yet they added that there were now 'additional charges exhibited against Col. Sydney', and they appointed a committee (including Ludlow) to examine them, and Sidney's answer.[21]

How far Ludlow was Sidney's friend at this stage is not clear; what we know is that four months earlier when Cromwell had asked his advice on an appropriate Commander of Horse to be sent to assist Ireton in Ireland, Ludlow 'told him, that in my opinion a fitter man could not be found than Col Algernon Sidney; but [Cromwell] excepted against him by reason of his relation to some who were in the King's interest'.[22]

[19] CJ vi pp. 382, 400, 431, 455, 482, 500, 517; B.M. Stowe MS 184 fols. 269, 272.
[20] CSPD 1650 pp. 89, 228, 256, 284, 289, 359, Longleat Bath MSS, Whitelocke Papers xxvi fol. 250; Worden, *Rump* pp. 248–9.
[21] CSPD 1650 pp. 89, 255, 387, 393, 399, 435.
[22] Firth C. ed., *Ludlow's Memoirs* (1894) i p. 247.

By early 1651 Sidney was threatened with a 'Court Martial' by 'divers officers of the army', and his brother Lisle wrote to Leicester: 'Truly I think he hath had very hard measure, and I know no grounds of it but his relation to a sort of people who are looked upon with a most jealous eye.' Junior officers at Dover seem to have been in the forefront of this pursuit, including the new deputy Governor, Cannon.[23]

A local court martial began to hear charges, but Sidney petitioned the House of Commons, and on 14 January the clearly affronted House ordered a suspension of all court-martial proceedings, and the return to Sidney of his impounded goods. A week later, when these orders were ignored, Parliament declared a 'Breach of the Order of this House', and summoned Major Audley, Captain Cannon, and Captain Wilson to the Bar of the House to explain themselves. The confrontation with Parliament caused unease within Army circles; Lambert wrote to Captain Adam Baines, who had 'appeared very ... forward in this business', that such 'needlesse zeale ... did rather tend to trouble than ye necessaire perservacon of ye discipline of ye Army'. Baines replied that: 'Col. Sidney doeth not apeale from the Judgmt of the Court Marshall But from the Jurisdiction [of it]', and that if MPs were not to be subject to court martials then they should not hold commands in the Army, for 'how absurd it will be for any man to have power to Judge others, by a Lawe which him selfe shall not be subject to'.[24]

In the end Parliament won this dispute over jurisdiction and the committee set up 'touching Col. Sydney' was left to continue its deliberations alone from January to mid April, before petering out without recorded conclusion. By making his case the subject of a uniquely sensitive constitutional issue Sidney secured its effective abandonment; but he lost any further opportunity to play his two (military and political) authorities off against each other, when he lost his last military command. He was replaced as Governor of Dover on 15 May.[25]

During the rest of 1651 Sidney continued his committee work on Irish Affairs, and combined his growing interests in military administration and finance with membership of a committee to supervise the finances of the Army and the Treasurers at War (along with Vane, Chaloner, Strickland, and others). He later helped to push its recommendations through the House; once again against the opposition of Marten (and Lord Grey). In the same year he secured himself appointment to a committee to consider a petition from his Uncle Northumberland for financial indemnity; and in good

---

[23] HMC De Lisle and Dudley vII p. 488; Sidney later sued Cannon in Chancery (1656) for allegedly pocketing his pay in this period. PRO Chancery C7 325/2.

[24] CSPD 1651 p. 118; CJ 1651 14, 22, 29 January; 28 March; 16 April; B.M. add MS 21426 fols. 7, 189.

[25] CJ 1651 (pp. 523, 529, 554, 562–3); CSPD 1651 p. 201.

classical republican fashion he voted (with Strickland) to retain strict
monthly rotation for all chairmanships in the Council of State and the
Houses' committees.[26]

Yet as I have said, it was in 1652, and particularly the Council of State
elections in November, that Sidney decided to commit himself completely to
the Republic. His work-rate had increased gradually throughout the year; it is
clear that the government's growing confidence following its conquest of
Scotland, and the urgency of the demands imposed after June by the Dutch
war, were catching Sidney's imagination. Certainly his work soon became
clearly focused on both war (naval) and conquest (Ireland and Scotland)
management. The family background to this outward-looking view has
already been discussed.

In Irish affairs Sidney had by now become the senior government figure,
and in August he headed the committee to draft the legislation necessary for
settlement by the Adventurers for Lands in Ireland. He was later assisted in its
passage through the House by Neville (again) against the opposition of
Marten (again). He was also closely involved with the sale of Church and
Delinquents' lands to raise money for the Navy, allying in this in divisions
again with Vane, and again against Marten.[27] In addition throughout the
year his involvement with foreign affairs increased, particularly in the
reception of foreign ambassadors – and it is in this work that he must have
had contact with John Milton. Finally, in September Sidney was placed on
Vane's committee 'in order to the Uniting of Scotland into one Commonwealth with England'.[28]

The vision of this committee paralleled the Vanist wish for the Netherlands: to unite Scotland into one nation with England, rather than administer
it as a conquered province. To do this the committee had to settle terms for
separate Scots representation at Westminster, and for administration of the
Scots judiciary, money supply, and other matters. It was intended as a
generous settlement, fit for a people who were fit for liberty: 'calculated for a
Commonwealth', explained Neville, 'and not for a Monarchy ... They must
not have Englishmen imposed upon them ... to enslave them and us too.' It
was the confident vision of a regime riding the crest of a wave of military
victories, and acquired for many the flavour of ancient achievement, of
Milton's dream of England reborn as a 'new Rome in the West'. This theme
resurfaced in nostalgia in 1659: 'You promised it to them, to take them into
your bosoms and make them one with you. The Romans never did well till
they did so.' Sidney attended twelve of the Scots-union Committee's eighteen

---

[26] This summary does not attempt to cover all the detail available about Sidney's activities in the
House in 1651. CJ vi pp. 567, 587, 599, CJ vii pp. 23, 41–2, 43, 55, 58, 61.
[27] CJ vii pp. 112, 156, 157, 159, 161–2, 163, 191, 218, 222, 238.
[28] CJ vii pp. 234, 189; cf. pp. 86, 154, 171.

meetings between the beginning of October and the end of November 1652; but after that both he and Vane stopped attending (though Whitelocke stayed on). The Council of State elections (in which Sidney became one of only three completely new members) had taken them to other more urgent concerns: from settlement of old (army) victories, to the management of new (naval) ones.[29]

Sidney's hectic workload on the Council of State centred on the Council itself, liaison with the House, and the work of two committees: for Trade and Foreign Affairs (with Vane, Say, Scot, and Strickland); and for the Affairs of Ireland (with Vane and Scot again, and Whitelocke and Morley). Of these the Committee for Trade and Foreign Affairs was the more important, and Sidney became within it, the Council of State, and the House as a whole, a principal spokesman on Foreign Affairs. Between December and April he met with the Public Ministers of Portugal, Spain, France, Sweden, Hamburg, Tuscany, Holland, France, and Austria; in each case it was he who reported the progress of the negotiations to the House.[30] At the same time, within the committee, he specialised, with Vane, in wartime and naval affairs, working on the accommodation of Dutch prisoners; communications with Holland; the provision of naval timber; and the sending out of naval ships from Harwich.[31]

The provision of naval materials involved Baltic trade, and on 9 February Sidney was given charge of a sub-committee to deal with the Hamburg agent about 'procuring Hemp and other Eastland goods from Hamburg' for the Navy. He worked on this with Vane, and with merchants in the City of London. In this work we see the germ of Sidney's later role as Vane's envoy to the Baltic in 1659, to protect English naval and trading interests in Hamburg and the Sound.[32] To underline the point, in this period he prepared with Vane the instructions for the proposed ambassador to Sweden, Philip, his brother. Algernon reported progress on this work to the House four or five times in March and April.[33]

At the same time Sidney was chaperoning through the House a major programme of legislation on the planting of Ireland (reporting it to the House on 1 and 4 January, and 5, 14, 15, and 19 April).[34] Thus by the eve of the dissolution (20 April) Sidney had worked hard to elbow himself to eminence

---

[29] *Burton's Diary* IV pp. 179, 183, 188, 190; PRO SP25/138.

[30] PRO SP25/132, 133, 138; CSPD CW5 1652–3 pp. 2, 9, 62, 83, 112, 157, 252, 178; SP25/68 5 January; CJ VII pp. 250, 252, 253, 262, 263, 269, 271.

[31] PRO SP25/33 p. 3 (11 March), p. 19 (25 March); SP25/132 p. 5 (15 December); SP25/68 p. 14 (3 December).

[32] CSPD CW5 1652–3 p. 155; PRO SP25/132 p. 47 (19 December).

[33] CJ VII p. 269; CSPD pp. 220–1, 250, 254.

[34] CJ VII pp. 241, 242, 271, 278; cf. p. 160 (more evidence of Sidney's tendency to adopt the hard line).

(Foreign and Naval Affairs) or pre-eminence (Irish Affairs) in at least two branches of policy, and two at least of his major projects (the Irish legislation and the embassy to the Sound) were coming to a head. It was at this moment that nemesis struck.

Blair Worden's analysis of the dissolution of the Rump Parliament by the Army has centred on the 'Bill for a New Representative', on which Sidney had worked in Committee, and which the House was feverishly attempting to pass, with Sidney sitting 'on the right hand of the speaker', the morning the House was dissolved. Worden has suggested that the bill was not, as Army propaganda claimed, a device to introduce 'recruiting' in the place of proper elections. Rather it was, in the face of growing Army pressure on the political process, an attempt to throw open the door to elections so free that they were, by Army standards, dangerous; it was a civilian attempt to take parliamentary revenge for Pride's Purge. This analysis fits in well with what we know about Sidney; about Vane, into whose particular care the bill was entrusted; and about Whitelocke, whom Sidney pictured with himself and Vane as the objects of Cromwell's ire on 20 April. These were lines Sidney had carried forward from 1649, and they were to serve him equally well again in 1659, when it was again Vane and Whitelocke with whom he became most closely associated in the Rump.[35]

Cromwell, Sidney recalled, paced:

> up and down the stage or floor in the middest of the House ... chid[ing] them soundly, and pointing particularly upon somme persons, as ... Whitlock ... [and] Sir Henry Vane to whome he gave very sharpe language ... After this he sayd to Corronell Harrison 'Call them in' ... and presently brought in ... five or six files of Musketeers ... It happened that day, that Algernon Sydney sate next to the Speaker on the right hand; the Generall sayd to Harrison 'Put him out' ... but he sayd he would not go out, and sate still ... then Harrison and Wortley putt theyr hands upon Sydney's shoulders, as if they would force him to go out, then he rose and went towards the doore. The Generall went to the table where the mace lay ... and sayd, 'Take away these baubles;' [and] sayd to young Sir Henry Vane ... that he might have prevented this extraordinary course, but he was a Juggler, and had not so much as common honesty. All being gon out, the door of the House was locked.[36]

6.2 MYTHOLOGY

It is clear from his political thought that Sidney's years in the Commonwealth government, and particularly his last few months in its Council of State, were politically the most formative of his life. To understand why it is necessary to look at the achievements of the Rump in general, and at those of Sidney within it in particular.

---

[35] Worden, *Rump* pt 5; *A Perfect Diurnall of some Passages in Parliament* no. 303, 15 May; Underdown, *Pride's Purge* p. 287.

[36] Blencowe, *Sidney Papers* pp. 140–1.

The Rump was ultimately hoist by the petard of revolutionary expectations it did not itself create. Caught between conservative hostility on the one hand, and radical critics on the other, this expediential regime was required to attempt to satisfy both, to fight three wars, to face universal European condemnation, and to handle the mountain of business necessary to consolidate (never mind extend) a revolution, all employing a form of government machinery improvised by itself, with no English precedent for its use at all.[37] Amid this sometimes grim and desperate adventure some MPs were responsible for periods of Herculean political labour by means of which, with the excellence of its armed forces, the Republic managed not only to survive but to secure itself against every foreign enemy it had, leaving only the enemy within which eventually destroyed it.

For these men (and in his last months Sidney became one of them), the experience of these achievements (as of that eventual betrayal) made an impact which never left them. Lacking political legitimacy, traditional machinery, or public support, the Commonwealth leaders proved to themselves not only that government under these circumstances could continue to function but that, indeed, in terms of military and naval achievement and, consequently, of European reputation, in four short years the regime stood the shame of Stuart weakness and martial negligence on its head. The civil war, and accompanying Parliamentary centralisation of government, had dragged England in one decade through the military and governmental revolution which had been transforming the *ancien régime* of western Europe since the shattering continental wars of the mid to late sixteenth century. The post-civil-war Republic was the first English government to inherit this new-found power and put it to the test against the nation's external enemies. Accordingly, and for the only time in the seventeenth century, England became one of the more powerful nations in Europe, courted by France and Spain alike. The impact of this experience, and of what it seemed to show about republicanism versus monarchy, lies at the core of Sidney's political thought, and of the mythology of the English Republic which he helped to create. It was this ideology which the American Republic imported through Sidney, Milton, and Harrington the following century.

It was Sidney's Council of State colleague Scot in 1659 who mused that: 'We never bid fairer for being masters of the whole World'.[38] In the *Discourses* Sidney produced the most strident evocations of all of the Republic's might in arms:

When Van Tromp set upon Blake in Folkstone Bay, the parliament had not above thirteen ships against threescore ... to oppose the best captain in the world, attended

---

[37] Worden, *Rump* p. 185.
[38] *Burton's Diary* III p. 112; on this theme see Trevor-Roper, *Religion, The Reformation and Social Change* (1967) p. 359.

with many others in valour and experience not much inferior to him ... But such was
the power of wisdom and integrity in those that sat at the helm, and their diligence in
choosing men for their merit was blessed with such success, that in two years our fleets
grew to be as famous as our land-armies; the reputation and power of our nation rose
to a greater height, than when we possessed the better half of France, and the Kings of
Scotland and France were our prisoners. All the states, kings, and potentates of
Europe, most respectfully, not to say submissively, sought our friendship; and Rome
was more afraid of Blake and his fleet, than they had been of the great King of Sweden,
when he was ready to invade Italy with a hundred thousand men.[39]

We have seen, of course, who was 'at the helm' during the Anglo–Dutch
conflict and exactly what it was he enjoyed about being there. We have seen,
too, in his tireless reception of foreign ambassadors how closely involved he
was in the diplomatic pay-off which resulted from England's new-found
strength. We can see, too, in Sidney's quote the emergence of 'merit' (rather
than birth) as the republican ruling principle. The point for Sidney, writing
after the Restoration with a Stuart again reduced to the status of a provincial
client of Europe's great power, was that:

The same order that made men valiant and industrious in the service of their country
in the first ages, would have the same effect if it were now in being. Men would have
the same love to the public as the Spartans and Romans had, if there was the same
reason for it. We need no other proof of this, than what we have seen in our own
country, where, in a few years, good discipline, and a just encouragement given to
those who did well, produced more examples of pure, complete, incorruptible, and
invincible virtue, than Rome or Greece could ever boast; or if more be wanting, they
may easily be found among the Switzers, Hollanders, and others: but it is not
necessary to light a candle to the sun.[40]

The *Discourses* invoked repeated 'testimonies of the difference between men
fighting for their own interests ... and such as serve for pay, and get
preferments by corruption or favour', the well-known Machiavellian doctrine also embraced by the Dutch republican leader De Witt. 'Compare',
insisted Sidney,

the justice of our tribunals, within the time of our memory, and the integrity of those,
who for a while managed the public treasure; the discipline, valour, and strength of
our armies and fleets; the increase of our riches and trade; the success of our wars in
Scotland, Ireland, and at sea; the glory and reputation not long since gained, with that
condition into which we are of late fallen [again; of] ... weakness, cowardice,
baseness, venality, lewdness, and all manner of corruption. We have reason therefore
not only to believe that all princes do not necessarily understand the affairs of their
people, or provide better for them than those who are otherwise chosen; but that, as
there is nothing of greatness, power, riches, strength, and happiness, which might not
be reasonably hoped for, if we had rightly improved the advantages we had, so there is
nothing of shame and misery we may not justly fear, since we have neglected them.[41]

---

[39] *Works, Discourses* pp. 240–1.
[40] *Ibid.* p. 184.
[41] *Ibid.* pp. 238–9.

We have seen, too, Sidney's glorification to Lantin in Paris of the parliamentary army, its Spartan discipline and its bible-toting piety, and his statement that the 'design of the English' had been to combine the best from the Hebrew, Spartan, Roman, and Venetian Republics. From this, Sidney elaborated to Lantin a wishful account of the Rump's constitution; a Roman-style senate and magistracy, with strict rotation of office at the top, and a mighty army beneath:

[that] there had been three Sovereign Magistrates, the General of the land army, the Admiral or chief of the naval army, and the Chancellor who had the administration of justice; that they had exercised their charges for one year only; that there had been a perpetual Council which had had inspection over all; that there had been officers of finance who had rendered exact accounts from time to time, under superior officers ... that there had been an army of sixty thousand infantrymen, and twenty thousand cavalry all ready to serve this republic, and sixty warships, well equipped ... [and] well paid ...[42]

What these reminiscences sum up again is not the Rump as it was but Sidney's own career and aspirations within it. In the Rump period Sidney was an army commander, a naval administrator, he worked on the Committee for Legal Reform, he voted in the House for strict rotation of office, and he was one of the Republic's senior financial committeemen.

As steeped as Milton in Livy, it seems likely that the precedent of the military greatness achieved by Rome following the overthrow of the Tarquins suggested itself to Sidney at an early stage.[43] Certainly when the General of these English military hordes himself overthrew the Republic, the parallel with Rome was to become overwhelmingly clear. The identification of Cromwell with Caesar in Sidney's conversation with Lantin was supplemented by the likening of Ireton to Pompey, and Lantin's own claim that Ireton's burial inscription was based on Pompey's.[44] Pompey had been, of course, the last great republican commander before Caesar, whose death had cleared the way for Caesar's coming usurpation. Lantin recalled at the end:

Le Comte de Sidney added that if Ireton, a relation of Cromwel had not died the Republic would have been Established, and that he would have prevented Cromwell from aspiring to domination.[45]

6.3 IDEOLOGY

In general, as Sidney's written republicanism was a retrospective creation, its focus sharpened by Cromwell's tyranny, and again by the bleak exile of the

---

[42] Paris BBN MS Fr. 23254 pp. 99–100: my translation.
[43] For Milton and Livy see Aubrey, *Brief Lives* (1972) p. 364.
[44] 'Lantiniana' p. 100: According to Lantin, Ireton's inscription read: 'Ireto regali tumulo jacet + Dorylaus /Rex Carlus nullo. Credimus esse Deos.' Pompey's had been: 'Pompeius nullo. Credimus esse Deos.' For another comparison of Caesar with Cromwell see *Discourses*, p. 331, and see, too, p. 315.   [45] 'Lantiniana' p. 100.

Restoration, we cannot be sure of the chronology of its assembly, particularly before 1664. In this last section, however, to understand something of the genre from which it grew, it is worth looking at some other republican theorists of the Rump whose writings were most like what came to be Sidney's own.

6.3.1 *Milton*

No theorist is closer to Sidney than Milton, and vice versa, a fact which has been noticed by scholars of English literature as much as by scholars of political thought. We have no evidence of their meeting but they not only worked in the same area in the same government, but each referred to the other: Sidney (discussing Milton's marital problems) to Lantin; and Milton paying tribute, in his *Second Defence* (1654), to 'Whitlocke ... Strickland ... [and] Sydney (an illustrious name, which I rejoice has steadily adhered to our side)'.[46] Specifically it has been suggested that Sidney wrote his reply to Filmer with Milton's reply to Salmasius in mind. This is not impossible, and its likelihood is increased by the role of Milton's *Defensio* in winning praise for the English republican cause from a Europe-wide audience, a context to which Sidney was particularly attuned.[47]

Sidney refers to Milton's epic encounter in the *Discourses* itself, with the sneer that 'Salmasius' story of bees [that they showed monarchy to be natural] is only fit for old women to prate of in chimney corners.' Both Sidney and Milton countered this argument with Aristotle (and Sidney tackled it in the *Court Maxims* as well). Like Milton's *Defense* Sidney's *Discourses* mounts the same paragraph by paragraph and contemptuously sarcastic refutation of its opponent's arguments. Both use the same biblical texts (especially Deut. xvii; 1 Sam. 8–10),[48] the same classical sources (especially Plato; Aristotle's *Politics* and *Ethics*, Tacitus, Livy, and Cicero),[49] the same comparison of the Stuarts with the Roman Emperors in general and Nero in particular,[50] the same praise for modern Dutch liberty, but especially for Livian Rome, which 'became glorious when they had banished their kings'.[51]

---

[46] Milton, *Prose Works* (NY 1933) III 234–5.
[47] Sensabaugh, *That Grand Whig Milton* (1952) pp. 99–103 (though Sensabaugh's particular examples are not very convincing); Sutherland James, *English Literature* pp. 359–60.
[48] Sidney, *Discourses* p. 79 (Salmasius). My references in this section will be focused on Milton; Sidney's writing and use of the same arguments and sources will be abundantly demonstrated in other sections. *Milton's Prose Works* ed. J. A. St John (London 1848), *A Defence of The People of England* pp. 33, 43, 56–7.
[49] St John J. A. ed., *A Defence* pp. 66, 68, 110, 132–4, 141, 160–1, 185.
[50] *Ibid.* pp. 69, 72, 137.
[51] *Ibid.* p. 117.

The two works use the same modern anti-tyrant writers, including Buchanan, 'Hottoman's Franco-Gallia', the *Vindiciae*, and de Comines.[52] Their use of natural-law theory in general, of its modern exponent Grotius in particular, and their Platonic/Aristotelian emphasis on meritocracy, on 'virtue, wisdom, and courage' in opposition to the corrupt and slavish principles of hereditary monarchy, are all substantially the same. So are the specific crimes they attribute to the Stuart princes (including complicity with the massacre in Ireland).

Also the same, interestingly, is their use of the medieval historian Matthew Paris to deny the reality of the Norman Conquest, and their assertion in its place, on the same authority of Tacitus's *Germania*, of the 'supreme authority' of the Saxon 'parliaments', the 'wittena-gemots'. Quentin Skinner, among others, has wondered why Sidney went through the ritual in the *Discourses* of denying a conquest Filmer had not himself asserted; the answer may be Sidney's model in Milton, who had indeed been forced by Salmasius's jibe at the antiquity of parliaments to make the Saxon case.[53] Certainly Milton's portrait of Saxon liberty is a much closer precedent for Sidney's English history than Harrington's description of flawed 'modern prudence'. This might also help explain why Sidney embarked upon the case of the Saxons at all, simply to make points about the conquest and the nobility which he had already made in the *Court Maxims* by the parallel mythology of the Plantagenet Age. Perhaps what all of these comparisons teach us is the extent to which both men were drawing on a wider and common political culture, the product of shared experience as well as ideas. Individual thinkers like Harrington are best seen as adapting this culture, not (as too often happens in intellectual history) the other way round.

Sidney's *Court Maxims*, too, finds an equally close model in an earlier Milton tract, the *Tenure of Kings and Magistrates* (1648). Sidney's *Maxims* uses the same sources and examples (e.g. Seneca, Trajan, Richard II) to justify and glorify tyrannicide, to produce a striking echo of Milton's conclusion: 'Ther can be slaine No sacrifice to God more acceptable then an unjust and wicked King.'[54] The *Tenure* anticipates Sidney's ridicule of the 'vain and empty titles' of the modern nobility, his references to 'The Massacre at Paris', his use of both Marian exile and French monarchomach sources, and again his use of Grotius, from whom Milton likewise concludes that tyrants who

---

[52] *Ibid.* pp. 164, 187, and *Second Defence* p. 280. Milton attributes the *Vindiciae* to Beza.

[53] St John J. A. ed., *A Defence* pp. 163, 167, 174; Fink, *The Classical Republicans* (1945) p. 114; Dzelzainis M., 'The ideological context of John Milton's *History of Britain*' Cambridge Ph.D. Thesis 1983 p. 275; Skinner Q., 'History and ideology in the English revolution' in *Historical Journal* VIII n. 2 p. 154. Skinner notes that (as in so much else) Locke echoed Sidney and Milton on this point.

[54] Milton, *Tenure* p. 18.

break the law make themselves liable to extermination as the 'common pest' of mankind.[55]

6.3.2 *Vane (and Stubbe)*

A great deal of Vane's ecclesiology and politics, and of the sceptical republicanism of Henry Stubbe's *Essay in Defence of The Good Old Cause*, written under Vane's patronage in 1659,[56] reappears in Sidney's writings in general, and in the *Court Maxims* in particular. I have mentioned Sidney's (and Milton's, and Stubbe's) adherence to the doctrine, with which Vane was particularly associated, of the separation of civil and spiritual jurisdiction. What Sidney's political thought in general shared with Vane's was an emphasis on 'Right principles' rather than any 'particular form of government'; 'It is not so much the form of the administration as the thing administered, wherin the good or evil of government doth consist.'[57] Vane's pursuit of inward principles, combined with a scepticism about outward forms, places him, as Judson has correctly observed, in a line of thought stretching from Plato to Rousseau, and separates him from the outward particular constitutionalism of Harrington. For Vane, as for Sidney, 'since the spirit [of good government] ... is set up [forever] by Christ in men' we need 'not be in bondage' to any particular outward form, even 'the judicials of Moses'; and 'no human ordinances or outward laws must expect to be perpetual and exempt from change'. 'Ancient foundations, whence once [they] ... prove hindrances, to the good and enjoyment of humane societies, are for their sakes, and upon the same reasons to be altered, for which they were first laid.'[58]

In Stubbe, likewise, 'God did not universally by his law tye all the world to one forme of government ... because the difference of persons, times, places, neighbours, etc, may make one form best to one people, and at one time and place, that is worst to another. Monarchy is best for some, Aristocracy for others, and Democracy for others ... How ignorantly done was it then [to attempt to] ... prove Monarchy alwayes best.' Stubbe's scepticism about

---

[55] Cf. Dzelzainis, 'Ideological context' pp. 225–36. On the titles of the nobility Milton indeed anticipates Sidney's own examination of what the words mean (in Milton's case 'Baro', which 'imported no more' than one considered fit to judge the king, in Sidney's case 'knight', which meant no more than one with sufficient means to equip and maintain a horse for battle). Many of the Stoic sources and examples (like Seneca, and the story of Trajan's sword) shared by Milton and Sidney, are to be found in Grotius, *De Jure Belli*, which may in much of this have been their common source.

[56] Henry Stubbe, *An Essay in Defence of the Good Old Cause ... [and] A Vindication of The Hon Sir Henry Vane From The False Aspersions of Mr Baxter* (1659).

[57] DNB xx 128.

[58] Judson, *Vane* pp. 19–21, 56, 30, 67.

outward forms, his Vanist religion, his identical use of Daillé, and his constant references to 'the severall interests, animosities, educations, and conditions of men', are strongly anticipatory of all of these elements in Sidney's writing.[59]

As Sidney attacked the stagnant constitutionalism of Venice, so Vane and Stubbe, too, attacked Harrington's materialistic faith in the perfection of his state's 'orders'. For Vane, as for Sidney, good government required not the 'methodical collection of the people' within an infallible constitutional maze, but the more uncertain (and potentially progressive) task of leading individuals, by education, self-discipline, and self-government, to a Platonic/natural-law theory knowledge of truth. This sought not to vanquish change but to direct it towards God, and 'all that was good'. This is the key, as we will see, to Sidney's *Discourses* as well as the *Court Maxims*; the object of politics is to seek not what is popular, or even stable, but what is good, and there is nothing more objectionable about Filmer than his predication of rightful government on what came first rather than what was best. This search for what was good – in politics 'the public good of mankind' – was a simultaneous seeking of God, and its light was the law of nature:

that law which God, at the creation of man, infused into his heart for his preservation and direction, the law eternal. Yet it is not this law ... in the heart of every individual man, that is [politically] binding ... but ... the act of a community, or an associated people, by the right dictates and persuasion of the work of this law in their hearts ... This ... is political power. (Vane)[60]

This, for Sidney and Milton, as for Vane, was the only way to lead the 'depraved, corrupted, and self-interested will of man', the consequence of his fall, 'to espouse [his] ... true public interest, and closely adhere to it'. And if 'the public good of mankind and the public good of human societies' was the object of politics for Plato, Vane, and Sidney accordingly; so the obstacle was self or private interest, the spirit of the devil in man. The struggle between the two in politics took place, like every other aspect of human endeavour, within the context of the greater struggle between God and the devil. Within this context Vane declared, and Sidney was to repeat in the *Court Maxims*: 'it is not in man to [completely constitutionally] order his own steps. Man, at his best, stands in need of ... God's spirit, to keep him steadfast.'[61] For both men this assessment of the fragility of the enterprise was to be sufficiently confirmed when such 'steadfastness' served only to bring them to the scaffold.

---

[59] Stubbe, *Good Old Cause* p. 22.
[60] Judson, *Vane* p. 62.
[61] *Ibid.* pp. 30, 50–1.

6.3.3 *Nedham (and Hall)*

What Milton and Vane do not adequately embrace is Sidney's Machiavellianism. In this Neville is closer, but the courtly language of his *Plato Redivivus* is well removed from the spirit of Sidney's thought, as is its Harringtonian preoccupation with Venice, and its soft-pedalling on Neville's friends the Medici, whom Sidney does not hesitate to ridicule.[62]

In fact by far the closest Machiavellian in spirit to Sidney was the radical and sceptical Marchamont Nedham; and he was not only the closest but the first.

Nedham's reputation as an accomplished turncoat continues to supply quite irrelevant moral distraction from the fact of his major importance as a political theorist, in two genres (both shared by Sidney): as pre-Restoration England's ablest 'interest' theorist; and as the first English writer ever to advance a radical and militarist Machiavellian republicanism.[63] Nedham did this in the Republic's own official journal *Mercurius Politicus*, for which he and his 'great crony' Milton were given joint blame in 1660 by a royalist pamphleteer, who commented darkly: ' 'tis incredible what influence they had'.[64]

Nedham, too, used the same range of biblical, classical, and modern sources as Sidney, particularly Plato, Aristotle, Plutarch, Livy, Seneca, Tacitus, Machiavelli, and Grotius (from whom Nedham, too, concluded that tyrants must lose their power by the 'law of arms'). Most of all Nedham shared the full extent of Sidney's scepticism, and emphasised, too, that the world was a place of perpetual change: '[All] Govts have their Revolutions and Fatal Periods'; 'There is a [perpetual] wheeling of all things and a revolution of manners as well as times'; 'all under the sun is vanity'. Like Sidney, Nedham acknowledged the source of much of this as being (as the imagery would suggest) 'learnt out of Plato'. Nedham's fellow editor of *Politicus*, John Hall, likewise acknowledged his debt to the 'Platonists', and announced: 'I [had] rather be Scepticall in my opinion, then maintain it upon grounds taken up and not demonstrated.' Identically to Sidney, particularly to the *Court Maxims*, the Platonist Hall emphasised the infinite and 'Noble variety' of nature, both between and within nations: 'climate and education ... so diversifie the minds of men ... even their understandings, and the different wayes of thinking so distinguish them, though of one Countrey'. Like Sidney's Platonic *Maxims*, Hall was to seek, in opposition to the disruptive private 'domestick Interest' of monarchy, the naturall 'poyse' by

---

[62] See, for instance, Robbins ed., *Two Republican Tracts* pp. 80, 143, 167–8.
[63] Pocock ed., *Harrington* p. 34.
[64] Anon., *A Rope For Pol* (1660), quoted in Anthony H. S., 'Mercurius Politicus under Milton' in *JHI* 27 (1966) p. 394. Worden, 'Classical republicanism' p. 192.

which this variety could be co-ordinated in 'beautifull harmony' for the good of all.[65]

Like Sidney's, Nedham's classical republicanism maintained a radical emphasis on the vigorous populist and militaristic Roman Republic, rejecting Venice as static, oligarchic, and oppressive, more so indeed than 'the Turk'. Like Sidney, Milton, and Vane, Nedham dwelt particularly on the relationship between government and manners: 'Freedom, Industry and Sobriety' versus slavery, luxury, and depravity – the familiar contraries with their familiar root. Week by week Nedham followed Machiavelli in rehearsing lessons from Livy's history of Rome, lessons connecting its greatness to its liberty. People who made their own laws, obeyed them; people who governed their own country had the bravery to defend it. This was sufficiently proved by 'our own Nation; whose high achievements may match any of the Ancients' – all of these claims, as we have seen, to be amplified in the *Discourses*. Greatness came to free states, when 'men have liberty to make use of that Reason and understanding God hath given them . . . to choose their own Government'; in Government by 'Birth and Inheritance', they lose that use of their reason, and that 'Freedom of choice . . . [which] must needs be the most irrationall and brutish [government] in the world'.[66]

Like Sidney Nedham insisted that the sovereign people retained the 'power of altering Government and Governors . . . [whenever] occasion [required]'. Like Sidney he mocked the 'Titular Nobility'; rehearsed the frequent 'bloudy disputes over Succession' which disfigured monarchies; and followed Machiavelli (unlike Harrington) in defending tumults in a commonwealth as not only preferable to tyranny but positively beneficial. Most interestingly, Nedham took on those who, in defending monarchy, 'are fain to run up as high as Noah and Adam . . . alledging [the origin of government in] . . . our first Parent . . . by deriving the pedigree of Govt from this Paternal Right'. Nedham may here have been answering Filmer himself,[67] and was led in the process to exactly the same scepticism and relativism as Sidney (and Stubbe): it was absurd to say that one form of government only was permissible regardless of time and place, for both people and, consequently, their governments, were different in all places and at all times, the variety was infinite, and this both justified and demonstrated the right of different peoples

---

[65] Nedham, *The Case of the Commonwealth of England Stated* ed. Knachel P. A. (Virginia 1968) pp. 7–9, 31–2, 35–6; Hall, *The Grounds and Reasons of Monarchy* (1651) pp. 14, 31, 39, 42–3.

[66] *Mercurius Politicus* no. 86 pp. 1367–8; 69, 1093–5, 1109–11; 105, 1642–3; 86, 1367–8; 85, 1349–52; and nn. 87 and 88.

[67] Filmer had by this time published three pamphlets attacking Plato, Aristotle, Cicero, Milton, and Grotius among others, and setting out the substance of *Patriarcha* clearly. See Filmer R., *The Anarchy of a Limited or Mixed Monarchy* (1648), esp. pp. 6–7, 12–13; *Observations Upon Aristotles Politiques* (1652), esp. Pref. p. 2; *Observations Concerning the Originall of Government* (1652), esp. pp. 14, 19, 25, 34–5, 37.

to choose. 'Thus you see how the world is subject to shiftings of Government.'
Like Vane, and Sidney, too, Nedham declared that the 'mystery of Iniquity'
and 'right hand of Antithrist [*sic*]' was the mixing of religion, which should
be 'spirituall and mysticall', with civil power and 'the wordly and secular
Interest'.[68]

Nedham's republican 'interest' theory described the 'Interest of an absolute
monarchy' as 'unlimited ... Power ... in the hand of a particular person, who
governs only according to ... his one Will and Pleasure', 'an Interest, that is
distinct from the true and declared Interest of State'. The Romans, he said,
realised this, which is why they cultivated in the people an 'irreconcileable
enmity' to kings. Nedham described the civil war as 'the Divided State of a
Commonwealth, where two opposit, or irreconcileable Interests, appear
upon the stage in Action', and illustrated the incompatibility of the 'Interest
of a Free State' and a 'Monarchick Interest' by a variety of historical examples
from Cesare Borgia to 'the King Craft' of James I. Finally, he named the
theoretical source for the 'vicious Monarchical Interest of State'; he attacked:
the 'violation of Faith, Principles, Promises and Ingagements, upon every turn
of time and advantage', the inventors of which (anticipating Harrington's
phrase) 'have had the luck to be esteem'd the only Politicians'. It was, of
course, 'Machiavel's own ... Book ... entitled The Prince '. To make his point
Nedham devoted issue 113 of *Politicus* to quoting 'verbatim' Chapter XVIII
of *The Prince*: 'In what manner Princes ought to keep their words.' These
'politick Maxims', he concluded, ought to be 'exploded out of all Societies
which bear the name of Christian'. In this way Nedham anticipated the spirit,
not just of the Machiavellian republicanism of Sidney's *Discourses*, but of the
anti-Machiavellian interest theory of the *Court Maxims* as well.[69]

[68] *Mercurius Politicus* no. 69 pp. 1093–5; 89, 1413; 95, 1489–92; 98, 1537; 99, 1540.
[69] *Mercurius Politicus* no. 100 pp. 1569–70; no. 79; no. 70 pp. 1109–11; no. 61; no. 92 pp.
1457–62; nos. 112–13 (esp. p. 1693).

7

Tyranny 1653–59

7.1 POLITICS

For Sidney, as for many of his republican colleagues from the disbanded Rump, opposition to Cromwell became something of a personal creed. He mentioned, in 1660, his reluctance to return to Restoration England, having 'too well learnt, under the ... Cromwells, what it is to live under the protection of thoes unto whome I am thought an enemy'. After seventeen years of exile, in Paris in 1677, his conversation with Lantin dwelled again upon the nature of tyrants in general and the actions of 'that usurper' in particular.[1] Then Sidney lionised the glory of the infant republic before 'ambition had turned [Cromwell's] head', leading him to destroy it, 'like an insolent servant ... [turning against] His Master ... although he knew well that he would not be able to conserve the Royalty in his family'.[2] At his trial in 1683 Sidney said of Cromwell again – in order to remind the jury of his opposition to this form of political illegality at least – 'he was a tyrant and a violent one (you need not wonder I call him a tyrant, I did so every day in his life, and acted against him too)'.

This refrain was taken up in the same year by Burnet, who said of Sidney: 'he was stiff to all republican principles, and such an enemy to every thing that looked like monarchy, that he set himself in high opposition against Cromwell when he was made Protector'.[3] Describing Major Wildman at the same time, Burnet continued: 'he [(Wildman) was] a great commonwealthsman, and ... both Sidney and he had appeared very resolutely against Cromwell when he began to set up for himself'.[4] Burnet's comment seems to imply that Sidney's 'high opposition' did not begin in earnest until the foundation of the Protectorate itself; it is certainly not particularly evident in a conversation

---

[1] Blencowe, *Sidney Papers* (1825) pp. 189–90; BBN MS Fr. 23254 'Lantiniana' p. 99: On tyrants in general Lantin recalled: 'Le Comte de Sidney ... me dit que ... Tous les Tyrans et les Usurpateurs ont feint d'estre Ennemis de usurpateurs et des Tyrans; et de vouloir retablir la liberte pour l'oprimer ensuite avec plus de violence, c'est ce qu'a fait Cromwel.'

[2] BBN MS Fr. 23254 (my translation).

[3] *Works* (1772) 'The trial' p. 32; Burnet, add MS 63,057 p. 341.

[4] *Ibid.* p. 143.

recorded with Whitelocke on 4 September 1653, under the short-lived rule of Barebones's Parliament.

Sidney had visited Whitelocke one evening shortly after the latter had, to his discomfort and alarm, received a personal request from Cromwell to undertake the embassy to Sweden initially intended (under the Rump) for Sidney's brother Lisle. Although Lisle had, unlike Whitelocke and Sidney, actually remained with the newly constituted government, he now wished to decline the mission on ostensible grounds of health (though in fact on grounds of discomfort and danger; the same reasons which made Whitelocke most reluctant to take up the baton). The object of Sidney's mission proved to be to get his brother off the hook by getting Whitelocke on it. Whitelocke attempted to probe his fellow-republican visitor's political conscience: 'I suppose he [Lisle] cannot scruple the authority which should send him, because he himself is one of their number...'

To which Sidney replied, unruffled: 'He doth not att all scruple it, and makes a difference between a judiciall imployment, and this, which is meerly ministeriall, to goe on a message which any one may doe for any persons.'[5]

Whitelocke eventually accepted the mission, earning Cromwell's personal gratitude. The episode illustrates the gap with Sidney, which we will encounter elsewhere, between 'high' principle in the mythology, and Machiavellian lack of scruple in the event. How far this attitude survived into the Protectorate itself is, however, another matter.[6] By late 1653 Sidney still had not split with his brother Lisle, despite the latter's loyalty to the new regime. By 1656, however, the breach was most overt. In the letter to his father in 1656 (quoted in Chapter 4), complaining about Algernon's 'extreamest vanity', and Leicester's inordinate favour of him, Lisle made clear that the offence was political as well as personal:

In my poore opinion the businese of your Lordship's house hath past somewhat unluckily, and that it had been better used to do a seasonable courtesy to my Lord Protector then to have had such a play acted in it of publike affront to him, which doth much entertayne the towne. I have been in some places where they have told me they were exceedingly pleased with the gallant relation of the chief actor in it, and that by applauding him they put him severall times upon it.[7]

This letter is the basis of one of the most famous Sidney legends, that the 'chief

---

[5] B.M. add MS 53727 pp. 53–7; Spalding R., *The Improbable Puritan* (1975) pp. 137–8.

[6] The possibility at least that Sidney *himself* might have accepted ambassadorial status under Cromwell's regime, is suggested by a mysterious piece printed among Thurloe's State Papers in Sidney's *Works*, ostensibly from a manuscript in Sidney's hand, entitled 'The Protector's Advice to Algernon Sydney ... [being] The Protector's avice to me, when I went from him to the king of Sweden in Poland'. Charles X was in Poland from 1655 to 1657. It would be unwise to discount the possibility, although in the absence of a surviving manuscript or any other corroborating evidence I am sceptical about this case. *Works* (1772), Letters etc. 'Taken From Thurloe's State Papers' p. 22.

[7] HMC De Lisle vi p. 400 17 June 1656.

actor' was Sidney playing Brutus in *Julius Caesar*. It is a fine story which lacks nothing except evidence. Even so, the legend fits Lisle's letter well enough, and the resulting picture of Leicester, with his history of dramatic patronage, and his shared Stoic belief that politics was a stage, colluding with his son's use of Penshurst to put the knife into Cromwell's claims to legitimacy, has a certain ring of believability about it.

What makes the suggestion of such a miming of tyrannicide at this time more interesting is the 1656–7 political context. For these years saw a republican literary campaign against Cromwell's government which again had close links with Sidney's own thought, and his own personal political associations. In 1656 there appeared 'R.G.'s' *A Copy of a Letter*; Harrington's *Oceana*; Nedham's *Politicus* editorials collected as *The Excellency of a Free State*; and Vane's *A Healing Question*. The following year the act of tyrannicide itself received a brilliantly punchy recommendation in Sexby and Titus's *Killing Noe Murder*. All of these works shared murky associations of personnel in which Sidney's friends among the ex-Rumpers, like Vane and Neville, linked with radicals and republicans in or attached to the army, like Sexby, Titus, Wildman, and 'R.G.' Sidney was to work closely with both Wildman and Titus in the period 1678–83. Indeed, in 1681, according to Burnet, he co-wrote with them an anti-royal tract, of 'great spirit and judgement [that] was by much ye best writ piece yt came out in all these Embroilments. It was ... penn'd by Major Wildman ... But many things were put into it by Colonel Sydney, and some few by Mr Titus.'[8]

I do not propose to discuss Vane, Harrington, and Nedham again, but the closeness of both parts of *A Copy of a Letter*, and the whole of Sexby and Titus's *Killing Noe Murder* to Sidney's *Court Maxims*, requires some comment. *A Copy of a Letter* remains regarded as a simple plagiarisation of Harrington's *Oceana*, interesting only for its audacious appearance before the masterwork itself. This interpretation dates back to Harrington's editor Toland, who accused the *Letter*'s author of 'trying to rob [Harrington] ... of the glory of his invention'.[9] Authorship at the time, Toland noted, was variously attributed to Wildman by some, and Neville by others (a Cambridge University Library copy features a contemporary attribution to Neville). While it may be true, this interpretation continues to reflect the perspective of Harrington editors, against the wider fact that Harrington's work was simply one of the most original outgrowths of a wider tradition of Machiavellian republicanism which initiated with the Rump, not with Harrington, and from which Harrington himself quite clearly borrowed. Thus if the *Letter* shares ideas with *Oceana*, and association by reputation

---

[8] Add MS 63,057 II p. 116; See Pocock ed., *Harrington* Intro., ch. II 'Oceana: The Circumstances of Publication'.
[9] Toland ed., Harrington, *Oceana* (1771) pp. xv–xvi.

with a Rumper like Neville, who had a history of association with the
tradition while Harrington apparently had no association with anyone but
Neville himself, it remains an open question who was borrowing ideas from
whom.[10]

A *Copy of a Letter* shares great pieces of Harrington's English history. But
its political focus, while equally Machiavellian, is in fact different from that of
Oceana: it centres not on a particular constitution, but on a series of general
maxims of interest theory, italicised for clear emphasis. *Oceana* itself does
use interest language, aiming as it does to 'raise ourselves out of the mire of
private interest into the contemplation of virtue', and settled upon the
conviction that 'the interest of popular government come[s] nearest unto the
interest of mankind'. But its discussion as a whole is not in fact framed in
interest/reason of state terminology, as the *Letter*, and as Sidney's later *Court
Maxims* are. What is interesting is that the *Letter*'s fundamental axioms are
exactly those of the *Court Maxims*: 'viz. That it is against the interest of a
Monarchy, to let his subjects grow rich'; that 'reason of state in Kings and
Tyrants, is to keep mankind poore and ignorant ... point blank contrary to
... the ... maximes of a Commonwealth, which is the nursery of vertue,
valor, and industrie'; and that, to 'conclude ... if all kingdomes be neer their
period and ruine, when the subjects under them grow rich, wise, and capable
of understanding their own good ... contrariwise ... Commonwealths do not
decay, but when their people in general grow poore; and ignorant.' These
'principles and maxims' themselves originate from Machiavelli's *Discourses*
Book II Chapter 2 (from where the Dutch republican de la Court also got
them), and we will see the use to which Sidney was to put them in the
Netherlands in Chapters 12–13. The *Letter* and both Sidney's *Maxims* and
the *Discourses* also share reference to a particular passage of Machiavelli's
History of Florence; again this shows not that they copied one another so
much as that they grew from a shared political culture.[11]

Even more wide-ranging in its anticipation of the *Court Maxims* is *Killing
Noe Murder*, advocating the assassination of Cromwell, and providing the
Cromwellian link in the tradition of anti-tyranny argument running from
Milton's *Tenure* for Charles I (acknowledged by Sexby and Titus as 'learned
Milton'), to Sidney's *Court Maxims* for Charles II. Once again it uses the

---

[10] Pocock ed., *Harrington* pp. 11–13.
[11] R. G., *A Copy of a Letter* (1656) pp. 4, 5, 8; *Oceana* pp. 169, 172 in Pocock ed., *Harrington*:
      A Copy of a Letter says that 'Florence ... did for manie thousand yeares maintain sixty
      thousand men, wheras the same Dominions now under a Duke, is not able to raise or
      maintaine twelve thousand'. The *Maxims* affirms: 'Machiavel says that in his time Florence
      and the valley of Arno were able to put into the field one hundred thirty and five thousand
      fighting men which cannot afford now above eight or ten Thousand att most.' *Letter* p. 5;
      Maxims p. 6. Machiavelli, *Discourses* II.2 (Penguin 1985 pp. 274–6). Sidney's *Discourses*
      (p. 225) repeats this story but amends the figure to 100,000. My thanks to Blair Worden for
      bringing this to my attention.

same common biblical and classical sources; 1 Sam. 8; Plato's *Republic*; Aristotle's *Politics*; Plutarch; Polybius; Tacitus; the Monarchomachs; Grotius; to arrive at the same conclusion, from the latter particularly, that tyrants 'the Laws of God, of Nature, and of Nations expose, like Beasts of Prey, to be destroyed as they are met'. It invokes the same examples of Nero, Tiberius, and Caligula; of the glory paid to ancient tyrannicides ('what Religion paid to such Men! What Songs What Elegies!'), both scriptural (Moses) and classical (Brutus), as Sidney does in the *Maxims*. It anticipates the *Maxims* precisely in quoting from Grotius that 'Against Common Enemies, and those that are Traitors to the Commonwealth, every Man is a Soldier.' In particular it anticipates the *Maxims* by stating its intentions in overtly Platonic terms, to undeceive a misguided people who 'judg of things, and name them by their exterior appearances, without penetrating at all into their Causes or Natures', perceiving things rather by their 'exterior Accidents and Qualities, than the defining their Essences'. Like Sidney the tract acknowledges Plato's *Republic* as its source for the political relationship between virtue and tyranny, and Aristotle's *Politics* for its premise that men enter society 'not just to live but to live happily'. Like the *Maxims*, *Killing Noe Murder* bitterly attacks both the spineless modern nobility ('What have we of Nobility amongst us but the name? ... poor wretches ... they have lost all Ambition and Indignation') and the virtueless 'mock' parliament upon which the tyranny rests. Finally, and most importantly, *Killing Noe Murder* goes beyond Milton's *Tenure* and to the heart of Sidney's *Maxims* by using against Cromwell not just 'Plato, Aristotle, Tacitus ... [but] his Highness's own Evangelist Machiavell' as well. The tract then rests, like the *Maxims*, and like Nedham's *Politicus*, on a sustained Machiavellian double act, using *The Prince* to describe the basis for tyranny ('Tyrants accomplish their means more by Fraud than Force') and the *Discourses on ... Livy* to describe what should be done about it by a people not yet reconciled to the slavery and degeneration tyranny begets, 'a Servile Fear they falsely call Christian Patience'. This involves a quite open process of both recommending and denouncing Machiavellian tenets as the occasion suits. Like Sidney's *Maxims*, too, the tract notes that Tyrants 'impoverish the People, that they might want the Power, if they have the will to attempt anything against them ... His Highness's way is by Taxes, Excise ... etc'. While lacking both its Dutch-developed interest theory, and its Vanist religion, *Killing Noe Murder* nevertheless thus anticipates the message and sources of Sidney's *Court Maxims* as completely as any English tract which preceded it. Given Sidney's later literary association with Titus, this point seems well worthy of note.[12]

---

[12] Wm Allen [Sexby and Titus], *Killing Noe Murder* (repr. 1689) pp. 6–7, 14–19, 22–3, 13, 2, 5, 9, 5, 7, 6, 21. Cf. Raab F., *Machiavelli* pp. 137–40.

7.2 LOVE

The memoirs of Charles II's brother James (eventually James II), contain an interesting accusation of involvement between two most improbable partners: Sidney himself and Lucy Walters, famous ex-lover of the restored King.

> Algernon Sidney (tho at that time a Collonell in Cromwell's army of Saints) having got notice of her, enter'd into Treaty about her and came to an agreement for fifty broad pieces (as he himself related this story to his R.H). But being in the nick of time comanded hastily out of London to his Regiment, he missed his bargain. After this she travelled into Holland, where she fell into the hands of his Brother Collonel Robert Sidney...

'This', recorded James in his memoirs, 'I had from his own mouth.'[13]

York's image of a laddish Algernon recounting to Charles II and himself stories of the (near) sexual conquest of one of the King's own mistresses is perhaps, even as slander, a trifle overwrought; (though no less effective for that: the story made at least one of Sidney's Victorian biographers very thin-lipped indeed). Yet it should not be automatically discounted. The image of Algernon as the stiff Puritan prig of the mythology, declaiming in the *Discourses* against the 'lewdness' of the Restoration, is, as usual, only half the story: Algernon's political propaganda, to be mistrusted alongside York's. Against it we must contrast Sidney the author of *Of Love*; the father of an illegitimate daughter in France; and the man who enjoyed telling stories over dinner in Paris about Milton's marriage, and Selden's sex life.

For although in matters of the public political stage, Sidney liked to judge both himself and others by the Stoic criteria of reason, gravity, and constancy (criteria by which he found both himself and others repeatedly wanting), in personal fact Sidney himself remained a creature, as his Platonic religion remained an expression, of passion. Some time (probably) before the Restoration Sidney wrote his earliest surviving work, the Platonic *Of Love*. It is a revealing look by Sidney at this relationship between real and ideal, passion and reason, in himself and, with no political posture to adopt, he comes out an earnest advocate of embracing the former, not banishing it. Passion, for Sidney, is part of the real and divinely created world, and by looking at his own relationship with that which is 'by all esteemed the most powerful ... [of] passion[s]', he comes to accord it the place it demands, in a world where balance and harmony between all the world's parts, even passion and reason, is the path to truth, not the absolute conquest, control, or

---

[13] Clarke J., *The Life of James II* (1816) vol. I p. 492; 'Life of James II 1660–98, written by Himself', in MacPherson J., *Original Papers* (1775) p. 76. The claim by his biographers that Algernon himself visited Holland in 1651 and 1654 derives from the mistaken attribution of his brother (also Col. Sidney) Robert's letters to him. See *Thurloes State Papers* vol. ii pp. 501, 522; Bod. Lib. MS Rawl A16 p. 467.

replacement, of any one by the other. This insight, in the most straight-forwardly Platonic of all Sidney's writings, takes us to the heart of his pro-harmony/anti-absolutist political theory as well.

Of Love is written following the Platonic love tradition, pursuing 'the Platonic Idea of perfect beauty'. This tradition was developed in Renaissance Italy by writers like Castiglione, Bruno, and Cavalcanti, and it linked itself with Sir Philip Sidney in England through the 'long and elegant' dedication by Bruno of his *De Gli Eroici Furori* (1585) to Sir Philip. Sir Philip's own writing was full of Platonic ideas about 'love of bewtie', concluding, like Algernon, that on the one hand Plato's allowance of homosexual love was not to be followed: ('abhominable filthiness', Sir Philip; 'the most unnatural of vices', Algernon), but that on the other 'the Platonics are the perfect patrons of that passion' under which, for Sir Philip 'I do burne in love'; for Algernon 'my passion hath made itself master of all the faculties of my mind, and hath destroyed all that is in opposition unto it. I live in it and by it, it is all that I am'.[14]

Sidney begins *Of Love* by examining 'the stoics, general enemies to all passions', before mocking their 'vanity ... who, for all their pretended austerity, have fallen as deeply under the power of that passion, as any other in the world'.[15] Man as he really is, says Sidney, has both 'absolutely sensual', and 'perfectly spiritual' parts to his nature; thus although 'the senses [are] uncertain', 'the mind being the only fixed power in us', 'his affections ought to participate of both his natures', 'a mixed creature must have mixed affec-tions'. The same idea underlies Sidney's concomitant political doctrine, that in the real (imperfect, variable, and changeable) political world good govern-ment must be mixed government, a combination of all the 'three simple species', a harmony of their variety, not any one of them absolutely. If the affection of the spirit is 'an affection for angels, pure and contemplative, the other for beasts, filthy and sottish', nevertheless 'man is a creature composed of both these', and so 'a man to love as a man, must have regard to both, and ... can fix his heart neither absolutely upon that which is too high to be understood, nor too low to be approved'. Such a balanced love, says Sidney, is 'the most strong, lasting, high, and perfect human passion ... in comparison of which all other wordly pleasures are vain and empty shadows'. 'Happy therefore is he', concludes Sidney, with a bravado which could be dismissed as conventional in anyone who took a different subsequent political road,

---

[14] Sidney Sir Philip, *Works* III 30, 33; *Astrophel and Stella* sonnet 25; Sidney A., 'Of Love' in Sir Walter Scott ed., *A Collection of Scarce and Valuable Tracts ... of the Late Lord Somers* (London 1809–15) vol. 8 pp. 613, 616. The manuscript is in the British Museum add MS 34,100.

[15] In this he was following Augustine, who had teased the Stoics from a similar Platonic perspective in the *City of God*, bk IX, 4 (ed. D. Knowles 1972 pp. 346–7).

'who hath [such] hopes and desires crowned with success, or that in search of them, being denied pleasure in this life, finds ease and rest in death.'[16]

Love, says Sidney, is love of beauty, and beauty consists in 'order, harmony ... unto which all ill actions have an absolute contrariety', a pithy expression of the vision and language which also dominate the Platonic *Court Maxims*. Stressing that he is 'aiming at real not fantastical excellence' Sidney begins the familiar Platonic progression from outward physical beauty as 'the image thereof', to true beauty, the 'outward resemblance of God'.

The glory of divine rays do appear in faces ... [and] more in minds ... Who can then without barbarity (I think I may say impiety) deny to suffer himself to be ravished with ... such an excellence of a created beauty, as is an image of the uncreated? ... If desires were absolutely sinful, they had never been given us; if beauty might not be desired, it had never been created; there is no forbidden fruit out of paradise; we have a free liberty of enjoying all that is good.

Love is accordingly not only permissible and good (as in his political thought, this is the key word), but indeed 'that same love, for which God created and beautified the world, is the only means for us to return unto Him, who is the fountain of our being; and, through the imperfections of our own natures, being not able to see or comprehend his greatness and goodness, otherwise than by his works, must take us from visible things to raise ourselves up to Him'. Again this attempt 'to return unto Him' and 'his goodness' is the essence of Sidney's political thought as well. Thus

by the power of God upon our hearts ... we may humble ourselves, and acknowledging God to be the author of all good depend upon him for a delivery from all interior and exterior ills, and [He] reserves the state of perfection to fill up the measure of our happiness when we come to that of immortality.[17]

Having thus established love's goodness, Sidney turns to its effects: and 'they be ordinary and vulgar spirits ... little understanding loves mystery', who preach moderation in the matter. 'This extremity of disorder and torment seems fabulous to those who have not felt it within themselves ... But some will say we ought to desire even the best things with moderation, which love destroys. Ah let that extend to ordinary things; desire, riches, honours and the like ... they cannot content the mind, therefore ought not to possess it ... [But] ... who can attribute too much ... to [love]?'[18]

Sidney closes with an enthusiastic tribute to women in general. Some men say that

they are only light creatures ... and have not such minds as can give delight to a wise

---

[16] *Ibid.* pp. 612, 613, 614.
[17] *Ibid.* pp. 614, 615–18.
[18] *Ibid.* The idea of love as an 'excessive force ... destructive of virtue in the sense that virtue requires a balance' was a convention of Cavalcanti's Florentine school. See Holmes G., *Dante* (Oxford 1980).

man. How great an ignorance is this! ... It is true, that women have not those helps from study and education as men have, but in the natural powers of mind are no ways inferior. They exempt themselves from ... those knotty sciences that serve only to deceive fools ... and, instead ... have a ... wit in conversation very much beyond men.

Even in military affairs, history 'shows they can, when it is needful, excel ours in gallantry as well as beauty ... Let not any man then, through a fond and ignorant presumption of his own merit, despise that sex.'[19]

Like all his other writings, then, perhaps this theory is a justification for something going on in Sidney's life in practice; an attempt not simply to come to 'know himself' with respect to the passion of love, but to come to terms with his feelings for a woman he loved.

7.3 MONEY

Whatever the distractions of power or love, however, these years Sidney chose to devote particularly, as we have seen, to matters of money. Moving from Petworth to London in 1655, and then permanently to Sterry in 1657, Sidney set about the challenging double bill of making his fortune, by repairing Strangford's.[20] In the end this attempt was thwarted on both fronts; according to Algernon through Strangford's continued outlandish expenditure; according to Strangford through Algernon's appropriation of the whole estate for his own rather than its owner's benefit. In fact what destroyed Sidney's attempt was the Restoration, which made it impossible for him to return to England to complete the execution of the Trust, so that the financial arrangements he had made collapsed, through Strangford's failure to honour them, and Sidney's inability to force him to by law.[21]

The Strangfords obediently left for Paris in 1655, not to return (and then only temporarily) until 1657. Sidney's first step was to pay £3,000 of his own money to Strangford's most urgent creditors. He then sold a piece of land called the Hoades for £300 to the Earl of Thanet, and in March or April 1656 borrowed upon a mortgage of part of the remaining Trust lands £1,000 from his old colleague from the Rump Council of State, the City financier Alderman Foot. He meant all of this £1,000, he later claimed, to go to Strangford's creditors, but he was in the event obliged to give £800 to the Strangfords in Paris. By December 1656, according to Algernon, Strangford

[19] *Ibid.* pp. 618–19.
[20] In June 1657, during Sidney's residence there, Sterry came under surveillance by Cromwellian intelligence. Thurloe had been informed that one Baron, a merchant who travelled between Calais and Dover, and a suspected royalist mail-carrier, often visited Sterry. This may have been the Cromwellian harassment Sidney later complained of. CSPD CW11 1657–58 pp. 3–4. In the Sidney papers a 'James Baron of Sterry' is recorded as having co-operated with Algernon in the capacity of attorney for the receipt of debts paid on Strangford's behalf from 1655 to 1656; De Lisle MS U1475 E28/8.
[21] De Lisle U1475 E28/5 PRO C7 327/50; C6 82/69; Kent R.O. U1475 E28/7; E28/8.

in Paris had 'by his extravagant ways of liveing ... fallen into new streights' and required some £1,500 more – and relying on his and Isabella's word Algernon had agreed to mortgage more of Swingfield and Boynton to raise the £1,200 on loan from the Earl of Thanet, on the understanding that Strangford would transfer the mortgage onto lands of his own as soon as he returned. The indenture with Thanet was accordingly signed on 18 February 1657.[22] Between 1657 and 1658 Sidney pressured Strangford to convey to the Trust a further piece of land to cover Thanet's mortgage as promised – and Foot's, and another £1,000 owed by Strangford to one Humphrey Tuckey: a total sum, with interest, of £3,300. Strangford duly did this and the manor of Postling was conveyed to Sidney in Trust in June or July 1658. Meanwhile, however, and before this conveyance, Sidney had in the course of 1657 'anxious to complete the trust and reimburse [my]self' embarked upon the probably legal but nevertheless rather sharp practice of selling off certain pieces of the original Trust lands despite their being now mortgaged (to Thanet), on the promise that the mortgage was to be taken off shortly and transferred to Postling. On this basis Sidney sold land worth £1,000 to John Symonds; £1,200 worth to John Carpenter and Thomas Andrewes; and £156 worth to Clement Rolph. These men were then legally indemnified against Thanet's mortgage by an agreement conceived by Sidney, and signed at his behest by the buyers, himself, and Strangford, promising in Strangford's name to transfer the mortgage to Postling as soon as it could be done.[23]

By 1659 Thanet had agreed to take over the whole Thanet/Foot/Tuckey debt on the security of Postling, and conveyances were being prepared to achieve this. According to Sidney, 'While this security was depending and before any execution thereof [I] was comaded [*sic*] by the then powers into Sweadland in the Quality of a publique minister ... where [I] continued for the space of about one yeare, and by reason of severall changes then happening ... could not returne home.'

In this stage of legal limbo Symonds, Andrewes, and Carpenter applied to Strangford for the removal of Thanet's mortgage of £1,200 from their lands, to Postling. Strangford refused to co-operate and they were consequently forced to sue for the money at common law. Strangford was later to claim that Sidney had tricked him into signing the guarantee of transfer in the first place – an absurd claim – and that Algernon had subsequently disappeared overseas with large quantities of the Trust's money – which is certainly at least possible. Exactly who robbed whom, how, and by how much, will have to remain unanswered – but the aftermath after 1660 was clear enough for both men. Sidney, through his absence, eventually lost control of the Trust lands by Act of Parliament (1665), and so also of security for any money he

[22] PRO C6 82/69; Kent R.O. U1475 E28/5.
[23] PRO C7 327/50.

had disbursed himself in execution of the Trust. Strangford's debts continued to multiply thereafter, much as they had hitherto.[24]

When the Strangfords had returned temporarily from France in November 1657, Algernon (living at Sterry) had 'offerd to play [*sic*] his industry and ease in having [their other, smaller] house [Ostenhanger] repaird and renderd convenient' for them to live in. To Sidney's disgust, this 'displeased them', and Isabella in particular 'not enduring to live at Ostenhanger, went to London, and Penshurst, and being soone weary of living there alsoe, about the end of the yeare 1658, desired to come to Sterry, wheare Alg: Sydney then was'. There 'Lady Strangford ... having neither mony nor creditte ... had [re]course to that only worldly help that never failed her, and acknowledg[ed] with many teares unto the sayd Alg: Sy[d]ney, hir errors, follyes, and evill dealing towards him, promised to ... [make amends] as well in relation unto hi[r]self, as unto him, and begged of him ... to trust hir, which he conf[es] seth, his kindnesse unto hir, render[ed] him unable to deny.'[25]

So Isabella, accompanied by 'twelve' hungry servants, lived with her severe brother at Sterry for the first few months of 1659. This uncertain domestic reverie was interrupted when, suddenly, 'Cromwell being throwne out of government [Algernon], had occasion to go to London.'[26]

---

[24] Cartwright J., *Sacharissa* (1907) pp. 166–7.

[25] Kent R.O. U1475 E28/5.

[26] De Lisle U1475 E28/5. Isabella's tribulations were not yet over. When she returned with Strangford to France they tried to persuade her younger sister Diana to accompany them. Diana, being 'overmuch importuned', eventually agreed, whereupon the Countesse of Leicester threatened to 'stricke' Diana out of her will if she departed. The barely solvent Strangford promised that if she came anyway he would make her a compensation payment of £2,000, in £100 per annum instalments, from the time of her return. She went, and a few months later the Countess of Leicester died – with a duly amended will. On their return from France in 1660 Diana's boat was taken by pirates and she lost her 'trunks, plate, and everything not on her person'. Once back Strangford pleaded insolvency and refused to pay. By 1663 Isabella was dead, and Diana, through acrimonious proceedings at both common law and chancery, had won the right to take her place in the queue behind Strangford's other creditors. PRO C10 70/104.

8

War and diplomacy 1659–60

8.1 BACKGROUND

Richard Cromwell's Protectorate was replaced by a restoration of the Rump Parliament in May 1659. This produced a sharp change in foreign policy, under the leadership of Henry Vane. Of this Sidney's mission to the Baltic Sound became the principal expression.

The nature of this change was prefaced as early as January 1659 by the republicans elected to Richard's Parliament. They included Scot, Haselrige, Vane, Neville, and Ludlow, and have become subsumed under the title 'neo-Harringtonian'. Again, however, their ideas grew from something wider and older than 'Harringtonianism'; they represented a revival of the Rump and army-officer opposition to Cromwell in 1656–7, an opposition which combined when army officers put the Rump back into power in May. Sidney took no visible part in this republican activity under Richard, though his contacts with those who did make it hard to imagine him at Sterry in ignorance of these events.

The reasoning behind their arguments may be seen in the republican Slingsby Bethel's *The Worlds Mistake in Oliver Cromwell* (1668). Bethel became a political colleague of Sidney's in exile in the Netherlands, and the close similarities between their writings will be shown in a future chapter.

Like all Bethel's writing (and Sidney's *Maxims*), the *Worlds Mistake* is a work of interest theory; and it identifies two overriding 'interests' for England (one domestic, one foreign). The first is trade, and Bethel contrasts the 'low condition of Trade in Oliver's time' with the fact that, 'When this tyrant turned out the Long Parliament, the Kingdome was arrived at the highest pitch of Trade, Wealth, and Honour, that it, in any Age, ever yet knew.' The second was that the interest of England in foreign policy lay in 'keeping the Ballance' between the two superpowers in Europe, something to be achieved by assisting the weaker wherever necessary. Under Elizabeth this had meant opposing Spain; but since the Thirty Years War Mazarin's France had emerged as the principal threat to the balance. Yet Cromwell 'by his ignorant' failure to understand this change, had 'contrary to our Interest, made an

124

unjust Warr with Spain, and an impollitick League with France', destroying Anglo–Spanish trade in the process. Similarly in the Baltic, where Sweden had by 1659 conquered Poland and was preparing to engulf Denmark, Cromwell and his policy successors had continued to support Sweden so that France and Sweden now threatened to divide the 'Western Empire' between them.[1]

Throughout the Protectorate Oliver Cromwell and Charles X of Sweden had 'lived in great conjunction of councels'.[2] Following in the footsteps of Gustavus Adolphus, Charles Gustavus had launched his reign in 1655 by invading Poland. When his absence emboldened neighbouring Denmark to invade Sweden, Charles X returned and defeated the Danes, forcing them in February 1658 to a decisive settlement at Roskilde. In this they ceded Blekinge, Bohuslan, Halland, and Scania, and so control of one (the northern) bank of the Sound to Sweden. Later in the same year, Charles X decided to destroy Denmark once and for all. He invaded without warning, breaking the Roskilde treaty, arriving rapidly at the walls of Copenhagen. There his military progress was arrested in late 1658 by the arrival of the Dutch fleet.[3]

Dutch involvement in the Sound stemmed from the same root as England's; it was there that the two nations' naval and trading interests coincided. Holland's traditional ally in the area was Denmark; England's had lately been Sweden, but there existed important potential common ground; both nations wished to keep Scandinavian political control over the passage divided, and the Sound open to third-party navigation. This desire was given potential teeth by the fact that both the Dutch and the English had far more powerful navies than either of the Scandinavian powers. Thus on this issue, under an English Republic, the potential for co-operation existed on the same basis, of common commercial, religious, and republican interests, which had underlain the Vane/Strickland/St John attempt at Anglo–Dutch union in 1651. When the Rump was restored in 1659 Vane was to seize this opportunity.

Concern about the Baltic situation quickly came to monopolise the foreign policy discussions of Richard's Parliament. Advocates of traditional Protectoral foreign policy like Thurloe, appealed for the immediate dispatch to Sweden of an English fleet to counter the Dutch, who would otherwise become 'insupportibly insolent'. Republicans, most prominently Sidney's friends Vane and Neville, countered angrily. 'He says', protested Neville, 'that the Dutch are already your enemies!' But 'interest of state, of trade, and of religion' suggested otherwise. Denmark was as protestant as Sweden, but did not pretend to more than the door to the Sound, while Sweden wanted

[1] Slingsby Bethel, *The Worlds Mistake in Oliver Cromwell* (1668) pp. 2–3, 5, 7.
[2] Burnet, *Own Time* (1823) 1 p. 139.
[3] Stellan Dahlgren, 'Charles X and the constitution' in *Sweden's Age of Greatness* ed. M. Roberts (1973) pp. 175–6; Geyl P., *The Netherlands in the Seventeenth Century Part Two 1648–1715* (1964) p. 44; Wilson C., *Profit and Power* (1957) p. 49.

'both the door and house too'. Why, then, might not England assist Denmark instead? Neville completed this realignment of sights by attacking the disastrous commercial consequences of the Protector's misconceived war with Spain. Vane rose to demand, too, that it be considered who started the present Swedish–Danish conflict, before it be assumed who England should be supporting in it. Why, he asked, should England and Sweden co-operate to dispossess Denmark 'like birds of prey'? Was it England's 'Interest' to make Sweden 'emperor of the Baltic seas'? In particular, why should it be assumed 'that Holland is your enemy already'? Vane's themes, both moral and tactical, were picked up by a number of other speakers, notably Ashley-Cooper (later to become famous for the opposite opinion).[4]

The republicans could not, however, command a majority in Richard's Parliament. On 16 April the government dispatched the Cromwellian Montague with a substantial fleet, to 'awe the Hollander' and protect Charles X from the Dutch. Vane protested angrily: 'The endeavouring to bring the two nations [England and the Netherlands] to a coalition ... had made great progress' before the Protectorate; now it was being jeopardised again. 'I see this affair all along managed but to support the interest of a single person, and not for the public good, the people's interest.'[5] Once in the Sound Montague tried to persuade the Swedish King to settle for a return to peace on the basis of the Treaty of Roskilde; Charles X attempted to persuade Montague to stop being silly and give him the use of the English fleet against the Dutch and the Danes, and Montague promised to write home for new instructions. There the situation remained in uneasy deadlock until the Rump's restoration in May.[6]

Sidney re-entered the Rump on the same terms as those on which he had been ejected: as a senior member of its Council of State, listed fourth in the Act after Fleetwood, Vane, and Whitelocke – confirmation enough of his position. Once again his work centred first on Irish, and then on foreign affairs.[7]

On the Council Sidney is credited again by Toland's version of Ludlow's *Memoirs* with membership of a group, including Haselrige and Neville, which insisted that the civilian Speaker, and not the Lieutenant-General

---

[4] Burton, *Diary* III pp. 384–5, 391, 401, 466, 469–71, 476. Rowe, *Vane* pp. 213–14.

[5] Burton, *Diary* III pp. 489–90.

[6] Burton, *Diary* III; Puffendorf Samuel Von, *Histoire du Regne de Charles Gustave* (2 vols. 1697) Livre II pp. 632–8; Harris, *The Life of Edward Montagu* (1912) pp. 145–6; *The Journal of Edward Montagu first earl of Sandwich* ed. R. C. Anderson (1928) x–xxvii.

[7] CSPD 1658–9 p. 349; Between May and his departure from England in early July, Sidney was voted onto several committees, but he only had time to complete one substantial political project before he left. This was to nominate and draw up instructions for a new set of Commissioners for Ordering and Settling the Affairs in Ireland. This he completed on 1 July, the day before receiving his final diplomatic instructions. CSPD 1658–9, pp. 362, 368, 378, 390; CJ VII pp. 650, 654, 656, 661, 663, 665, 677–8, 689, 691–2, 694–5, 699–701.

(Fleetwood), formally grant commissions in the Army. Vane and Ludlow opposed this, pleading with their colleagues not to insist upon 'things indifferent' which might reinflame Parliament/military relations at such a delicate early state. While Toland's account fits Sidney's attitude to the Army from 1649 to 1653, it needs to be set once more[8] against Sidney's clear association in activity in this period, and in correspondence in the next ten months, not with Haselrige and Neville, but with the other side of Ludlow's fence, Vane and Whitelocke, both of whom were to go with the Army when the first breach with Parliament came on 13 October. Sidney wrote to Whitelocke on 13 November, to denounce exactly the touchy hard-line civilian conduct Ludlow attributed to him, and on exactly Ludlow's own grounds: 'I cannot imagine what could put them upon so contrary a course, destructive unto themselves, and dangerous to our long defended cause.'[9]

An expedition to the Baltic was Vane's immediate foreign-policy priority.[10] His first choice as 'plenipotentiaries' to conduct it were Whitelocke, Sidney, and his own brother-in-law Sir Robert Honeywood (who had just returned from living in Holland). Whitelocke refused to go, because he was, for the same reasons of expense, danger, and discomfort, as reluctant to undertake this embassy as he had been to undertake the last. He also harboured fears about one of his prospective colleagues, for 'I knew well the overruling temper and height of Colonel Sydney.' Whitelocke's justified concern was that Sidney would refuse to concede to him the 'precedency' which he would expect as the previous ambassador to Sweden. Accordingly he was replaced by Thomas Boone, a one-eyed Dartmouth merchant and MP (and, like Honeywood, an ex-member of the Rump's 1651 Council of Trade) who was not to discover the overruling temper and height of Colonel Sidney until they were well out to sea.[11]

As Sidney informed the alarmed Swedish ambassador before his departure, his instructions left him very wide powers, to use as he thought best on behalf of the Commonwealth of England. The expedition gave Sidney, as its senior member, not only some real power and autonomy, a combination of which he was inordinately fond, but the opportunity to perform upon the great stage of Europe, and among foreign heads of state. It was an opportunity for which he had been prepared by family and political background, and which he – in

---

[8] See above ch. 6 n. 12.
[9] *Ludlow's Memoirs* II p. 89; Blencowe, *Sidney Papers* pp. 169–73.
[10] Professor Everitt sees, in 1659, a core group of six Kentish republicans who formed a controlling interest in the Council of State: Vane, Sir Robert Honeywood, Sidney, Lisle, John Dixwell, and Michael Livesey. Everitt A., *The Community of Kent in the Great Rebellion* (1973) p. 309.
[11] CJ VII 670, 677, 680–1, 694–5, 699–701; Rowe, *Vane* pp. 221–2; Cal. S.P. Ven. 1659–61 p. 30; Cooper J. P., in Aylmer ed., *The Interregnum* (1972) p. 133; Whitelocke, *Memorials* IV p. 351; Ludlow, *Memoirs* p. 93.

contrast to both Whitelocke and his brother Lisle – seized upon with alacrity.[12]

Talks were instituted with the Dutch in London, through their ambassador William Nieupoort, and in Holland, through the English ambassador George Downing. Nieupoort summed up the aims of the pre-negotiations as to re-establish the ancient Dutch–English partnership of the time of 'Queen Elizabeth of immortal memory' when 'the Wisest men of these and other Nations have Considered England as a Strong Cittie fortified by the Out-workes of the United Netherlands'.[13] Both Vane and Sidney did intend the mission to serve as a model in protestant republican co-operation, and Vane considered that the restored Rump badly needed the stability a firm foreign partnership with the Dutch would bring. Other, more pragmatic reasons, however, underlay the urgency of Vane's preparations. There was deep concern about the fleet still in the Sound under Montague, and about its allegiance under the new regime. There was equally the need to secure England's naval and trading interests in the Baltic, something much more likely to be achieved, at this moment, in partnership rather than competition with the Netherlands. The outcome of the negotiations was the Treaty of the Hague (14 July), in which the two republics, with the diplomatic co-operation of France, agreed to act together to negotiate, and if necessary actually force by combined naval action, a peace between the two northern kings. The peace was to be based on the Treaty of Roskilde, with minor amendments if necessary, provided that control of the Sound remained divided.[14]

In London Sidney assured the increasingly apprehensive Swedish ambassador that 'there would be no exception to the peace of Rothschild, which did not accord with justice, reason, and the public good', a nice example of the language Sidney apparently employed in political practice as well as theory, and one which presumably gave the Swede a good deal less satisfaction than it gave him. Sidney also explained that since the English Republic had already made for itself a great name, at home and abroad, it did not seek at this time new conquests, or the hazard of new enterprises, but merely the protection of what it already had.[15] What his hearer made of all this is uncertain; what is clear is that in Sidney the new role of diplomat lay very thinly over the old of commander of cavalry.

Algernon left in early July, neglecting to say goodbye to his father, with whom he had apparently argued. The row was possibly about his accepting a

---

[12] Puffendorf, *Histoire* II p. 657.
[13] Longleat Bath MSS Whitelocke Papers XIX fols. 96–7; CJ VII pp. 653, 680–1, 694; Rowe, *Vane* pp. 221–2; Geyl, *Netherlands* pp. 42–4; Ludlow II p. 93.
[14] Venetian SP 1659–61 p. 30.
[15] Puffendorf, *Histoire* (1697) vol. II p. 657.

mission that would take him away, possibly about his rejoining the politically bankrupt Rump regime at all. Whatever the cause, Leicester noted: 'You went away angry, and so I thinke you continewd for I heard nothing from you ... [for] 3 months.' And so it was. The ambassador had other things on his mind.[16]

8.2 GUNBOAT DIPLOMACY

a few shots of our cannon would have made this peace (*Sidney 1659*)

We shall soon see the results of such unprecedented methods of negotiation (*Venetian envoy in North Germany 1659*)

As befitted a nation with a 'great name, at home and abroad', the plenipotentiaries arrived on 20 July at Elsinore (Sweden) on board 'the Langport and Maidstone frigates', '*avec une magnifique escorte*'. On 22 July they dined with Montague on board the *Naseby*, where they communicated their instructions. These were to agree a balanced joint naval force with the Dutch, so that both nations could return part of their fleets home, and in general to speed the treaty as much as possible.

In his first letter home (to Whitelocke) Sidney found the fleet:

of good strenght [*sic*] and in all appearance well affected [to the new republican policy], both the Generall and all the officers, expressing very great inclinations to serve the Parlmt, to pursue the English interest against forrainers, or old enimyes at home, and very much to slight any family interest that should endeavour to set itself up against that of England.[17]

The English envoys requested an immediate interview with the Swedish King who was out inspecting his far-flung troops and so not available. It was, besides, normal diplomatic practice to let foreign ambassadors – particularly unwelcome ones – cool their heels for a few days before admitting them. In the intervening time, therefore, Sidney arranged to meet the Dutch commissioners, to finalise terms for co-operation, on board a 'frigat' to circumvent the diplomatic formalities that would be necessary on land. They met on board the *Langport* midway between Copenhagen and Elsinore on 27 July.

The Dutch had two fleets in the Sound, under Opdam and de Ruyter. Sidney, seeking to establish the basis for a 'joint fleet ... equal in all respects', sought Montague's advice, who suggested combining fifteen of the (larger) English ships with twenty-five of the Dutch. The Dutch responded positively, but required formal confirmation from home, and promised to write immediately, a delay which Montague was later able to use as a pretext for deserting

---

[16] Add MS 32680 fol. 11.
[17] Puffendorf, *Histoire* ii p. 657; Rowe, *Vane* p. 222; Harris, *Edward Montagu* p. 144; Bath Whitelocke Papers xix fol. 66 Elsinore 28 July; Montague's journal p. 41, 20–2 July.

the negotiation in breach of his instructions. Under the Treaty of the Hague, fifteen days were required to elapse between a decision that persuasion was proving ineffective, and joint English–Dutch naval action against the refuser.[18]

The decision of the English commissioners to meet with the Dutch before even presenting their credentials to the Swedish King was a serious breach of diplomatic etiquette, or as Sidney put it: 'I confesse ... contrary to the ordinary way of ceremony.' It was strongly resented as such by Charles X who, after all, regarded the Dutch as his mortal enemies; and it served to confirm his worst fears about the new English policy. On the embassy in general Sidney quickly became obsessed with seeking ways of 'waving all ceremony', 'finding nothing in our business more necessery than a speedy dispatch'. His general contempt for empty external ceremonies of any sort asserted itself. 'Wee are wearied to death with all the tedious and frivolous disputes of theis northern people about formes and titles.' '[We] have been soe farre retarded by the tedious ceremonyes and disputes that are usuall in theis northerne courts', and so on.[19] In fact Sidney's iconoclastic temperament and style were entirely inappropriate for the formalistic cat-and-mouse of seventeenth-century diplomacy. He knew this; his reliance lay from the outset, not on the negotiations, but on the Navy.

Charles Gustavus met the English on 31 July, 'with as much respect and ceremony as ... could be', at Fredericksburg. Both sides were polite and Charles attempted to correct the envoys' suspected lack of sympathy with Sweden with a quick verbal military history of the country from the time of Gustavus Adolphus. He then inaugurated his tactics of delay by requesting a written assurance from the King of Denmark that he seriously wished to treat. The English thus returned to Elsinore, met the Dutch ambassadors the next day, and travelled with them 'through the Swedish camp to Copenhagen' the day after.[20]

The next four days were spent at Copenhagen, while the Danes were 'pressed' by Sidney through their customary initial prevarication 'for an immediate and particular treaty upon the grounds of that of Roschild'. The Danish King agreed, if he could treat through the three mediating powers, rather than with the Swedes directly which, they claimed, would give too much offence to their [anti-Swedish] German allies. This was important, since it effectively took the management of the treaty out of the hands of the

---

[18] Montague's journal pp. 42 and 49–59, esp. pp. 58–9; MS Rawl A.65 pp. 259–63; Sidney, *Works*: 'Letters of 'Algernon Sydney Taken From Thurloe's State Papers' pp. 4–7; Puffendorf, *Histoire* p. 657.

[19] Bath Whitelocke MS XIX fol. 66 p. 2, fol. 74 p. 4; Blencowe, *Sidney Papers* (1825) pp. 163, 172.

[20] Puffendorf, *Histoire* II p. 658; *Thurloes State Papers* 10 August 1659 pp. 724–5; Montague, p. 42.

two Crowns involved, and put it into those of the mediators, something Denmark, as the weaker power, had little to lose by proposing. Sidney was pleased, seeing in it, by cutting the direct contact between the antagonists, a way of putting 'a speedy end to the business, the disputes of titles, precedence, time, place, powers, persons, and great animosities between the parties'. Montague and Boone returned to Elsinore on 6 August, and Sidney and Honeywood the day after, where they requested another audience with Charles X.[21]

At this point Samuel Puffendorf's pro-Swedish *History of the Reign of Charles X* begins a new chapter entitled: *Etrange Conduite des Ambassadeurs Anglois*. Already rattled by the news of the Hague Treaty, at the receipt of which, three days before, Charles X was reported to have 'raged horribly', he now found the English determined to 'regulate everything according to their fantasies'. He expressed amazement at this 'wish to command all, as if they were masters'.[22]

The English demand to see Charles in person was accordingly evaded, as Sidney put it, out of pique, and the English were made to deal with Swedish diplomats. The next day, while Boone stayed on the *Naseby* to administer the oath to the fleet, Sidney and Honeywood met the Swedes, at Sidney's request, at the undiplomatic hour of 8 a.m. The Swedes protested at the high-handed plan of dealing through the mediators; Sidney protested at the use by the Swedish King of his own middlemen. Finally, convinced that he was getting nowhere, and to cut through these 'cavils' and the 'loss of time in vain talking' Sidney retired and dictated onto paper, in conjunction with the Dutch envoys, a formal treaty proposal based on that of Roskilde. This was to be presented, in line with that of the Hague, to each of the two northern kings, with direct naval action to be taken against the refuser.[23]

This early resort to gunboat diplomacy was too much for some. According to the Venetians, who watched the northern manoeuvres of their Dutch and English trading rivals with fascination, 'The French Ambassador refused to put his hand to this as being too violent and unusual . . . we shall soon see the results of such unprecedented methods of negotiation.'[24] Danish consent to this treaty obtained, there followed two interviews with Charles Gustavus. The first was a fruitless attempt to overcome the Swedish King's objections to a Roskilde-style peace, which would require him to give up all of the conquests of his recent campaign. In the course of it Charles X seems to have made some disparaging remarks about the English Commonwealth government, and Sidney replied by attacking the Swedish ambassador in London,

[21] *Thurloes* SP p. 725; Montague, p. 42.
[22] *Thurloes* SP p. 726; Venetian SP 1659–61 pp. 63–4, 66; Puffendorf, *Histoire* II pp. 661–4.
[23] *Thurloes* SP p. 726; Puffendorf, *Histoire* II p. 664.
[24] Venetian SP 1659–61 p. 64.

correctly assumed to be the source of Charles's information. To this, it was reported, 'there was exception taken by the King'.[25]

The second meeting, on 18 August, produced a major diplomatic incident. Harassed into it by the impatient Sidney, the unwilling Swedish King received the envoys in a public room full of 'officers, courtiers and servants, not fit for any discourse'. Unfortunately Charles had chosen the one tactic least likely to cool down this particular adversary; a stage and an audience. Sidney had decided to do two fateful things. The first was to enter the King's room in the company of his partners, the Dutch, which had never been attempted before; and the second was to formally hand over to Charles the mediators' treaty, at which point the fifteen-day fuse to naval action would begin to burn.[26]

As the mediators entered the room together the French ambassador Terlon lost his nerve, turned, and walked out again. The Swedish King saw the Dutch, strode over to Sidney and demanded to know what the paper was in his hand. In a nicely hubristic response Sidney replied, 'It contains the desires of three great powers.'

Charles X exploded: 'to see the profession that you make of friendship: to see that you take it upon you to lay down the law'. Are you, he said, mediators or dictators? 'And you', he barked at the Dutch, 'I recognise not even as mediators, but as my enemies.' The Dutch attempted to calm him and excuse themselves, but were silenced. Charles paced around, and then exclaimed: 'You make your projects, with your fleets, but I make mine, and I decide them, with my sword', and seized upon the hilt of his own, as general gossip afterwards agreed. The mediators marched out.[27]

There were enough breaches of etiquette in this meeting to fund a small war, and the fallout in all directions was considerable. The Swedes formally complained to England, and were rebuffed; because Henry Vane, they said, managed all things there and conformed himself in all things to the Dutch. De Witt, when he heard how his envoys had been publicly humiliated, *jettoit feu et flamme* and issued dark threats – which, to his credit, he eventually carried out. Gossip reverberated around the English Parliament that the Swedish King had drawn his sword on Sidney. 'Everyone is amazed', it was reported, 'how Sidney stood up to him'. 'Even the enemies of this government', wrote the French ambassador from England, 'praise the high-spirited manner in which Col Sidney answered him.'[28]

The event soon became the basis of a specifically republican legend; as Ludlow put it, 'the King of Sweden had expressed his discontent that . . . two

[25] Puffendorf, *Histoire* II pp. 663–4; *Thurloes SP* pp. 732–3; Ranke, *History of England* III p. 250, in Harris, *Edward Montagu* p. 146; Montague, p. 44.
[26] *Thurloes SP* p. 733; Puffendorf, *Histoire* II pp. 664–5.
[27] Puffendorf, *Histoire*; *Thurloes SP*; Sidney, *Works*, 'Letters' pp. 14–16; *Venetian SP* p. 82.
[28] Puffendorf, *Histoire* II p. 665; Guizot, *Richard Cromwell* I p. 160, in DNB; Sidney, p. 205.

Commonwealths should form conditions to be imposed on crowned heads'. The Danes, scarcely able to contain their glee, played upon this line with reports back to England that Charles X had expressed amazement that such 'parricides' had ever dared to enter his court.[29] In the midst of all this, Sidney, content to wait for the fifteen days to elapse, returned to Copenhagen. It was probably at this moment that the Danes presented their new (and temporary) hero with the signature book of the University of Copenhagen. In it the fêted 'mediator' wrote:

PHILIPPUS SIDNEY
MANUS HAEC INIMICA TYRANNIS
EINSE PETIT PLACIDAM CUM LIBERTATE QUIETEM[30]

Most people, of course, would simply have signed their name. This famous inscription was subsequently reproduced at the head of all editions of Sidney's works, expanded, turned in America into verse, incorporated into many whig gentlemen's coats of arms, and remains to this day the official motto of the State of Massachusetts, USA.[31] As the inscription was later related by Sidney to Lantin during a discussion of Cromwell, he was probably the tyrant in mind when he wrote it. But it was the applicability of the inscription to the recent débâcle with Charles X which delighted the Danes. That it later delighted whigs as a denunciation of Stuart tyranny is a tribute to the universality of the legend.

Unfortunately Sidney's problems were just beginning. The violence of the Swedish meeting had severely unsettled the mediator community in general, within which 'Sidney was most generally blamed, as a man hard in his actions and in his discourse and altogether incapable of managing an accomodation.' Sidney argued that the interview had put the Swedish King in the clear role of refuser, and he pressed for literal adherence to the Treaty of the Hague after the fifteen days had elapsed. But trouble for Algernon's military plans was brewing from a crucial quarter.[32]

Sidney's initial suspicions about Montague had been aroused when he had recognised a royalist agent, Whetstone, attempting to approach him in Copenhagen. Another royalist correspondent reported to the still-exiled Charles II that Sidney had said of Montague 'your majesty is in his heart'. Also in Montague's heart were his Cromwellian friendship with the King of Sweden; his dislike of the Dutch; his corresponding disapproval of the new Commonwealth foreign policy, and his particular horror at the scene at

[29] Ludlow, *Memoirs* II p. 117; Puffendorf, *Histoire* II p. 666.
[30] 'Lantiniana' p. 101: 'This hand, always an enemy to tyrants, seeks a little peace under liberty'; Add MS 32680 fol. 9.
[31] Winthrop R. C., *Addresses and Speeches 1852–1867* (1867) pp. 154–6; Robbins, 'Sidney', *WMQ* ser. 3, vol. 4 p. 276.
[32] Puffendorf, *Histoire* II pp. 665–6; Bath MS Whitelocke, XIX fol. 74 p. 1.

Charles X's Court. At this crucial juncture he thus began to talk openly of taking the whole fleet home, an inclination to which he was earnestly encouraged by Charles X, who was beginning to feel that under Sidney's direction the English fleet represented a greater threat than the Dutch themselves. Montague admitted that his desertion would be a 'breach of faith' with the Dutch, and 'a means of dissension between the [English and Dutch] States, the contrary whereof we are obliged to endeavour, a more stricter amity'. But he complained of the Dutch delay in finalising ship numbers, and the want of victuals in the English fleet, and declined Sidney's suggestion that they take personal responsibility for ordering provisions on the credit of the English government, 'that way being somewhat hazardous to our own particular estates [so that] I found no great willingness but difficulty in all (except Col Sidney) to do it'.[33]

Sidney's subsequent confrontation with Montague in Copenhagen, in the four days following that with Charles, followed a classic pattern which we will see repeated throughout his life with recalcitrant political colleagues. It began with a battle for the allegiance of their team-mates, which tipped Boone at least in Montague's favour. Sidney accused Montague of treating with the Swedish King, which Montague admitted, pointing out that that had been the purpose of his mission. 'He [Sidney] replied no but it is because the King of Sweden is against a Commonwealth that you are so earnest in this and that the King of Sweden was otherwise looked upon now than in the late Protector's days. I told him it was otherwise.' Sidney then accused Montague of treating with the would-be English King; and added

if he should give his opinion, for sendinge away the whole fleet he thought he should deserve to lose his head; ... that if his own father commanded the Fleete, yet if he could any wayes in the world hinder the saylinge of it, though by makinge the saylors mutinye against him, he would doe it.[34]

Over the next three days 'Col. Sydney was high again in expressions'. He finally appealed to Montague to leave fifteen ships, to which the admiral replied that there was no guarantee that the Dutch would not make off with them. Sidney expressed himself content with the word of 'a state that never have violated their public faith', but Montague would not agree. Sidney 'leaned in the window by himself apart, in a discontented manner', and 'walked about the room with Mon Slingerland [a Dutch envoy] alone discoursinge'. Finally, having (as Montague said), 'worked on them secretly', Sidney brought in all the other commissioners in the negotiation, Dutch and French, and demanded that Montague formally acquaint them with his

---

[33] Montague, pp. 52–3, 56; Harris, *Edward Montagu* pp. 144–56; Puffendorf, *Histoire* pp. 671–3; Pepys S., *The Diary of Samuel Pepys* ed. Latham and Mathews, *Vol. IV 1663* (1971) p. 69.
[34] Harris, *Edward Montagu* p. 149.

intentions. He did, protesting lack of provisions, 'whereat they seemed troubled', and told him he could obtain them 'at Lubeck or I cannot tell where else'. Montague denied the possibility, at which 'Col Sidney standing by said Messieurs il se mocque de vous'. On 24 August, less than a month after Sidney's arrival, Montague left with the whole fleet, and a diamond set portrait of the Swedish King.[35]

Sidney wrote to the Council of State, setting out all he had done to oppose Montague's action, and outlining the damage it had caused to the English side of the negotiation. It not only made joint naval action under the Treaty impossible, but put England at the mercy of continued Dutch goodwill for their share of the final result. In fact Montague's departure was a disaster for Sidney; he had overreached himself, and the centre of gravity now pitched away from the English envoys and towards the Dutch, who had the power. Sidney was now to suffer a great deal of the ceremony, nit-picking and equivocation which he detested, unable to do anything about it; though not, even now, for want of trying.[36]

Months later, Sidney was to lament: 'a few shots of our cannon would have made this peace'. At Montague's departure he was mindful, in a letter to Whitelocke, of the danger 'of bringing soe great a fleet all together into England without victualls, or mony, in a time of soe great disturbances'. His mind wandered homeward: 'it is very uneasy for me to be heare treating of peace betweene tow forraine Kings, when I think I might possible [sic] be a littell more serviceable at home.'[37]

8.3 AFTER THE FLEET 1659–60

The Council of State condemned Montague's departure unequivocally. For the next three months Sidney's letters were full of diplomatic detail which failed to disguise the central message: 'Since [the going of the fleet] we have been able to make very small progress.'[38]...

Charles Gustavus felt free now to opt wholeheartedly for the tactics of obstruction and delay, relying on his military strength if push came to shove with the Dutch. He continued to object to their accreditation as mediators, and Sidney, to his credit, continued to insist on their inclusion as a precondition for English ratification of any peace. Gradually, as the Dutch began to discuss unilateral military action independently of his advice, Sidney moved away from them and into a closer partnership with the (similarly fleetless) French envoy Terlon. But he did not abandon them immediately, and

[35] Harris, *Edward Montagu* pp. 151–4; Puffendorf, *Histoire*; Pepys, *Diary*; Montague, pp. 53, 63, 66.
[36] MS Rawl A.65 pp. 431–2; *Works*, 'Letters' pp. 13–14.
[37] Blencowe, *Sidney Papers* pp. 172; Bath Whitelocke MS xix fol. 74 pp. 1–4.
[38] *Works*, 'Letters' p. 17; Venetian SP p. 72.

certainly not before they abandoned him. As late as mid-September he wrote to his father:

> I hope that whatsoever be the issue of our negotiations, as mediators of peace between theis two northerne kings, wee shall have this fruite of our journey, as to be able to lay a good foundation of a neare alliance between the United Provinces and England.[39]

Indeed the English did not instantly lose the central negotiating position they had wrested for themselves. As late as 14 November Venetian observers reported: 'It is not believed there that any other English fleet will arrive this year, because the season is so far advanced, but this does not prevent the English from being held in great respect and practically the arbiters of the whole business.' Sidney's style had clearly made some impression.[40]

The battle of attrition over Dutch accreditation continued and on 25 October Sidney and Terlon represented the Dutch and the Danes at a series of meetings with the Swedes at Nicoping. Charles X refused to deal with Sidney's written statement of the Danish position, until he had personally struck out the word 'mediators' from beneath the Dutch names. By the beginning of November the Dutch had lost patience. The last of the Nicoping meetings was abandoned as de Ruyter's Navy attacked the island of Funen. This had a marvellous effect on Charles X's concentration; a fact which offers considerable endorsement of Sidney's own original approach. The King immediately offered the Dutch concessions, but he had left it too late, and on 14 November Funen fell to the Dutch, a disaster which shook the Swedish monarch badly. On 29 November he offered an Instrument of Reconciliation to the Dutch, and it became the subject of talks throughout December. Finally, the Dutch undertook to Charles X to bring the Danes to an acceptable settlement for him, and left well satisfied for Copenhagen.[41]

Not surprisingly, Sidney was extremely upset. With Stoic constancy he had continued to insist on a literal agreement in accordance with the Hague treaty, involving all three mediating powers. He had no time for private initiatives being hatched between the Dutch and the Swedes. He refused to accede to the 'frivolous desire' that they return to Copenhagen; they had already been there and settled terms. He refused to begin the negotiation over again. As he had defended the Dutch claim to involvement against Charles X, he now turned to defend the tripartite basis of the treaty against the Dutch themselves.[42]

Towards the end of the year the English government recognised the English loss of initiative in the negotiation by licensing their plenipotentiaries to return home if they wished. Boone returned, Honeywood stayed on but

---

[39] Blencowe, *Sidney Papers* p. 168; Puffendorf, *Histoire* pp. 674, 678.
[40] Venetian SP p. 90.
[41] Puffendorf, *Histoire* pp. 678–9; 684–5.
[42] Bath Whitelocke papers xix fol. 94.

became bedridden with gout, and Sidney went on alone, teaming up increasingly with Terlon. At Penshurst his mother had died, and Sidney's letter of condolence to Leicester tried to be elegant but was really slightly awkward, and soon gave way to a monologue of the details of his negotiation which he seemed to hope would cheer his father up. As only his second letter since he left England it cannot have gone far to assuage the feelings of loneliness and neglect beginning to cloud over the Earl.[43] At the same time Sidney expressed growing concern about the deteriorating political situation in England. About the October breach with the army he said to Whitelocke:

I was never more surprised with anything then the votes and acts of the parliament, upon the petition ... the contents of it being so modest that, for ought I can see, they gave a very fair way and opportunity unto the parliament of gratifying them ... but ther is a vis abdita which sweyes all human things, turns them which way it pleaseth [and] blasts the best weighed councells ... Wee have seene much of this in our age ...[44]

This was the scepticism which underlay the emphasis in Sidney's conduct as well as thought on constancy and military strength. He continued, to Whitelocke:

Your Lordship sees how much I am in the dark as to thoes actions amongst you, wherein I have the nearest concernment both as an Englishman, and as one that, for theis many years, have bin engaged in that cause, which by the help of god I shall never desert.[45]

On 12 February 1660 a second national disaster struck the Swedes when Charles X himself died of a fever. As the point of friction in the negotiations had for Sidney begun to centre less on the Swedes and more on the Dutch, he had begun, as early as mid November (1659), to describe the Swedish King as a man who, though 'violently transported by ambition and choller' was nevertheless 'a man of exceeding good wit, valiant, industrious, vigilant, thinks nothing well done either in military or civill businesse, which passeth not through his hands; and he is thought to understand affaires of both natures, better than any man in his court or army'.[46]

In short, Sidney recognised in the Swedish King qualities very like his own. He was quite capable of praising such in opponents, and in kings; virtue was more fundamental to his political thought than any particular constitutional title. We get a closer view of the exact qualities Sidney admired, from a letter to Whitelocke:

I thinke it not unworthy to be knowne, that this Prince, whoe, by the many and great actions of his short reigne, deserves to be remembered with honour, had not so noble a stage to act his part upon as his predecessor Gustavus; [but] the constancy and serenity

[43] Collins, *Letters* pp. 683–5, 690; Blencowe, *Sidney Papers* p. 171.
[44] Blencowe, *Sidney Papers* pp. 169–70.
[45] Blencowe, *Sidney Papers* pp. 170–1.
[46] Collins, *Letters* p. 685; Blencowe, *Sidney Papers* pp. 166, 174–6.

of mind shewed in all the time of his sicknesse and the certaine approaches of death, deserve not lesse praise if they are well considered.[47]

Such was Sidney's eventual admiration for Charles X that he wrote a 'Character' of him, alongside that of Vane. This, with another of Oliver Cromwell, has been lost.[48] The qualities he attributes to Charles in his letters, however, are exactly those of the character of Vane: above all, constancy; greatness as a military commander; and finally a particular resoluteness in the face of death (the nearest imperfect mankind could come to triumphing by virtue over the transitoriness of their condition). The setting is mentioned here too: a 'stage'; as is the end result: 'honour'. Again the world is a stage, and Sidney's values are those of Stoicism. It should be unnecessary to point out here that again, as in the 'Character' of Vane, Sidney was prefacing exactly the characteristics that were to make his own life and death legendary.[49]

Burnet later reported: 'Even Algernon Sydney, who was not inclined to speak well of Kings, commended [Charles X] to me, and said he had just notions of public liberty.' Sidney added that 'queen Christina seemed to have them likewise', a judgement with which Burnet could not agree, though the nature of Sidney's obligation to Christina we will see shortly. For now Sidney applied his own sense of constancy to an attempt to espouse the interests of the late King's 'virtuous mother' and infant heir.[50]

Sidney's hope that the King's death would at least speed up the conclusion of the negotiations proved ill-founded.[51] The Danes, faced now with an infant King and fledgling Swedish protectorship, recovered their courage entirely. They began to make difficulties over terms, and to demand reparations for the damage inflicted upon them by the Swedish occupation.

Sidney, still charmingly constant to the obsolete Treaty of the Hague pointed out to the Dutch that this put the Danes in the role of refusers and demanded Dutch naval action against them. The Dutch equivocated, implying agreement but actually encouraging the notion of reparations, with the idea of taking a share of them themselves. Simultaneously they kept up the

---

[47] Blencowe, *Sidney Papers* pp. 177–8.

[48] It was originally 'recovered at Montpelier' by Vane's son Christopher, Lord Barnard: HMC Buccleugh Montagu House Papers Rept 45.3 vol. II 'Journal of The Duke of Shrewsbury 1700–1706' p. 756.

[49] Blencowe, *Sidney Papers* pp. 166, 177–8; Collins, *Letters* p. 694.

[50] Blencowe, p. 166; Burnet, *Own Time* (1823) vol. I p. 139. Cf. also Sidney's *Discourses* p. 443; and his other letters to his father: 'I must ... confesse ... the King of Sweden had such Qualityes as I did love and admire, though I knew his errors alsoe. I had inclinations to serve him, as farre as my Orders gave me Leave, and did think it would be a great Honour to me, to doe a Thing, which such a Prince should acknowledge to be an Obligation; he did expresse a Sense of it, with kindnesse, four Howers before his Death, which I thought did more oblige me to continue the same good offices unto his Sonne ...', Collins, *Letters* pp. 685, 694; MS Rawl A.67 p. 82.

[51] Blencowe, p. 177.

pressure on the Swedes to submit to a private two-nation accord with them, to the exclusion of the English and French, on the basis of the old Swedish–Dutch Treaty of Elbing.[52]

On 2 April Sidney composed a solemn letter of protest insisting that Holland force Denmark to terms, or he would be obliged to declare that the Netherlands had violated the Convention of the Hague, and the English Parliament would have the right to demand reparation for its injury. He closed with a naked attempt to rekindle Dutch fears from 1652 to 1653, hinting at possible future English naval action 'whensoever it should please God to put us into a condition of demanding right and satisfaction'.[53]

Meanwhile, the Dutch had successfully concluded their treaty with the Swedes. Sidney insisted that Dutch possession of the Norwegian province of Drontheim, for which they were angling as reparation, was inconsistent with English naval interests, and would be opposed with every means at England's disposal. He demanded to know if the new Dutch–Swedish treaty committed the Swedes to help the Dutch in the event of another Anglo–Dutch war. He refused to continue with the talks until a clause had been written in promising no Swedish naval action under the treaty against any of the three mediating nations, a move for which he harnessed Terlon's support.[54]

The Dutch would not comply, and the Swedes felt powerless to do so, though they privately attempted to assure Sidney that the treaty was commercial not military and that Sweden had no wish to be 'engaged in the frequent conflicts between England and Holland'. This was not enough, and tension between the mediators escalated to paralyse the negotiations. 'Matters went so far', reported the Venetians, 'that mediators were required between the mediators.'[55] The peace was drawn up between the Swedes and the Danes, but Terlon and Sidney refused to sign, and they pleaded with the Swedes not to sign either, until they had satisfaction. Sidney reported:

Having composed the Quarrell between the tow Kings [!], our next business must be ... to breake the Alliances, that either of them have made to our prejudice, which are principally with the United Provinces; that state, hath ever since the warre with England, endeavoured to strengthen itself, with defensive alliances, with almost all the Princes of Europe.

Thus had the English republican experiment of a 'neare alliance' with the Dutch, as in 1651, turned within a year to open hostility and talk of war, as in 1652.[56]

Finally, de Ruyter sent his fleet into action against the Swedish Navy,

[52] *Works*, 'Letters' pp. 20–1; Puffendorf, *Histoire* II pp. 739, 746; Collins, *Letters* p. 694.
[53] Puffendorf, *Histoire* pp. 739–40; B.M. MSS Rawl A67 pp. 324–5; Bod. Thurloe MSS vol. VII p. 741.
[54] Puffendorf, *Histoire* p. 743.
[55] Venetian SP p. 150; Puffendorf, *Histoire* p. 746.
[56] Collins, *Letters* p. 687.

blockading it off from the sea. Amid Sidney and Terlon's howls of protest the Dutch handed the treaty to the Swedes and demanded their signature. Even at this eleventh hour, with his own government in tatters behind him, Sidney presented the Swedes with a counter-treaty, dictated by himself, and backed by a promise of guaranteed English naval action in the future. Sidney and Terlon formally broke from the Dutch, explained to Sweden that by their naval action they had 'put themselves out of the negotiation', and insisted that the Swedes henceforth deal through the two remaining mediators only. Both ambassadors made, in the names of Mazarin and the English Council of State respectively, promises of future military and naval support for the Swedes which amounted to declarations of war against the Netherlands.[57]

But the Swedes could not survive on promises, particularly promises which Sidney, at least, had no authority to make, and no longer any government to execute. The English and French resistance could not be sustained.

At 5 p.m. on 27 May 1660 a treaty was finally signed by the Danes, Swedes, and all three mediating powers. It followed the original lines of the Treaty of Roskilde, but in addition the Dutch kept their separate alliances. The Restoration of Charles II, a relative of the Danish King, had not only ultimately doomed Sidney's approach, but his signature reflects his realisation that his own, now extremely precarious, personal position in England could only be further imperilled if he were forced to return home with nothing to show for his long negotiation. The interesting fact is that apart from the separate alliances, which Sidney did not mention in his letters home, the final treaty was entirely satisfactory in terms of England's original aims. Control over the Baltic channel remained divided; moreover, the Dutch did not gain Drontheim, or any other territorial reparations. Sidney informed his father that it was a good peace, which safeguarded England's interests, and owing in no small part to his own dedication. In this there was some truth.[58]

[57] Collins, *Letters* pp. 686–7, 694; Puffendorf, *Histoire* pp. 746–50.
[58] Blencowe, p. 185; Puffendorf, *Histoire* pp. 750ff; Collins, *Letters* 689–91, 694.

Part Three

RESTORATION AND EXILE

9

The Restoration

To begin with Sidney, far from openly condemning the Restoration, attempted to conform himself to it, and even hoped for continued political employment under the new regime. This attitude hinged again on the role of Parliament:

Since the Parliament hath acknowledged a king, I knowe, and acknowledge, I owe him duty and the service that belongs unto a subject, and will pay it. If things are carried in a legall and moderate way, I had rather be in employment, than without any.[1]

In late June Sidney heard (wrongly) that his father had been restored to his old post as Lord Lieutenant of Ireland, and wrote: 'if that weare true, I should not be content to stay heare, believing, that if I am capable of doing Service in any Place in the World, it is theare, wheare I have somme knowledge of Persons, Places, and Businesse...'. As late as 1660 therefore, Algernon was ready to return to his 1642 beginnings; employment in Ireland under the royalist mandate of his father.[2]

But Sidney's skies darkened. He heard that the Court of Charles II disapproved of his negotiations on the ground that he had too much favoured Sweden. This was, of course, hardly a fair criticism of his conduct as a whole; but his 1660 role at least had been pro-Swedish to the extent that it was anti-Dutch and Danish; and he felt obliged to excuse himself for this. Indeed he went further; he set out to his father a plan whereby the English Court could, by threatening to withhold ratification of the treaty, turn the existing peace more to the advantage of Denmark:

I doe not only propose this, but will pawne my Life and Reputation upon it, that if his Majesty will give me the Powers that are requisite, I will effect it ... [indeed] if his Majesty is not contented with this, I have discovered soe much of the Affaires of theis Parts ... I will shewe the Way, how to drive the Naile a good Deale farther, and not stop, untill you shall say it is enough.[3]

[1] Blencowe, *Sidney Papers* (1825) p. 186.
[2] Collins A., *Letters and Memorials* p. 691.
[3] Collins, p. 695.

143

This is again salutary matter for reflection for adherents to the myth of Sidney as a doctrinaire ideologue, 'stiff to all republican principles'. Once again he showed himself to be flexible — literally Machiavellian — in the pursuit of employment and power. It is a feature of his political conduct which was demonstrated again when Sidney admitted to his father he had illegally claimed backing from the new King during an attempt in Sweden to have an acquaintance removed from prison: 'I confesse, the Alleaging of th[at] ... Arguement, might look sommething strangely from me; but I did not care, if I could have done the Businesse by it.'[4]

Nevertheless, Sidney did have a bottom line: it was hinged not on external but internal criteria. When he was pushed to it he became self-possessed and immovable. Further news from England was to push him to it.

The English Court had begun to register stories of Sidney's strident republican behaviour in Copenhagen. On 30 August the Earl of Leicester wrote a long and bitter letter to his son, detailing the actions of which he had been accused. The Earl made it quite clear that he took these political actions personally, and reminded Algernon how he had left him 'sick, solitary and sad, at Penshurst'.[5]

Leicester had been visited at Penshurst by a Mr Pedicom, whom he had met on his own embassy to Denmark in 1632, and who 'much commended my sons good parts, yet he said that he was rough, and had bin so to the King of Denmark, as also to the King of Sweden'. Pedicom told Leicester about the Copenhagen University album inscription, which, he noted, 'must needes be known to many, and may do your son some harm because he hath declared himself to be a defender of a Commonwealth'. He also related Algernon's having termed the King-in-exile a 'bandite', and his spirited defence of the execution of Charles I: 'Guilty? ... do you call that guilty? why it was the justest and bravest acti[o]n that ever was done in England, or anywhere...' '...to wch I answerd', noted the hurt Earl:

that this seemed very strange to me, because I knew that my sayd son was none of [the late King's] judges, nor had anything to do in the death of the sayd King, but if it were true that he had sayd such words, he must not thinke of comming into England, when that acsion was so much abhorred by all men, and by me in particular, that am his father.[6]

Sidney was understandably deeply upset by this letter. His position was complicated by the intertwining of two related problems; the political, in England, and personal, with his father. In both cases he had seriously burned his bridges but in neither case, by August 1660, was the situation a hopeless

---

[4] Collins, p. 693.
[5] Blencowe, pp. 205–10.
[6] Brit. Mus. Add MS 32680 fols. 9–10.

one. What made it hopeless was his inability to back down or acknowledge fault; to exchange stridency for contrition of even the most utilitarian variety.

[The King] will have all to submitte, to recant, renounce, and ask pardon ... I can doe the first, cheerfully and willingly, as he is acknowledged by the Parliament. Noething of the others.[7]

Once it became clear that that was what his reacceptance would require, Sidney completely shipwrecked the idea and refused thereafter to discuss it, preferring 'this voluntary exile' instead. This was at the root of his political constancy; it was a constancy not initially to any external political principle; but to self, when self was the only thread of constancy left in a disintegrating external political world. For Sidney, 'liberty' meant never having to say you were sorry. Instead he fell to blaming those around him:

In all theis alterations and variety of accidents, I doe not find any that help me ... when I was fallen into as deepe a degree of inconvenience and mischiefe, as one could be cast into, by the destruction of the party which for many yeares I had followed, and the ingratitude of somme of my friends, whome I had obliged in every manner ... possible ... I was troubled to finde your lordship lesse carefull to give me some reliefe, than I hope [sic] you would have bin: Especially, when I could accuse myself of noe other fault ... [than] an unhappy constant adherence unto both.[8]

Sidney was angry, too, with his collapsed 'party'; their having 'of late runne into extream great extravagances, and the ill management of theire power is the cause of theire destruction'; a criticism which he could surely have equally levelled at himself.[9]

Sidney wrote frequently in this period to his father, to Sir John Temple, and to Northumberland. In a letter to Northumberland he enclosed another for the King. Of this he said to his father: 'I know the points that upon such changes give most satisfaction, that few do omitte, are not mentioned; but whether that makes the paper fit for the fire, I leave it to your lordship to judge.' The omitted points were, of course:

congratulation and acknowledgement of our faults, in having bin against this king, or his father. The truth is, I could hope for no good in a business that I should beginne with a lye and I shall be better contented with my fortune, when I see theare was noe way of avoiding it, that is not worse than ruine.[10]

Sidney's inability to back down was thus clearly enough tied to his greatest fear; dishonour – only that could be 'worse than ruine'. His consequent inability to 'accuse myself [of anything except the Stoic virtue of] ... constancy', and his inability to 'acknowledge ... faults' were features of his behaviour over which there was no flexibility at all during his lifetime. This

---

[7] Blencowe, p. 233.
[8] *Ibid.* pp. 182–3, 190.
[9] *Ibid.* p. 185.
[10] *Ibid.* pp. 187–8.

was crucial to his martyrdom; Sidney went to the scaffold with a catalogue of the world's crimes against him and the illegalities of his trial, the effectiveness of which have never been in danger from the fact that he was probably guilty as charged.

Under these circumstances there was a limit to what his father and uncle – and even George Monck whom Sidney heard makes 'Discourses . . . much to my Advantage' – could do. His father counselled him to wait for the situation to cool, in northern Germany or Holland. But on 28 July in Copenhagen, after receiving some letters from England about the situation, Sidney suddenly made a definite decision to abandon all thoughts of returning home for the time being. It was no longer adequate for the King to allow him to come back on his own terms; Sidney would require 'some [positive] act of favour or trust, [to] showe that he is reconciled to me'. '[F]or though I can very joyfully retire myself, into as private a life as any man in England is in, I have too well learnt, under the Cromwells, what it is to live under the protection of thoes unto whome I am thought an enemy.'[11]

In his next letter, having heard that his father was still 'very intent upon finding a way of bringing me into England', he thanked him but said firmly: 'I desire you to lay that out of your thoughts; it is a designe never to be accomplished.' Needless to say, this did nothing to improve relations between the two men. Algernon added: 'I have not yet resolved on my place of residence; but I dislike all the drunken countries of Germany, and the north, and am not much inclined to France. I think I shall choose Italy.' This was an assessment of northern habits at least which Leicester must have found hard to fault. He had recorded of the Danish King on his own visit in 1632: 'a strange life he leads, drunk every day, lying with a whore every night . . . the prince is likewise debauched, as all in this country are'.[12] This was not enough, however, to rescue his son from his displeasure.

Sidney lingered on in Scandinavia for some time after his diplomatic powers had expired. Characteristically, one of the reasons he finally left was to avoid the 'shame' of no longer having the money to maintain the lifestyle appropriate to a place where he was known to have been 'long under a character that rendered me not inconsiderable'.[13] There was also, by the end, some political urgency about his departure from Copenhagen; the Danes had become hostile, and rumours circulated that he would be arrested and handed back to the English Court as a regicide. Sidney recounted an incident in which he and Terlon had been fired on by a Danish shore-cannon in Copenhagen harbour while setting off in a small boat to greet a Swedish vessel there.

[11] Collins, p. 688; Blencowe, pp. 189–90.
[12] Cant Rev. 'The Earl of Leicester's Embassy to Denmark 1632' in *Economic History Review* LIV p. 258. Blencowe, pp. 190–1, 195.
[13] Collins, p. 690.

Sidney had demanded to know who had fired the cannon and was told the Danish Queen had just been there. She felt obliged to send a note to Sidney disclaiming responsibility for the shot. Sidney replied with the sarcasm which will be familiar to all readers of his *Discourses*: 'saying that all things which came from her Majesty weare favours, even bullets, and if that shee had a mind to try her skill, I would goe againe to the same place, and make myself her mark as long as she pleased'.[14]

Algernon, having asserted, over his father's recommendation of Germany, his intention to go to Italy, added as he left that if he received any particular and written rather than general and verbal commands from Leicester about where to reside, he would, of course, obey them exactly.[15] His father responded with a positive written statement that he was 'wholly against' Italy, and wanted Algernon to stay in Germany for the time being, preferably Hamburg. By the time Algernon received this he was well south of Hamburg and about to make the Alps crossing. He wrote to Leicester that he could not assume he wished him to go all the way back to Hamburg, where he had found 'great inconvenience in staying'; and so he would proceed to Rome or Florence, though 'if your Lordship doth dislike either, I will upon your command remove from thence into Germany or France, or into England...' This sort of sophistry did nothing to mend the Earl's temper. He complained: 'what to advise you, truly I knowe not; for you must give me leave to remember, of how little weight my opinions and counsel have been with you ... which in much affection and kindness, I have given you on many occasions, and in almost everything, from the highest to the lowest'.[16]

As Sidney travelled through Hamburg, Frankfurt, and Augsburg towards the Alps, he noted the general post Thirty Years War poverty and the bareness of the German countryside. He paid particular attention to the state, and type, of each town's military fortifications: the worst, he said, were no more than 'lines cast up in the night'. He observed that he was being forced to use French (which he knew well) and Latin (which he had not known as well), in order to help himself to the conversation of 'persons of quality', and 'priests' respectively. He found the priests extremely ignorant, but the eminent among them learned English and 'their Libraryes are full of [Goodwin], Baxter, Burroughes, and other English Puritane Sermon Books'.[17]

It was in Hamburg that Sidney met Christina, ex-Queen of Sweden and now a celebrated catholic convert, on her way north from Rome to visit Stockholm. He sought her reassurance that she was not going to rock the boat

---

[14] Blencowe, pp. 220–1.
[15] Blencowe, p. 191.
[16] Blencowe, pp. 208, 213, 239–40.
[17] Collins, pp. 696–8. The name 'Goodwin' does not appear in Collins's published version of this letter. In the De Lisle papers the name 'Goodwin' has been crossed out in Collins's editing ink. Food for thought about whig preferences for Sidney's religion.

of succession in Sweden. In a long meeting she perfectly satisfied him on this point; Christina was evidently quite a woman and Sidney emerged from the interview a little sheepish. He rallied, however, in reporting the event to his father: 'I do not believe this barely because shee sayd it (for I am in this Yeares Employment, growne much lesse credulous then I was) but because the impossibility of effecting any Thing [else] is soe plaine.'[18]

This meeting was important to Sidney, for it was to Christina's city that he now made his way. In Rome she moved in the highest clerical circles, and it was to these that she evidently gave him an introduction. Her closest friend – some said lover – was Cardinal Azzolini, and it was Azzolini who was to become, in turn, Sidney's closest friend in Rome.[19]

On his way through Germany Sidney also produced the defence of his conduct around Charles I's execution that we have examined. He confessed, however, that he had publicly defended the regicide in Copenhagen, for 'Your Lordship may judge how good a servant I had been, if I had waved justifying the authority that had employed me.' On the question of his general stridency on behalf of the Republic, Sidney summed up his approach to the negotiations:

The work was only to be carried one with vigour and boldnesse; I was forced to take that part, my collegue grewe slack. By this Denmark was brought to the peace. If I had showed any faintnesse, I should have had noe more credit than my footboy.[20]

It was from this period, too, that there emerged the most famous Sidney letter of all: 'The Hon. Algernon Sidney's Letter Against Bribery and Arbitrary Government.' This was first published in England in the 1690s, in Rochester's *Familiar Letters*. It enjoyed an immense vogue in eighteenth- and nineteenth-century England and America, and became the basis of the Sidney legend for a great many people who never read anything else he wrote. It was a strident and uncompromising critique of a Restoration England where 'all things' are 'vendible', virtue has expired, and the nation is ruled by a weak lust-crazed King and his coterie of parasitic favourites. Unfortunately (or fortunately) Sidney did not write it; it was forged in the early stages of the Sidney whig myth industry.[21] It has no address and no date, and the overblown style, full of exclamations: 'Ah no!'; 'Miserable nation!'; 'Infamous traffic!'; 'Detest-

---

[18] Collins, pp. 685, 696–7.
[19] Pastor L., *The History of the Popes* vol. xxxi (1940) p. 68 (and ch. ii in general).
[20] Blencowe, pp. 216–17.
[21] Blencowe, pp. 199–204; Worden, 'Sidney' p. 28. Blair Worden first drew my attention to this fact. Other products of the same late seventeenth-century Sidney forgery factory survive in the Bath MSS at Longleat; including 'Algernon Sidney's Letter of Advice to his Friend on the Education of his only Son', written in couplets which conclude: 'Your old friend Ludlow is in good health / And hopes to live to see a Commonwealth.' Longleat Portland Papers vol. xvii fols. 65–6.

able bribes!' is well over the top, even for Sidney, and unlike anything else he wrote. More to the point the whole letter, purporting to have been written from Germany, is quite politically premature. Sidney's line towards the Restoration took some time to harden, and he did not become so strident or bitter for at least two years, until the execution of the regicides, and then Vane. At this stage he didn't even have sufficient access to news to know what was going on.

There is, however, a letter which Sidney *did* write at this time, to his father from Hamburg on 30 August, which is quite different in tone and style, and perhaps the most interesting he ever wrote. In it Sidney wrestles with all the issues concerning his own conduct which this chapter has discussed. In the process, and under the strain of his difficult situation, he comes closer to admitting personal defects of judgement – though he cannot admit personal responsibility for them – than anywhere else; and from this struggle with self emerges a clear statement of the bottom-line motives by which Sidney acted, and which were to frame his conduct in the face of the Restoration and for the rest of his life.[22]

He explained to his father that his refusal to make 'vile and unworthy submissions, acknowledgement of errors, asking of pardon and the like' provided him with the only comfort he had amid his collapsing political world.

[If I lose that] I shall from that moment be the miserablest man alive, and the scorne of all men. I knowe the titles that are given me of fierce, violent, seditious, mutinous, turbulent . . . I know people will say, I straine at knats, and swallow camels; that it is a strange conscience, that lets a man runne violently on, till he is deepe in civill blood, and then stays at a few words and complements; that can earnestly endeavour to extirpate a long established monarchy, and then cannot be brought to see his error, and be persuaded to set one finger towards the setting together the broken pieces of it . . . I have enough to answer this in my owne minde; I cannot helpe it if I judge amisse; I did not make myself, nor can I correct the defects of my own creation. I walk in the light God hath given me; if it be dimme or uncertaine, I must beare the penalty of my errors: I hope to do it with patience, and that noe burden shall be very grievous to me, except sinne and shame.[23]

This introspective side of Sidney was not one which he often exposed to the world, and even now would only expose to his father. It was a side of which the eighteenth century were ignorant; Collins's collected letters, published in 1742, focused on the dry, public and political. Somebody – almost certainly his sister Dorothy – had removed from the Sidney papers at Penshurst all the letters which exposed the vulnerability, and charm, of Sidney's private as

---

[22] Blencowe, pp. 194–8.
[23] *Ibid.*

opposed to public persona.[24] In 1825 these letters were published by Blencowe; by that time the popularity of the Sidney political mythology in England was already in decline.

As this quoted letter makes clear, 'shame' and 'the scorne of all men' were Sidney's greatest fears: 'contempt might procure safety; but I had rather be a vagabond all my life, than buy my being at soe deare a rate'. He meant it, too, as his preference for the scaffold over an 'unworthy' offer made to him for the saving of his life at the last moment in 1683 sufficiently shows. 'It is ill enough to satisfy the malice of my most bitter enimyes, and not easily capable of an aggravation, but by doing something that would dissatisfy myselfe.'[25]

In this 'severity and obstinacy' Sidney believed he had now 'noe companions'. He was subsequently to find he had been wrong, and to write his *Character* of the man who showed him wrong on the scaffold in 1662: Henry Vane. Having formulated his stand, Sidney consolidated in his own mind and that of others the political principles on behalf of which it was taken. It was not surprising, he said, that he should be persecuted by the English Court for his 'stiffe adherence to the party they hate':

I did not take the warre in which I was engaged to be a slight matter, nor to be done by halfes. I thought it undertaken upon good grounds, and that it was the part of an honest man to pursue them heartily. It is not strange that this should raise great animosityes against me. It is usuall to desire to destroy thoes that will not be corrupted.[26]

By the time he arrived at Rome, therefore, Sidney's Tacitean mythology of himself in relation to the Restoration, a model of the incorruptible virtue which republics employed, and which monarchies sought to destroy, was already building its foundation. But the anger and despair which moulded it into a political ideology, and impelled him into political action against the government, was produced by events which still lay in the future, and a growing sense of loss for which there seemed no other remedy. Before that came the rest, relaxation, and companionship of Rome.

---

[24] The manuscripts of these letters are now in Sevenoaks Library, Kent, MS U1000/7 Z1. They had come into Blencowe's hands through 'Mr Lambard, of Sevenoaks', to whom they were given by 'his sister, who received them from her friend Lady Smythe'. Lady Smythe was the descendant of 'Mr Smythe ... who married [Dorothy Sidney]'. Blencowe, *Sydney Papers* (1825), Introduction.

[25] Blencowe, pp. 224–5. There was another problem about his political recantation which Sidney raised, in typically sceptical terms, and re-demonstrated in the process that it was another aspect of the same old need; for, in the chaos of changeable particulars, something solid to grasp onto. 'Whoe can answeare for what he hath sayd in eighteen years of a party unto which he professed utter enmity ... I can noe sooner justify myself in one point, but a multitude of others will be alleged against me ... where is the law or rule, to which such pleadings should be reduced?' Blencowe, p. 232.

[26] Blencowe, p. 222.

Rome 1660–63

I sought nothing here but rest and good company
22 December 1660

The most unusual thing about Sidney's time in Rome is that he does not seem to have argued there with anybody. This is a powerful sign that he was not, at this early stage, engaged in any sort of political activity. The other remarkable feature is the company he chose; he shunned the English community and instead assiduously cultivated his *entrée* to the society of the papal Court. So successful was he that within a year he had moved to live in the private palace of Prince Pamphilio, nephew of the previous Pope, at Frascati and was sending home to his father a collection of twelve 'Characters' he had written of each of the cardinals.[1]

As his commonplace books show, Sidney's father the 'puritan' Earl harboured something of a fascination with the intrigues of papal politics. This was the world his son now entered. The family had long-standing ties with Italy (Tuscany, Venice, and Rome in particular) and, as we have seen, Algernon had visited Rome before. For Algernon, as for the family in general, disbelief in the Roman religion was no barrier to appreciation of its intellectual culture. This applied equally to Spain; the Earl's commonplace books are full of Spanish authors; and one of the two works Algernon told his [Catholic] friend Lantin in Paris that he 'esteemed above all . . . for perfecting himself in [the] Science . . . [of] politics' was 'the Spanish book entitled *El Gobernador Christiano*' (by Juan Marquez, Salamanca 1621). When Filmer later accused his opponents of taking their theories from the Jesuits, Suarez and Bellarmine, he scored a palpable hit which left Sidney, writing in the aftermath of the Popish Plot, flailing amid unconvincing denials. Even as he did so he could not resist conceding the point by sniping that Filmer 'might as well have joined the Puritans with the Turks because they all think one and one makes two'.[2]

---

[1] Collins A., *Letters and Memorials* pp. 711–16, 718.
[2] *Discourses* p. 4; Indeed the Earl's own notes mention 'le Cardinal Pamfilio neveu du Pape' Z9 19–20, 5; Z1/9, esp. 9–10, 15, 51–4; Z1/4 1–6; 430–34; 523/6; Z22; Worden, 'Classical republicanism' pp. 184–6; 'Lantiniana' p. 101.

With Sidney's Roman sojourn we are once again observing the gap between the real person, and the cardboard cut-out character of the political mythology, born in part of Sidney's own political propaganda. Beyond his own confident protestant faith Sidney knew, as the relativist and sceptic he was, that the world contained a myriad range of religious opinions, many as deeply felt as his own. He felt their errors, but he understood them as part of the (imperfect) human condition – the many 'opinions and fancies of men'. It was for this reason that faith had to be personal, based upon the judgement and conscience of individuals, not the coercion of an external church or state. Thus, while in Rome, he enjoyed the intellectual and political conversation of the cardinals, and the entry which these contacts gave him to witness the curious ceremonies and festivals of the Roman Church. The only things he bitterly criticised *as such* in letters to his father, were the religious trials he witnessed; the incidents of persecution.[3]

Sidney never, with his family background, lost his distrust of papism on this account, as the religion to which persecution, and ultimately massacre, attached itself when it acquired political power. He would write in the *Discourses*, under the shadow of a popish plot and threatened popish succession, that

the fatherly care shewed to the protestants of France ... the mercy of Philip the second of Spain to his pagan subjects in the West-Indies, and the more hated protestants in the Netherlands; the moderation of the dukes of Savoy towards the Vaudois in ... Saluzzo and ... Piedmont; the gentleness and faith of the two Maries, queens of England and Scotland; the kindness of the papists to the protestants of Ireland in the year 1641 ... in a word, the sweetness and apostolical meekness of the inquisition, may sufficiently convince us that nothing is to be feared where that principle reigns.[4]

Yet the Roman religion itself and this persecution still remained distinct in Sidney's mind. He thus remained as noted for being 'a Friend unto Roman Catholics' in private in England (where they were a persecuted minority), as he did for the zeal with which he opposed any attempt by them to acquire political power. Moreover, during the Restoration's own immediate persecutions it became increasingly clear that papism itself had no monopoly on the crime of compulsion against which he fought. Accordingly, the *Maxims* said bitterly, a feature of modern protestantism in Europe seemed to be that it had learnt to persecute as bloodily as, if not more so than, papism. The *Maxims* thus proceeded to ridicule the Anglican Church for aping the intolerance of Rome while having renounced the theological justification for it.[5] Accordingly again, in 1670, attempting to engineer through Turenne in Paris a settlement in England based on religious toleration at home and a French

---

[3] See below pp. 5, 7; *Court Maxims* pp. 90–3.
[4] *Discourses* p. 494.
[5] *Court Maxims*, pp. 38–9, 79–81, and pp. 73–96 in general.

alliance abroad, Sidney was to claim that he 'preferred catholicism to the rule of the Bishops [in England]'. This was because in 1670 catholic France was more tolerant of protestant religious dissent than protestant England.[6] As late as 1679 Sidney remained intriguing with France on the same basis, but when, by 1682, the situation in France had changed, and with a huguenot refugee in his own home, Sidney's attitude to catholic France was changing sharply too. Changing times and circumstances required changing tactics and responses; this was the relativism, in conduct as well as thought, ignored by the whig myth of Sidney the inflexible protestant patriot. When a mere hint of Sidney's French, never mind his catholic, intrigues began to leak out Sidney was repudiated by the culture that had claimed him from the scaffold. This was the living person lurking behind the dead, with none of the rigor mortis that made the latter so politically serviceable. This less two-dimensional Sidney was more consistently devoted to the liberty to believe and practise any faith in any country than whig culture could readily take on board. We must strip this two-dimensionality away to find the 'doctrinaire' republican who wrote a 'Character' of the Swedish King; this hero of protestant English radicalism who lived with the cardinals of Rome; this whig martyr who 'feared the Prince of Orange more than the Duke of York'. The key to much of the difference lies in Sidney's internationalism: that his education, experience, and beliefs were European rather than simply English. The importance of this fact will become increasingly clear in the chapters which follow. We see the dimensions of that internationality emerge for the first time clearly in Rome.

We do not know for certain how long Sidney stayed in Rome, or Italy. In his 'Apology' he wrote:

I hoped that noe man would ... disturbe me in a most innocent exile; and that the most malicious of my enemyes should not pretend that I practiced anything against the government, I made Rome the place of my retreat, which was certainly an ill scene to act any thing, that was displeasing unto it. But I soone found, that noe inoffensivenesse of behaviour could preserve me ... and was defended from such as there designed to assassinate me, only by the charity of strangers.

He then spoke of being in Flanders and Holland in 1663. Since we next hear of him (after his letters from Frascati in mid 1661) with Ludlow in Switzerland in autumn 1663, his biographers have pictured him staying at Rome for the full three years, 1660–3. It seems likely that he went elsewhere in Italy at least; his last letter of the period (Frascati, 14 July 1661) stated that he had 'somme Inclinations this Autume, to goe to Naples, and from thence to Sicily, and Malta, to passe the Winter in somme of those places, and returne to Rome in the Springe'. He was to make several references to the Naples revolt

---

[6] Paris, Ministere des Affaires Etrangeres Corresp. Politique Angleterre vol. 99 p. 270.

of 1647 (which had briefly erected a republic)[7] in both the *Court Maxims* and the *Discourses*. He had also spoken of his desire to go to Florence, and his gift to Ludlow in 1663 of a pair of pistols from Lombardy suggests that he may have done so.[8]

Following his meeting with Christina, Sidney had communicated his intention 'to meet in Rome somme eminent persons, that I have lately bin acquainted with, to see whether I can, upon conference, fix upon anything'. Rome clearly attracted him at this point as a suitable opposite to the poverty, the climate, and the threadbare culture of Scandinavia, Germany, and 'all the drunken countries of the North'. In his political theory Sidney praised the honest simplicity and martial vigour of the northern 'Gothic' polities, in contrast to the luxury and decadence of once-great Rome. In practice, however – at least at this moment – he much preferred the latter.[9]

'I think', he wrote soon after his arrival,

the councell given me by all my Friends, to keepe out of England for a While, doth too clearly appeare to have bin good, by the Usage my Companions have already receaved ... I must either have procured my Safety, by such Meanes as Sir Arthur Haselrig is sayed to have used; or runne the Fortune of somme others, whoe have shewed themselves more resolute.

He had been most reluctant to remain in Germany, he repeated, 'finding myself too apt to fall too deepe into melancholly, if I have neither Businesse, nor Company, to divert me; and I have such an aversion to the Entertainements of that Country, that if I had stayed in it, I must have lived as a Hermite, though in a populous Citty'.[10]

He quickly after his arrival began to seek out his high social contacts. 'I have already visited severall Cardinalls; to Morrowe I intend to pay the same Respect to the Cardinal Gizi, Nephew to the Pope: He hath allready granted me the Liberty of waiting upon him, which was signified unto me by another eminent Person of the same Robe and Degree.' Rome, he commented, did not 'beare such signs of Ease, Satisfaction and Plenty' as on his first visit, but 'the Company of Persons excellent in all Sciences, which is the best Thing Strangers can seeke, is never wanting'.[11]

Sidney spoke to his cardinals about local papal, and general European politics. He enjoyed, following the death of Cardinal Mazarin in late 1660, offering his opinion about his likely successor in the French Court, a matter of much concern at the curia. He advised, with the grave and learned scepticism of an elder statesman, 'that he will be chosen, that can finde most Favour with

---

[7] Pennington D. H., *Seventeenth Century Europe* pp. 333–4.
[8] 'Apology' p. 3; Collins, *Letters* p. 721; Worden ed., *Voyce* Introduction p. 33.
[9] Blencowe, p. 226; see p. 6 below.
[10] Collins, *Letters* p. 700.
[11] *Ibid.*

the Ladyes, and that can with most Dexterity, reconcile theire Interests, and satisfy their Passions. I look upon theire thoughts, as more important then thoes of the King, and all his Councell; and theire Humors, as of more Weight, then the most considerable Interest of France.' This view of Court politics later resurfaced as a passage in the *Discourses*.[12]

Sidney's friends among the cardinals clearly took him up with interest; as Burnet commented: 'Sidney had a particular way of insinuating himself into people that would harken unto his notions, and not contradict him.' They took him to see various political and church ceremonies. 'I went Yesterday with a Cardinal to the Palace ... wheare I saw Mr Colebert receaved.' On another occasion: 'the Cardinal Azzolini had invited me to see [him] ... assist as Deacon Cardinal. I went, and, upon the Staires going up to the Vaticane, found him, and Cardinal Palavicini, who brought me into the Chamber whear the Cardinals weare all assembled ... The Pope soone came in.'[13]

It was, as I have said, Christina's friend Azzolini with whom Sidney spent most time. He was only thirty-five years old, close to Sidney's own age, and it was his age which Sidney chose to remark upon particularly in his 'Charac-ter'. It seems fair to assume that their social circle included Christina herself, following her return to Rome. Pallavicini, a Jesuit scholar, the Pope's confessor and eventual biographer, had Sidney's intellectual admiration for having written a *History of the Council of Trent* which he praised and offered to send to his father. Sidney's contacts among the Cardinalate as a whole were wide: 'I have visited nine or ten of that Order, somme of them the most extraordinary persons that ever I met with, others equall with the rest of the World.' His praise for them as a group was unequivocal: 'I doe not find, that ... [they] want any Quality, that makes Men estimable; and they are soe farre from that Loosenesse of Life, of which they have bin formerly, and ordinarily accused, that I have not yet seene any of that Order doe an indecent Thing, nor speake a loose Word; and yet I mark them as narrowly as I can ... Theare is a great Alteration in that Kind, for the better, since I was heare last.' (This is to be contrasted with the later sneer in the *Discourses* at the moral depravity of the manners of modern Rome, 'refined by the pious and charitable Jesuits'.)[14]

On their own parts the cardinals admired Sidney's 'Parts and Wit', as well, perhaps, as his birth and family. Once again also, while the Sidney of his theory is better known – the iconoclast critic of vain 'flattery' – the Sidney of practice showed himself to be fully possessed of all the graces most useful in high society – including flattery – as we might expect from his upbringing as a

---

[12] Collins, *Letters* pp. 700, 704, 707; *Discourses* pp. 115–16.
[13] Collins, *Letters* pp. 703, 710; Burnet, add MS 63,057 fol. 342.
[14] Ranke L., *The History of The Popes* (London 1908) II 361, 365, 368; Collins, *Letters* pp. 705, 707.

diplomat's son in Paris. Speaking of Cardinal Zachetti, Sidney noted: 'He seemed pleased once, when I told him, That he had found a Way of attaining that Dignity which is equall to Kings [the Cardinalate], by meriting it; and had ascended unto that which is above them all [the Papacy], to the Compleating of his Glory and Fortune, if he had not merited it too well. Which, though a complement, is exactly true.' Thus did this scion of protestant anti-clericalism assert to cardinals that the Pope's position was above that of kings – a clear application, if there ever was one, of the (relativist) proverb 'When in Rome...'[15]

Sidney's admiration and pursuit of the society of the Roman clerical nobility is to be contrasted with his low opinion of the other groups to which he might have turned while there: the secular nobility, and the English community. Of the former he said exactly what he would later say in his political theory of the modern English 'nobility': 'I have much more Aquaintance amongst the Prelates, than the nobility of this place ... the most auncient Familyes [here], have lost all the Vigour and Virtue of their Aunceſtors; theire most remarkeable Qualityes, are now Pride, Lazinesse, and Sensuality.' As for the English and other foreigners in Rome, Sidney avoided them altogether, partly for political reasons: 'having never found any Inconvenience heare, but by theire Company, and Neighbourhood'.[16] The sentiment was reciprocated; as one of the Englishmen himself reported to Sidney's old parliamentary enemy Sir Philip Percival:

Here is one Colonel Sidney here, that was by the Rump sent Embassador into Sweadeland, and has no mind to return home. He has put himselfe here into very great equipage, his coach and three lackeys; he is very gracious with some of the Cardinals, which some impute to his own Parts and wit, others to some recommendation from the Queen of Sweade, but as he converses here with few of the English, so have they little devotion to treat with him.[17]

The political caution Sidney felt about the foreign community was caused in part by 'one Plunket, a young Irish Priest that gives me somme Trouble, by foolish Discourses ... he sayes I am an Atheist, and bred up in your Lordships House under a Master, from whome I learnt thoes Opinions. He was answeard, that was very improbable, and that my Life and Conversation gave Testimony of the Contrary'; an answer Sidney says produced an 'Apology' from Plunket, and a good illustration of the internal and moral, rather than external and doctrinal, conception Sidney had of true religion. It is in these terms that Sidney's praise for the morality of his friends the cardinals is of interest.[18]

[15] Collins, *Letters* pp. 709, 712.
[16] *Ibid.* p. 705.
[17] *Ibid.* pp. 701, 710; HMC Egmont 63.2 p. 616.
[18] *Ibid.* p. 709.

Nevertheless, the papal court made its own inquiries about Sidney

to the Internuntio in Flanders ... of me, my Birth, Person, and Quality. To whome Information was given ... that I was ever found to be violent against Monarchy, a Freind unto Roman Catholiques, one that in our last Troubles, meddled littel with private Businesse, and that had made my Fortune, by the Warre ... Part true, and Part false; but none that I can learne which doth me any Prejudice. They were put upon this Enquiry, by the foolish prating of some Priests, who spoke of me, as the only Enimy the king had left, and that I being taken away, his Majesty might reagne in Quiet.[19]

During this period Sidney apparently played host to Dr John Mapletoft, tutor at Petworth to Northumberland's son Joceylin, who was in Rome for a year. Mapletoft was a close and lifelong friend of John Locke – one of a number of acquaintances Sidney and Locke had in common, though no record of their meeting survives.[20]

Sidney related to his father the details of doctrinal struggles within the Roman Church: between 'the Scotists and the Thomists', for instance, over the divinity of the Virgin Mary; and concerning the internal position of the Jesuits, under suspicion for being 'a commonwealth within a commonwealth'. He described many church ceremonies, particuarly the spectacular festivals of Christmas and Easter, though he did not see all he could have, 'finding the Curiosity usual in Strangers, to be very littell suitable to my Age or Humor'. His protestant perspective intruded as he ridiculed clerical taxes (and the ruses employed to levy them), and remarked sourly on the punishments inflicted on heretics after public trial. He narrated with amazement the devotions of 'tow hundred persons' in a public street who did 'whip themselves most cruelly, so that somme of them, through the extreame Losse of Blood, fainted'.[21]

It was in mid April 1661 that Sidney sent his father his 'Characters' of the cardinals, already mentioned. Given his other efforts concerning Vane, Cromwell, and Charles X it was obviously a literary form which pleased him; indeed he was to finish his life by writing a 'Character' (his *Apology*) of himself. The purpose of the Roman portraits was to display knowledge, to instruct and entertain, and above all to judge – both morally and intellectually. What is most interesting about them is Sidney's criterion for judgement. Pio 'is more a gentleman than a prelate ... He doth not pretend to be very zealous.' Chigi 'is rather innocent than good, or good than wise ... He thinks the use of pleasures is an advantage justly belonging to greatness.' Barromeo, on the other hand, 'is a principal ornament to the college; few excel him,

---

[19] Collins, *Letters* p. 709. The informant was 'one White, an Irish Man', secretary to the Spanish ambassador Don Alonso de Cardenas, with whom Sidney had negotiated for the Republic in 1650.

[20] Maycock A., *Chronicles of Little Gidding* (1954) p. 110; Cranston M., *John Locke* (1979) pp. 28, 117, 113–14, 137, 142, 145.

[21] Collins, *Letters* pp. 703, 708.

either in natural parts ... or strictness of life ... He drinks but eight ounces at a meal. His delight is in study, and conversation with learned persons.'

Albizzi is 'little favoured at court for the plainness of his language, expressing his dislike to all things that deserve it ... Virtuous in his life, zealous in his religion ... his countenance ... though something hard, and severe, hath so much of vigour, vivacity, and constancy, as renders him not unlovely ... He is ... learned, especially in divinity ... [and] deserves the triple crown, but is not likely to wear it ... as too strict and dangerous, both to cardinals and prelates.'[22]

Sachetti by contrast is 'gentle, affable ... [but] not much learned with books'. His vice is that he 'loves to talk a little too much, and often makes his own actions the subject of his discourse ... [these actions are] very considerable ... [but] might sound better from others, than from himself'. It is to Sachetti that Sidney offered the elaborate piece of flattery mentioned above. Like Sidney, then, Spada 'doth not much love dissimulation, but knows how to do it, when it is necessary ... No man is thought to excel him ... in human learning ... He is a living history; and his memory is a magazine, where the records of all the affairs of the world are kept in so good order, that he knows when, and how, to bring forth every piece to ... best advantage.' Even he, however, 'is more pleased with the praise given to one of his epigrams, than some think is suitable to his age, dignity, and person'.[23]

Sidney's admiration for Pallavicini is tempered by a repeat of the Machiavellian caution quoted from the *Discourses* in Chapter 3. On the one hand

Italy hath not a finer wit ... nor hath any convent a monk of stricter life ... six pence a day serves him in meat ... The use of [women] is unknown to him ... [and] He hath showed it is possible for the same man, to be most excellent in the Belle Lettere, and the most deep and abstruse sciences ... [Yet] I do not think he hath so well joined the theory and practice of business ... he hath lived more among books and papers, than men. He ever aims at perfection ... forgetting that the counsels, as well as the persons of men, are ever defective; and that in human affairs, governors and ministers are not so much to seek what is exactly good, as what is least evil, or least evil of those things, that he hath the power to accomplish.

That this conviction lies at the heart of both Sidney's own 'theory and practice' needs no emphasis; its meaning in practice will become evident in the following chapter.[24]

The point receives emphasis when Sidney describes his friend Azzolini as

Inferiour to [Pallavicini] in learning, but much above him in practice, and knowledge of worldly business ... The one is more speculative, the other hath an understanding far better suited to government ... He is [universally] esteemed, though he hath no

22 Sidney, *Works*, 'Letters taken from the Sydney Papers' pp. 42, 46.
23 'Letters' in *Works* pp. 42–44.
24 *Ibid.* pp. 42–3.

prerogative above his companions, but their voluntary yielding to him, for his merit ... If he lives, he is likely to meet with no greater obstacle [to the papacy], than [the jealousy] ... which accompanies those that come so young to be eminent.[25]

These characters, and the minute relations of day-to-day events with which Sidney's letters from Rome to his father are full, were belated attentions seeking to recover the Earl's favour; thinking it 'lesse Ill to fill my Paper, with the Trumpery I find in the Streets, then with the Fruites of my owne Imagination; I knowe tow well, what Opinion your Lordship hath of them'. Accordingly Sidney also attempted to find for his father products of Roman culture which would be acceptable to him; whether ornaments for his 'new Buildings [such] as Pictures, Statues, Marble Table, or of Mosaik Work', or, most importantly, books for the Earl's library. Sidney made a list of the books available which he thought would interest the Earl, and sent it to him for selections to be made.[26]

It was at the beginning of the summer season of 1661, when life in Rome became unpleasant on account of the 'Grossenesse of the Ayre', that Sidney was invited to lodge in the Villa de Belvedere at Frascati, 'one of the finest in Italy', by its owner Prince Pamphili. He gratefully accepted, and consequently turned down a second similar offer made the following week by Sachetti. From Belvedere he wrote soon after his arrival:

Heare are Walks and Fountaines in the greatest Perfection ... My conversation is with Birds, Trees, and Books: In theis last Moneths ... I have applied myself to studdy, a littell more then I have done formerly; and though one whoe beginns at my Age, cannot hope to make any considerable Progresse that Way, I find soe much Satisfaction in it, that for the future I shall very unwillingly ... put myself into any [other] Way of living ... Whatsoever hath bin formerly the Objects of my Thoughts and Desires, I have now [the] Intention of seeking very littell more than Quietnesse and Retirement.[27]

This was not, of course, the first of Sidney's 'retirements', nor was it to be his last. But these periods of study were probably important to the development of the self-confidence that prompted his eventual forays into political theory; forays which did not begin, so far as we know, until after the Restoration. In later letters from Belvedere Sidney wrote: 'I ... live now as a Hermite in a Palace. Nature, Art, and Treasure, can hardly make a Place more pleasant

[25] *Ibid.* p. 45.
[26] Collins, *Letters* pp. 701, 706, 709. There is, among the De Lisle MSS, a seventeenth-century Italian political tract, copied by hand in 'the Tuscan language', which is traditionally claimed as the work of Algernon, written or copied in Rome and then sent from there to please his father. Contrary to claims on its cover, the book is not in Algernon's hand, and there is no particular reason to connect it with him, but the text makes conspicuous mention of both Plato and the Athenian Academy, and so may be a work of Florentine or Tuscan neo-Platonism. This would make it appropriate to, and of interest for, Sidney family culture in general, and a translation would be informative. 'Discorso politico, in Lingua Toscana, miento authore' U1475 Z22.
[27] Collins, *Letters* pp. 718–19.

than this.' He hoped that the 'Knowledge of my Manner of Life' might make 'they, whoe the last Yeare at Whitehall, did exercise theire Tongues upon me, as a very unruly headed Man ... soe farre change theire Opinion of me ... as to believe me soe dull and lazy as to be fit for nothing. When that Opinion is well settled, I may hope to live quietly in England, and then shall think it a seasonable Time to Returne.'[28]

But despite his happiness at the Villa, Sidney felt the temporariness of that, as of everything else. 'I cannot', he wrote,

be soe sure of my Temper, as to knowe certainely how long this Manner of Life will please me. I cannot but rejoice a littell to finde, that when I wander as a Vagabond through the World, forsaken of my Freinds, poore, and knowne only to be a broken Limbe of a Ship-wrecked Faction; I yet find Humanity and Civility from thoes, whoe are in the Height of Fortune and Reputation. But I doe alsoe well knowe, I am in a strange Land, how farre thoes Civilityes doe extend, and that they are too aery, to feed or Cloath a Man.[29]

Indeed Sidney's restlessness and concern with his difficult personal situation was growing. He complained of his ignorance of what transpired in England: 'my Frends theire doe (as it seemes) think the knowledge of that, would disturbe my Solitude, by making me as much a Stranger unto all that is done theire, as to the Affaires of China'. The overriding problem, however, as the end of the previous quote made clear, was money.[30]

By his reported 'great equipage' in Rome as well as on his embassy, Sidney obviously had plenty of money after he left England. Whether this was his own, from the Strangford Trust, or drawn upon the public account in Denmark and Sweden, is uncertain.[31] What is clear is that it would not last forever, and Sidney was now in the uncomfortable position of needing financial consideration from a father whom he had deserted, neglected, and offended. Characteristically, what Algernon feared most was not so much being left to starve – there was no danger of that – but of being 'in a Place farre from Home ... wheare I am knowne to be of a Quality, which makes all lowe and meane Wayes of living shamefull and detestable'. Such thoughts drove him to conclude: 'My only Hope is that God will somme Way or other put an End to my Troubles, or my Life.'[32]

He was further exasperated by Leicester's deliberately sluggish response to these hints. Eventually, having heard through a third party (probably Sir John Temple) that the Earl's response to the suggestion that he help his son had

---

[28] *Ibid.* p. 721.
[29] *Ibid.* p. 720.
[30] *Ibid.* p. 720.
[31] Certainly he asked to be indemnified against prosecution for money drawn upon the public account in Scandinavia, as a condition of his accepting the offer to return home in 1677. Bath MSS Coventry Papers app. vol. II fol. 135.
[32] Collins, *Letters* p. 717.

been, in Algernon's words: 'I had made a Provision for myself, and discharged you of that Care', Sidney's long-maintained attempt at chattiness broke down:[33]

> I did intend to have said no more, but it is a folly to conceal the evils that oppress me . . . If theare be no difference in living, but he that hath Bred hath enough, I have some hopes . . . If theare be noe Reason for allowing me any Assistance out of the Family, as long as theare is a Possibility for me to live without it, I have discharged you. If thoes Helps are only to be given to thoes that have neither Spirit nor Industry . . . to help themselves, I pretend to deserve none . . . And as I have for somme Yeares runne through greater Streights, then, I believe any Man of my Condition hath done in England, since I was borne, without ever complaining . . . I shall with Silence suffer [what remains] . . . I confesse I thought another Conclusion might reasonably have been made upon what I had sayd . . . but I leave that to your Lordships Judgement and Conscience . . .[34]

In fact Sidney had here been forced to put his cards on the table, and that, as the Earl apparently felt, was a step in the right direction. A straightforward admission of dependence and request for aid would have opened Leicester's coffers, but it was the element of dependence implicit in the situation which Sidney could not bear, and so he continued the façade of basic self-sufficiency overlaid with heavy hints for some sort of 'voluntary' paternal gesture. It was a combination which Leicester found peculiarly irritating.

If Sidney was receiving any sort of independent income in Rome, it may have been from Swingfield and Boynton, access to the rents of which remained legally his until 1665. The Strangfords had, in 1660, as he later claimed, 'contrary to Law, justice, common honesty and humanity . . . violently seased [u]pon his horses, goods, household stuf[f] and that part of his stock which the Lady Strangford and hir family had not already eaten', at Sterry. His temper had not been improved by Strangford's arrest on charges of complicity with Booth's rebellion in 1659, and subsequent release upon Lady Strangford's use of his (Algernon's) name.[35] Some sort of search of Sidney's papers was inevitable since the Trust was paralysed without him, and he steadfastly refused to sign over his control until satisfied for the debts incurred in its execution. He was later to claim that among papers taken were deeds showing at least £800 to be due to him in rents from Swingfield and Boynton. Isabella offered him £500 in Rome, which he rejected indignantly, insisting on £1,500 as the bare minimum and a good deal less than he was owed (which sum he was later to put at closer to £6,000). '[If] they refuse to

---

[33] *Ibid.* pp. 703–4.
[34] 'Letters taken from the Sydney Papers' in *Works* pp. 30, 49.
[35] Kent R.O. De Lisle MS U1475 E28/5, Henning D. ed., *The House of Commons 1660–1690* (London 1983) III p. 450.

doe this, after having robbed me, railed at me, and in all respects dealt soe unworthily with me, I shall be innocent of what prejudice may befall them.'[36]

In England Sir John Temple politely pestered the Earl to show Algernon some sign of affection: 'You may please to consider, what a dangerous place he now resides in, what fates he shall meet withall, to work upon his discontents ... I confess I think ... that he may run such a course (for he speaks of going to serve against the Turk) as will deprive his friends of all means of his recovery.' Temple himself did his best for Algernon's affairs, advising him on what might please his father, and sending him deeds to sign in Rome which put into Leicester's hands Algernon's control of part of Swingfield, apparently in the hope that the Earl might take up the mortgage on it. But there was a limit to what Temple could do; he could not manage Sidney's messy affairs forever, and he could not reconcile him with his sister and brother-in-law. Eventually he was forced, in mid 1661, to return to Dublin, leaving the Earl of Thanet's mortgage still on the lands, Strangford having no intention of transferring them to his own land as had been agreed. This, said Sidney, is 'the sorest Mischiefe that ever fell upon me since I was borne'.[37]

In July 1661, however, Temple wrote from Ireland to Leicester to say that he was 'extreame glad to finde your Lordship's resolution to helpe your son Algernon'. In the same month Sidney received from the Earl a sum of money – though still no letter – at Frascati. He replied, thanking him for it, and asking him to make use of what remained of his beloved stables, where

theare weare good Store of Mares and Colts, and I believe, the best in England of that kind ... I beseech your Lordship hurry, they that have robbed me of allmost all I had, will not leave me any Thing, that is worth takeing; Before all be gone, I wish your Lordship would take soe many as you shall care to have.[38]

What Sidney desired most of all, however, was liberty from the tyranny of dependence upon others; what he therefore wanted most from his father was that the Earl might be prepared to lift the mortgages upon Swingfield and Boynton, to give him an independent regular income:

if you will please to Favour me soe much in the Ruin of my Fortune; as to take off that Burden, so that I might have that Land free for my subsistance; I shall as long as I live endeavour to deserve it ... [for] at my Age, growing very neare Forty, and giving Marks of declining by the colour of my Haire, it is Time that I had sommething which I may call my owne ... when Fortune hath taken from me all Meanes of gaining it, by my Industry.[39]

But it was not to be. Whether or not the Earl complied in the short term (we

[36] Blencowe, *Papers* pp. 192, 240.
[37] Blencowe, *Papers* p. 246; HMC De Lisle vi pp. 506–8, 512–14; Collins, *Letters* pp. 717, 721.
[38] HMC De Lisle vi p. 513; Collins, *Letters* p. 722.
[39] Collins, *Letters* p. 709.

do not know), by 1665 Sidney had lost the lands by Act of Parliament anyway.[40] He later stated that he received no regular maintenance from his father from 1642 to 1664;[41] it seems therefore that from 1665 onwards the Earl paid him a regular allowance, probably inspired by the loss of the lands in that year. It was then, in 1665, when the nightmare of complete dependence became real, that Sidney became involved in a campaign among the exiles to overthrow the English government.

[40] Cal. SPD 1665 26, 27 January; 1, 7, 10, 17 February.
[41] B.M. Eg. 1049.

$\twoheadleftarrow$ 11 $\twoheadrightarrow$

The exiles 1663–66

11.1 INTRODUCTION

By mid 1663 Sidney was angry enough to be gravitating towards political activity again. In England not only the regicides had been executed, but Vane too, and the religious persecutions had begun. Abroad Sidney himself had narrowly escaped a royalist assassination attempt, and was to survive a second; others of his exiled colleagues, despite living in a 'state of siege', were not to be so lucky. Sidney's 'voluntary exile' had become involuntary; his request to make a private visit to Penshurst had been denied.[1]

As Sidney was to find, to his chagrin, individual reactions to this situation varied. Throughout the next three years, of all the exiles, he proved the foremost advocate of action, and – in the difficult circumstances under which they operated – the least particular about the means to be employed to bring it about. Sidney's impatience, brusqueness, and lack of scruple grew to alienate an increasing number of his colleagues; their naïvety and ineffectuality grew to increasingly infuriate him. To Sidney it seemed that Rome was burning and his colleagues would only fiddle about making moral stipulations about the fire brigade. To many of them it came to seem that the means Sidney was prepared to employ, and his dictatorial style in employing them, constituted an affront to the cause itself.

As Sidney struggled through these frustrations in practice, he set out his political vision in theory. From the *Court Maxims* emerges the centrality, to Sidney's feelings of urgency at this time, of the English religious persecutions. Although the *Maxims* is an argument against monarchy in general, people could at least in the short term live under monarchy. What was killing hundreds of 'God's people', and what made the Restoration regime accord-

---

[1] 'The first that I ever did ask, and the least that I ever can ask (I meane Assurance of being permitted to live quietly for a few Months at Penshurst) not having bin granted, I am like to make fewe Requests, for the future.' Sidney, Brussels, 1 December 1663 Collins, *Letters* p. 275.

ingly a 'work of the Devill', were the persecutions unleashed by the Clarendon Code.

It is impossible to appreciate what Sidney felt to be at stake in this period without trying to correct the effect of historical hindsight. One certainly cannot suppress a smile at the claims which hopeful exiles like William Say – severely out of touch as they usually were – were inclined to make of the 'great party' which they could expect to rise for them at home. Say did not see, in 1665, how Charles II could possibly survive when 'the whole body of the people are so enraged against him; and many very many of the considerablest p[er]sons in England doe now apply to and courte the phanatiques'. Yet the English government themselves took the threat far more seriously than we are now inclined to. Aside from the Dublin and Yorkshire plots in 1663, reports by government agents in 1664 and 1665 of networks of 'anabaptists' throughout the countryside, '200 horsemen [ready to rise] in Suffolk', and 'a list of size subscribed by 52 officers to Ludlowe' are legion.[2]

In 1665 the government had only been in power for five years, significantly less time than many exiles and regicides themselves beforehand, and therefore no proof at all, as they knew better than anybody, against eventual internal discontent and collapse. Unable to see ahead, the exiles looked behind them, to precedents like that of the Marian exiles, who had not only successfully waited out a period of English tyranny and persecution from abroad, but returned home to produce a religious revolution in Scotland that changed the face of British politics forever, not least in helping to spark off the English Civil War, the beginning of the exiles' own cause.

Indeed historians have allowed themselves to be led, partly perhaps by the unanimous joy of 1660, into severely overestimating the security and stability of the restored Stuart regime as a whole, something which any close study of either the gathering crises of Charles II's reign, or the final débâcle of James's, should be sufficient warning against. What indeed did the Restoration really restore? Certainly not Charles I – and not Charles II either since he had never been in government to *be* restored. Not the basis for a degree of eventual political stability or consensus; that had to wait until 1688. Not even poor old Clarendon, for more than a short period overridden by the reactionary vengeance of a younger generation in Parliament, and the equally distasteful dilettantism of an equally trying younger generation among Charles II's ministers. By the end of 1667 Clarendon and Sidney had become fellow exiles in Montpellier.

In fact the 'Restoration' administration was not restored, but brand new, and young too; as Sidney put it: 'a parliament full of lewd young men chosen by a furious people in spite to the puritans, whose severity had disgusted

[2] Ludlow, *Voyce* p. 1065; PRO SP29 no. 109 p. 93, no. 101 p. 66; CSPD 1664–5 pp. 148–9.

them'.[3] As such it had to take its chances, in distinctly turbulent times, along with the rest. No one understood this, and the inherent instability of the situation, better than the King himself. Unable to believe his good fortune in 1660, Charles II spent his first year getting up at 4 a.m. every morning, determined to use every minute allowed to him. This gave way to a more enduring principle of kingship: long-term survival.[4] As soon as that priority had fallen from the throne, with the death of Charles himself, the days of the 'restored' regime as a whole were numbered.

Indeed this regime, centred upon two one-time exiles corrupted by foreign women and foreign religion, was to prove as narrowly based, as politically off-balance and religiously radical, and so as inherently unstable, as its predecessors from 1649 to 1660. For this reason it was to meet a similarly ignominious fate in unanimous rejection in 1688. It is quite wrong to blame that 'revolution' solely on James II personally, although it suited both Tories and whigs to skirt the wider constitutional implications at the time by doing so. The 'revolution' of 1688 was in fact the true Restoration; a second attempt at the sort of moderately conservative Clarendonian settlement which had eluded the nation in 1660. By sharply restricting, rather than extending, the provisions for liberty of conscience in operation at the time of its occurrence; by establishing satisfactory guarantees against further innovation from the throne; and by centring itself around a known conservative protestant, the anti-republican anti-French Prince of Orange, the settlement of 1688 successfully established the basis for a government which truly expressed the fundamental conservatism, intolerance, and anti-catholicism which were the bases of English parliamentary policy in 1640–8, 1660–3, 1672–3, and 1687–8. Moreover, it did so without the reactionary overkill which had helped to destabilise the 1660 attempt; without, that is, the alienation of a large part of the élite whose acquiescence had been instrumental in making it possible in the first place. In 1689 the Tories, however uncomfortable, were kept on the bandwagon: in 1662 the Restoration had helped narrow and undercut itself by throwing the 'Presbyterians' (as well as all other non-Anglican groups) off. Consequently it was only after 1688, not 1660, that religion ceased to be one of the major concerns and the major destabilising factor in English politics; it was only after 1688, not 1660, that the ruling élite in England recovered the level of unanimity and cohesion which it had lost between 1640 and 1642, with the disastrous result of the civil war. It was only after 1688, not 1660, that England began its 'growth of stability', dominated by the cohesion of, and deference to, a recovered, enriched, and unchallenged aristocracy. And it was in 1688, not 1660, that

---

[3] *Discourses* p. 502.
[4] Miller J., 'The Potential for Absolutism in Later Stuart England' in *History* vol. 69 p. 195.

Sidney's fellow republicans in England and in Holland saw their hopes of tipping the prevailing political and religious situation their way finally dashed permanently. England's second seventeenth-century 'revolution' was in fact nothing more or less than the final victory by England's conservative parliamentary élite over the non-parliamentary debris remaining from the first. That debris included monarchs as well as nonconformists and republicans; the events of 1688 were a response to an alliance between the two former.[5]

Parliament, rather than the monarchy, had been the conservative obstacle to political and religious change, and later toleration, in England throughout the period 1625–88; it had had to be purged to allow radical change in 1648; it had reasserted its traditional religious conservatism in 1662 and 1672; it had to be manipulated and bypassed again to achieve full religious toleration in the last years of James II's reign. In the reaction against that final attempt, Parliament had at last established its own solution and the era of innovation, religious strife, and instability, 1625–88, Personal Rule, Republic, and Restoration, was gradually superseded.

In practical terms, then, the events of 1660–2 constituted not a conservative 'Restoration' (though that was the intention), but in fact a Reaction: narrow, ideological, and temporary; the flip side of the same coin of political/religious instability as 1625–60, revolving around the same issues. These continued to resurface until the final settlement within the ruling élite of the grounds for political, religious, and social control, and the mechanism by which debate would be conducted (the rage of party superseding the clash of steel) in 1688. What it restored were the problems and the instability of seventeenth-century political and religious life; what it did not restore was harmony and settlement.

The ingredients of the 'Restoration' regime's basic instability, in particular its religious instability, were variously illustrated in the years 1661–2, 1672–3, 1678–83, and 1686–8. The principal difference between the destabilising extra-parliamentary radicalism of 1647–60, and that of 1660–88, was that in the latter case much of it came from above rather than below: from the Crown. We have accordingly perhaps been slower to recognise it for what it was, and make the comparisons with the 1640–60 period that can be made. Seventeenth-century radicals themselves were quicker to recognise it; Sidney and Stubbe, for instance, supported Charles II's Declaration of Indulgence in 1672, because it was, complete with a Dutch war, the closest thing to a return

---

[5] In 1688 some sort of Anglo–Dutch political federation was at last achieved by the forces of monarchy, not republicanism, as had been attempted in 1651, 1659, and 1665. This sealed the fate of republicanism as a political force in both countries. In this fact lies the historical illegitimacy of the appropriation of the republican Sidney, a product of the first revolution, for the propaganda purposes of the second.

by the government to the religious and foreign policies of the English Commonwealth that England was ever to see again.[6] The major difference was that the 1672 religious policy was more radical than that of the Rump, and so found itself the subject of even more parliamentary outrage. The man Charles II would have needed to get the Declaration through the House in 1672 was Colonel Pride. Instead, mindful of the hard lessons of the past, he chose to back off. When, later in the decade, he found himself confronting Parliament again over an issue on which he could not bring himself to back down, he endured the most dangerous period of his reign, and one which grew to produce the widespread public fear of 1641 again. Many of the ingredients of 1641 were there again in 1679: the chief minister impeached; Parliament angry and hostile; a Scots rebellion; the breakdown of censorship; and the full-blooded resurrection of protestant panic over a popish plot. What pulled the nation back from the brink of civil war was, first and foremost, public memory of the previous experience of civil war. This time it was not the King, but the nation at large that remembered the lessons of the past and backed off. This left the civil-war-age insurrectionaries like Sidney exposed and they were swept up in the tide of the (second) loyalist reaction.[7]

The period of the 'Restoration', then, from 1660 to 1688, was not a *fait accompli*, but a fragile and unstable situation in which many of the political and religious issues of the 1625–60 period remained alive, and undecided. Accordingly Sidney and his friends were to try to influence the direction of Restoration policy by attempted radical alliance with the Crown on some occasions (1672, 1687), and against it on others (1665, 1679–83). After 1660, whether in England or in exile, when domestic or foreign affairs threw up an opportunity, there still seemed to Sidney everything left to fight for.

The chapters which follow will draw extensively on two manuscripts recently discovered by Blair Worden: Edmund Ludlow's *A Voyce From The Watchtower*, and Algernon Sidney's *Court Maxims*. Both have immeasurably increased our knowledge of Sidney's concerns from 1663 to 1666. Both

---

[6] This reflects Stubbe's and Sidney's scepticism; for them the means of politics were flexible in relation to the ends. This was not the case with all Interregnum-era men who supported liberty of conscience, however. Andrew Marvell regarded the 1670 Conventicle Act, which Charles II's Declaration was designed to circumvent, as the 'Quintessence of arbitrary malice', but nevertheless called the King's own attempt to dispense with it 'a Piece of absolute universal Tyranny'. (Wallace, *Destiny* pp. 186–90.) The comparison of Charles II's policy to that of the Rump was recently made by Christopher Hill in *The Experience of Defeat* (1984) p. 270, but Sidney himself made it first – as we will see in ch. 14.

[7] Other historians who have studied both the civil war and the Exclusion Crisis have arrived at the same general conclusion. After 1600, said J. H. M. Salmon (*Religious Wars* p. 123), 'all the conflicts of the preceding age were implicit in the new settlement, and only the king's political genius kept them temporally quiescent. The position of Charles II was not unlike that of Catherine de Medici before the onset of the Religious Wars. The balance of the constitution was far from clear and religious hostilities threatened its uneasy equilibrium'.

have also changed forever the (whig) political and religious picture we had of both men.

The nature of the change in Ludlow's case, and the questions raised in Sidney's, are devastatingly demonstrated in Dr Worden's introduction to the published section of the *Voyce*. We now know that Ludlow's *Voyce* is the manuscript upon which Ludlow's *Memoirs* were originally based, and that the *Memoirs* are a posthumous fabrication, less than a quarter of the length of the original and entirely different in tone. They were first published by their probable creator, John Toland, in 1698. The principal effect of Toland's rewrite, notes Worden, was to excise 'the spiritual dimension of the manuscript', which 'would have wrecked the *Memoirs'* chances of political success in the post 1688 age'. There is a great chasm between the measured 'country whig' Ludlow of the *Memoirs* and the biblically obsessed Puritan enthusiast of the *Voyce*.[8] It is from the same rediscovered world of exiled Puritan enthusiasm that Sidney's *Court Maxims* emerges.

The *Maxims*, too, is, as I have said, different in tone and more religiously 'enthusiastic' than the later-published *Discourses*. This is particularly important since Sidney's *Discourses*, too, were published in 1698, probably also by John Toland, and no manuscript survives to check their veracity. Yet I believe both texts to be genuine, tampered with, if at all, only superficially. That Sidney wrote both is shown conclusively by the countless specific repetitions between them, and between each and Sidney's other written work, both in style and substance. The difference in tone reflects (as we must by now expect from Sidney) the difference in their context, their intended audience, and above all their political purpose. As in the following two chapters I will show how the language of the *Court Maxims* arose from the need to persuade the Dutch, as well as the 'godly' English; so in *Algernon Sidney and the Restoration Crisis* it will be demonstrated that Sidney (like Locke) answered Filmer in the language of the natural-law theory Filmer was himself attacking. That language was undergoing a revival in London from 1678 to 1683 as an effect of the revival of the civil-war independency from which it had previously grown; this itself in part underlay the decision to republish Filmer.

Sidney was thus capable of speaking in several political languages (and in the case of Filmer he added those of classical republicanism and ancient constitutionalism – both also attacked by Filmer – to natural-law theory). The tone and content of both of these two works, however, are echoed elsewhere in Sidney's life and writings: he was to repeat the interest-theory argument of the *Maxims* to Barillon in 1679, and its religious enthusiasm in his *Last Paper* and *Apology* in 1683; the tone of the *Discourses* in turn is like the tone of his letters to his father. The change in tone was not, in other words,

---

[8] Worden A. B ed., Ludlow E., *A Voyce From The Watch Tower* (1978) Intro.

an effect of the passage of time *per se*; all of these modes of expression were part of Sidney's permanent political arsenal. As this study as a whole will make clear, what is more remarkable than the difference in tone between the two works is the continuity of substance. Not only their general sceptical republicanism, but a host of particular arguments, examples, paragraphs, and turns of phrase are shared between them. The religious content of the *Maxims* is not different from that of the *Discourses* (in both it is Platonic), it simply receives more emphasis, and at a higher emotional volume, as is appropriate to Sidney's task of opposing the English religious persecutions in the former. Finally, the range of their sources is fundamentally consistent, but there are some interesting differences in weighting and visibility among them. The *Court Maxims* makes heavier use of the Greeks (especially Plato and Aristotle), and of Grotius, in conjunction with biblical sources, for its task of morally arming the Christian soldier. The Romans (Livy and Tacitus) appear, with Machiavelli, but their role is ambiguous and Sidney's use of Machiavelli in particular is often disguised. In the *Discourses* the Greeks, Scripture, and Grotius remain crucial, but by then Livy, Tacitus, and Machiavelli have moved openly to the forefront (in response, again, to Filmer's own attacks on the Roman Republic), and the basis for Sidney's 'Roman Whiggism' has been laid. Had Sidney written again later, the weighting, and accompanying tone would probably have been different again; but the message as always the same: a call to rebellion.

11.2 SWITZERLAND, FLANDERS, AND GERMANY, 1663–64

In mid 1663 Sidney passed through Switzerland on his way to Flanders and the Netherlands. In its customary whitewash, his later *Apology* spoke only of the time 'When the care of my private affairs brought me into Flanders and Holland, anno 1663.' Yet the implication that his movement had no political content from the outset is belied by the record, in both Vevey and Geneva, if indeed it is not sufficiently cast into doubt by the visit to Vevey itself.

Sidney arrived in Vevey in the autumn of 1663 and stayed there with Ludlow and his fellow exiles (including Nicholas Love, Andrew Broughton, John Lisle, William Say, and others) for three weeks. The reasons he gave there for his journey, and indeed as usual the principal content of his conversation, were political. Ludlow recorded:

The Divisions of our Enemyes, began to heighten ye hopes of friends touching ye Approaching of our deliverance, In so much, that Colonell Algernon Sidney ... having bin Instrumentall to conclude ye [Northern] peace ... and having chosen Rome for his retirement as a place that might render him less Suspected to ye Usurpers in England; Now thinkes it seasonable to draw towards his Native Country, in Expectation of an Opportunity wherein he might be more Active for their Service; and in his way was pleased to favour us with a visit ... expressing himselfe to us, w[i]th much affection and freindship; and to ye Publique w[i]th much honour and faithfulness not in ye least declyning to owne us, and ye despised Cause for wch we suffred.[9]

Sidney charmed Ludlow by presenting him with a finely crafted pair of Italian pistols, and subsequently by lending his eloquence and 'quality' to the performance for the exiles of a 'signal service' in neighbouring Berne, which he visited 'in his Way to flaunders, where for ye Ensuing Wynter he intended to repose himselfe'. In Berne Sidney spoke to two high officials of the magistracy of Berne canton

assuring [them] that all ye good people of England would take the Civillityes and kindness extended to us [the English exiles at Vevey], as done to themselves ... [and] upon the whole our Noble friend ... by ye freedome and Ingenuity of his discourse ... of ye Estate of our Affaires in England, gave [Mr de Graffery ye Avoyer] such satisfaction, that as he Judged he left him in a temper to add to the favours they had already done us, rather than in ye least to wthdraw from them.[10]

It was in the same fortifying Swiss republican atmosphere (by the end of this year Sidney had visited all three major European republics: Venice, Switzerland, and the Netherlands) that Sidney visited the Calvinist Academy at the university in nearby Geneva. There he was asked again, as in Copenhagen (one begins to wonder exactly who asked whom!) to sign an inscription in the visitor's book. This has survived,[11] and it leaves no doubt about his political mood: SIT SANGUINIS ULTOR JUSTORUM (Let there be revenge for the blood of the just).[12]

Two months later, at the beginning of December, Sidney was at Brussels, from where he wrote his father two letters. The first was a recapitulation of his involvement with the Strangfords from 1652 to 1654, supplied at the Earl's request, in the face of another legal action.[13] The second concerned 'a Businesse ... relating unto myself'. Sidney had been informed that 'young Culpeper' (Strangford's half-brother and steward)[14] had a command in 'a regiment of thoes Men reported to be raised for the Service of the Emperor'. Culpepper advised that Sidney himself 'might have a good Employment' by a command in the same service. While deeply suspicious of the 'Reallity in the Proposition' Sidney was sufficiently interested to ask his father to make further inquiries. If it were true, he said

[9] Ludlow E., 'A Voyce From the Watchtower' Bodleian MS Engl. Hist. C.487 p. 977.

[10] Ludlow, 'Voyce' p. 978.

[11] Other English signatures in the same place include those of Essex (Robert Devereux the third Earl), Halifax, and Manchester, and both Henry Neville (Sidney's colleague's father) and James Harrington (1635).

[12] Neville's signature is in a different book, the 'Album Amicorum' of Jean Durant, calvinist refugee from the massacre of St Bartholemew and friend of Beza. Sidney's inscription is reproduced photographically in Charles Borgeaud, *Histoire de l'Universite de Geneve: l'Academie de Calvin 1559–1798* vol. I pp. 442–3 (see also pp. 147, 149).

[13] HMC De Lisle VI pp. 520–3.

[14] Henning D., *The House of Commons 1660–1690* (1983) vol. III p. 450.

I can ascribe it only to the Desire that thoes in Power may have, to send away thoes that are suspected by them ... [if so] I will undertake to transport a good strong Boddy of the best Officers and Soldiers of our old Army, both Horse and Foot ... and it will be very suitable unto my Intention, whoe as I told you in a Letter about three weeks since, have Thoughts of passing the next Summer as a Volunteere in Hungary.

In this letter Sidney also asked his father to communicate the prospect of his renewed military employment to 'the Lord Sunderland', which implies that he may have met his nephew as he journeyed to Italy the previous year accompanied by Henry Sidney and William Penn (the latter just emerged from Saumur).[15]

Needless to say the English government did not feel tempted by Sidney's proposition. This was wise, since it is far from clear what Sidney – who communicated the prospect of this command to Ludlow – really intended to do with the troops had he been granted them.[16] This initial approach to Flanders and Holland in 1663 may indeed have had its background in the subsequently failed Yorkshire plot of that year, which had its own Dutch connection, and the defeated remnants of which subsequently made their way to Holland in early 1664.[17]

We certainly know from Sidney's own account that he moved on to Holland after Flanders at this time. He later recounted of this period to his quaker friend Furly in Holland:

[In retirement] I [had] lived almost three years, seldome much disturbed, but in the end I found that it was an ill-grounded peace that I enjoyed, and could have no rest in my owne spirite, because I lived only to myself, and was in no wayes usefull unto God's people, my countrey, and the world. This consideration, joined with thoes dispensations of providence which I observed, and judged favorable unto the designes of good people, brought me out of my retirement into theis parts. [But] The spirits of those who understood seasons farre better than I, seemed as yet not to be fully prepared. This obliged me againe to withdraw myself.

Sidney accordingly withdrew, sometime during 1664, to Germany; perhaps seeking military service from some German princes, or the Emperor. (He was later to remark in the *Discourses* [p. 470]: 'The present emperor ... passed his time in setting songs to music with a wretched Italian eunuch, when he ought to have been at the head of a brave army, raised to oppose the Turks in the year 1664.') By the end of the year he was living at Augsburg, and it was to that city that a group of royalist assassins, led by Andrew White, activated by news of growing political intrigues among the exiles, were despatched to kill him in April 1665.[18]

[15] Collins, *Letters* p. 725.
[16] Ludlow, 'Voyce' p. 1004.
[17] Walker J., 'The republican party in England from the Restoration to the revolution' Manchester Ph.D. 1931 pp. 142–3.
[18] Ludlow, *Memoirs* II p. 382; 'Voyce' p. 1063; Sidney, *Apology* p. 2.

'The asperity of this persecution', Sidney later recorded in his *Apology*,

obliged me to seeke the protection of somme forraine princes and, being then in the strength of my age, had reputation enough to have gained honourable employments; but all my designes were broken by letters and messages from this court, so as none durst entertaine me; and when I could not comprehend the grounds of dealing with me in such a way ... A man of quality, whoe well knew the temper of the court, explained the mistery unto me, by letting me know, that *I was distinguished from the rest, because it was knowne, that I could not be corrupted*. Noe man could have thought it strange, if this had cast me into the utmost extreamityes; and perhaps occasions of being revenged would not have been wanting, if I had sought them; but, instead of that, I cast myself into unsuspected retirement, in the most remote part of France...[19]

If the italicised section of this quote shows Sidney most shamelessly drawing up the terms of his own mythology, the last sentence shows him at his least truthful. For it omits the small matter of his leadership, over the eighteen months before his retirement to France, of the exiles' design to invade England and overthrow the government. The 'fower bloodhounds' sent to hunt him at Augsburg missed their mark, because by April 1665 'through mercey Colonell Algernon Sidney the prey they sought after was removed to Holland before'. Sidney had broken his second retirement at the turn of the year. As he explained to Furly once back in the Netherlands:

I found farre less satisfaction in my second retirement than the first, and, by the advice of friends, am once more comme upon the stage. I doe not knowe what success God will give unto our undertakings, but I am certaine I can have no peace in my owne spirite, if I doe not endeavour by all meanes possible to advance the interest of God's people. Others may judge from whence this temper doth proceed, better than I can; if it be from God, he will make it prosper, if from the heat and violence of my owne disposition, I and my designes shall perish. I desire you and all our friends to seeke God for me, praying him to defend me from outward enemyes, but more especially from thoes that are within me; and that he would give me such a steady knowledge of truth, as I may be constantly directed in seeking that which is truly good.[20]

11.3 THE NETHERLANDS, 1665

Algernon Sidney went then to Holland and pressd De Wit [to think] of invading England, and shewed him great probabilities of success. But in that ... his hatred of the King and Monarchy blinded him for the people were not then under such Discontents as ... could have been wrought on to a Revolt.[21]

By late 1664 relations between England and the Netherlands were rapidly deteriorating towards war. From the *Court Maxims*, part of which was written in Holland after the results of de Ruyter's expedition to Guinea

[19] Sidney, *Apology* p. 4.
[20] Blencowe, *Sidney* pp. 259–60.
[21] Burnet, add MS 63,057 vol. 1 252.

became known (late 1664), but before the final outbreak of war (22 March 1665),[22] it would seem that Sidney arrived back in the Netherlands around the turn of the year. Even while in Germany he had been instrumental in encouraging initial exile contacts with the Dutch. As Ludlow noted, when William Say – a colleague of Sidney's on the Foreign Affairs Committee in 1652–3 – suggested that the time had come to 'feele the pulse of ye Dutch, touching their uniting wth ye honest pty in England against Charles Steward ... he was encouraged by Col. Algernon Sidney a pson full of affection and zeale for ye publique'. Somebody in the Netherlands was accordingly written to and 'made a very hopefull progress therein; Insomuch that Mr Say upon the Advice of Col Sidney repaires to Holland'. Whether Sidney was already there to meet him is uncertain. 'Coll. Sidney', said Ludlow, 'had bin long very earnest with me to meete him in some place for ye carrying on of this designe, and had appointed to remove his station to Basle [northern Switzerland], in Expectation that I and some other freinds should have come to him thither ... But that wch was ye bone of contention betweene us, was touching the Tearmes on wch to Engage wth ye Hollanders.'[23]

This term 'bone of contention' should be seen, in its long-term context, as an all-too-rare example of Ludlow's capacity for understatement. Ludlow's doubts about the Dutch, as he expressed them, had three dimensions: specific, general, and what he called 'collaterall consideration[s]'.

His specific grievance concerned the regicides Okey, Barkstead, and Corbet, who had been extradited from Holland in 1662 and executed upon their return. In fact after the extradition treaty with England was signed in 1662, the Dutch republican government had by and large successfully sought to avoid fulfilling its literal terms. Since the breakdown of relations with England during 1664 the danger had lessened further and the number of exiles gravitating to the Low Countries had increased accordingly. The particular tragedy of Okey, Corbet, and Barkstead had occurred as the result of the outfoxing of De Witt and effective kidnapping of the regicides by the English ambassador at the Hague, Downing.[24]

Yet Ludlow held the Dutch responsible for their surrender: 'The blood of any one pson [*sic*] unavenged pollutes a whole Land', and anyone who contracts with such magistrates 'becomes a ptaker [*sic*] of their sin'. More generally, Ludlow could not (or did not want to) convince himself that God was really with the Hollanders, 'they being looked upon as those who preferr their Trade, before the honr of God and Christ'. Finally, there were the

---

[22] 'the business of Guiny succeeding very contrary to expectation, and other obstructions occurring, the [English] King endeavours to continue the peace'. *Court Maxims* p. 177; On de Ruyter's coup in Guinea see Geyl P., *The Netherlands* pt II pp. 84–5.

[23] Ludlow, 'Voyce' p. 1056.

[24] Walker J., 'Republican party' pp. 121–53; Rowen, *John De Witt* (Princeton 1978) p. 454.

'collaterall considerations': prospects of safety in the Netherlands worried him.[25]

Sidney found Ludlow's reservations not simply irrelevant, but positively perverse, and a threat to the design. 'Nothing', he wrote to Ludlow, 'would so much contribute to a peace between them [the Dutch] and England as the Apprehension that was upon them' that the destruction of 'ye kings pty' in England would only throw them into the hands of those who wished to avenge the handing over of the three regicides. Accordingly Sidney required from Ludlow not simply the suppression of his private doubts but positively 'pressed the giving of [the Dutch republican government] satisfaction in this pticcular, as the letting them know, that I [Ludlow] looked upon that Act as done [only by their domestic political opponents] the Prince of Orange his pty'.

Had Sidney been content, Ludlow claimed, with 'ye saying nothing of it at present ... there had bin some hopes of Accord; but he insisting upon it as a ridiculous thinge to looke backward, and as unjust and unchristian to Joyne wth them as freinds, and to expect their Assistance', while maintaining private reservations, Ludlow found he could not agree. He concluded: 'those who looked not upon it wth such an Eye I left to act according to their Consciences, choosing to wayt for what the Lord would bringe forth by this Extraordinary Providence'. What to Sidney, then, was a God-sent opportunity for action, was to Ludlow a sign which could be relied upon to further reveal itself independently of human activity. Already 'Divisions', which all agreed had been responsible for the destruction of the cause in 1659, were threatening its revival.[26]

Sidney's response to Ludlow, consistent with his temperament and relativism (the need to take the Dutch on their own terms, and the folly of 'looking backward'), was also determined by the political problems he faced in Holland. Burnet recorded:

Algernoon Sidney ... came to de Wit, and pressed him to think of an invasion of England and Scotland ... and they were bringing many officers to Holland to join in the undertaking. They dealt also with some in Amsterdam, who were particularly sharpened against the King, and were for turning England again into a Commonwealth. The matter was for some time in agitation in the Hague.

The King's spy in Flanders, Aphra Behn, reported, too, that 'Collnll [*sic*] Sidney is in great esteem with Dewitt.' However, De Witt's first concern with the proposal was: 'what would the effect be of turning England into a

[25] Ludlow, 'Voyce' pp.1056–7.
[26] Ludlow, 'Voyce' p.1056; For a view on Sidney's disagreements with Ludlow based on the printed Ludlow *Memoirs* see Ashley M., *John Wildman* pp.199–200.

Commonwealth, if it could possibly be brought about, but the ruin of Holland?'[27]

This was the first of Sidney's two great problems: the historical legacy of the Rump Parliament. As Sidney knew better than anyone, De Witt had good reason to fear a revival of English republicanism, for the Dutch had suffered their most damaging war of the century at their hands. Accordingly the overriding consideration for Sidney and, as we will see, the great wheel upon which the *Court Maxims* was to turn, was the need not simply for unanimity between the Dutch and English republicans, but to argue a precise unity of 'interest' between them, essential to the survival of *both*, in the face of an identical unity of 'interest' between their two respective enemies, the houses of Stuart and Orange. This emphasis on the Stuart–Orange connection, apart from its clear basis in fact, was a shrewd pitch by Sidney at internal Dutch republican government sentiment. The Stuart–Orange alliance had contributed importantly to the growing fear of Orangist monarchical aspirations which had helped to put De Witt and the republicans in power in 1650 in the first place. It was to contribute equally to the same sentiment (and its renewed exploitation by Sidney) following the new Stuart–Orange match of 1677.[28]

Accordingly Sidney argued in the *Court Maxims* that:

The last war [between the Dutch and English Republics] was not brought on by a contrariety of interests ... but both found themselves unawares involv'd in it by a fatality that none could understand. The effects of it were so pernicious to both, that they were endangered and we destroyed by it.[29]

The Stuart–Orange alliance was personified in Holland, Sidney said, by Downing, who laboured, assisted by De Witt's enemies the 'Orange faction', to undermine the internal political unity of the Netherlands itself, as well as the unity between the Dutch and English republicans, thereby weakening the Dutch war effort on two fronts. 'The fanatics', says the English Courtier in the *Court Maxims*,

are fatter of spirit than formerly, and could not let slip so fair an opportunity of destroying us [as] when engag'd in a war with Holland ... [so we must] lull [the De Wit government] asleep, and divert them from using their present power against us 'till we have strengthened the Orange faction and destroy'd the Phanatiques.[30]

Indeed the whole object of this section of the *Maxims*, which praises

[27] Burnet, add MS 63,057 p. 393; Cameron W. J., *New Light on Aphra Behn* (1961) p. 73; PRO SP29 171 fol. 65; Burnet's own visit to the Netherlands had, he admitted, permanently influenced both his religious and political views, in the directions of toleration and (even, for a while) republicanism respectively. See his account in add MS 63,057 I fols. 186–9.

[28] Smit J. W., 'The Netherlands and Europe in the seventeenth and eighteenth centuries' in Kossman E. H. and Bromley J. S. eds., *Britain and The Netherlands in Europe and Asia* (1968) p. 21, cf. Geyl, *Netherlands* pt II p. 57.

[29] *Court Maxims* p. 172.

[30] *Maxims* p. 164.

hopefully De Witt's ability to see through such tactics, is to produce that action: to send the Dutch thundering into war, with the English republicans riding on their backs. This section was thus written before the final declaration of war in March 1665, and when Downing was still present in the country, and shows that the *Maxims* was written to convince a sceptical Dutch government, as well as an English republican audience. It describes a threat to the Anglo–Dutch republican unity it seeks to establish.

The methods Sidney attributed to Downing's attempts to sow division between the Dutch and English republicans centred on his harping on two principal negative themes in the history of their relationship: the 1652–3 war; and the delivery of Okey, Barkstead, and Corbet. This latter event, of course, said Sidney in the *Maxims*, was 'Not to be imputed to the States Generall, who were surprised and cheated by Downing', working in conjunction with 'some of the Orange faction'.

It will be clear, then, why Ludlow's attitude seemed to Sidney to risk jeopardising the whole design. Unfortunately, however, his absence threatened to do so even more. For the second and other great obstacle to the acceptance of Sidney's proposals by De Witt was Dutch scepticism about the exiles' ability to deliver. In Burnet's words again: 'there was no reason to think that, while the parliament was so firm to the King, any discontents could be carried so far as to a general rising, which these men undertook for'. These suspicions were deepened when Ludlow's continued non-appearance seemed to testify to some disunity among the exiles themselves. The Dutch accordingly fastened on Ludlow's absence as a pretext for delaying concrete commitment until he appeared.[31]

Their early negotiations with the Dutch, Sidney and Say performed through their old acquaintance Lord Nieupoort, ambassador to the Rump during the last attempt at Anglo–Dutch republican co-operation, as they 'were enterteyned at and lay private at a country house of ... Newports'. It was from here that Say wrote to Ludlow of the size and strength of the Dutch fleet, begging him to come: 'England, Ireland, and Scotland will be Engaged for you.' He insisted that the Dutch government were not to blame for Okey, Corbet, and Barkstead, and that 'ye present most Considerable pson at ye Hague, did lately very much Enquire after you...' Say also reported that plans were afoot to spring Lambert from prison, and that the Dutch wanted Ludlow, Lambert, or both at the head of the invading regiment.[32] English government sources, meanwhile, reported that 'Sidney and Ludlow (who is now sent for to reside here) are to be the chief'.

On 22 May Say wrote again and this time his letter was accompanied by one from Sidney. Say confirmed 'ye conjunction of Scotland wth England on

[31] Burnet, add MS 63,057 p.393.
[32] 'Voyce' pp.1058–9, 1065.

ye tearmes aforesayd, and that they are ready to rise at 5 dayes warning; that a very considerable Body is ready to draw together in ye North, and also in ye West of England', that 4,000 foot was being assembled in Holland, and that they planned to land at 'Newcastle wch is promissed to be delivered to them'. He informed Ludlow that he was sending Colonel Bisco to him to persuade him to come.[33] Sidney's letter, up to a point, 'was much to the same effect', but in addition 'many other thinges [were] said too long for a letter'. Among them, Ludlow recorded, Sidney

having expressed his dissatisfaction, in that I had not hitherto psued his advice . . . he was pleased to acquaint me, that ye duty he owed to his Country, and the profession he made to be a Lover of it obliged him to tell me, that since he came into those ptes he found all thinges suitable to his Expectation; [but] . . . that ye only obstruction he discoverd proceeds from mistrust that at heart we have other Counsels, and the small appearance of freinds doth encrease it, wch is caused by Ludlow . . . thinges are ready, ptyes will appear in ye North, the West, and London, Newcastle will be delivered . . . Ludlow is named for this, if he will not harken unto freinds, he may probably overthrow ye designe, he can best Judge whether that will prove for his honr or Advantage; I know Mr Say writes of sending Bisco to you; but that will not doe the worke, too much time will be spent, if you will doe any thinge effectuall, you must make all Imaginable hast; and [closed by] giving some pticcular Instructions relating to my Journey . . .[34]

'These', Ludlow concluded, 'I looked upon as Lowd Calls, yet I could not get over that of ye blood of our frends . . .'
    Soon

other Letters . . . I received thence intimated, that by reason of the Divisions that are amongst our pty, there is not ground for so great hopes; Notwthstanding which, my correspondents and frends in Holland are so possitive in their former advise for my repaire unto them; that the little patiense they had, began now to be converted into passion, Coll Sydney [now] chardging me upon that acco[un]t wth not only disliking the meanes, but the thinge itself, to wit, the publique cause, and going on, adds these words
    I leave you to consider of this . . . and when you finde that wch some doe now plainly see, that this proceeding of yors hath stopped . . . freinds in their designe, and proved ye greatest service to the king of England, that he hath this many yeares received from any man, you will be able to Judge, whether it had bin better for you to have hearkned unto ye Advises and desires of freinds resolved upon by Comon consent after maturre deliberation, and that knowledge of thinges wch men usually have who are upon the place where they are acted, or to fixe yourselfe unmoveably upon your own Imaginations, grounded upon the vainest, and most frivoulous mistaken Informations that can possibly be given in thinges of such Importance . . . I confess this troubles me by reson of my affection to the Comonwealth, and my Respects to yorselfe; I wish you would consider that wch so nearely concernes you in reputation and Interest. I may say, I thinke . . . [in] duty too . . . you may thinke of this at Leysure . . . you will phaps Judge whether it had bin more suitable unto ye condition of a man who is not Prince

---

[33] 'Voyce' p. 1065.
[34] 'Voyce' p. 1066.

nor master of a Nation, but Joyned with many others in a pty for the obteyning of publique Ends to followe the Advises and reasons of freinds, or answering all wth saying I am of another Oppinion. But this concernes you more then me, I will say no more of it, but leave you to answer for yor proceedings before God and man; I have pformed my pte and am ... [yours etc, Alg: Sydney][35]

Immediately after this letter Ludlow received three others from the Netherlands: from Slingsby Bethel, who 'was lately come into those ptes'; from Say; and from Phelps, who had recently left Ludlow in Berne to join the intrigue. Bethel argued, much more gently, that immediate satisfaction over the three regicides was impossible, but that Ludlow was enormously important to them, and that he would be safer in the Low Countries anyway. Say offered his customary range of inducements. But after the mailed fist, it was too late for the kid glove. Severely rattled by Sidney's letter, particularly its grandiloquent invocation of 'God and man', Ludlow dug in further and composed a grand remonstrance in vindication of himself:

That I was to follow my owne light, and not that of others ... that I acknowledged not my selfe bounde to yeild active Obedience to ye *absolute commands* [my emphasis] of any, save ye Lord Christ ... in fine, I tooke the Liberty to offer it to Coll. Sydney as my oppinion ... That till ... I observe a greater spirit of meekness and condescention amongst us then yet I doe ... [we are not ready] but when ye Lord hath humbled a people and fitted them for himselfe ... he wil certeinly ... bringe them to honour. And truly to me the Lord by his Providencyes speakes his people rather fitter for suffering then action ...[36]

This was the last straw. Never one for 'suffering', Sidney replied with a furious

Letter stuffed with Invectives from the beginning to the End. Justifying the Dutch in what they did as to the delivery of our three freinds to be butchered, avowing it an Act they ought to doe, and all wise and virtuous States had ever done the like; ... [and saying] that I must prove the putting of ye King [of England] to death to be no Murther, before I could conclude their delivery of our friends to be so.[37]

Thus heavy became the calibre of Colonel Sidney's artillery. It is most unlikely that amid the resulting acrid smoke Ludlow grasped the lesson in political pragmatism Sidney was offering. Should not Ludlow the regicide understand that in politics, in 'thinges of such Importance', drastic means might sometimes be necessary to achieve vital ends? Had not Sidney, though himself free of the taint of regicide, publicly defended that act as necessary 'just', and 'noble', 'not in the least declyning to own us and ye despised Cause for wch we suffred'? Yet, of course, Sidney could not have made the point to Ludlow in a less provocative way. Ludlow broke off communications

[35] 'Voyce' pp. 1079–80.
[36] 'Voyce' pp. 1080–2.
[37] 'Voyce' p. 1105.

completely, 'hoping that tyme and Providences might make a clearer discovery of psons and thinges'.

By the end of 1665, then, Sidney's practical plans in the Netherlands were not very much further advanced. By this time the group of exiles around Sidney, including Phelps, Lockier, William Scot, Bisco, Say, and Bethel, were based in Rotterdam.[38] There Sidney remained in contact with De Witt, and was reported also to be 'often in Consultation with Benjamin Turly [Furly] the quaker, beeing resolved to shape som designe for England'. As she reported his friendship with Furly in Rotterdam, Aphra Behn also noted: 'Sidney is at present writinge a Treatise in defence of a Republique, and agst Monarchy, and designes it soone or late for ye presse.' Furly not only had the local Dutch contacts to get the *Court Maxims* published: as we will see, he and Sidney were again co-operating thirteen years later in 1678 to bypass English censorship laws by getting English political and religious writing published in Holland.[39]

Furly, 'the quaker ... who ye fanatics do so confide in', had come to the Netherlands from England in 1658. By 1665 he had become a prosperous Rotterdam merchant, buying a new house with 'a fine larg garden' in April of that year. Sidney may well have stayed with him there, we do not know; but he was to correspond with his 'deare freind' for the rest of his life. Furly represented a blend of quaker theology with political activism which Sidney found particularly attractive. In addition he was a scholar, linguist, and bibliophile, with a penchant for philosophical and political discussion as well as activism. He was not simply heavily involved with Sidney in shaping the 1665–6 design, he was also involved with local Dutch religious and political issues and groups. Finally, as a merchant he was not only in touch with contemporary Dutch trading theory and practice, he was a supporter of the Dutch republicans, the Louvesteiners, whose political ideology took its basis from a series of arguments on the paramount importance of Dutch trade. Furly held, in fact, just the combination of Dutch Louvestein political, religious, and mercantile sentiments which went together to create Sidney's *Court Maxims*. He also possessed the local contacts and Dutch language necessary to make these ideas fully accessible to Sidney himself. The following two chapters will try to show not only what use Sidney made of these ideas; but that Furly's importance lies not simply in his involvement with Sidney and the early Restoration exiles in 1665–6; but in his friendships with other important English political theorists among the second wave of

---

[38] From this period on Ludlow speaks collectively of 'the whole body of freinds in that Citty'. 'Voyce' p. 1111.

[39] Cameron, *Aphra Behn* pp. 47, 73; Forster T., *Original Letters of Locke, Algernon Sidney, and Anthony Lord Shaftesbury* (1830) p. 95; The originals of most of these Sidney letters (including this one) are in Bodl. MS Engl. Letters C200 (fol. 23). CSPD 1665–6 pp. 118, 146.

Englishmen who fled for Holland following the arrests of Sidney and others in 1683. This group included most importantly John Locke.[40]

Sidney's political hopes of the Dutch were by now becoming hampered not simply by Ludlow's failure to appear, but by the not unconnected phenomenon of growing disunity among the exiles in Holland itself. As usual, he himself was squarely at the centre of all tensions. Colonel Joseph Bamfield, a complicated individual who had spied for Cromwell, commanded a regiment in Holland, and was now spying for De Witt, hoped to lead a regiment of exiles on the English invasion. Basing himself at the Hague, he had 'skrued himselfe into the young Pr: of Orange his favour, has been frequently wth him ... supps with him, meets him in the park, shares his coach to Schievlinge'. Not surprisingly, then, it was reported that 'Sidney and Bam[field] do not agree'. The fact that Bamfield was establishing his Orangist links as a spy in the pay of De Witt does not seem to have been known to Sidney, and it is unlikely that it would have made any difference if it had.[41] At the same time it came to Ludlow's attention about:

> Mr Saye ... and Col Sidney ... that there had bin great heates betweene these two, the one charging ye other wth having obstructed me in Joyning wth them, Col Sidney beleeving that Mr Say had underhand advised me against coming to them; and Mr Say affirming that Col Sidney had used all meanes to discourage me ...[42]

Amid this wonderfully abject state of affairs, God by His providence chose to hurl one last fireball of hope. De Witt hit upon a new idea. He would fob Sidney and his nagging coterie off onto the Court of his new ally Louis XIV, who had recently, and reluctantly, declared war against England in Holland's support.[43]

II.4 FRANCE, 1666

At this point Sidney moved into a clear role of leadership among the exiles in Holland.

He was introduced to the French ambassador in the Netherlands, d'Estrades. He told the ambassador that he was prepared to put himself under the protection of the French King, 'and go immediately himself to France to offer his services if the occasion presented itself'. D'Estrades wrote an enthusiastic account of the interview to the French government, praising particularly 'M. de Sidney' himself, '[un] personne de qualite et de grand merite, et qui a ete employe dans de grandes ambassades par le feu Protec-

---

[40] Hull W., *Benjamin Furly and Quakerism in Rotterdam* (1941) pp. 8–10.
[41] Cameron, *Aphra Behn* pp. 23, 73; PRO SP 29 172 fol. 81 II; Rowen, *De Witt* p. 665.
[42] 'Voyce' p. 1113; Ludlow, *Memoirs* II p. 391.
[43] Ashley, *Wildman* p. 202 (and see pp. 198–203 generally).

teur.' The plan as finalised, however, contained only one awful hitch. As d'Estrades wrote to Louis XIV:

Mr de Witt has asked me to supply a passport, to travel into France, to Monsieurs Sidney and Ludlow. They are two persons of great ability . . . and desire to come to find your Majesty over matters of considerable importance.[44]

The plan, poor Ludlow was informed by Say, was that the Dutch ambassador to France would provide accommodation in his house in Paris, 'where a Treaty should be carried on Joyntly by the King of France and Holland with Collonell Sydney and myself'.

The same problem thus remained, but the causes of it had changed: they emanated not from the negotiating governments, but from the exile community itself. Despite Sidney's now clearly established credentials as the persuasive man of 'quality' required at the top for the forthcoming negotiations, he still lacked one crucial element necessary for the leadership of the military expedition itself: popularity among his troops. Sidney's tense and dictatorial approach had ensured that, however much he charmed the French King's diplomatic representative, among the 'masses' themselves he was, as he later put it in 1683, 'no popular man'. Increasingly, this level of unanimous enthusiasm seemed only prepared to kindle at the still absent, and therefore increasingly legendary, name of Ludlow.

Consequently, although Say wrote initially of the French design: 'the whole body of friends in [Rotterdam] . . . had fixed their Eyes and heart upon me [Ludlow] and Col Sidney, to whom they let me know they had writ for the same purpose', his next letter clarified the bottom line somewhat: 'that all there [Rotterdam] will goe with me if I goe, but if I refused, he beleeved, not a man would stirr'.[45]

Poor Sidney thus found himself facing again a serious question of bridges burned. There was nothing for it, he would have to write to Ludlow again. This time, however, he would not make the mistake of giving him time to answer; he would follow the letter to Switzerland himself.

Consequently Ludlow, who could by now have been forgiven for living in as great a fear of the postman's whistle, as of the assassin's dagger, received a long message. In it Sidney assured him that everything he had

formerly said, was as a freind proceeding from his affection to me, and earnest desire, that I having a farr better opptunity than any other, might Improve such advantage as God had given for ye good of ye Comonwealth, and to express wth much confidence, that he could easily remove any scruples of conscience I could have, might he but speake wth me; and though he knew I tooke ill what he had written, yet he made no doubt but I should see he sincerely and affectionately sought my good, whilest those to whom I gave more credit, and wth whom I was farr better satisfied, did ye contrary.

---

[44] Guizot M., *Portraits Politiques* (1874) pp. 87–8.
[45] 'Voyce' pp. 1112–13.

and in the conclusion [he invited] . . . me to give him a meeting at Bazill [Basle] in Order to continue our way from thence to Paris.[46]

Having thus attempted to lob a grenade into Ludlow's relations with others, whom he continued to suspect of sabotage in preference to himself, Sidney made all possible haste in travelling through Germany towards North Switzerland, putting his faith in the persuasive power of a personal meeting. He was accompanied on the way by two colleagues, Phelps, and Colonel Blood, the latter travelling under the pseudonym of 'Morton'. At Frankfurt Sidney met his French contact, the French King's resident at Metz, who gave him the letters of safe-conduct for both himself and Ludlow, ordered by d'Estrades. From there, too, he sent Phelps and Blood on ahead to Berne, to flush Ludlow out and make sure he turned up at Basle. A matter of hours after their departure Sidney received at Frankfurt Ludlow's reply.[47] In it Ludlow protested the unsuitableness of his 'condition and principle' for such a work. He complained that Paris was where Riordane and the royalist assassins were based. He objected to co-operation with Louis XIV as much as with De Witt, perceiving him 'no less a montayne in xtes way'. In short, Ludlow concluded, without putting too fine a point on it, the 'designe might be much better managed by those who had a greater Latitude therein then myselfe, wch I found Col Sidney had; who was well experienced in Businesses of this Nature'.[48]

Sidney sent the letter on to overtake Phelps and Blood, presumably for them to better prepare themselves to counter its arguments, but with instructions to otherwise ignore it and press on. Their irritated and besieged quarry thus found himself compelled to meet them in neighbouring Lausanne. There poor Ludlow attempted to argue his superior usefulness where he was, in case the design should have recourse to Swiss mercenaries. He presented the envoys with an extensive list of conditions after the satisfaction of which he would now be prepared to co-operate with the Dutch (though not the French). There was nothing further Phelps and Blood could do.

There ensued, predictably enough, a great row between Sidney and Phelps: 'upon the Jealousy that Colonell Sidney conceived of Mr Phelps doing ill offices, both in relation to his freinds in Holland and myselfe [Ludlow]'. The result was that 'there arose such heates, that they could not any longer draw together'. Arguments with Sidney then engulfed Blood, 'wth whom Col Sidney could not accord'. Accordingly Blood returned to England, and Phelps 'repaire[d] to Holland much discontented'. Amazingly, reserves stepped

---

[46] *Ibid.*
[47] 'Voyce' p.1114; *Memoirs* II p.393.
[48] 'Voyce' p.1114.

forward, and Sidney was accompanied on his way to Paris by two others, John Lockyer, and Colonel White.[49]

There, Louis XIV recorded his meeting with Sidney himself:

Sidney, an English gentleman, promised me to produce a great uprising [in England]; but the proposition he put to me to advance him 100,000 ecus ... was more than I wished to expose on the word of a fugitive [so] I offered him only 20,000 with the promise of furnishing the rest when it was clear that he was really capable of doing what he promised.[50]

Sidney's biographers have portrayed a contemptuous refusal of the paltry 20,000 by Sidney at this point, and an end to the whole affair. But this seems to be mistaken. Ludlow's 'Voyce' reports:

[It is said that] 20,000 [is offered] ... and 400,000 [*sic*] after with what forces should be desired ... if satisfaction could be given that this supply would be rendered advantagious ... this satisfaction is Laboured to be given, it is given forth, that my being there, would have answered all; but how groundlessly, is most evident.

Indeed in Paris Sidney, presumably aware of his crumbling base of support in Holland, had finally stepped over the brink and committed definitive political suicide. He had volunteered to command the invasion directly from Paris leading French troops.

Coll Sidney offers to goe in ye Head of them [French troops], or be Hostage, But freinds in Holland though they are willing to accept of ye King of France his mony yet not of his men; and besides other distastes, the Treaty wch Mr Phelpes, and our other freind [Blood] received from Col Sidney renders him unacceptable to most of them; and as they writ he was not well approved by those of the States, who had a good will to this affaire.[51]

Phelps, meanwhile, wrote to Ludlow:

We cannot but be sensible with you of ye apparent difference betweene treating with the french King a monarch, and these heere a free State, and we are glad to heare that ye same principles that Reasons you against treating with ye one, enclynes you to the other; when you see your call.

Phelps and his colleagues thus abandoned Sidney altogether and fell again to the tedious and indeed pensionable business of trying to persuade Ludlow to leave Switzerland. Others of the Dutch exiles continued to wait. In September Aphra Behn reported of the Rotterdam community, 'they can not come to any

---

[49] 'Voyce' p. 1123. For the plotting career of Lockyer, both earlier with Blood and Michael Livesey in a plot (1663) to assassinate Charles II, and at this time with Henry Danvers in England (1666), see Greaves R. and Zaller R., *Biographical Dictionary of British Radicals in The Seventeenth Century* v II p. 198. Later in 1680 Lockyer once again joined up with Sidney and Danvers, by then working together in London to get Sidney elected to Parliament.

[50] Louis XIV *Memoires 1661 et 1666* (1923) ed. Longnon, p. 213, my translation (see also pp. 172–3).

[51] 'Voyce' p. 1123.

resolution to doe any thinge ... before Coll Sidneys returne, who is expected som 10 days hence'.[52]

But Colonel Sidney was never to return. In Paris, increasingly abandoned, he tried one last card to supply the 'Ludlow factor'. With French assistance he attempted to spring Lambert out of prison on Jersey. The 'two french men ... Imployed' for this purpose were caught, carrying a letter from Sidney, and executed. Lambert convinced the government during interrogation that he knew nothing of the plan and so narrowly escaped the same fate. Subsequently, 'upon pretence [by Louis XIV] that satisfaction could not be given him, that what he should doe, could be made use of to Advantage, our freinds were dismissed without any thinge being done'. Sidney's political involvement with the exiles was over. Holland's and France's war with England ended the next year, after the Dutch raid up the Medway, guided by the English exiles who accompanied it.

[52] Cameron, *Aphra Behn* p. 79.

12

The 'Court Maxims'

God had deliver'd us from slavery, and shewd us that he would be our King; and we recall from exile one of that detested race, as if the war wch destroy'd so many thousands of men, had bin only to drive him into forreign countreys, where if possible he might learn more vicious and wicked customs, than what had bin taught him by his father . . . We set up an idol and dance about it, tho we know it to be most filthily polluted with innocent blood . . . We promise ourselves peace but there will be, can be no true peace till by the blood of the wicked murderers a propitiation be made for the blood of the righteous . . . our madness has bin such as not to have bin taught by experience . . . the mistress even of fools. Burnt children dread the fire, but we more childish than children, tho oft scorch'd and burnt, do agen cast ourselves into the fire, like moths and gnats, delighting in the flame that consumes us . . . I pray you pardon this digression. I speak this in the anguish of my spirit, broken, through the abundance of my sorrow, sighing for the iniquity of my people, praying to God, that his wrath may not overflow the whole land.

Court Maxims p. 203

But in the midst of judgement God . . . kept a lamp still burning in the house of David.

Court Maxims p. 200

12.1 CHRISTIAN SOLDIERS

The *Court Maxims* is a monument not simply to Sidney's 'anguish of . . . spirit', but to the situation of exile which confronted him. Like the Marian exiles before him Sidney seeks to persuade the English people, but he cannot help lashing at them at the same time. Like the Marians, too, his tract is radical and unrestrained in comparison to other contemporary English literature. While Milton and Sexby and Titus had at least rehearsed the traditional huguenot resistance theory distinction between lesser magistrates and people, Sidney is well past even raising the matter. While other English tracts of the same period dealing with the dilemma of the persecuted, by Wolsely or Owen, for instance, strove to play down the damaging association of religious dissent with political sedition, Sidney's

186

tract, with its readvocation of civil strife to an exhausted world, strove to make the connection necessary and clear:

For if it be said these and other nations after wearied with Civil dissensions have sought Monarchy as their port for rest I answer; few or none of them have sought Monarchy as their rest, but have fallen or been driven into it as a Ship upon a Rock. Wee may as well conclude death better then life because all men doing what they can to preserve life doe yet end in death. That free states by divisions fall oft into Monarchy only shows Monarchy to be a state of death unto life. And as death is the greatest evil that can befall a person Monarchy is the worst evill that can befall a nation.

The cloaked figure lurking behind this appeal is one that no amount of nautical window-dressing can disguise. Machiavelli's statement that while civil war is a disease of the state tyranny is its death, is one of the central quotations upon which Sidney's later *Discourses* is built. But here and elsewhere in the *Maxims* Machiavelli is not openly acknowledged, for the *Court Maxims* is itself nothing less than a maxim by maxim refutation of the amoral 'policy' of Stuart tyranny; drawn, says Sidney, from Tacitus and Machiavelli's *The Prince*. Following the huguenot tradition of Du Mornay, Beza, and Gentillet, Sidney portrays his tyrants wandering around with *The Prince* instead of the Bible in their back pockets. After describing traditional Aristotelian and Christian political virtues Sidney comments:

By this you can see whether the name Policy be fittly given to that wicked and malicious craft, exercised with perfidy and cruelty, accompanied with all manner of lust and vice, directly and irreconcileably contrary to virtue and piety, honesty and humanity, which is taught by Machiavel.[1]

When Sidney's commonwealthsman in the *Maxims* quotes from St Paul the courtier replies:

I desire if you would prove anything to me by authority of Authors you wold cite Machiavile [*sic*] Tacitus or others in which I am better versed, and not of your St Paul, who is too obscure for me ... How should Charles the 9th of France contrary to faith, honour, law and religion have found men to committ the tragedy of St Bartholemews Eve, unless he had plenty of such [authorities]? And how may princes in our dayes have by reason of state bin obliged to kill their fathers, wives or Children ... if such persons could not have bin found: As soon as Cromwel came to be a Monarch he well understood the[se] Arcanii Imperii too ...[2]

---

[1] *Maxims* p. 20; Church, *Richelieu* pp. 47–9; Andrea A. and Stewart D. eds., Innocent Gentillet, *Discours Contre Machiavel* (Firenze 1974). Gentillet had close connections with Beza; Du Mornay denounced Machiavelli as the cause of France's troubles in the preface to the *Vindiciae*. Sidney's maxim by maxim chapter structure is very reminiscent of Gentillet's own. See, too, Skinner Q., *Foundations* II pp. 308–9. For Beza, Hotman, and Mornay I have used Franklin J. H., *Constitutionalism and Resistance in the Sixteenth Century* (NY 1969); for the coincidences of sources, ideas, and examples between their and Sidney's work see especially pp. 33–5, 37–8, 40–3, 159–61, 167 (on the corruption of the nobility), 179 (on the book of Samuel), and 188 (on the variety of civil governments).

[2] *Maxims* p. 203.

What Sidney does not mention is that it is precisely these two 'politic' writers, Tacitus and Machiavelli, who become the most important sources for his later *Discourses*, and indeed he uses them (positively) frequently in the *Maxims* as well. For the device with which Sidney chooses to confront monarchical reason of state in the *Court Maxims* is republican reason of state; that is, Machiavellian interest theory itself. Sidney's work is an attempt to combine sceptical and politic insight with the moral and religious high ground; to define a 'right' policy, in conformity with 'reason' and 'truth', but in tune with the special demands of 'that science they call Policy', of all 'sciences' the most 'abstruse and variable according to accidents and circumstances'. The result is not without some obvious tensions. But the attempt was not without precedent either. One man who sought to combine Machiavellian and Tacitean politic insight with Stoic and Christian morality was Lipsius, whose connection with Sidney's family we have already noted. Another, in a different sense was the Sidney's second Dutch connection, Grotius. A third was the Spanish Augustinian natural-law theorist, Juan Marquez, whose *El Gobernador Christiano* (Salamanca, 1621) Sidney nominated to Lantin as his favourite political text after Grotius.[3] Like Lipsius, Marquez recognised the need to define for politics a special moral field of action; a code of statecraft, though he, like Ribadeneyra with whom he is associated, drew the moral reigns tighter. He shared with Sidney his Aristotelian and natural-law categories, and his classical/Christian sources: 'Greek and Roman [including Stoic] philosophers, the Fathers, and the Bible.' But what might have interested Sidney in particular in Marquez were three things. Firstly, Marquez maintained the complete superiority of religion over politics, of the knowledge of God and the natural law over all things temporary and human, both rulers and ruled. Secondly, like Lipsius, Sidney, and Machiavelli, Marquez laid special emphasis on the military science; on the need for military training, discipline, and strength. Thirdly, then, Marquez attacked Machiavelli's *The Prince*, not just for undermining political morality, but in particular for undermining military morality; for Machiavelli's claim that Christianity made men pacifists and was thus a militarily subversive religion. For Marquez the key to military success was strength of belief and faith in the cause for which one was fighting. Nothing, accordingly, was more invincible than the Christian soldier, armed with the moral rectitude of his cause – a suitably Spanish contribution to what remained in essence a sixteenth-century debate. In these terms, by sowing

---

[3] Like Lipsius, Marquez considered monarchy the best form of government, but as usual with Sidney constitutional forms were not the essence of the matter. He shared with Sidney, however, a particular interest in the Hebrew republic, which was exceptional because it was God's own creation, 'une maniere d'anarchie aidee par la Providence divine'. *El Gobernador* p. 295, quoted in Maravall, *La Philosophie Politique Espagnole au XVII Siècle* (Paris 1955) p. 135.

doubt, Machiavelli's doctrines were themselves the most militarily subversive of all.[4]

With this we know that Sidney, heir to the Christian soldier *par excellence*, Sir Philip Sidney, agreed. In the *Discourses* Sidney, though protestant, praised both the military might, and the iron faith, of the Spaniards, before absolutism unmanned them. 'No people ever defended themselves with more obstinacy and valour than the Spaniards'; 'among nations that have any virtue, or profess Christianity ... the French and Spaniards ... had certainly a great zeal for religion, whatever it was; and were so eminent for moral virtues as to be a reproach to us, who live in an age of more knowledge' (pp. 183, 481). For Sidney (as for Grotius) 'great zeal for religion' was the key 'whatever it was'. Indeed in 1665–6 it was a fiercely Christian army, the 'phanatiques', that Sidney was trying to recruit, for a crusade on behalf of God's persecuted and innocent people. As Grotius said in *De Jure Belli*: 'the duty of the Christian soldier' is to fight 'on behalf of the safety of the innocent'. The problem for Sidney was not just to furnish them with arms but, as his relations with Ludlow illustrate, to persuade the defeated and quietest Godly of the 1660s, in religious and moral terms which they could accept, to take up those arms once more. It is this seduction which the *Court Maxims* attempts, one in which the naked insurrection of Machiavelli's *Discourses* appears clad in the flimsy négligé of moral anti-Machiavelli directed at *The Prince*.

The *Court Maxims* is 212 pages long, and divided into fifteen chapters. These comprise an introduction, the discussion and refutation of thirteen *Court Maxims*, and a conclusion. The work is a dialogue between 'Eunomius ye Commonwealthsman' on the one hand, and the improbable 'Philalethes a morall Honest Courtier and Lover of State Truth' on the other.

The chapter organisation and order of the *Maxims* as it survives is the result of a visible job of editorial surgery which was never completed and which has left some notable irregularities of content and juxtapositions of tone within the text itself. Moreover, the manuscript survives in the hand-writing of two copyists: the first half in a seventeenth-century hand, and the second half in an eighteenth-century hand. The change in tone from one to the other is obvious; the first half ends with the word *Finis*, and the second rather as Sidney himself was to do, with unnatural abruptness, half-way through a political point.

Accordingly I propose, for the purpose of the following discussion, to set aside the editors' own chapter order and substitute my own. Judging by the tone and content, rather than the editorial organisation, of the text itself, the

---

[4] Maravall, *Philosophie Politique* pp. 131, 143, 216–18; 271, Church, *Richelieu* pp. 58–60, 69; Burke, 'Tacitus' p. 165 (on Ribadenyra).

Maxims's fifteen chapters can be grouped into five sections, each, though containing different numbers of chapters, of surprisingly similar length.

12.2 (CHAPTERS 1–3, 15) THE OBJECT AND VARIETIES OF GOVERNMENT

Sidney's Introduction (Chapter 1) sets the scene. The courtier cannot understand why, only a few years after 'the People of England ... did so passionately desire a King', everyone is now unhappy. After a series of particular points – 'he is not happy that hath what he desires but desires what is good and enjoys it' – Sidney makes the general claim which sets the tone for the whole of the following inquiry. In line with the tract's outward form of Platonic dialogue, it is a Platonic claim about essences. The people, says Sidney, have been disappointed in their hopes of the Restoration[5] because in opting for the glitter of monarchy they have been deceived by the bare surface appearance of things. Surface appearances are transitory, insubstantial, and subsist only by fickle passions and desires. The wise man, the 'man of truth', must use reason to probe beneath surface appearances and 'examin the [true] nature of things'. 'Reason', admits the courtier, is 'repugnant unto those maxims which att court wee look upon as certain truths.'

The object of political science, moreover, says Sidney, is like that of every other human science: to advance what is 'good'; in this case the public or political good of mankind. Again this is the Platonic 'good', and it is not to be confused with what is commonest, easiest, or longest lasting; what is of 'value' is not what is done by the greatest 'number of ... Nations' but the 'best' – the 'most learn'd, valiant, noble-spirited nations ... If that was best that was practis'd by the major part of mankind 'twold be better to play the fool than act as a wise man.' This object of the 'good' amounts, like that of all other human endeavour of value, to the seeking of God: 'acknowledging God to be the author of all that is good'.[6]

Sidney accepts the courtier's claim that order is a paramount consideration for society, and he quotes Aristotle's *Politics* to argue that only the order society provides can raise man from the level of beasts. He agrees equally that sovereignty is indivisible, denying, however, following Grotius, that this means that the sovereignty must be centred in one man. He gives examples of commonwealths and 'mixed monarchies' which show that society can be established, order maintained, and sovereignty exercised without depending for it upon one man. He then turns, as in the *Discourses*, to a discussion of the infinite variety of governments in the world, and of the universal right which

---

[5] This was not mere wishful thinking: 'In short I see no content or satisfaccion anywhere in any one sort of people.' Samuel Pepys, *Diary* 1661 (1970) p. 167 (and see p. 156).

[6] *Court Maxims* p. 10, *Of Love* p. 614.

this illustrates people have, of choosing whatever sort suits them best in their own particular situations. In the process he denies the apparent 'natural' resemblance between monarchical and paternal power; it involves a confusion of categories: 'Paternall Government extends only to a family and so belongs not to the matter of this discourse.'[7] Quoting Aristotle again 'following his master Plato' Sidney argues that the only form of monarchy which is 'naturall' is one over men who are incapable of governing themselves, or in a society where one man has more natural political virtue than the rest of the inhabitants put together. What is most striking about this section as a whole is the extent to which Sidney's courtier anticipates most of Filmer's case. The *Discourses* and the *Maxims* cover much of the same ground.[8]

Sidney then discusses monarchy by right of conquest, arguing from Grotius again that such a right may or may not exist, depending on 'the justice of the cause' for which the war of conquest was fought. 'States are to consider not only whether such conquests may be usefull to them but whether they have a right of war.' Even if they do, the conquest then belongs to the nation that made it not the man that led it, an argument which Grotius himself had raised in order to *refute* it. This discussion of conquest involves a series of moral qualifications quite absent from the unbridled expansionism of the *Discourses*, and represents, at a theoretical level, an adherence to Grotius later abandoned in favour of a wholesale acceptance of Machiavelli. Conquest and expansion are not necessarily good in themselves, says Sidney here, as 'If the end of Government were ye enlargement of dominion'. Since the end of government is rather 'that in Society wee may lie free happy and safe' a conquest is not good 'unless it conduce to those ends' for the nation that made it. He then instances the Roman Republic, eventually destroyed by the effect of its 'conquests till the prodigious power it arrived to brought in Luxury and pride destroy'd discipline and virtue for then ruin necessarily followed'. Modern Spain, too, has been ruined by the extent of its conquests. The contextual point of this qualification becomes clear in the ensuing elaboration when Sidney argues that some states are suitable for conquest and some are not, according to the varying 'constitution nature and situation' of each. In particular, 'as a body opprest by a disease nourishes not itself but the disease by taking meat ... so a Nation discomposed by some man or order of men too much prevailing can never be better for Conquest'. Sidney is writing from the enemy camp on the eve of Charles II's first foreign war.[9]

Soon enough indeed even here Sidney argues, in expanding the point, and

---

[7] *Maxims* pp. 8–9, 10; cf. *Discourses* pp. 472–3.

[8] As an example of the latter Sidney gives the Incas of Peru. *Maxims* pp. 9, 30; cf. *Discourses* pp. 65, 67.

[9] *Maxims* pp. 10–12, 13, 14; cf. *Discourses* pp. 130–1; and Machiavelli, *Discourses* bk II ch. 19.

as in the *Discourses*, the superior value of republics to monarchies in war and conquest generally. He instances the valour of Rome, of Venice against the Turks, of the United Provinces against Spain, and finally of England and its conquest of Scotland and Ireland 'in five years'. Yet even this last achievement, so gloriously elaborated in the *Discourses*, is here strikingly undercut: 'the actions performed in that time seem rather Prodigies than the effects of man's valour and virtue'. Moreover, 'God [then] suffer'd divisions to arise amongst us for the punishment of our Sins and so we came to be betray'd.'[10] Nevertheless, like Filmer, Sidney's courtier is told that, contrary to royalist mythology, divisions and internal strife are more common in monarchies – among 'people driven to despair by a Tyrant' – than in republics. Sidney then demonstrates the basic fickleness, instability, and changeability of royal counsels, instancing the changes in policy from Olivares to Don Louis de Haro; from Richelieu to Mazarin; and from Henry IV to Louis XIII, as well as between 'Somerset, Buckingham, Strafford, and [Laud] ... every one differing from his predecessour'.[11] Such unstable variability in monarchies is inevitable because, just as they are dependent upon the irrational lottery mechanisms of inheritance, so they are government based on will – the will of one man – not on reason. They therefore share the instability of passion and the world of surface appearances: all are part of the same uncertain and fluctuating world. Accordingly monarchy, since it is not rooted in 'virtue ... the dictate of reason', far from being the most natural of all governments, is in fact the least natural, for 'man is by nature a rationall creature everything therefore thats irrational is contrary to mans nature'.[12]

Inequality among men, says Sidney, is natural or artificial. Inequalities of 'wisdom, virtue ... fidelity, valour, experience' are natural. Inequalities of power, status, social and political position are artificial. Artificial inequalities are only just when they derive from natural ones. Since natural, as opposed to artificial qualities, are not inheritable, hereditary monarchy breaks this rule. There is nothing naturally superior about kings: 'We all breath the same aire are composd of the same materials have the same birth, and tho they or their flatterers sometimes say they are Gods, they shall die like men they are naturally no more then men and can justly therefore pretend to no more then others.' Another way of putting this is that only *natural* inequality may justly regulate natural liberty. 'He that pretends a power over me must shew how I have lost the liberty God and nature gives me; That is the power over my self ffor [*sic*] I am naturally equal to him in freedom.'[13]

---

[10] *Maxims* pp. 15–16.
[11] *Maxims* pp. 17, 22.
[12] *Maxims* p. 27; cf. Benjamin Whichcote: 'Man is a rational being; ... in virtue of reason ... he is made in God's image'. Powicke, *Cambridge Platonists* p. 61.
[13] *Maxims* pp. 27–30.

Accordingly the hereditary rule of a 'Private family' or person involves 'the utter ruine and violation of all Laws of Nature and reason'. It is accordingly a violation of the only things which hold civilised societies in existence. Against such a threat to human society and order, says Sidney, quoting Grotius (in turn quoting Tertullian), 'Every man is a souldier.'[14] For 'he that pretends to a power that enables him to do evil and remains unpunished seems to me like a thief or a Murderer who pretends exemption from the penalties of the law because his father and other ancestors were accustomed to committ the like'. The extent to which Sidney (like Milton before him) is here anticipating Locke's similar use of Grotius will be discussed in the next chapter.

In this way Sidney prepares the ground for the elaboration of his positive doctrine: for the replacement of the 'Chaos' of the human will in politics, with the ordering principles of reason and law. Like the God of Milton's *Paradise Lost*, the God of Sidney's *Maxims* created the world from Chaos by the ordering principle of reason. Man can order the societies he creates by establishing that reason in law. By doing so societies cope with the 'infinite variety' and particularity of their condition – not by seeking to eradicate it; that is not possible – but by seeking to harmonise and co-ordinate it for the good of the whole. Again Sidney's imagery here is purely Platonic, with its Pythagorean ingredients of harmony. Men's interests are infinitely various: the job of 'that Science they call Policy' is therefore to frame laws by which society holds in tuneful balance 'the severall humors, natures, and conditions of men'. 'Ten men are not to be found but one of them will have more witt, another more courage then the rest; one will be precipitous and rash, another dull and heavy, one Industrious, another lazy, besides many other differences proceeding from their complexions education and interest.'[15] And as

that tune in Musick is well framed in which the sharpness of one tone is sweeten'd by ye gravity of another, And the perfection of the Harmony consists in the due proportion of one unto the other. So in Civill Societys those deserve praise that make such laws as conduce to a civill Harmony wherin the Severall humors, natures and conditions of men may have such parts and places assigned them that None may so abound as to oppress the other to the dissolution of the whole ... but every one in his own way and degree may act in order for the publick good and the composing the civill harmony in which our happiness in this world doth chiefly consist.[16]

Sidney's politics was thus premised on a central belief, not in the basic equality, but rather in the inequality – the variety – of men. Men were not

---

[14] *Maxims* pp. 30–1, 54.

[15] This is strongly reminiscent of Hall, and Harrington: cf. Harrington, *The Prerogative of Popular Government* in Pocock, *Works* p. 485: 'A political is like a natural body. Commonwealths resemble and differ, as men resemble and differ; among whom you shall not see two faces, or two dispositions, that are alike ... one may have his greater strength in his arms, the other in his legs; one his greater beauty in his soul, the other in his body; one may be a fool, the other wise; one valiant, the other cowardly ...'

[16] *Maxims* pp. 18–19.

equally 'good', or equally capable of providing for the good of mankind. This premise was made equally clear in the *Discourses* (p. 65) where Sidney said: '[Aristotle], and his master Plato, did acknowledge a natural inequality among men [which is] ... nothing to [Filmer's] purpose. For the inequality, and the rational superiority due to some, or to one, by reason of that inequality, did not proceed from blood or extraction, and had nothing patriarchal in it, but consisted solely in the virtues of the persons, by which they were rendered more able than others to perform their duty, for the good of the society.'[17] There was, however, one natural quality which all political men did hold from God in equal measure: and that was liberty. Sidney's society sought to cater for all its members by accepting as its basis, on the one hand, variation and inequality among individuals; and by according them, on the other, the mechanism – liberty – by which that variety could be effectively registered and find its ('natural') level in the ('artificial') construct of the whole. Only in this way could artificial political society reflect and harmonise the natural variety of God's creation.

This is the absolute core of Sidney's political thought, and it is important to realise that by it Sidney would have regarded the modern conjunction of 'liberty, equality, and fraternity' as a contradiction in terms. It was inequality which made liberty necessary; and it was liberty which gave that inequality true expression. It is accordingly inequality that the concept of liberty as 'free enterprise', to compete, and (in Sidney's words) 'to increase our fortunes [or dominion] by honest industry' in relation to others, assumes. This concept, too, Sidney shared (like his relationship with the Cambridge Platonists) with John Locke. The object was not to achieve equality for all, but to remove impediments to the advance of the 'best', and in *that* sense advance the (total) 'good' of mankind. The survival of this political ideology today in the service of a purely material object is the replacement of its original basis – which was moral and religious – with one of its external 'accidents'. That the best should prosper was God's will, for the good were His children; that they should be subject to 'the worst' was the government of the devil. To bring the 'public good' of mankind to prosper by such political means (by the grant of liberty) was to bring the whole of mankind closer to the nature of their creator. Politics had the power, by advancing the public good, to narrow the gap of the Fall. It was after the collapse of this political enterprise in England that Milton wrote *Paradise Lost*.

12.3 (CHAPTER 9) 'THE CORRUPTION OF LAWYERS IS USEFULL TO YE KING'

Charles II's monarchy, says Sidney, following the Machiavellian common-

---

[17] Cf. Aristotle, *Politics* III 12.

place,[18] must be maintained by force or fraud. Of these fraud is more important, for 'we so well remember the temper of [our subjects'] swords, we avoid all disputes that are determin'd that way'. In the service of fraud the monarchy has two principal instruments: the bishops and the lawyers.

Our 'Ancestours', says Sidney, 'through a vertuous simplicity had made their Laws so plain and easy' that justice was 'speedy and certain ... and the number of Lawyers was not great'. Now, however, by 'kingcraft', and 'dexterous' manipulation of Parliament, the laws have become complex and confused, rendering 'questions in law subject to a variety of interpretations, and ye number of suits infinitely multiplyed'. 'Lawyers and their dependants are growing exceeding numerous' as a result. Moreover, 'Judges, Pleaders and all officers are ye king's Creatures.' The law has become an instrument for the advancement of private, rather than the public interest: it is no longer managed for 'justice', only for 'mony'. This whole corrupt 'union of interest': the 'Spies, Trepanners, false witnesses, counterfeiters of hands and seals, knights of ye Post, perjur'd jurymen, and those that corrupt them'[19] is united by this common bond of private interest, in opposition to that of the public. It is the interest of the monarch, who seeks the destruction of that barrier by which the people's 'lives, liberties [and] estates' are traditionally protected, for the establishment of his power. Accordingly royal and legal private interest agree in allowing the lawyers to grow fat by administering the law for their own, rather than their clients' benefit.[20] Here, then, Sidney establishes the central ideological mechanism of the *Court Maxims* as a whole: the 'direct contrariety' between this private, and the public interest; between the private interest of monarchical rule, and the public 'interest of mankind'. This 'proceeds from contrariety of principles, and those principles from contrary root. All that's just, good and true begins and ends in God; that which is contrary must be by the impulse of ye Devil, whose devices and designs are against God ... this quarrel began with the fall of man, and will never end till the powers of sin and death be destroyed and swallow'd up in that victory, which the son of man shall have over all his enemys in earth and in hell.'[21] So long as this struggle continued, said the *Maxims*, echoing Vane, 'Man is not able to stand in his own strength. If he leave dependance on God he must become the servant of the Devil.' It is, once again, on account of this general

---

[18] Cf. Machiavelli, *Discourses* II p. 13; Milton, Sexby and Titus, and many others use the same terminology.

[19] Compare Nedham in *Mercurius Politicus* (no. 65 p. 1031) on how Empson and Dudley (to be favourite butts, too, of Sidney's *Discourses*), established the usurper Henry VII by 'Informers, Promoters ... Knights of the Post'.

[20] *Maxims* pp. 97–99, 106. These claims, of course, echo many of the basic arguments for legal reform voiced in England during the 1650s by army and other political radicals.

[21] *Maxims* pp. 100, 101.

unsteadiness of the human condition: 'the infinite variety of human accidents
... such as allows no steddy assurance unto any man in any condition', that it
is necessary to establish human societies on the basis of law, and that positive
law on God's law of nature, the 'universal law of mankind'.[22] Man's fall, said
Vane, had set up in him 'that great idol', 'self interest', or private interest. This
was the first work of the devil, and 'a frame of spirit in direct contrariety to
Christs ... serving to promote and advance the great designe and interest of
the Devill in the world'.[23] Milton likewise emphasised that the need for
government stemmed from 'the root of Adam's transgression', and that all
human magistracy, 'if it does not proceed ultimately from God, must needs
come from the devil'.[24]

Law accordingly for Sidney must have three characteristics. First, 'It must
be consonant to the Law of God, the great soveraign Lord and Creator of
Mankind whose authority is above all.' Secondly, 'It must agree with the light
of Nature and reason in man ... [which has] its beginning in God.' Thirdly,
'No Law can be just, which destroys or impairs the ends for which Laws are
made. If they are made to preserve Societys: Societys established for obtaining
of justice; justice sought because good and helpfull to mankind; what Law
soever is made, prejudicial to those of that society [i.e the public interest],
perverting justice destroys the end for which it [ought] ... to be established
and is therefore utterly invalid.' By a tour through Scripture, ancient Greek
and Tacitean Roman history, plus the preceding two centuries in Europe,
Sidney finds examples of monarchs who have corrupted the law that it might
then be an instrument to ensnare the 'Liberty, estates, lives' it was designed to
protect: 'They therefore helped forward the great work of turning a
legitimate monarchy into Tyranny.'[25] Sidney considered this 'great work' a
general feature of the modern European political landscape, which is why,
although the *Maxims* employs the usual Aristotelian distinction between
monarchy and tyranny, any actual distinction in his mind has in practice
disappeared. It is not long before we hear there is a categorical 'contrariety
between God and a King'. The end result of the 'great work' is a reign like that
of 'Queen Katherine de Medici' whose political 'interest' Sidney depicts as so
'directly contrary' to that of her people that she presided over the French
religious wars equally delighted with 'those [casualties] that fell on both sides
... she would say God be thanked, we are delivered from [that many]
enemys'.[26]

[22] *Maxims* pp. 102, 104, 109.
[23] Vane, *Retired Mans Meditations* To The Reader, and p. 383.
[24] Milton, *Tenure* p. 16; *Defence* ed. St John p. 41.
[25] *Maxims* pp. 114, 121–2.
[26] *Maxims* pp. 107, 136; cf. *Discourses* pp. 116, 151.

This political dichotomy of 'interest': public and private; republic and monarchy; good and evil; God and the Devil; and the fundamental 'contrariety' between the two, Sidney describes as 'the principle [*sic*] comprehension of all civill and morall things'. Whichever interest rules in a state can only do so by destroying the other. The results of this internal dialectic determine the fate of the state as a whole: advance or regress, progress or decline. Public-interest government, uncorrupt law, and the consequent 'political perfection of Liberty, security, and happiness' result in a situation whereby 'understanding advanceth in the discovery and knowledge of truth through the rectitude of the will ... Where things are in this right order, there is a perpetuall advance in all that is good.' This optimism; this belief in the progressive discovery of truth through an institutionalised rectitude of the will is again Platonic. As Plato said in his *Republic*: 'the State, if once started well, moves with accumulating force like a wheel. For good nurture and education implant good constitutions, and these constitutions taking root in a good education improve more and more ...'[27] Private-interest government, however, results in a situation where

a defect in ye Law ... leaves an easy entrance for corruption in ye administration as ye will wch is not guided by a right understanding is easily overcome with the allurement of vice, or deceits of the Devil ... This corruption of the law perpetually adds to ye evill of the administration. Thus these two plagues, if suffered to continue still feed one another, till the body that was strong healthy and beautiful becomes a carcass full of ulcers, boils, and putrid sores.[28]

12.4 (CHAPTERS 4, 8) 'THE TYRANNY OVER CONSCIENCES'

Alongside the tyranny over men's 'lives, liberties [and] estates', there is the 'tyranny over consciences'. Sidney devotes two chapters accordingly to examining Scripture, and the authority of the bishops in particular. The first addresses the 'Court Maxim' that the Restoration regime represents the sort of government 'most conformable to ... Scripture'.

Sidney prefaces his use of Scripture with the clear proviso that 'in civil things God has ... left us a liberty of choseing and constituting such a Govenment [*sic*] as according to the time and nature of the place and people we find most convenient'. This does not stop him, however, from then using Scripture in a literal and prescriptive way for purposes of demolition.

Sidney's key texts here, as in Milton, and as in the later *Discourses*, are

---

[27] Plato, *Republic* bk IV in Buchanan ed., *Plato* p. 419.
[28] *Maxims* pp. 124, 144; cf. Machiavelli, *Discourses* I p. 33 on 'corruption' of 'the administration of the law'.

1 Samuel 8–10, and Deuteronomy 17 ('raise not your hearts above your brethren').[29]

In 1 Samuel 8 by the republican reading, the Israelites, determining 'to follow [their neighbouring] nations in their beastly Idolatry . . . [did] reject the Civil Government of Gods own institution' and demand from God a king. They were punished for their folly by God when he granted them Saul. 'The Israelites', explained Sidney, '[had been] seducd by' the Devil to set up his government and worship. The point is that this is exactly what has happened again in Restoration England. Sidney emphasises that in England, as in Israel, the destructive wickedness of a tyranny has been introduced by means of the 'stiffnecked people' 's 'most democraticall election'.[30]

For Sidney the Restoration is not just a repeat of the Israelites' sin and punishment, it is worse, for the reign of Saul knew no such religious persecutions. 'I may even wish we had that only which was threatened by Samuel as a punishment to the Israelites. It would be a favour to us wee are fallen into such a condition.' He appeals passionately to God against those 'who persecute and endeavour to destroy thy church and people throughout all the world, adorning the gates and Towers of the City with the mangled limbs of thy choicest servants to gratify and uphold the interest of their two masters the King and the Devil . . . Oh Vane how ample a Testimony hast thow born to this truth thy condemnation was thy Glory, thy death gave thee a . . . never perishing Crown.' Sidney opines hopefully on the number of people alienated: 'Tis no matter whether a man be an independent Presbeterian or Anabaptist if he can pray or preach he's a fanatick with them. Our prisons are full of such our churches are empty.'[31]

Yet this punishment of the idolatrous people by God is not to be permanent: it is 'sent for a season to scourge them'. In a passage like many in Ludlow's *Voyce*[32] Sidney says to Charles II: 'I know not how long you may be continued as a punishment for the sins and exercise of the graces of Gods

---

[29] *Maxims* pp. 32, 33, 40, 48, 49; *Discourses* pp. 28, 102, 106–7, 274–5, 279, 283–91.

[30] The Marian exiles before him had used the same text (1 Sam. 8) in the same way. Sidney echoes one tract in particular, Goodman's *How Superior Powers Ought To Be Obeyed* (1588), not just in its use of the Samuel text but in the whole range of Goodman's attacks on the English people, clergy, and nobility for their 'shame', 'follie', and 'disobedience' to God in co-operating with 'bloodthirstie wolves . . . agaynst God and their conscience'. His conclusion, too, is the same as Goodman's, that 'Not to withstand such rages of Princes . . . is to give them the bridle to all kinde of mischiffe, to Subvert all Lawes of God and Man, to let will rule for reason and thereby to enflame Gods wrathe agaynst you.' Goodman, *Powers* pp. 34–5, 140, 150 (also pp. 12, 30–2, 48–50, 57, 59, 206–7). There are many similarities, too, between the *Maxims* and Ponet's *A Short Treatise of Politike Power* (1556) pp. 29–31, 44, 47, 50 (56–7, 104–6 Saul text, 109, 152 on the nobility), 153.

[31] *Maxims* pp. 41, 46, 48, 70.

[32] See, for instance, Worden ed., *Voyce* pp. 10–11.

people';[33] 'that which makes me hope the end near, is that the measure of your iniquity seems to be full, the harvest ripe. The blood of saints also crys aloud against you, and God will not long delay his appointed vengeance.' Again Vane had said that when 'iniquity ... prospers for a season against the saints ... [still] Christ is able to grapple with it, and in due time will visibly undertake it and triumph over it'. The task for the *Maxims* becomes to address the Saints; men who 'live in and by faith, they see things that to other eyes are invisible ... We trust in God, not men; persecution makes us ripe for mercy and our persecutors ripe for vengeance ... They that depend upon him fall not into impatience for the delay of his coming.'

Yet displaying something very like impatience, Sidney goes on to uproot all religious arguments for non-resistance; to make God's instruments willing. Dismissing the quietism of a very few misguided 'Quakers and Socinians', Sidney argues that pacifism is something preached to the people by the bishops to make them docile. While religiously good in itself, it is political madness to renounce the use of force before the bishops and those in authority themselves do. While they remain 'most savage wolves' and persecution continues, Christian pacifism on the part of the oppressed only makes society ungovernable: it is 'disallowing the use of force, without which innocency could not be protected, nor society maintain'd'. For Sidney this is so important, and so at the centre of the *Court Maxims*'s message, as well as its tensions, that it leads him to a startling admission. In politics, 'the most difficult and abstruse of all sciences', resistance against those who seek to destroy society or its members is justified, even where in itself it amounts to 'the hard necessity of sinning against God'. There is, after all, 'perfection in God only, not in the things he has created'.

Sidney pillages Scripture and ancient history for a succession of increasingly bloodthirsty precedents for action. He concludes, like Milton: 'The blood of an Idolatrous Tyrant was then a grateful sacrifice to God; it will therefore be so forever.' Moses and Joshua slew thirty-one kings; no two people therefore 'better deserve the name of regicides' or are 'more deserving of imitation'. The ceremony by which kings are anointed is not from God, says Sidney, but from the devil. He recommends to Charles II the procedure of

---

[33] Sidney uses this term 'graces' a great deal. What he means by it here may be suggested by Henry Hammond's *Of The Reasonableness of Christian Religion* (1650), pp. 204–5 where Hammond finds earthly sufferings to have this consolation: 'They are admonitions ... disciplines of the Soul, to awake us out of secure, and stop us in wilful, sinning ... [and] there is yet a ... sublimer benefit of such dispensations of God ... And that is the exercise of many Christian Graces ... in the sight of God, and such as shall be ... mostly richly rewarded by him, which were it not for such changes ... would lie by us unprofitably; such are Patience, Meekness, Humility, Contentedness with whatsoever lot, Dependence on God in all outward things ...' It was precisely Sidney's dilemma that he accepted the religious truth of this teaching, but could not content himself with the political crumbs it offered. Hence his extraordinary admission (see above).

the Greek Tyrant Polycrates, who was crucified and then held so close to the sun that it 'melted his fatt and so anointed him with his own [oil]'.[34]

Seeking to delegitimate the persecuting Church of England in general, Sidney attacks with equal venom the bogus claims to religious authority of the clergy (the 'English Rabbies') on the one hand, and of the state ('No religion is to be suffered but what is established by Authority of Parliament') on the other. He ridicules the Henrician Reformation itself as a kidnapping of religion by an evil alliance of King (Henry VIII), Archbishop (Wolsey), and 'Three Acts of Parliament'; the intended analogy with the Clarendon Code is clear. The result was the idolatrous grafting of 'a temporall head on[to] a spiritual body ... the head of a filthy devouring fish' onto the 'body of a beautiful woman ... the pure and undefiled spouse of Christ'.[35]

Sidney then turns to the English bishops in particular. From whence do they derive their authority? Is it external or internal: the outward church or the inner spirit? If it is external, and so translated through the Church's own outward traditions, then it is tainted by over 1,000 years of what they themselves call popery, and 'An obscene spirituall adultress [Rome] living in errours and Idolatry cannot be a true church.' Yet the Church of England lacks even the authority of Roman traditions – it left the Roman Church and therefore can derive no authority from them. The powers of Catholic priests are crucially those of the keys, and of 'sacrificing for the living and the dead which is done in saying mass'. But the Church of England has renounced these powers in their own clergy. In doing so it has renounced the basis of outward clerical power.

If the source of their authority is rather internal then it rightly belongs to the 'phanatiques', 'the pure and spiritual christians', and clearly cannot be imposed from outside, by the bishops or anyone else. Accordingly, Sidney concludes, the English bishops are a theologically laughable hybrid, trapped between Rome and the 'phanatiques', trying to use the arguments of each against the other, and lacking the arguable bases of authority of either.[36] They are a 'lifeless branch' of Rome, and the best way to deal with such men is to 'cut them into five pieces'. Finally, as we saw in Chapter 3, Sidney brings the huguenot sceptic Daillé's work to bear on the authority the bishops are accustomed to claim from the Church Fathers.[37]

The end result of the 'tyranny over consciences', Sidney concludes, would be that the English people would 'lose their patience at last', and gather to defend themselves, taking 'sharp vengeance on their oppressours'. The

---

[34] *Maxims* pp. 36, 47, 89.
[35] *Maxims* pp. 82, 86. Ludlow, too, called Henry VIII a 'monster of mankinde' who had checked the Reformation, Worden, *Voyce* p. 7.
[36] *Maxims* pp. 78–80, 95.
[37] *Maxims* pp. 82, 94–6; cf. *Discourses* pp. 308–10.

punishment of the bishops, he warned, would extend to that interest 'which sets them up and maintains them': the throne. Even Grotius[38] though a 'gentle spirited man', considered resistance to authority justified in such cases 'of the extremest injury', because such a transgressor 'breaks the comon pact by which humane society is established ... [and in doing so] renders himself a delinquent'.

Finally, Sidney attacks the logic of religious compulsion, since belief is not 'an act of the will'. To illustrate he takes, typically, a Euclidean example:[39] 'I can be forced to say the 3 angles of a triangle equal 3 rather than 2 right angles; but not to believe it.' He counters with four questions: 1. Whether belief can be compelled?; 2. Whether compelled worship is acceptable to God?; 3. 'Whether those who are not spiritual men are fitt to judge of spiritual things'?; 4. Whether a prudent man can be so sure 'he is in the right as to dare force others to his way'? Again it was the scepticism of the last point which lay at the heart of the[40] matter, and typically Sidney personalises it:

so I shall take my liberty to differ from them [the forces of external authority] when I see them apt to fall into the lowest path of sin and darkness, as well as I, wanting light and therefore subject to the same errours I am.

In the same place he makes the religious–political liberty connection explicit. 'The Power of Princes [could] not be fully established unless they had a power over consciences.'[41]

12.5 (CHAPTERS 5–7, AND 14) 'DOMESTIC INTEREST'

The rest of the *Court Maxims* Sidney devotes to the development of his central argument concerning 'interest'. In these chapters he illustrates the theory in its domestic context.

This argument holds, as we have seen, that government in the hands of one person or family is inevitably 'private-interest' government; that the government of a republic or commonwealth is 'public-interest' government; and that within any state there is an 'irreconcileable contrariety' between the two. Since each cannot help but pursue its own interest ('interest will not lie' is the maxim) each can only survive by destroying the other. A republic will always, therefore, serve the public interest, and seek to destroy any 'private interest' which might aspire to political power in the state. A monarchy conversely can

---

[38] *De Jure Belli ac Pacis* bk 1 ch. 4: This is Sidney's favourite chapter of Grotius, cf. *Discourses* pp. 23, 190, 229, 280, 318.

[39] 'Arithmetic and geometry' were, as I have noted, the world of (relative) absolutes by which Plato, too, sought to 'rise out of the sea of change and lay hold of true being'. *Republic* vii p. 561 (see pp. 558–65 generally. Cf. Cornford, *Before and After Socrates* (1932) pp. 63–74 [esp. p. 67]).

[40] As it had for Stubbe: see Zagorin, *Political Thought* p. 160.

[41] *Maxims* pp. 81, 83.

only secure its private interest by seeking to destroy the 'public interest'; which means the wealth, health, and happiness of its subjects. This makes the resulting tiny, private-interest coterie of king, courtiers, bishops, and lawyers, parasitically undermining the strength of the main body, an irrational basis for government which results in the eventual destruction of all concerned (governors included). That is how England, in a few years, has fallen from its 'flourishing state' under the Commonwealth, to become 'one of the most miserable nations at home and ... despicable abroad'.

In each of these chapters Sidney takes a segment of the population and shows this 'private-interest' mechanism at work upon it. The first centres on the nobility, and the Court Maxim, 'Monarchy is not secure unless the Nobility be suppressed, effeminated and Corrupted.' It shows the decline and extinction under monarchy of the once vigorous, war-like Plantagenet nobility in England, a picture already discussed in Chapter 2 above. To the 'establishment of absolute power at home' a 'virtuous warlike Nobility', thirsty for 'glory', 'is of all things most destructive'. The King cannot let them remain strong, for as such they would remain an internal force capable of defending the 'public interest' from his depredations. The result of their destruction conversely is that it destroys the basis of the nation's power at home and abroad. The result is a modern English state in which an effeminate 'titular nobility', entirely lacking 'spirits suitable to their birth ... spring out of Dung' and submit 'their honour and conscience to [the King's] interest'. The only group with the spirit to challenge this debilitation in modern times, says Sidney, were 'the roundheads'.[42]

In the next chapter Sidney shows how monarchy goes to work on the people as a whole. The Court Maxim is: 'As long as the people continue strong numerous and Rich ye king can never be happy.' Rebellions against tyranny always begin from the richest cities: the war of independence 'in the Low Countries began in Antwerp Ghant [sic] and Bruxelles ... the French league in Paris ... the [Fronde] att Paris Bordeaux or Rouen; those in Naples grew within its walls. And all ours [the Civil War] grew from the greatness and strength of London.' In general 'all people grow proud when Numerous and rich ... the least injury putts them into a fury; But if poor weak, miserable and few they'l be humble and obedient.'[43] This view of Europe's cities in the seventeenth century is interesting; and it reminds us (as I will suggest in Chapter 14) that Sidney lived his life in the world of those cities – Paris, London, Rome – rather than any one country. Republicanism was, of course, a city–state form of government, and the English Republic certainly was a product of the victory of London in the civil war.

---

[42] *Maxims* pp. 55–9.
[43] *Maxims* pp. 59–67.

The King, then, must impoverish his people to maintain his control. He 'loves his people . . . as a butcher his oxe, in hopes of what he shall make of his carcass. His business is so to tye his oxe, that he may not kick or push him; thats to kill him.'[44]

The argument, the effects of which are repeatedly demonstrated on a Europe-wide scale, thus becomes that monarchy, the old style of government in Europe now degenerated into tyranny, actively impedes economic improvement and progress as a matter of policy; it must do so to survive. So in modern Europe there are, on the one hand, the monarchies: ravaged Germany, poverty-stricken Italy, wooden-shoed France, and declining Spain; and, on the other, wealthy Venice, bulwark against the Turks and, above all, the free United Provinces, centred on Amsterdam, which Sidney calls 'the richest and most powerful city in the world'. Sidney appeals to London, and England, after their famous attempt to break out from one camp into the other, to once again choose their road.[45]

Having focused attention on the cities as centres of wealth and insurrection, Sidney then describes the ways in which monarchies attempt to destroy them. In particular, 'to effect this work of Impoverishing and bringing the people low we find it to be the Kings interest to destroy trade', that force which 'Sir Walter Raleigh found [to be the strength of] . . . the comon-wealth of Carthage'. Sidney focuses on the Dutch cities, examining their great wealth by 'increase of trade', and explaining how 'The hollanders in all business of warr or peace with any nation doe principally consider trade.'

It is easy for monarchs, says Sidney, to ruin trade in their own cities through the crucial role modern government plays in the maintenance and promotion of trade. Merchants cannot operate without the backing of their own government against foreign competitors; without a willingness on the part of government to judge and, if necessary, intervene in foreign mercantile disputes involving their nationals; and without the support of a government policy which will hold to reasonable customs and excise charges. Monarchies habitually remain idle; extract all they can in customs and excise, and choke the trading activities of their subjects under the control of a few great monopolies, given as gifts to fawning and incompetent courtiers. The merchants cannot compete internationally and so lose the basis of their and the people's prosperity for the short-term interest of a gaggle of 'Courtiers and Gallants . . . fidlers, players, whores, Cooks, and other instruments of idle and lasciveious pleasures'. Again, the great English challenge to this came when the King's subjects began to resist these 'illegal burdens such as Hamden Sr Arthur Haselerigg etc' and 'the peoples party [grew] powerful . . .

---

[44] *Maxims* p. 41; cf. *Discourses* p. 231.
[45] *Maxims* pp. 41, 61, 66.

their liberties and priviledges defended ... at the beginning of the long Parliament'.[46]

Finally, Sidney devotes a chapter to demonstrating how the 'interest' of a monarch requires him to destroy all those in his nation with 'virtue, valour, and reputation'. The reason, of course, is the same; the argument this time draws (as in the *Discourses*) particularly on Tacitus, and the Roman emperors who excelled in this regard. Unlike the more careful *Discourses*, however, the *Maxims* soon enough turns from Tacitus to Buchanan to show that the Stuarts, too, and their 'ancestours understood the arts of reigning by taking away the principall persons for nobility power and vertue'. It then relates bitterly how Charles II, aided by 'this supple Parliament', continued the work. Again, to this fact, 'No testimony ... is equal to that of Vane.'[47]

12.6 (CHAPTERS 10–13) 'FOREIGN INTEREST'

Finally, in these chapters, Sidney adds a second – foreign – dimension to his interest theory; to illustrate how the English monarchy acts as contrary to the public interest abroad as it does at home. In the process he takes the argument one step further: Stuart 'private-interest' foreign policy acts not simply contrary to the interests of its own people, but to the 'public interest' of Europe as a whole, seen as an interdependent community of states. This endangers the stability, in particular the balance of power, of Europe generally; the maxim of the Stuarts in foreign policy is: 'Let other States look to the publick interests of Europe we endeavour to secure ourselves.' The point this leads to is the Stuart–Orange 'private-interest' alliance mentioned in the previous chapter, and so to Sidney's war aims: the need for a 'public-interest' alliance between Dutch and English republicans in response.

To begin with Sidney examines the Stuart foreign-policy maxim 'Union with France is necessary to uphold Monarchy in England.' By the introduction of French customs 'the [English] people by their example [may be] brought to beggary and slavery quietly'. This alliance is so close that 'Theres nothing so secret at our court, but by the next post tis known at Paris.' The power of Louis XIV is growing and were English power 'rightly employed they might curb and oppose him more than any other'; but the English people have a government acting contrary to 'their true interest'.[48]

There follows a religious critique of Stuart foreign policy. While England should be championing and uniting the protestant cause in Europe, Charles II, like his father and grandfather, prefers to do the contrary: to ally with catholicism (France), and against protestantism (the Netherlands). The

---

[46] *Maxims* pp. 61, 62, 64.
[47] *Maxims* pp. 185–9; cf. *Discourses* pp. 114–15, 151–2.
[48] *Maxims* pp. 148–51.

Stuart Court leaves consideration of the 'publick good, and advancement of the cause of christ in the world, and diminishing the power of antichrist, to the Fanaticks'. The Stuarts indeed are antichrist, says Sidney, as their involvement with Antrim and the massacre (and continued plans for the extermination) of protestants in Ireland sufficiently shows.[49]

Sidney then moves to an explanation of European balance-of-power theory, in terms of the true 'interests' of each state, and arrives at two general conclusions. The first is that 'There is ... a perpetuall contrariety between the interest of Spain and France.' The second is that 'The interest of every nation that cannot pretend to a Universall Monarchy or more limited superiority over its neighbours is to keep any others from attaining it, and maintain its own freedom', a clear enough parallel to Sidney's personal case against Monarchy, and a parallel which he draws himself.[50]

Accordingly, in the sixteenth century the interest of England, correctly pursued by Elizabeth I, was to help the Dutch 'raise and foment troubles in Flanders ... to oppose the terrible power of Philip II of Spain'. Now, however, when Spain was weak and France grew to be a threat to Europe, England should be allying with Spain, for its own preservation as well as that of Europe as a whole: 'England to keep the ballance even between France and Spain should ever cleave to the weakest.' Instead, of course, it not only allies with France and Portugal, but overthrows the Elizabethan inheritance, too, by attempting to destroy the Dutch. This is because 'the prosperity they enjoy in a Comonwealth [is] ... a most pernicious example to England'. Through 'good government and liberty of traffick [the Netherlands] is so rich powerful and prosperous' that it is bound by example to occur to the English people eventually that

England, if so governed may promise itself incomparably more; abounding in all they [the Dutch] want; and being free from all the inconveniences they suffer'd or fear'd, apprehending no opposition but that of ye Stuart family, wch is left weak and naked ye first moment we come to discover its reign inconsistent with our welfare.[51]

'Queen Elizabeth assisted these Provinces ... but as soon as the Scotch line came into England a new policy entred. James from his first coming to reign here apply'd his thoughts to render himself absolute.' Accordingly, his first move was to ally with Prince Maurice of Orange to destroy Dutch liberty as well. Their first victim was the Dutch republican leader, and patron of Grotius, Oldenbarneveldt, and so a

vertuous head, wch had so long and so successfully laboured in ye service of his country was cut of[f], to facilitate his way who sought to oppress it ... This and the rendition of Flushing and ye Briel [the Dutch Elizabethan cautionary towns; Sidney's

---

[49] *Maxims* pp. 180–2.
[50] *Maxims* pp. 151–2.
[51] *Maxims* pp. 153, 158, 159.

grandfather was governor of Flushing under James I] wholly depending upon the Prince of Orange were the two principal arts of that king towards the advancement of the House of Orange.[52]

Thereafter Sidney traced how the Stuart–Orange alliance had become hereditary, Charles I allying with Prince Henry to make him 'Lord of the United Provinces', now Charles II allying through Downing with young Prince William. The object of the alliance is, as always, in Holland as in England, to establish power by 'setting up a private interest in each ... contrary to the welfare of the whole'. Its methods are the use of deceit to sow the 'seeds of division between them [the Dutch] and ye Phanaticks', and between the Dutch provinces themselves. 'The ways and ends of deceit are of such infinite variety, through different humors, designs, natures, passions, conditions, interests and abilitys of men, that no man that can well apply them need fear losing the opportunity.' 'Downing is a fit instrument for this work'; he has 'ye arts of an inquisitive spye ... by wch from a beggarly boy, he is raised to riches and power'. Fortunately, says Sidney hopefully, De Witt and the Dutch republicans know that

the power of a Prince, and the subsistence of their Comonwealth is inconsistent, that their Liberty is their life. [So] They think it much better to have a sharp contest with the King of England now, who seeks to advance his nephew to their ruine, than when he [the Prince of Orange] shall be of Age in his own person to enter the quarrel ... In fine the King seeking the ruine of the English trade and people, and ye ruine of the Holland Commonwealth, those two nations may see their joint interest against him and Orange, and unite in Councells and actions, joyning their hands, hearts and heads to extirpate the two detested families of Stuart and Orange ... The opposition between us and them, their concernments and ours, is universall and irreconcileable. Their safety is our destruction: our safety is their destruction. We desire to be governed by good Laws, possess our goods in safety, with the full enjoyment of our Civil and spiritual Libertys. We seek to increase our fortunes by honest industry, advance our persons [and] familys by vertue and ye service of our Country, and by merit gain that, which truly deserves the name of honour. All this is contrary to ye interest and maxim of Tyrants who with their own inherit all manner of vices, pride, avarice, cruelty, lust, and perfidy ... These rare Kingly qualities cannot be freely exercised, till their power be unlimited, and the misery of those under it inexpressible. Those who see and well consider this will, to ye utmost, lay out themselves and all they have to secure a multitude of innocents, by the overthroe of a few guilty heads.[53]

[52] *Maxims* pp. 159, 160.
[53] *Maxims* pp. 164, 165, 169, 178–9.

$$\twoheadleftarrow 13 \twoheadrightarrow$$

The Dutch connection

13.1 INTEREST (I) FRANCE AND ENGLAND

The political language of 'interest' was a sceptical and potentially (though in Sidney's use not actually) 'morally ambivalent' form of analysis which captured the high ground of political discourse in western continental Europe by the end of the first half of the seventeenth century, particularly in the Netherlands and France.[1]

In the first half of the seventeenth century, in France, two theorists established this language beyond all others: Richelieu, and the Earl of Leicester's friend du Rohan. It was during the Sidneys' period in Paris that du Rohan published his *De L'Interest des Princes et des Estats de la Chrestiente* (1638), which helped to popularise among English protestants (particularly those, like Sidney, Penn, and Halifax, with French huguenot connections and/ or education) many of the standard maxims of interest analysis: 'Interest never lies'; 'princes rule people and interest rules princes ... The prince may be deceived and his council ... corrupt, but interest alone is forever sure.' Du Rohan's work also advanced the vision of international power politics put forward by Sidney in the *Maxims*: the view of an interdependent community of European states, each pursuing (or failing to pursue) its own true 'interest', around the axis of the balance between France and Spain.[2]

Interest was an autonomous political law held to operate independently of changeable human passions, and human imperfection and error. This was the basis of its appeal to the sceptical seventeenth century (it followed major civil conflict, and the resulting flowering of scepticism, into France, the Netherlands and, eventually, England in that order) and the meaning of 'interest alone is forever sure'. In addition, in this analysis of the 'interests of the state'

---

[1] Skinner Q., *The Foundations of Modern Political Thought* (1978) vol. II pp. 248, 253–4; Keohane N., *Philosophy and The State in France* (1980) p. 169.
[2] Keohane, *Philosophy* p. 155; Du Rohan's work spawned, over the following thirty years, a whole genre of 'interest' analyses on this model, within which the foreign-policy section of Sidney's *Maxims* clearly belongs. Cf. Church, *Richelieu* pp. 352–5; Hirschmann A. O., *The Passions and The Interests* (Princeton 1977) p. 36.

the true interests 'of one special individual – the prince – were assumed to be identical with the interests of the public and the state'; an identification which Richelieu, in his *Testament Politique*, helped to turn into the theoretical basis for French absolutism. The public interest was not only held to be 'identical with the interests of the prince himself'; in Richelieu the latter defined the former. The fact that the Prince, regardless of the vagaries of human will or perception, was considered incapable of acting contrary to his own personal interest helped set the seal on this identification, and its political usefulness. This theoretical victory, of course, left potential questions unanswered. It was easy to say that the interests of prince and people were politically identical; 'that the prince had no interest in ruling over a population of slaves'; 'that the interest of the prince and glory of the state required a flourishing populace'; but, in the words of Nannerl Keohane, 'the exact nature of the relationship between public and private utility [remained] open to question'. At this time, however, the questions were not asked: 'Little attention was paid to the potential dissonance between the Prince's personal desires and the good of the whole polity.'[3]

The language and ideas of 'interest' established themselves increasingly in England during the period of the civil war and after, from Parker and Herle onwards. Their progress shadowed Sidney's own very closely, from their use by the New Model Army in late 1648, to an increasing foothold under the Republic and then within republican circles of the opposition to Cromwell, and finally to their most complete flowering in the brief republican renaissance of 1659. By 1660, interest language, though still (by continental standards) used only in the simplest way, was becoming standard discourse for England's politicians of all persuasions. Ireton's *Humble Remonstrance*, delivered to Parliament on 16 November 1648, was the earliest clear forerunner to Sidney's use of the theory, arguing a public/private interest dichotomy between King and people, and exposing the 'force' and 'fraud' of Charles I's duplicitous Court Maxims.[4] The following year Warr's *The Priviledges of the People* developed, from 'Machiavils Prince', the theme that 'The Interest of the king [had] advanced it self into a Principle of Distinction, Separation, and Superiority above the Interest of the People.'[5] Nedham's *Mercurius Politicus* had drawn from the experience of the civil war (experience, what is more, on both sides of it) to combine with his interest language (drawn principally from du Rohan) the idea of 'fighting contraries' of interest. Yet this stopped well short of the full development of a republican

---

[3] Keohane, *Philosophy* pp. 155, 174–5.
[4] [Ireton] *The Humble Remonstrance of his Excellency the Lord General Fairfax*, in *Old Parliamentary History* pp. 159–338; see pp. 166–8, 173–6, 183–4, 187, 190, 194, 212. Kishlansky M., 'Ideology and politics in the parliamentary armies 1645–9' in Morrill John ed., *Reactions to the English Civil War* (1982); Underdown, *Purge* pp. 123–4.
[5] Raab, *Machiavelli* p. 124.

theory based on the laws of continental 'interest' analysis. Even Nedham's later *Interest Will Not Lie* (1659), a work with much in common with Sidney's *Maxims*, does not live up to the promise of its title. Its use of 'interest' language is piecemeal and superficial, and it offers no systematic interest analysis at all.[6]

In fact the *Court Maxims*'s republican interest theory goes beyond anything visible in English political thought by the time it was written. While everyone from Hobbes to Harrington had debated the extent to which monarchy could be assumed to operate for or against the 'interests' of its subjects, Sidney's work both sharpened and extended the terms of the question, in two ways.

Firstly, Sidney did not simply challenge the assumed identity of interest between monarch and people; he replaced it with an opposite of equal theoretical exactitude and rigidity: the 'irreconcileable contrariety' of interest, 'the principal comprehension of all civil and moral things'. The rigidity and breadth of Sidney's doctrine came from its acceptance of the terms of classic French interest theory itself: it was not a matter of Stuart experience, or proof by example, but a general *a priori* political law which operated independently of particular circumstances or the will of any particular monarch. Richelieu's absolutist theory based itself on the assumption of identification, and then used the mechanical laws of interest theory to carry it through. Sidney's theory based itself on the assumption of contrariety, and then used the same laws. The result was a hijacking of Richelieu's theory to the service of republicanism.

The second thing about Sidney's tract, within the contemporary English context, was its sophisticated illustration of interest theory in foreign as well as domestic affairs. J. A. W. Gunn found this development occurring in English political thought for the first time in 1679, in the work of William Penn, in his *One Project For The Good of England*. In *One Project*, says Gunn, Penn developed, for his description of *internal* interest, on 'all those commonwealth republicans who founded the common interest in each man's concern for preserving his personal rights', to conclude that 'each private man could adequately interpret the good of society because each man knew his own interest in preserving his liberty and property'. This led, says Gunn, to a 'new concept of a common interest: the mutual preservation of individual private rights'. Whether or not this concept was new – and to the question of the origin of Penn's ideas we will return shortly – this was certainly, as we have seen, the basis of Sidney's theory; and it was also the basis of John Locke's. Secondly, however, Penn extended his interest analysis for the first time into a second dimension mirroring the first: the public interest of the

[6] Nedham M., *Interest Will Not Lie* (1659).

state internationally, as well as of its citizens internally. According to Gunn this 'twofold meaning of interest served to capture the bastions of State power for individualism'.[7]

13.2 INTEREST (2) THE NETHERLANDS

In fact Penn was not the first English theorist to do this; his personal friends Sidney and Bethel were; and they were both living in the Netherlands at the time that they did so. Another thing which distinguishes Sidney's *Maxims* (and Bethel's writing) from an English point of view, is its interest in trade, and Sidney's location of his political perspective in the world of the European cities, with an accent on Amsterdam. We need now to look at the local context of Sidney's work, to see where he might have found some of these ideas. It is a picture into which Penn, Locke, and others will be drawn.

If Sidney's doctrine of 'interest' can be seen as the French theory of absolutism inverted to the service of republicanism, no nation had a more obvious use for such a doctrine than France's neighbour, the Dutch Republic. As already mentioned it was the Netherlands which shared most completely with France the use of interest language. From the foundation of the Dutch Republic in 1650 the De Witt regime developed a new and distinctive ideology to justify the existence of republicanism as the natural government for the United Provinces. It was the first complete republican interest theory, and was called the ideology of 'True Liberty'.[8]

The doctrine was closely associated with De Witt himself, and he was personally involved in its formulation. Burnet described De Witt by reference to some of its features:

he laid down this for a maxim, that all princes and states followed their own interests; so by observing what their true interests were, he thought, he could without great intelligence calculate what they were about ... he [also] had an hereditary hatred to the House of Orange. He thought it was impossible to maintain their liberty, if they were still Statholders.[9]

During the build-up to the 1665–6 war itself, De Witt had sighed with exasperation: '[The English are] a marvelous nation who decide on action not on the basis of equity or their true interests but undertake or abandon all things with passion but no thought.' At the same time, writing the *Court Maxims*, Sidney was explaining of English policy: 'the lightness and

---

[7] Gunn, *Politics and the Public Interest in the Seventeenth Century* (1969) pp. 171–6.

[8] Smit J. W., 'The Netherlands and Europe in the seventeenth and eighteenth centuries', Bromley J. S. and Kossman E. H. eds., *Britain and the Netherlands in Europe and Asia* (1961) p. 22.

[9] Burnet, add MS 63,057 p. 383; On the De Witt/Orange opposition see Roorda D. J., 'The ruling classes in Holland in the seventeenth century' in *Britain and the Netherlands* II (Utrecht 1964) pp. 124–6, 129.

uncertainty of court counsells begets this variety of proceeding ... [lacking] generall maxims ... there is a perpetuall uncertainty in all their actions'.[10]

The Dutch government's ideology of 'true liberty' was first definitively set out in *Het Interest Van Holland* (1662), later published in England in the early eighteenth century as *The True Interest and Political Maxims of the Republic of Holland*. The tract was written by Pieter de la Court, who enjoyed the same position of patronage under De Witt as Grotius had under De Witt's republican predecessor Oldenbarneveldt. De Witt himself had 'read over the manuscript, toned down some of its most forthright passages, and contributed parts of several chapters'. The work's publication, two years before Sidney's arrival in the country, aroused a furious public controversy, although De Witt managed to resist Orangist attempts to have it banned. It was reprinted in an expanded form in 1666.[11]

'I am no slavish Courtier', said de la Court, 'who can be unconcerned for the welfare of his country ... [so] I have endeavourd to inquire into the true interest and maxims of our republick.' In looking for the ideas with which Sidney chose to challenge the 'interest' and 'maxims' of the English monarchy, a closer look at de la Court's work is most instructive.

De la Court's origins as a theorist lay within a similar classical republican tradition to that with which Sidney was associated in England. His works employed the same Aristotelian forms, the same Polybian idea of mixing them, the same selection of Hebrew, classical, and modern republics, and the same particular fondness for Machiavelli. De la Court's choices within the tradition were equally radical; like Sidney and Nedham he criticised aristocratic Venice, and praised democratic Athens. Above all de la Court, with his brother Johan, shared Sidney's (and Nedham's) Platonic and neo-Stoic influence and their scepticism, to a point which led them not only to Tacitus, Seneca, and Machiavelli, but Montaigne, Descartes, Hobbes, and Spinoza as well.[12] What de la Court brought to his theory that Sidney didn't have, was membership of the merchant élite of Leiden, and a central concern with cities and trade.

For de la Court '[The] true interest of all countryes consists in the

[10] Rowen, *De Witt* p. 464; *Maxims* p. 177.
[11] Pontalis A. C., *John De Witt* (1885) I 302; Wilson C., *Profit and Power* pp. 11–18; Rowen H., *The Low Countries in Early Modern Times* (1972) pp. 200–1.
[12] Hobbes's sense of the disorder of the non-political state, and the need for strong centralised sovereignty, they (and Sidney) adopted. (They did not achieve it, it must be said, in the constitution of the United Provinces.) See Eco O. G., Haitsma Mulier, *The Myth of Venice and Dutch Republican Thought in The Seventeenth Century* (1980) ch. IV, esp. pp. 121–9, 131–3, 134, 137–51. Thus Sidney criticised Hobbes's absolutism, and his anti-humanism, but endorsed his concept of 'bellum omnium contra omnes' in the *Discourses* (pp. 42, 48, 378; cf. p. 188). Cf. Kossman E. H., 'The development of Dutch political theory in the seventeenth century' in *Britain and the Netherlands* I 91–110; and Tuck R., *Natural Rights Theories* p. 142.

prosperity of all the inhabitants.' Because 'in all societies or assemblies of men, self is always preferred; so all sovereigns or supreme powers will in the first place seek their own advantage in all things', therefore 'true interest cannot be encompassed by a government unless the generality of the people partake thereof; [and] therefore the publick welfare will ever be aimed at by good rulers'.[13]

This leads de la Court to the 'generall maxims of all rulers'. First, he considers monarchy. Monarchs and courtiers 'follow their [own] pleasures'; they rule for their 'private interests'. Therefore, says de la Court (acknowledging Aristotle's *Politics* Book 5, Chapter 11), ''tis the interest of monarchs to weaken and impoverish the subject that they may assume to themselves what power they please'. A prince's subjects are accordingly like horses which 'they [must] reduce and keep so tame and manageable, as not to refuse the bit and bridle'. 'For which end', in particular, 'it is highly necessary to prevent the greatness and power of their cities . . . to render them weak and defenceless . . . the reason is so strong and clear, and confirm'd by experience, that the history of all former ages, as well as the age we live in, teach[es] us.'[14]

De la Court accordingly denounces 'the ungodly Maxims of monarchical government', and on three counts: its corrupt 'administering justice'; its oppression of religion; and its destruction of trade. The object is to show that 'no country ever fell into greater slavery than Holland lay under during the service and government of those Princes [of Orange]'; and their courtiers 'those blood-suckers of the state . . . [who] cry up monarchical government to the very heavens'.[15] De la Court locates the origins of the evil of monarchy in Scripture: the text 1 Samuel 8: 'altho God did at first mercifully institute no other but a comonwealth government, afterwards in his wrath [he] appointed one sovereign over them'.[16]

'The interest of republican rulers', on the other hand, 'is to procure rich and populous cities.' Thus because the interest of the Netherlands in general is 'the prosperity and increase of the subjects' the 'true interest' of the Dutch lies in having a 'free commonwealth government'. While (again acknowledging Aristotle) several nations in 'Asia and Africa, as well as Europe, that lies southerly' are naturally 'of that temper and disposition that they cannot govern themselves', it is clear that this does not apply to the Netherlands. Moreover, the Dutch republican government is based on the recognition that the 'members of this Dutch republic are of different natures and manners'; just as, in Europe as a whole, the 'diversity of rules, subjects, countrys, and

[13] De Witt [and De la Court], *The True Interest and Political Maxims of The Republic of Holland* (London 1743) pp. xxx, 2.
[14] *True Interest* pp. 2–3.
[15] *True Interest* pp. xi, 7, 106.
[16] *Ibid.* p. 7.

situations, must needs cause a diversity of interests'. Accordingly the government of a state must be one which allows for this diversity by the liberty –
political, economic, and religious – that it grants to its citizens. Only this
policy will produce 'the prosperity and increase of the subjects'. Everyone
knows, says de la Court, the great importance of liberty of conscience for the
prosperity of Holland, as well as for the good of religion. Persecution is
irrational: belief cannot be compelled. That liberty and prosperity are
intertwined was sufficiently illustrated by the state of Holland's prosperity
compared to that of the 'many [nations] that are near us'. Both England and
France possessed huge natural resources the Netherlands lacked, but both
remained comparatively poor, because both possessed monarchical governments which operated against the wealth, happiness, and increase of their
citizens: 'neither in France nor England was there any liberty of religion, but a
monarchical government in both, with high duties on goods imported and
exported'.[17]

Finally, de la Court's work expounded the 'interest' of the Dutch Republic
in its international, as well as domestic, context. The Netherlands' true
interest abroad was to maintain peace for the good of its trade. This required
it to attempt to maintain the stability and Franco–Spanish balance of power
in Europe by all means (short of war); and to avoid entering into any offensive
engagements with other nations by which this might be upset. Hindrances to
Holland's international position would have been much worse over past
years he noted, had there been but one of those nations 'that are near us, well
suited for fishing manufactury, traffick and navigation, which during our
wars and troubles had seen and followed their own true interest'.[18]

Here, then, in this Dutch republican recipe for liberty and increase, had
already been set out not simply many of Sidney's central ideas and arguments
in the *Court Maxims*, and much of the basis for the ideology of 'liberty and
property' to the development of which he and Locke were later to contribute
in England, but also that 'two-fold meaning of interest' in Penn's 1679 work,
that for Gunn 'served to capture the bastions of state power for
individualism'.

I have discussed the local political context of the *Court Maxims* sufficiently
to show the obvious benefit to Sidney of adopting the political ideas of the
Dutch republicans themselves to argue his case. In particular we have seen
how he used the stick with which he was beating monarchy in general – the

---

[17] *Ibid.* pp. 6, 8, 10–11, 15, 16, 38, 44, 49–56; De la Court detailed all the ways in which a
monarchical 'interest' habitually destroyed trade and prosperity: imposing guilds and
monopolies, and other imprudent restraints like customs charges and high taxation; and
persecuting religion. Even now, he warned, all Holland's present prosperity could be ruined
by one mistake, 'which is the electing one supreme head over all these inhabitants, or over
their armies'. *Ibid.* pp. 37, 60–1, 68–70, 70–8, 78–88, 88–105.
[18] *True Interest* pp. 37, 60–1, 68–70, 70–8, 78–88, 88–105.

argument from interest – as the staff with which to try to link his cause with the anti-Orangist sentiments of the Dutch. In the process he openly held up the De Witt regime's 'good' government and 'liberty of traffick' as the example for England to follow. It was completely typical of Sidney that in order to argue an ideological case for unity with his host regime he should attempt to do so in their own political terms and language. And it is natural that the republican exiles should have sought to bolster their case with Dutch arguments, as they sought to do with Dutch arms. Indeed there seems little doubt that Sidney's problem was that he did so only too well.

For if we take Sidney's *Court Maxims* as roughly indicative of the arguments he put to De Witt in person then we can see that it furnished the Dutch leader, in his own political language, with every possible reason why he should deny Sidney help. Not only was the sort of offensive alliance argued for by Sidney anathema to Louvestein ideology, but Sidney had himself made, in the *Maxims*, as an enticement to his English audience, de la Court's point that an England, with its vastly superior natural position, defences, and resources, run effectively for the first time in accordance with its own 'true interest', could not only emulate but promise itself 'incomparibly more' than the Netherlands itself. It is thus no surprise that, as Burnet recorded:

De Wit was against it, and got it to be laid aside. He said it might engage them in a long war, the consequences of which could not be forseen ... [and] what would be the effect of turning England into [such] a Commonwealth, if it could possibly be brought about, but the ruin of Holland?[19]

As Sidney himself, like du Rohan, understood only too well, though states might have temporary common interests, like maintaining the balance of power (or breaking it), and although they might express these in temporary alliances, in general, by the terms of interest analysis, 'success in the game of [international] politics depended upon the accurate perception of one's own interests and those of the rulers of other states; and these were understood to be fundamentally opposed'.[20]

13.3 INTEREST (3) ENGLAND REVISITED

The idea of a continental, and, particularly, Dutch ideological context for Sidney's *Court Maxims*, both receives support from, and throws some light upon, the work of some other English Restoration writers.

The influence of de la Court's ideology of 'True Liberty' on the English republicans in Sidney's circle in Holland is even more obvious in the work of Slingsby Bethel, who took it and its economic preoccupations over wholesale and transported it to England. We have already discussed Bethel's *World's*

---

[19] Burnet, add MS 63,057 pp. 383–4.
[20] Keohane, *Philosophy* p. 174.

Mistake (1668), published soon after the Dutch period, and reproducing de la Court's 'interest' language and policy priorities exactly, in both domestic (trade) and foreign affairs (peace, and maintenance of the balance). In 1671 Bethel further developed his theories in *The Present Interest of England Stated*, written on the eve of the second Anglo–Dutch war. The key to England's 'Interest' abroad he argued, was a 'firm peace and amity' with the Netherlands; England must 'look upon them as the out-works, which must be first taken in by any invader that will attempt them', a repetition of the statement in 1659 by William Nieupoort (Dutch host to the republican exiles in 1665) that we saw in Chapter 8. At the same time Bethel praised the Dutch, among all

Countries [having] observed their Manners, and read their Disputes, and Transactions with other Nations ... in the generality of their Morals, they are a reproach to som Nations ... [and] I cannot think their Trade, or Wealth (although I believe, that Holland singly taken is the richest spot of ground ... since the Creation) to be a good or honest foundation for a quarrel; for their commerce [is] ... alone the effects of Industry, and Ingenuity.[21]

Nine years later, fifteen years after their political co-operation in Holland, Sidney and Bethel were together in action again. In 1680 Barillon, the French ambassador, reported from London 'the party of the independents and other sectaries [who] ... were masters during the late troubles ... are strong [again] in London; and it is through the intrigues of Algernoon Sidney that one of the two sherriffs, named Bethel, has been elected'. It was in this year that Bethel published a much extended second edition of his *Present Interest*, called *The Interest of Princes and States* (1680).

It was a complete reproduction, for an English audience, of de la Court's ideology of 'True Liberty'. His tract, Bethel announced, was an explanation of the two concepts of domestic and foreign 'Interest', according to the general political law that 'the prosperity or adversity, if not the life and death of a state, is bound up in the observing or neglecting its Interest'. 'When publick Principles do not govern men ... private Interest will.'[22] Domestically, the 'corruption' of a ruler was defined as the pursuing of 'private ends' over the 'Interest of his country'. In foreign affairs, Bethel explained that the general 'interest of European Princes' had changed since the decline of Spain and rise of France had altered the balance of power. England's 'Interest' was to keep the balance in Europe. This, he said, necessitated now above all a close alliance with the United Provinces. Under Elizabeth England had united with Holland to defeat Philip II; it was now the 'Interest of King and Kingdom of England to do the same against France'.[23]

---

[21] Bethel, *The Present Interest of England Stated* (1671) pp. 30–1, 33.
[22] Slingsby Bethel, *The Interest of Princes and States* (1680) pref. pp. 3, 6; text p. 2.
[23] *Ibid.* pref. pp. 4–6; text pp. 6, 28, 65.

Bethel laboured not only England's 'identity of interest' with the United Provinces abroad, but also the value for its own internal 'true Interest' of following that nation's cardinal policies. These he listed as keeping the peace; keeping down the Prince of Orange; maintaining liberty of conscience and, above all, promoting trade: 'the Netherlanders ... certainly understand the Interest of Trade ... equal to any people living'. Corrupt courtiers, lawyers, and other parasites, said Bethel, could only impoverish a nation; trade could only enrich it. Indeed trade was so naturally prone to advance a nation that 'nothing ... except violent obstructions (as imposing upon consciences etc) or want of good laws ... [are] capable of hindering the inncrease of it'. He concluded that England was so blessed with its situation and natural resources that under an 'active and ambitious' government 'so wise as ... to know [our] own Interest and pursue it', there could be no holding it back.[24]

As in 1670 when he spoke of his admiration of the Dutch upon reading their political literature, here Bethel came as close as he could to openly acknowledging the source of his ideas: this work, he wrote, was 'the result of the observations made by the Author long ago, in the time of his Travels, and writ some Years since'.

Let us return now to William Penn. Penn's theory has a great deal in common with Sidney's besides his use of interest language, something that will be discussed in the next book. What should be noted in this context are some obvious connections in experience between Penn and Sidney themselves. Penn in fact shared with Sidney the crucial aspects of every branch of context I have drawn in here: French, Dutch, and English.

Penn was, like Sidney, educated in France at the huguenot academy at Saumur. He then travelled in Europe with Sidney's nephew Sunderland, and may have met Sidney in Italy in the process.[25] He returned to England in 1664 through the Netherlands, staying in Rotterdam *en route* with none other than Benjamin Furly. After Sidney's own return to England, and probably through the common relationship with Furly, Sidney and Penn became friends and political partners. In 1679, accordingly, they formed an electoral partnership to get Sidney into the Commons. It was in the course of this campaign, during which time Sidney stayed frequently with Penn at his country house in Sussex, that Penn's *One Project*, of interest to Gunn, was published. It was during this year, too, that the similarly 'interest'-termed tract, *England's Great Interest in the Choice of This New Parliament*, was produced. This was the Sidney–Penn election manifesto, and informed England's 'Free-holders and Electors' of the 'True and Just Interest' each had in their own 'Lives, Liberties, and Estates'. It warned against 'men of mean spirits ... that would sell the

[24] *Ibid.* pp. 6, 10, 10–14, 28, 60–1, 65; pref. pp. 4–6.
[25] Hull, W., *William Penn* (N.Y. 1937) pp. 81, 83; For Penn at Saumur see Wildes H. E., *William Penn* (1974).

Interest of the People', and recommended instead 'Men of Industry and Improvement ... those that are Ingenious and Laborious to propogate the Growth of the Country, will be very tender of weakening or impoverishing it.' It was probably written by Penn (though it was – unusually for him – signed with the pseudonym 'Philanglus') but is so clearly the result of the joint intellectual, as well as practical, political enterprise of Penn and Sidney that the point of precise authorship is almost irrelevant.[26]

Another important English writer of the same period, Halifax, was also a prominent interest theorist ('interest will not lie is a right maxim') and his political theory, too, bears an uncanny resemblance to Sidney's in a range of respects.[27] Halifax had also lived in the huguenot South of France, and subsequently had his own eldest son educated at Saumur, during which period Sidney met him and courted his company. For indeed Halifax, like Sunderland, was Sidney's nephew. It was partly as a consequence of this relationship that in the same year – 1679 – Sidney, Halifax, and Penn were all involved together in a co-operative political enterprise to secure some measure of liberty of conscience in England. This was the period when Sidney, as Burnet put it, 'set upon all men yt he thought might be his tools ... [he] plied Hallifax much'.[28] At the same time, Sidney was maintaining his links with the Dutch republicans in general, and with Furly in particular, to whom his letters (with regular news of Penn) survive. When both Sidney and Furly accordingly provided Penn with criticisms of his proposed Frame of Government for Pennsylvania they were substantially the same. After his return from the first trip to Pennsylvania, in 1686, Penn again stayed with Furly in Rotterdam. There he met Furly's new house guest, another English theorist who had been involved in the same political movement as Sidney in England from 1679 to 1683, and the same theoretical enterprise of answering Filmer, but who had escaped Sidney's fate and subsequently fled to become what Sidney had been twenty years before: an exile in Furly's house in Rotterdam. This was John Locke.[29]

I have often mentioned the important bases Sidney's and Locke's political thought had in common. One is the equal reliance of both upon Grotius, the theorist of the first Dutch Republic; and the consequent stress of both on the

---

26 Philanglus [Wm Penn], *Englands Great Interest in the Choice of This New Parliament* (1679) pp. 2–3. My judgement that Penn wrote the tract is based only on style, but Sidney's presence in its content is equally apparent.

27 A point noted by his biographer Foxcroft; the discovery of the *Court Maxims* makes the similarity even more obvious. Foxcroft H., *The Life and Letters of George Savile* (London 1898) vol. II pp. 279, 282, 288, 289, 297, 335, 497.

28 Add MS 63,057 v II p. 138.

29 Sidney described Penn's *Frame* as 'worse than the Turk'; Furly as 'unsavoury and unjust'. Nash G. B., 'The framing of government; Pennsylvania' in *William and Mary Quarterly* 23 (1966) p. 202. Dunn M. M. and R. S., *The Papers of William Penn* (1981–2) II 82, 127–9, and doc. 82.

nature of civil society as a compact of law established by the consent of its members for the protection of (to use Locke's words, identical to Sidney's) 'life, liberty, estate'.[30] For both theorists, men move from an unstable and primitive state of nature to a commonwealth by resigning up their private right of judging and punishing transgressors over these things, collectively defined as 'property', to a common tribunal. For both theorists, accordingly, life under an absolute monarch or tyrant, whose will stands above the law, represents, for the subject, a miserable state of no legal redress in which (in Locke's words) '[any man's] property is invaded by the will and order of his monarch'. For both, therefore, a monarch who places himself above the law in this way accordingly places himself outside civil society, and so becomes a public delinquent against whom, in Sidney's phrase, quoted from Grotius, 'every man is a souldier'; or in relation to whom, in Locke's, every man is in a 'state of war'. Their identity on this point leads Locke to his most striking echo of Sidney's *Discourses*, given that it is a point which we have seen Sidney took from his father's own musings on Livy. In undermining by force, said Locke, the legal 'umpirage' by which relations between society's members were kept harmoniously ordered, tyrants reintroduced, by the law of nature, a state of war against themselves; for 'rebellion', comes from the Latin 'rebellare – that is, [to] bring back again the state of war'.[31]

Sidney's and Locke's works contain many other echoes, particuary revolving around their use of their basic natural-law sources, Aristotle and Grotius. But their common relation to Dutch theory does not end with the ideology of the first Republic, and Grotius. Locke's definitions of the nature of public and private 'interest' in the state; of the political relationship between them; and of the other specific objects for which society is set up, are not only also identical to Sidney's *Maxims*: they are as strongly reminiscent of the theory of the second Dutch Republic, of de la Court.[32]

In Locke's *Second Treatise* commonwealths are established 'under several constitutions and manners, according as chance, contrivance, or occasions happened to mould them'; the function of their internal laws, accordingly, is to regulate and harmonise 'the variety of opinions, and contrariety of interests, which unavoideably happen in all collections of men'.[33] The good commonwealth's function, accordingly, is 'by established laws of liberty to secure protection and encouragement to the honest industry of mankind, against the oppression of power and narrowness of party'. This protection, says Locke, has become in modern times particularly necessary since 'ambi-

---

[30] Locke, *Second Treatise* Gough J. W. ed. (1966) ch. VII no. 88.
[31] Locke, *Two Treatises* II XIX 226 (ed. Laslett p. 112).
[32] The other clear common ancestor Locke and Sidney have is Milton. Cf. Laslett ed., *Two Treatises* (1964) p. 32.
[33] Locke, *Two Treatises* no. 76; ch. VIII no. 98.

tion and luxury in [later] ... ages ... aided by flattery, taught princes to have separate interests from their people'. 'Those who speak as if the Prince had a distinct and separate interest from the good of the community, and was not made for it; [are] the root and source from which spring almost all those evils and disorders which happen in kingly governments'. It is above all his experience of this phenomenon, says Locke, which has moved him to write his tract, to 'examine more carefully the original and rights of government' in general, and the uses of royal power 'contrary to the ends for which society was created'.[34]

Although Locke's relationship with Shaftesbury put him in a different wing of the 1678–83 opposition movement from Sidney the two men nevertheless retained important contacts in common, which became more important – as Sidney himself did – when Shaftesbury died.[35] In 1682, for instance, Locke visited the country house of the Earl of Essex, at the time when Sidney had 'fataly subdued Essex so to him, yt he turned him which way he pleased'.[36] Locke also displayed a level of concern at Sidney's trial which has moved Laslett to suggest that it may have been responsible for the destruction of the bulk of his *First Treatise*.[37]

But as the thing which stands out about Sidney's *Maxims* in an English context is its emphasis not simply on 'Interest' but on cities and trade, so, too, the thing which strikingly characterises Locke's *Two Treatises* is the way in which it examines the *economic* origins and basis for the society of 'liberty and property' which it advocates. As society was set up, said Locke, to provide 'laws of liberty to secure protection and encouragement to the honest industry of mankind' (compare Sidney in the *Court Maxims*: 'we seek to increase our fortunes by honest industry ... to be governed by good laws, possess our goods in safety, with the full enjoyment of our Civil and spiritual Libertys') so man, said Locke, laid the foundations of the property society was set up to protect 'by being master of himself and proprietor of his own person and the actions and labours of it'. And as 'different degrees of industry were apt to give men possessions in different proportions, so [the] ... invention of money gave them the opportunity to continue and enlarge them'. Not only does Locke then discuss this increase of property primarily in terms of the growth and exchange of money; he also deliberately seeks to establish the superior value, in terms of this desired increase, of labour to land. In his words: 'This shows how much numbers of men are to be preferred to largeness of dominions.' This, of course, was the basis claimed by the near-

---

[34] *Ibid.* ch. IV 22; ch. VIII 3; ch. XIV 163 (Gough p. 83).

[35] Cf. Ashcraft R., 'Revolutionary politics and Locke's two treatises of government' in *Political Theory* vol. 8 no. 4 (1980), esp. pp. 444–50.

[36] Add MS 63,057 II 138. Burnet seems to have attributed to Sidney's political influence a debilitating effect not unlike that attributed by Sidney to monarchy.

[37] Laslett, *Two Treatises* pp. 63–4.

landless Dutch for their economic miracle performed in the face of their amply land- and resource-endowed neighbours, particularly France and England. It is also the basis of the focus we saw in de la Court, and so in Sidney, on an increase in population, trade, and cities, as the crucial indicators of success for the sort of society which they wished to set up. The nature of this society, as an artificial construct of law (Grotius), securing public over private 'interest' (de la Court), and protecting liberty in trade, politics, and religion together, as the basis for a culture of industry and increase, is the same in de la Court, Sidney, and Locke.

I do not mean to suggest that these ideas were unknown in London, or that Locke could not have developed them there. What is interesting is that Locke did not actually publish them in the form we know until his return from six years' living in the Netherlands. We should therefore be interested that he spent almost half of that time in the house of Sidney's, Bethel's, and Penn's friend, Benjamin Furly. There is a very real possibility in consequence not just that Locke's *Two Treatises* and Sidney's *Discourses* were written to answer the same opponent (Filmer) but that the *Two Treatises* and Sidney's *Court Maxims* were written, in part at least, in the form that we know them, in the same house. It was in Furly's house that Locke 'resumed writing, though whether on philosophy, toleration, or politics is not clear'. It was from there also that he requested from England the remaining 'half' of a tract which may have been the manuscript *Two Treatises*.[38] The suggestion that we should be interested in this contextual coincidence is reinforced by what we know about Locke's personal relationship with Furly.

The formative influence of Locke's Amsterdam period on his religious views, and his resulting *Essay on Toleration* has been long established.[39] No equivalent study has been undertaken of his subsequent Rotterdam period. There Locke became not only Furly's lodger but, like Sidney, a close friend who continued to correspond with him for the rest of his life. There, too, he attended meetings of Furly's Lantern Society, for religious and political discussion. In the process he was, as he freely admitted, strongly influenced by Furly's own views. Locke wrote to him in this period: 'I should suspect that you handle me thus smoothly with designe to draw me in to be hereticated by you. The truth is I finde you have gone a great way towards spoiling of me already.' Most importantly Furly, of course, was not just a republican and a quaker – he was also a merchant. And soon after Locke moved in he teased this English medical man for being naïve and 'unversed in matters of exchange'. Locke's biographer finds this hard to understand since Locke was

---

[38] Ashcraft, *Revolutionary Politics and Locke's Two Treatises of Government* (Princeton 1986) p. 536.

[39] See, for instance, Colie Rosalie, 'John Locke in the republic of letters' in *Britain and The Netherlands* I pp. 111–29.

later, as he points out, to establish himself within English philosophical circles as 'such a notable economist'. There seem to me grounds to ask then exactly when and under what circumstances he became one.[40]

There were other Restoration writers who equally argued the case for liberty of conscience in terms of 'Interest'; who linked the 'interest' of religious liberty with that of trade; and who used the Netherlands as a reference point for both. In 1668 Charles Wolsely condemned that wicked 'Policy ... destructive to all Publick Interest, to say subjects must be kept ignorant ... They must be kept poor. They are Maximes only fitted for a Tyrant, and such who only govern [for] themselves, and calculate all Interests ... as they concentrate [on] their own'; in its own knock-kneed fashion as concise a summary of the *Court Maxims* as could be desired. It is thus of interest again that when Sidney and Penn were campaigning together in Bramber in 1679 the candidate upon whose behalf Sidney gave a 'learned oration' was Charles Wolsely.[41]

Unlike the works of Penn, Locke, Bethel, and Wolsely, however, Sidney's *Court Maxims* was too vitriolic to be published in his lifetime. Like Ludlow's *Voyce* it was too religiously enthusiastic to be published, without a drastic rewrite, for an audience of whig admirers after his death. Unlike the *Voyce* it was also clearly written to promote a specific design, and the moment had long passed.

But there was another reason why the *Court Maxims* could not possibly have been published like the *Discourses* in 1698. The English King was William Prince of Orange, whose extermination it earnestly advocated. In the back of the second edition of the *Discourses*, however, published (shortly after William's death) in 1704, a list of books appeared being brought out in English for the first time by Sidney's publisher J. Darby. It included 'The True Interest and Political Maxims of the Republick of Holland ... Treating of Liberty in General, of Manufactures, Fisherys, Traffick ... Toleration of Religion ... Impartial Justice ... And of its Interest ... as to the Government of a Single Person. Written by John de Witt and other Great Men in Holland ...'

---

[40] Cranston M., *John Locke* (1979) p. 295.
[41] Wolsely Sir Charles, *Liberty of Conscience The Magistrates Interest* (1668) pt II 8, 10–11; Wolsely was a friend of Sidney's brother Lisle as early as 1656, de Beer E. S. ed., *The Diary of John Evelyn* (Oxford 1955) III 164–5.

14

Le Comte de Sidney 1666–77

The Earl of Northumberland is of the house of Percy, a rich, great, and ancient family that because it claims descent from the house of Lorraine boasts of its imaginary rights to the crown of France on account of the usurpation of Hugh Capet. With these visions is always associated the name Algernon, which was that of the Duke of Lorraine of their branch, who at that time should have succeeded to the throne.

Lorenzo Magalotti 'On the Nobility of England' 1668[1]

We shall soon prove, that the Kingdom of France neither was, nor is, disposable as a patrimony ... the law, by which such divisions were made, having been abrogated by the assembly of estates in the time of Hugh Capet.

Sidney *Discourses* p. 371

Hugh Capet, could neither pretend title nor conquest, nor any other right than what was conferred upon [him] ... by the clergy, nobility, and people.

Sidney *Discourses* p. 91

14.1 INTRODUCTION

We left Sidney in Paris, in 1666, amid the debris of his latest political design. Once again 'the broken limb of a ship-wrecked faction', he received a royal pass in August to change his residence from 'Germany' to Montpellier, in the south of France. He now faced the longest and most important of his several 'retirements'; an exile, indeed, from which he would never entirely return.

This period has always been the greatest hiatus in Sidney biography, principally because all accounts of his life have relied on English historical materials. As the reception accorded the Dalrymple evidence suggests, the resulting perspective was a matter of choice as well as convenience. To seek out Sidney's French experience risked an uncomfortable reappraisal of 'the whig Patriot' himself. Nobody spends eleven years anywhere without being influenced by it, and Sidney's total French experience was a good deal longer than that.

---

[1] Knowles W. E. ed., Middleton, *Lorenzo Magalotti at the Court of Charles II* (Ontario 1980) p. 118.

I have already shown the extent to which the perspective of Sidney's political writing was European rather than simply English. If we add to this eleven-year exile Sidney's earlier life and education in France we find that he spent eighteen years there, which is not much less than he spent in England. The absence of surviving evidence has allowed all Sidney's biographers to portray the French exile of 1666–77 as a dormant interlude in which the 'Patriot' prepared himself (e.g. by reading for the *Discourses*) for the later political role in England which was their principal interest. In fact this perspective needs to be reversed; there is much less to be learned by seeing Sidney's time in France from England, than by seeing his later activities in England from the standpoint of his experience in France. In the context of this chapter, what marked Sidney off most from his English contemporaries in the later period, 1677–83, was the fact that his political behaviour and writing partook less of the outlook of the English than of the French nobility, practitioners of insubordination and rebellion *par excellence*.

We must also, in the course of this chapter, travel some distance in time between the disillusioned 43-year-old who retired to Montpellier 'in the strength of my age', and the grateful 54-year-old who accepted a pass to visit England eleven years later. The distance is not simply one of years but of personal expectation, as in the latter period Sidney combined increasing personal sickness with references (e.g. in 1677) to where he proposed to 'finish' his days. This psychological ageing was accentuated by the strain of exile: a consciousness of past political failure combined with the various constraints of the present. In the end Sidney fell into the peculiar predicament of the long-term exile. He lost his personal country (Sidney's Republic) forever, and became suspended between two worlds: England and France, the past and the present; unable, while living in either, to completely belong to either, and increasingly on both counts the 'Patriot' of a country less real in geography than in memory. The most significant political outgrowth of this process was to be the *Discourses*, as much the work of an irritable old man as the *Court Maxims* is of an angry young one. It brings the knowledge and nostalgia, the moral authority and the repetition of an old man to bear against the heedless young world of the Restoration; it is an attempt to call to a sense of itself an age too inclined to forget, by an author insufficiently able to do so.

Sidney's time in France was divided between Languedoc in the south-east (from 1666 to some time between 1670 and 1672) and Guyenne/Bordeaux in the south-west (from 1672 or 1673 until 1677), with extended visits to Paris throughout the period (in 1666, 1670, 1676, 1677). From the whole, two most obvious themes emerge, both related to Sidney's family's historical contacts in France. The first is that the areas in which he based himself: Montpellier and its hinterland in Languedoc; and an area of Guyenne/Bordeaux bounded by Nerac in the south-east and La Rochelle in the north-west, were the two principal huguenot territorial strongholds in France.[2] Indeed Leicester's friend du Rohan and his family had led huguenot rebellions in both, in the sixteenth and seventeenth centuries respectively.

The second theme is that while in France Sidney entered a particular French aristocratic circle whose political experience and perceptions have a great deal to tell us about his own. It was here that 'Colonel Sidney' of the English civil wars became 'Le Comte de Sidney' of Nerac, for the south of France did not share England's rigid primogeniture and so aristocratic titles were inherited by all a noble's sons. When we see Sidney occupying a place of title within the French aristocracy which he could never (barring the death of Philip) have occupied at home, we can begin to see why he returned to England temporarily, not permanently, and specifically to secure against Philip a share in the Leicester estate that would give that title some independent basis and meaning in France. When we see the circle concerned we can also begin to understand why we find behind the cause of English parliaments in which his activities were housed, the associates, the attitudes, and the posture of the aristocratic frondeur. It is no accident that Sidney's closest associate in 1683 was the Earl of Essex, husband of Elizabeth Percy and brother-in-law of the last Earl of Northumberland. And if part of Sidney's own aristocratic self-image derived from his own Percy heritage, it was to be accentuated in France by the friendship of a group of nobility whose claims to such territorial power and political near-independence were less a matter of distant historical memory. This group were, as Sidney's one surviving letter from Nerac reveals to us, the related families of de Bouillon, Turenne, and de la Rochefoucauld, the principal aristocratic powers of the South-west. Together these men and their families made up (with another relative, Condé) the principal remnants of the last great noble rebellion – the noble Fronde.

As J. H. Elliot put it, compared to France's 'congenitally insubordinate nobility', even the aristocracy of Spain were tamed and domesticated in the seventeenth century; they 'displayed none of the French nobility's addiction to armed faction and rebellion'.[3] While the 'age of Louix XIV' retains the image of military greatness dominated by the brilliant spectacle of the royal court, it is easy to dismiss as bravado Sidney's comment in the *Discourses* that 'The beauty of it is false and painted . . . there is no real strength in it.' Yet modern scholarship tends to agree that the reality of France's internal situation in no way matched the external show. Apart from the continued independent powers and pretensions of the greater nobility, widespread poverty accentuated by unprecedented military taxation produced a great

---

[2] Mousnier Roland, *The Institutions of France under the Absolute Monarchy 1598–1789* (Chicago 1974) p. 384.

[3] Elliot J. H., *Richelieu and Olivares* (Cambridge 1984) pp. 93, 134.

wave of popular provincial uprisings, centring on the times and places of Sidney's own residence in France.[4]

It is certainly true that from Richelieu's ministry onward the French nobility were under continuing and cumulatively successful pressure to submit to rule from the centre; pressure which produced not only reactions like the noble Fronde but an ideology of the corruption of the 'ancient aristocracy' very like Sidney's own.[5] But unlike their English contemporaries they not only continued to possess important powers and independent judicial functions on their lands, but the role of military leadership remained 'a monopoly of the "sword" nobility'.[6] Louis XIV's conquests were led by one-time frondeurs like Turenne. It was the huguenot Turenne (Mareschal of France and Louis XIV's own military instructor) who was Sidney's own principal acquaintance at Versailles in this period. It was probably through Turenne that Sidney met his nephew Maurice-Godefroi, Duc de Bouillon, and thus came to take up residence at Nerac, part of de Bouillon's Duchy d'Albret. 'The great semi-independent Duc de Bouillon'[7] held a special position within the French noble hierarchy as a *'prince etranger'*, second only to the princes of the blood. This derived from his title as an independent Prince of Sedan, as well as a Lord subject to the French Crown. The result was that in addition to his military role in relation to the state he enjoyed across his own vast landholdings in the south-west the right to administer local justice quite independently and for his own profit; a right which gave him effective power of life and death over his own 'subjects'.[8]

It will thus be no surprise to us to find 'Le Comte de Sidney' writing to the Duc de Bouillon at length from Nerac in 1677 telling him how he should be running his estates; and at the same time imbibing some ideas about the relationship between noble and royal power which were a good deal more controversial transplanted to London than they had been in the Duchy d'Albret. In Nerac Sidney was to combine the role of adviser to princes with that of petty princeling himself.

In fact this life in Nerac provides us with a number of clues to Sidney's later political behaviour in England, particularly his courtship of the French ambassador Barillon in that period. Sidney believed that in his political role, and in his relationship to Louis XIV, Charles II was less the powerful

---

[4] The most important occurred in 1668–70 in Guyenne, 1670 in Languedoc, 1674 in Tours and Guyenne, and culminated in 1675 in Brittany and Bordeaux. Mettam Roger ed., *Government and Society in Louis XIV's France* (London 1977) pp. 265–6; Coveney P. J., *France in Crisis 1620–75* (London 1977) pp. 48–9; Pierre Goubert, *Louis XIV and Twenty Million Frenchmen* (London 1970) pp. 133–5.

[5] Rothkrug Lionel, *Opposition to Louis XIV* (Princeton 1965) pp. 114–15.

[6] Coveney, *France in Crisis* p. 48.

[7] Bishop Morris, *The Life and Adventures of La Rochefoucauld* (Ithaca 1951).

[8] See Lough John, *An Introduction to Seventeenth Century France* (London 1954) pp. 62, 68–9.

monarch of an independent country than a sort of overseas Prince of Sedan. And if he retained independent powers of judicial administration and revenue raising then it was apparent that in all other respects (foreign, military, and extra-territorial revenue) he was tied to the French King. This was a matter of deliberate policy: Charles II preferred to accede to this relationship with a brother monarch than with his own Parliament, and no one mindful of recent English history could blame him. In a sense the whole 'Exclusion Crisis' was an attempt by the Parliament to rescind this decision and it was one made possible not by any inherent strength in the position of Parliament itself but by an unseemly squabble between the monarchs themselves. When that relationship was restored Parliament was dispensed with once and for all, and those opposition leaders who had placed all their reliance and predicated all their strategy on Parliament (Shaftesbury) were ruined and led the cause to ruin with them. In the book to follow I will argue that Sidney, on the other hand (despite his own strategic errors), was quite right in seeing the King's *external* political relations (with Paris) and so the prospect of influencing them as the key to both the outbreak of the crisis in the first place and the nature of the resolution that would eventually emerge. Indeed Sidney's analysis of the true nature and springs of English politics from a continental perspective proved a good deal more realistic in general than the views of his more insular contemporaries, and for this reason: that the Restoration monarchs had themselves been continental and French exiles and shared the same perspective.

Thus it was that Sidney described in his *Discourses* 'the great [French] dukedoms and earldoms, little inferior to sovereign principalities'.[9] From the same premise it will be equally clear why from all the *Discourses*'s discussions of France one central idea emerges: that to all intents and purposes the aristocracy and monarchy remain interchangeable. The monarch is nothing but a hyper-aristocrat and is made so by nobody but the aristocracy (and people) themselves. Intertwined with this theme runs a constant refrain recounting the shocks given to the French Crown in the seventeenth century by its nobles and people. And it should come as no surprise that within this catalogue certain names and places not unknown to Sidney personally occupy the places of honour.

The commotions in Paris, Bordeaux, and other places, together with the wars for religion, shew, that though the french do not complain of every grievance, and cannot always agree in the defence and vindication of their violated liberties, yet they very well understand their rights ... [and if] the king ... do [any]thing against their laws ... they may oppose him.[10]

---

[9] Sidney, *Discourses* p. 144.
[10] Sidney, *Discourses* pp. 254–5.

The Duke of Orleans was several times in arms against Lewis the thirteenth his brother ... [and] Those who understand the affairs of that kingdom make no doubt, but that the count de Soissons would have set up for himself, and been followed by the best part of France, if he had not been killed in the pursuit of his victory ... Since that time the kingdom has suffered such disturbances as shew, that more was intended [by the noble Fronde] than the removal of Mazarin: and the marshal de Turenne was often told, that the check he gave to Condé at Gien ... had preserved the crown upon the King's head ... And to testify to the stability, good order, and domestic peace that accompanies absolute monarchy [let us remember also the rebellions of] ... the dukes of Angoulesme, Vendome, Longueville ... the houses of Guise, d'Elbeuf, Bouillon, Nemours, Rochefoucault, and almost all of the most eminent in France, with the parliaments of Paris, Bordeaux, and some others, joining with them.[11]

Elsewhere we get the same roll call: 'the houses of Conde, Soissons, Montmorency, Guise, Vendome, Angoulesme, Bouillon, Rohan, Longueville, Rochefoucault, Espernon, and I think I may say, everyone that is of great eminency in that kingdom, with the cities of Paris, Bordeaux, and many others, in the space of the last fifty years, have sided with the perpetual enemies of their country'.[12]

It will be observed that this 'space of the last fifty years' covers the period from Sidney's initial residence in France with his father to the time of his own final departure. The catalogue of rebellious names includes his father's friends from the earlier period, Rohan and Condé, as well as Sidney's own from the latter: Turenne, Bouillon, and de la Rochefoucauld. The two groups were indeed closely related, by family, by religion (though not uniformly), and particularly through the central event of the noble Fronde. In 1650 Conde had joined with Turenne, his brother Frederic-Maurice Duc de Bouillon (the father of Godefroi-Maurice), and de la Rochefoucauld to bring it about, just as in 1652 Turenne had finally turned against Condé at Gien to bring it to an end. It was as these men commanded the South-western rebel army centred in Bordeaux, and Mazarin laid siege to the city and sacked de la Rochefoucauld's estate at Verteuil (where Sidney was later to visit him during the Nerac period), that Bordeaux became a centre for radical political ideas (including regicide) imported from the English Republic.[13]

The records of the de la Tour family, Ducs de Bouillon, reveal that all the incidents Sidney mentions in the *Discourses* are actually episodes in their family history; and it is a history which reads remarkably like that of Sidney's own family (and of Sidney himself). Thus Frederic-Maurice was famous for

son espirit independant[,] et ses sentimens passiones le firent participer aux divers complots du regne du Louis XIV. [Under Louis XIII too] Il s'unit au comte de

---

[11] Sidney, *Discourses* p. 211.
[12] Sidney, *Discourses* p. 144.
[13] One of those who imported them was Colonel Sexby, co-author of *Killing Noe Murder*. Bishop, Morris, *The Life and Adventures of La Rochefoucauld* (Ithaca 1951) pp. 177–219. The losers were eventually pardoned: La Rochefoucauld lived until 1680.

Soissons [the rebellion mentioned in the *Discourses*, quoted above] *contre le roi et Richelieu et contribua a la victoire de la Martee en 1641.*[14]

Sidney's own relationship with 'the brave Monsieur Turenne' (as he called him in the *Discourses*) may not have been unrelated to the fact that he was the de la Tour second son; one who had risen to power in the state by his own military merit.

We don't know how far the Sidney–de la Tour relationship stretched back or whether Sidney's father Leicester himself had known the Duc de Bouillon and was responsible for his son's introduction, as seems likely. But the father of both Turenne and Frederic-Maurice was the huguenot *Henry de la Tour, ancien compagnon d'Henri IV, et marechal de France* and I have noted earlier how the Château de Nerac had been an important centre for Henry IV's *noblesse de robe*. Among the de Bouillon family papers are preserved letters to both Henri de la Tour (Prince of Sedan and Duc de Bouillon) and his wife Elizabeth de Nassau (Duchesse de Bouillon) from Philippe du Plessis Mornay; and de la Tour's children and grandchildren were to have subsequent close relations with Christina of Sweden. It was, of course, as Christina's ambassador in Paris that Grotius had become friendly with Leicester.[15] Christina's other friends included not only Algernon himself but de la Rochefoucauld as well (an edition of his *Maximes Morales* annotated by her has been published). We are reminded how much not only Sidney's education but also his character and subsequent experience fit the model of this circle of French nobility when we read not only of Frederic-Maurice's rebellious *'espirit'*, but how, following the failure of the rebellion of de Soissons, he went to the papal Court of Urban VIII in the early 1640s, and there decided (with a commission from Cardinal Barbarini, described among Sidney's 'Characters') to fight against the Turks instead.

Thus the history of these families was like (and at some point probably connected with) the history of Sidney's own; their country was the country in which Sidney had been educated and to which he had now returned; their religion was in many cases more meaningful to him than that of his own country; and above all their political experience and attitudes helped to form his own ideas about the contest between (aristocratic) independence and absolutism in a formative way. For his entry into this society he had been prepared by the aristocratic culture of his family in general and father in particular; and it was a culture, a religion, and a political cause which transcended national boundaries in a way that no distinction between nation and exile can adequately capture. After Sir Philip Sidney's own, no career more clearly exemplified this internationality in all these respects than that of Grotius, with the roles (shared by Algernon) of diplomat and exile by which it

---

[14] d'Huart S., *Inventaire des Archives Rohan-Bouillon* (Paris 1970) p. 113.
[15] *Ibid.* pp. 78, 115–17, and 142–3.

was attended. Thus also it was the exile Grotius who most squarely captured the perspective of this internationalism for political theory in his *Law of War and Peace* (creating 'international law' in the process); and so creating the basic textbook for Sidney's own political thought as well. And as it was in Paris that that work was written; as it was in Paris that Grotius met Leicester and Sidney himself was educated; so it was in Paris a generation later that Sidney was to identify that work's importance to him to Lantin.

As I have already suggested in Chapter 12, it is thus less true to Sidney's life and mind to speak of him as an Englishman in exile in France, than as a citizen of the European cities, particularly London and Paris (though also Rome, Amsterdam, Venice, Geneva, and elsewhere). The place he felt exiled to was not France as such but the countryside; and it was this exile which he was to punctuate with regular visits to the capital throughout the period. Paris itself remained as full of the European (and so also English) aristocratic and diplomatic community in general, and of members of Sidney's family in particular, as it had been in his father's time. As Mazarin – another immigrant to France – put it in 1637: 'To a gentleman, any country is a homeland.'[16] This was a return for Sidney to the environment in which he had been raised: paradoxically its internationality is harder to imagine now after 300 years in which the most significant political development has been the solidification of the separate nation state. It was in the early modern period that Europe was beginning to lose (through religious division) the belief by which it had been nominally united like a collection of provinces, and to gain in its place separate and (eventually) more secular nationalisms backed by the new centralising and military forces of the nation state. We now live in a world where nationalisms support all the old wars and atrocities once committed for religion, and the separate identities of states (including some European states) are now protected with the zeal of weapons offering global (and to this extent unifying) annihilation. With their schemes for European protestant unity, Sir Philip Sidney, Grotius, and Leicester were among the last of the backward-looking would-be unifiers; their great contemporary enemy was Richelieu, architect of the nation state and the ideology of reason of state. Richelieu (and others) wrested the state from the ruins of religious division and the equally centripetal force of aristocratic independence; Sidney, his family, his aristocratic friends in France, and their shared culture, represented this opposing and nostalgic force in both its religious and aristocratic respects. The rebellion of de Soissons and Bouillon against Richelieu in 1641 perfectly expressed its aspirations, as the two men issued in Sedan a manifesto promising 'to restore everything to its former place; re-establishing the laws ... the immunities, rights and privileges of the provinces, towns and

[16] Parker, G., *Europe in Crisis* (1979) p. 270.

personages that have been violated ... ensuring respect for churchmen and nobles';[17] all at the same time as men like Northumberland were preparing action against Charles I on the same basis across the Channel. This force was (in modern terms) 'international' in that it was an enemy of, and a challenge to, the nation state, and Sidney's anti-absolutism amounts in large part to an expression of that enmity. It was an enemy not simply to the internal centralisation but also to the narrow (amoral, and irreligious) conception of external interest involved; by which the state refused to involve itself any longer in religious crusades abroad. When Richelieu finally took France into the Thirty Years War, it was not for religion but for reasons of state which put the nation on the wrong (protestant) side of the religious divide. The opposition which he aroused was only slightly less serious than that eventually incurred by Charles I for refusing to become involved at all. Both nations were in their own ways turning their backs on the sixteenth century; not everybody was prepared to make the change.[18]

14.2 MONTPELLIER, 1666–70

Montpellier was not only a principal huguenot centre in the south of France but a favourite resort for Englishmen also. Sidney's arrival there was followed a year later by that of the Earl of Clarendon, and John Locke, too, spent fifteen months there from 1676 to 1677.[19] One of its attractions was a prestigious medical faculty, and it is to some form of medical indisposition on Sidney's part that we owe this memoir (written twenty years later) by Thomas, Earl of Ailesbury:

I remember great clamours there were relating to the executing Colonel Algernon Sidney. It was well known how he behaved himself during the time of Cromwell and after his death, and when he had the mortification to see the King happily restored, he ... lived [abroad] shifting about in Republican governments for the most part. Being at Montpelier he had like to have killed Mr Barberai, my physician after, who told it me there; and for what? Because a medicin he had taken by his order had not operated to his mind! I mention this one particular, but I knew from many of what an amplacable [sic] spirit he was of, and towards kingly government most of all.[20]

Clearly Dr Barberai had not read Sidney's *Discourses* p. 342:

---

[17] Parker G., *Europe in Crisis* (1979) p. 268.
[18] As Sidney noted in the *Court Maxims*, the Thirty Years War was not a war of religion – it was a war of state-building, employing the formidable new arms of the State, and in this respect the internationalist response it drew from Grotius (1625) was to be duly overridden and ignored. Sidney's position is, however, more complicated than this, since he also picked up aspects of the new unifying tendencies: for instance reason of state ideology in his own political theory, as well as zealous centralising autocracy in his own (republican) political practice.
[19] Lough John ed., *Locke's Travels in France* (1953).
[20] Ailesbury, *Memoirs* p. 136.

A physician does not exercise his art for himself, but for his patients; and . . . I send for him of whom I have the best opinion . . . but I lay him aside if I find him to be negligent, ignorant, or unfaithful; and it would be ridiculous for him to say, I make myself judge in my own case, for I only, or such as I shall consult, am fit to be judge of it.

From Montpellier in 1666 Sidney wrote to Benjamin Furly, enclosing in his own hand a copy of 'A Prophesy of St Thomas the Martyr'.[21] This 'Prophecy of Thomas Becket', re-'discovered' in the seventeenth century by William Lilly, had been attributed variously to Bede, 'Mr Truswell Recorder of Lincoln', and (by the quakers) to Boehme.[22] It described an apocalyptic conflict between the Lily, the Eagle, the Lion, and the Son of Man which interpreted politically depicted a European conflagration in which France would be dismembered by its protestant English, Dutch, and German neighbours. While this application may have been Sidney's intention, and while it made the 'Prophecy' most suitable for publication by Furly in 1688, the political identifications made on the manuscript itself are additions and are not in Sidney's hand. Whatever the intended substance of the prophecy, the tone is clear enough:

[A]nd after shall be a deluge of blood . . . [and] many batailes amongst the followers of faith. The greatest part of the world shall be destroyed. The head of the world shall fall to the ground . . . and then there shall be peace over all the [world] and the sonne of man shall take the wonderful signe and passe to the land of promise.

Apparently the placidity of life in Montpellier was already getting Sidney down.

In April of the following year a less apocalyptic communication was received by the new English ambassador in Brussels, Sir William Temple, son of Algernon's friend Sir John. Temple informed Secretary of State Arlington:

Hee [Sidney] desired my conveyance of two [letters] enclosed, one to my Lord Northumberland and one to my father desiring my pardon for the trouble hee gave mee, wch hee was tempted to by the miscarriage of all his letters of late both from and into England. He assurd mee that the letter to my Lord Northumberland concernd nothing but the provision hee was making of some barbary horses for Him, and the other I suppose was concerning his lands in the Fenns, about wch I know my father was intrusted . . . I remember I asked yr Lsp upon my coming over, what my carriage should bee, if I mett him in any of my journeys, wch I thought my father's former acquaintance with him and some little of my owne might bring to pass, yr Lsp then told mee I might bee civil to him, and just so much I have been, upon this occasion.[23]

Temple replied to Sidney, informing him that

I had letters very lately from Petworth and Penshurst which left Health in both those

---

[21] Surviving and endorsed by Furly in the Bodleian. MS Engl. Letters C200 fols. 24–5; Furly had the Prophesy printed in 1688, in English and Dutch: copies are in the BL 1103.f.27(15) (English); 1103.f.27(16) (Dutch).

[22] Thomas Keith, *Religion and the Decline of Magic* (London 1971) p. 395.

[23] Temple, *Works*, Swift J. ed. (1750) vol. II p. 31.

Places ... Your present Abode was no Secret to me ... that Information having been given me ... by some English Gentlemen, who passed from Italy through Germany and these parts into England, where I cannot think they made a greater secret of it ... than they had done here. I am sorry your Dispositions or your Fortunes have drawn you so far out of the Reach of your Friends services, and almost Correspondence ...

Within three days of Temple's letter Arlington was also informed from Brussels by another (unidentified) hand:

I received yesterday a letter ... from Coronel Sidney from Provence from where I heerd not a word This very long time; I am apt to believe he would be glad [if] he were permitted to returne home and live quietly there, he is a man of excellent parts, and knowledg in the affaires of Europe; I think it would not prove disadvantageous to his Majesty's service to give him this liberty and by that means take him of[f], from casting his thoughts anywhere else and from all affayres ...[24]

This suggestion produced no recorded result, leaving Sidney to make his own advances three years later.[25]

14.3 PARIS, 1670

In 1670 Sidney paid an extended visit to Paris, to attend to his 'particular affairs'. These involved among other things a visit to Turenne at Versailles. His presence in Paris at this time also coincided with that of the Northumberland family who occupied the Hotel Bationere for the first half of the year.[26] Members of Sidney's own family also spent time in Paris: Dorothy in 1677 and probably earlier; Henry in 1675; Sunderland (with Lady Northumberland, Mapletoft, and John Locke) in 1672–3.

Someone else in Paris cultivating French political contacts at the same time was the Duke of Buckingham. From London the Duke of York noted this geographical proximity darkly and concluded that 'it was by his [Buckingham's] order that Sidney waited in Paris, for them to hatch together some plan prejudicial to the service of the king'.[27]

There is no evidence that this was so, but certainly somehow by mid 1670 Sidney showed himself well aware of the new drift in Anglo–French relations in that year. Accordingly, after the secret Treaty of Dover in May, but before the public one in December, Sidney used this knowledge as the context for a

---

[24] PRO SP Flanders 36 fol. 205.
[25] From Montpellier Sidney was also, according to Ludlow, in correspondence with a friend in Geneva. And on 'le 6 Octobre 1668 a Montpellier il [Sidney] delivrait a Mr David Abrenathee, ministre protestant, un certificat portant temoignage de l'anciennete de sa femille d'origine Eccosaise'; whether this refers to Sidney's family or Abernathy's (and what it means if the former) is not clear. Archives de Lot et Garonne, Serie J fonds Lagrange-Ferregues p. 185.
[26] Ministere des Affaires Etrangeres Corresp. Politique Angleterre vol. 99 Du Roy a Colbert 29 July 1670 p. 269; PRO SP France 129 nos. 6a, 265. PRO SP France 136 pp. 104, 126, 207; 137 p. 220.
[27] PRO Baschet 31/3 4 August 1670 no. 125.

proposal for his own political rehabilitation. His unsolicited counsel to the English King was relayed through Turenne, and transmitted in August by Louis XIV himself.

The French King described Sidney as 'An English gentleman named Philipe Sidney ... one who was a great parliament man', and who had made a series of points to Turenne which might be 'worthy of some consideration'. He enclosed Turenne's transcript of the conversation and requested Charles II's and Arlington's opinion. Turenne recorded:[28]

The said Sidne after several discourses of things passed which it would be superfluous to relate testified that ... he had a strong disposition to render his services to the King of Great Britain. He avowed that his sentiments had always been entirely parliamentary, and that if the party into which he had entred (which was not that of Cromwell but of Parliament) had had the direction of affairs instead of the Protector, they would have established for their conduct three principal maximes, Firstly, the ruin of the Dutch, second the humiliation of the Spaniards, and thirdly a strict union with France by which they hoped to augment their commerce.

Concerning England's internal affairs Sidney claimed 'that the Presbeterians and independents would never rest quietly until they had liberty of conscience; and that he personally had less hatred for the Catholic religion than for the government of the [English] bishops'. He 'was persuaded that in accordance with liberty of conscience the state would become extremely tranquil, and that those who had at other times supported [civil] war, would then wish for nothing but peace'. He insisted, again emphatically, 'that in consultation with the heads of the various sects and some measure of liberty of conscience, the King of England would have nothing to fear from them; on the contrary he would be able to depend upon their fidelity ... and from that he could take all his security'. One of the hearers at the other end of this advice was the Duke of York who, as James II, was to institute just such a policy in 1687–8.

Finally, Sidney claimed that he was sure 'all the people of England generally supported the ruin of the Hollanders'. Turenne recorded at the end that his companion did not seem at all to have a 'broken spirit', but that he 'supported himself with many reasons' to argue his case.

For those who would like to find consistency in all Sidney's conduct the Turenne transcript presents a greater obstacle than any other episode in his life. It is much more difficult to explain in this respect than the later negotiations with Barillon, which were simply in pursuit of the same Anglo–Dutch republican strategy that Sidney had followed in 1665–6. In its foreign policy suggestions, however, the Turenne transcript flatly contradicts the pro-balance of power and thus ultimately anti-French drift of both these

---

[28] For the Turenne transcript see Paris, Ministere des Affaires Etrangeres, Du Roy a Colbert 29 July 1670.

periods, and thus of both the *Court Maxims* and the *Discourses* as well. The anti-Dutch animus of Sidney's arguments to Turenne may owe something to his disappointment with De Witt in 1665–6, but principally it simply reflects the transfer of his hopes to the Anglo–French alliance (as earlier the Anglo–Dutch war) as the means for influencing policy in England. In this respect the transcript is simply a typically (relativist) Machiavellian attempt to make what political gains could be made by exploiting the circumstances of the time.

As such its principal interest (aside from its opportunism, and its emphasis on trade, both instructive) is Sidney's willingness to overlook, in the short term at least, the political issue of the monarchy itself in order to secure the religious goal of liberty of conscience. This is entirely in accordance with the political scepticism we have examined, in which political effect is more important than form, and (as in the Netherlands itself) all means available (including monarchy itself) are to be used to secure the given effect. In this respect it is no more surprising to find Sidney volunteering support for French policies in 1670 than to lead French troops in 1666; he was always adept (as later with Barillon from 1678 to 1680) at attempting to serve his own purposes by telling his contacts what he thought they wanted to hear. What is more difficult to know here is what in their entirety those purposes were, and what effects (apart from liberty of conscience) Sidney really hoped might flow from this advice in England. In view of his past and future behaviour it would be naïve to assume he had reconciled himself to the monarchy in England; indeed given his stated belief that the superstitions of monarchy and religious uniformity depended upon one another he presumably hoped that by removing one the conditions would eventually be created for the removal of the other. Naïvety, however, was probably the weakness from which Charles II suffered least.

Certainly 'he knew the said Sidney', replied Charles II, 'for a man of great courage and spirit, though also the most opinionated republican he had in his whole realm ... [Sidney] had promised (and that was the least he could do) that he would not do anything against him as long as he lived' – the first we hear of any such agreement, and one in exchange for which Sidney had presumably secured himself against further royal harassment. He certainly knew, continued the King

that everything Sidney had said to Turenne was exactly right; that he [too] is certain that the majority of the English support the ruin of the Dutch; that he too is persuaded that his realm will never be at peace if liberty of conscience is not accorded to all the principal sects, as he himself desires; and ... he believes that by giving [this liberty] to others, they will not take it ill accordingly when he also takes it for himself.[29]

[29] PRO Baschet 31/3 no. 125 (4 August 1670).

What is most interesting about this whole episode, then, is not Sidney's proposals so much as the King's response; and from them must arise the possibility that in formulating the strategy of 1672 the King was encouraged or influenced by what Sidney had said. What emerges from the exchange as a whole is how well the two men seem to have understood one another and how much common ground they had. The common ground was as members of the same generation, their lives dominated by the experience of the civil war and the respective exiles which followed. Both intrigued in the Netherlands against the government of the other; both retired to France when their overtures were rejected by De Witt. Both became (pro-trade) sceptics with a continental perspective on English politics and religion and so a distaste for the persecuting self-righteousness of the insular Anglican Church. As Sidney's understanding of the King is suggested by the nature of his proposals, so the King showed that he understood Sidney well enough by agreeing with his policies and refusing to take the hand by which they were offered. He told the French King that he did not care whether Sidney lived in Paris or Languedoc, provided that he did not 'return to England, where his pernicious sentiments, supported by such great parts and courage could do much harm'.

Nevertheless, three weeks later Arlington again raised the possibility of making use of Sidney. He suggested that if the French King were to offer him '*quelque petite assistance*' to retain him in Paris then the 'great correspondence' he kept up with the republicans and sectaries in England could make him very useful. But he could not convince the King, who showed increasing uneasiness every time Sidney's name was mentioned. Finally, Charles 'after speaking several times of the dangerous intentions of the said Sidney, concluded that it would be best if he were sent back to Languedoc, and that he could not be far enough from England'.[30]

14.4 LIMOGES AND THE FIRST PASS, 1673–75

Yet if Sidney was disappointed in 1670 we nevertheless now know that only three years later the Earl of Leicester was able to win him permission to visit England. The peculiar matter of this first pass, and the mystery still attaching to Sidney's failure to take it up, form a small chapter in the continuing saga of Sidney's relations with his family which was to culminate in the battle over Leicester's will. I can best treat it separately here, before proceeding with the account of Sidney's remaining years in the south of France.

The confusion still surrounding this episode stems in large part from the nature of our evidence for it: it became the subject of yet another chancery dispute, this time between Algernon and his brother Henry in 1682. Accordingly we have only Algernon's later and partial account (Henry's reply was

---

[30] Baschet 31/3 no. 125.

never returned), shrouded by the claim and counter-claim of intra-family legal strife.

In 1672 the Earl of Leicester found himself facing new legal action, over plans for developing his property of Leicester Fields in London. His problem was his (at least titular) heir Philip's refusal to legally bind himself to maintain any improvements after the Earl's death, an obstruction which made the necessary long-term leases for the buildings impossible. It was on account of this situation that in April 1673 the Earl desired 'that Algernone Sydney should come into England ... that he might be assistant unto him in his affaires ... complaining unto Henry that he would not assist him'.[31] Leicester applied himself to Arlington and a pass was granted for Algernon to return in July 1673.

It is far from certain what happened next. Algernon's bill of complaint of 1682 accuses Henry and his steward Gilbert Spencer of an orchestrated conspiracy from 1673 to 1677 to keep him out of England and so out of first place in his father's affections and inheritance. Behind the detail we will recognise an old obsession, yet we would be unwise to dismiss Sidney's story as mere paranoia. Most of the facts it relates to are documented and, while his interpretation of them is the highly suspect outgrowth of a later legal dispute, without it or some alternative some of the facts are very difficult to explain away. The central problem may be simply stated. If the pass was valid (as Sidney claimed, and as it seems to have been)[32] and Sidney himself knew that it was at the time (which he denied), why didn't he use it? Why then, too, did he never mention the first pass before 1682, even during his negotiations for a second one in 1676–7? And if he didn't know it was a valid pass then why not?

According to Sidney, in 1671 Leicester had drawn up a codicil to his will dividing all his personal estate evenly between Henry and himself: all 'books, writings and papers, goods, chattells, and moveables, and all mony plate and jewells'. Two years later, however, and seven months after the issuing of Algernon's pass and his failure to return upon it, the Earl annulled this codicil and replaced it with another giving Algernon £5,000 out of the personal estate and Henry the rest

Sidney said he was first informed that his pass was pending one month before it was granted, in early June 1673. The Earl had entrusted the task of liaising with Sidney on the matter to Henry, who in turn employed Spencer to write to him. Spencer's letter told Algernon of the pass 'but warned him not to comme away, untill the end of the summer, nor then without positive directions from the Earle his father'. In August Spencer sent a copy of the pass

---

[31] De Lisle MS U1475 L5; one of Leicester's opponents in these disputes over Leicester Fields was one 'Robert Filmore', cf. Chancery C6 205/51 (1672).

[32] CSPD 1673 p. 459.

itself 'withal shewing it to be very imperfect, and renewing the warning given, not to comme upon it, and not long after [Spencer] sent severall letters unto Alg Sydney as by the command of the sayd Earle, seeming to be greatly discontented with him, that he did not comme'.[33]

Almost two years later, in July 1675, following the replacement of the first codicil with the second

Henry came unto Alg. Sydney then at Limoges in france[34] and told him of the second codicile made (as he sayd) [for the benefit of] . . . the sayd Alg [Sydney, as available] . . . immediately unto him, wheare the other parts consisting in house hols [*sic*] stuffe and arreares of ren[t] would be hard for him to [bring o]ver, unless he could comme into Ingland, which Alg: Sydney believing to be true, did rest satisfied with, only desired he might have so much household stuffe and plate as would furnish a littell house for him [in France], whereupon Henry Sydney sayd all that [would be] given unto him.[35]

At this stage, then, far from being disgruntled with what he was later in the suit to call 'only 5000', Sidney now wrote to thank his father for his care and generosity. In Limoges 'Henry Sydney alsoo sayd that the forementiond passe given by hi[s] Ma[jes]ty had bin deliverd unto him by the Ld Arlinton and that he would have brought [it] unto him but that it was defective, and would be of noe use, but [he] would endeavour to get . . . [a] better [one].'

Summing all this up in 1682 Sidney concluded that he had been kept in France 'by the fraud of Gil: Spencer, whoe by [Henry's] order had sent him a false coppy, to deterre him from comming over, that he might the better work upon the infirmitys of his father in his extreame age'. The second codicil 'doth by its date shew that the Earle made it, when he was discontented with Alg Sydney because he did not comme over, whilest his passe was fraudulently detained . . . and commands pretended from the Earle, that he should not'. Following his eventual return in 1677, said Sidney, he discovered that the £5,000, far from being equivalent to half the personal estate 'appeared not to be the [fift – crossed out] sixt part of it'. He also spoke to Arlington in London who told him that the original pass had been 'as lar[ge] and full, as any that his M[ajesty] had ever granted'. The level of wickedness implied by this account reached a suitably Gothic climax in the traditional deathbed scene:

The Earle seemed to have discovered theis frauds when he was too farre spent to repaire the prejudice done by them, and Alg: Sydney comming to him the day before he dyed, thinking of nothing lesse then to trouble him with any concernements of his owne he with a dying voice and eyes sayd severall times I cannot, indeed I cannot, I would if I could, I would if I could and then his speech failed him but [he] sayd enough to be understood by Alg: Sydney, and such as were then present.

There is no question that this story bears strong marks of the immediate circumstances of its creation, when (as the next book will relate) a last minute

---

[33] De Lisle MS U1475 L5 pp. 1–2.
[34] Henry left England for France in April: CSPD 1675–6 p. 67.
[35] *Ibid.*

piece of legal non-cooperation by Henry combined with the nature of the final will settlement (which favoured Henry) threatened to throw the whole joint settlement against Philip into jeopardy. It must have been easy, at that point of extreme frustration, for Algernon to take refuge in historical paranoia, concluding that the cards had been stacked against him by the 'fraud' of his younger brother from the beginning.

Moreover, if, without believing something of this story, it remains difficult to explain why Algernon failed to avail himself of a pass which seems clearly to have been good, it is equally true that the story itself suffers from some significant lacunae. A minor one is the question of why Sidney remained silent about a fraud he discovered in 1677 until 1682; co-operation with Henry in that period was a legal necessity but it is hard to believe he could have swallowed such a monstrosity for so long and with so little difficulty. A corollary to this is that it is hard to understand how, if Algernon really believed his own story, he could have forgiven Henry sufficiently by the following year to make him the major recipient of his will.

But the major problem with Sidney's account is that it involves accepting that he received instructions from his father not to come (which he took at the time to be genuine), followed soon after by expressions of discontent that he did not come, and with no explanation offered of how this confusion was resolved. That it was is made clear by the fact that Sidney and his father were on sufficiently good terms by 1675 for Algernon to take the new codicil as an expression of favour and to thank him for it.

We must thus at least consider the possibility that Sidney may for reasons of his own have been reluctant to accept the pass home in 1673 to reinvolve himself in his father's legal affairs. He may therefore himself have quibbled about the form of the pass (as he was to do in 1677) or he may have done so because he was genuinely anxious about the political safety of such a move. He may, in other words, have shown the same reluctance in the face of his father's efforts as he had in 1660, and with the same paternal disgruntlement as a result. Only a firm sense that Algernon would never be returning – rather than temporary difficulties about the form of a pass – would seem to explain either Leicester's action to convert Sidney's share of the legacy to movable money, or Algernon's preparedness to accept the change at the time as having that intention. When after his subsequent return, Sidney found that this share of the legacy seemed not to match Henry's after all, it must have been easy to read this (probably wrongly) as an expression of his father's disapproval, and to blame the apparent beneficiary for knowingly exploiting or even creating the situation.

Neither explanation is entirely satisfactory, and the deficiency of evidence permits us to go no further. It is to the life that Sidney was living in the south-west of France at the time that we must now turn our attention.

14.5 NERAC AND THE SOUTH-WEST, 1672–7

Notwithstanding the seeming prosperity of France, matters there are not much better managed. The warlike temper of that people is ... worn out by the frauds and cruelties of corrupt officers... *Discourses* p. 239

If in 1670 Sidney had returned from Paris to Languedoc, by the turn of the year 1672/3 he had moved west to Nerac, where he was to be based for the rest of his exile. Nérac is near Agen on the Garonne river, well inland from and slightly south of Bordeaux. From here he visited a number of places north and north-west (Limoges, Verteuil, Ruffec, almost certainly Bordeaux itself) enclosing a rectangle of south-western France bounded by Poitiers in the north-east and La Rochelle in the north-west. This great expanse of rolling green countryside and small villages was the domain of Le Comte de Sidney for five years. It was a long way from Paris.

Most of what we know about Sidney's life there comes from one letter, albeit a long one.[36] It is written to Monsieur Bafoy, an agent of the Duc de Bouillon in Paris, and was preserved for posterity by the wealth and detail of the accusations it makes against local residents and officials. Even by Sidney's standards it is a sanctimonious monument to the frustration and boredom he must have been feeling in such a place by 1677. Aristocratic men of affairs spent most of the year at Versailles; there was little to do in such a hamlet except ride and hunt. After five years of riding and hunting Sidney succeeds in making the management of the game park a political issue.

If even part of the judgemental tone of Sidney's letter was reciprocated he can hardly have been the most popular man in the village. His letter was first discovered by Nerac's local historian, Monsieur Lagrange-Ferregues, who noted its tone with interest: *'[la] lettre révélent un charactère ardent, autoritaire, se ressentent d'une origine élevée et d'une habitude de commandement longtemps exercé.'* Observing this autocratic bearing and noting the close contacts suggested by the letter with de Bouillon and de la Rochefoucauld, Lagrange-Ferregues became intrigued by Sidney and succeeded in the end in composing a little biography of him. He imagined the astonishment the arrival of this unknown 'Comte' must have caused in the village: *'[Les] Neracais durent etre saisis d'etonnement en voyant descendre d'un equipage un grand seigneur et ses laquais dont ils ignoraient l'origine, accueillez avec di[e?]fience sans doute pars des notables.'* As the letter shows, this picture of Sidney surrounded by his 'lackeys' is not exaggerated.[37]

---

[36] Archives Nationales R2/82; the letter is dated Nerac, January – almost certainly January 1677, just before his departure. For notice of it I am indebted to Carswell J. P.; for assistance with its translation to Martin Roberts.

[37] Agen R.O., Archives de Lot et Garonne, fonds Lagrange-Ferregues Serie J pp. 180–9. The pass granted him to enter France (De Lisle MS U1475 F20/1) made provision for 'Mr Sidney Son to the Earl of Leic[este]r ... with his Domesticks'.

His letter opens with a suitably damning report on the state of local judicial affairs.

To aquit myself of the promise I made you to give you news of the affairs of this country, I have to tell you that the business concerning the consulate of Castel Jaloux [a neighbouring village] is making a great deal of noise, the authority of M le Duc de Bouillon, having been inappropriately exposed ... I have not heard of any other trial begun by Masellieres [Paul de Mazelieres, Governor and Intendant d'Albret, the Duc's senior local official] to have succeeded any better, but having been badly [begun], and badly conducted, they have finished badly, and there are those who believe that if someone more informed dosn't manage that of Julien, the result will be the same.[38]

More junior officials do not fare any better.

They say M de Bouillon took Poale the assessor, and Mesparote ... to be [of] his counsel, but they are not the sort of people to put his affairs in better order. The first is simply an idiot, who signs false [acquittances] when Masselieres orders him to do so, and the other serves him in the villanies of the town house, but is so little esteemed that ... few people wish to entrust him with a one-ecu trial. They say that Masselieres is trying to introduce his two brothers Casimon into the service of M. le Duc de Bouillon, but in addition to their life, which you could hardly describe as good ... the younger of the two is absent for having recently assassinated an officer in his bed ... One should not be surprised at this, for everyone likes those who are like them: people of bad life always have affairs in which those who are worth more do not wish to become involved, and when they are overwhelmed in debts, disputes, and crimes, they look for their security in those who have equal need of their assistance, but M de Bouillon, doing nothing which is not just and honest, he has no need of such canaille.[39]

We see here glimpses of the moral tone and the linguistic devices ('They say ... there are those who believe') of the *Discourses*, as well as glimpses of the sort of man Sidney was becoming – increasingly soured by the fortune that made him a commentator upon, rather than actor in, affairs. And if the moral standards which he was later to demand of the Restoration state in England were unrealistic enough, they were even less appropriate to the provincial Wild West of the Duchy d'Albret. Soon the letter's drumbeat of 'debts, disputes, crimes' in relation to the Duc's officials gives way to Sidney's own prospectus for rectifying the situation, centred upon a series of 'honest' men known to him and distinguished by their freedom from these things.

If [Mr le Duc de Bouillon] ... considers it appropriate ... there is one here who will take [charge of] Nerac and Castel Jaloux ... [and] It would be easy to find a faithful and responsible receiver here. M d'Andaison will be able ... to provide for the hunt: he has no dispute, debt, or crime on his head ... By this means, the pay of a great number of [unnecessary] officers will be saved: M de Bouillon would have no other business than his own, and honest people being no longer exposed to insults, would always be ready to serve him.[40]

[38] Paris, Archives Nationales R2/82.
[39] *Ibid.*
[40] *Ibid.*

In the course of the letter, too, we discover one way in which Sidney had been occupying himself.

Since my return [from Paris] I have been hunting three times, and have found that there are some hares, as always when the snow falls on the high ground. In these three days, I saw eight and only caught two, but I did not see a dozen partridges in all, and didn't catch a single one.

This subject then brings in its own rich harvest of complaint; the usual administrative bungling and corruption being exacerbated by the fact that someone has had the unbelievable cheek to question the Comte's own inroads into what game there is available.

They tell me there is no-one here who wishes to conserve the game, who had to take care to keep soldiers away ... the Captains have been with me ... and protest that they have nothing to hunt ... [but] their subalterns ... at the beginning [of the season] killed twenty five or thirty partridges [and by such depredations, and others by] some rascals who are in league with the guards ... [and] by Perez [who] had more than thirty partridges and [forty] of other game ... one has surely never seen it less stocked, and ... there's hardly anything left between Barbance and Durance ... Last week a gentleman told me ... there is not a single stag at Durance ... M de Bouillon believes that one cannot prevent this, but it is said that he is badly informed ... he would be able to ... if his guards did not receive money from those who do harm ... I never go for a walk without hearing gunshots and often I see fire in the hills, but I havn't yet seen a gamekeeper in the country. They tell me that d'Orient is not around for a quarter of the year, and that is only to collect the wood revenues or to insult somebody, but as for his job, when he is sitting with a bottle in front of the fire, he does not even take the trouble to get up at all the gunshots that he can hear.[41]

On what had been passed on to M de Bouillon that someone called David, who was with me for some time, had destroyed much game ... I have diligently enquired, and cannot find, that he ever went out without my order, or killed four pairs of partridges without my being present. I must not believe, that M. de Bouillon requires of me an account of game that has been killed, but for my satisfaction, I have asked my men, and they tell me, that in four years, the whole does not amount to more than sixty pairs of partridges, of which two thirds were from the last year. After this, you will be astonished that anyone has had the impudence to make accounts such as you have heard, but a man who lies perpetually, and who has no other purpose than that of making his master look bad to everybody, is capable of anything.[42]

Finally,

I request you to give M. de Duc de Bouillon my very humble *baise-mains* [hand-kisses] and Mme la Duchesse [Marie-Anne Mancini], and in passing this on to tell them, that to put an end to these disorders it is necessary to follow the method of M. de la Rochefoucauld. On his land, no-one has ever spoken of poison or violence. A gentleman is looking after the hunt, and a businessman looks after affairs of revenue: both are good to the country, and serve it without offending anybody. The most honest people guard what is close to their houses, the others are discovered and

[41] *Ibid.*
[42] *Ibid.*

punished, and the lord is liked and revered by all. Mme d'Hautterine does little different at . . . a piece of land . . . near to Verteuil (la Rochefoucauld's seat), where two miserable rascals earning only twenty ecus protect the forests so well that there is hardly any place in France where there is more game of every sort. The same thing could be done here . . . but while affairs are in the hands of those who are odious to the country . . . full of crimes, wickedness, and ignorance, and who introduce into his service scoundrels who resemble themselves, it is impossible that he should often avoid scandals, and that he should not suffer such notable prejudices as these are, to his reputation, and his interests.

I think he will do me the justice to believe, that it is for this consideration that I give myself the trouble of describing all this, where I can [myself] have neither passion nor interest. Those who know me even a little will see well, that I can think nothing of an enemy like Masellieres, and that his master has a greater interest in the chastisement of his insolences, than I can have in helping him. Besides [even if] I . . . [had] an interest in anything here . . . the letters that I received from England the last week [from Henry Savile, enclosing his pass to return to England] would detach me from it.[43]

Apart from its interest as a window into an otherwise unknown part of Sidney's life, this letter is a complete reproduction, within the parameters of its particular environment, of the mobile mental construct which was to culminate in the *Discourses*, and which we may call Sidney's Republic. Here for the Duchy d'Albret we find anticipated the shape of the *Discourses*'s message for England. The country is in a grim state; the disease from which it suffers is both moral and constitutional, infecting both individuals and the administrative framework. Its greatest illustration (and the primary obstacle to its rectification) is the head of government (in this case Mazelieres; later Charles II), and because such men always surround themselves with others like themselves this evil infects all other officers and the government as a whole. The result is that the people are oppressed; they who should be the principal beneficiaries are the principal victims of the administration, and the law itself has become as corrupt as the people administering it. 'This corruption of the law perpetually adds to ye evill of the administration . . . [and] these two plagues, if suffered to continue still feed one another.'[44] In this administration there is therefore insult and violence where there should be law and order; idleness, drunkenness, and corruption where there should be vigour and virtue. As in the *Discourses*, too, this picture forms the backdrop for Sidney's alternative vision – the same combination of public virtue, popular support, and correct administration – the obvious benefits and real possibility of which are underlined (along with the contrast itself) by concrete examples. The benefits of de la Rochefoucauld's way of doing things is no less obvious than those of the English Republic's. 'When things are in this right order, there is perpetual advance in all that is good.'[45]

43 *Ibid.*
44 *Court Maxims* p. 124.
45 *Ibid.*

Moreover, in this case Sidney's description of the situation around him was almost certainly based on fact. The local government of such semi-autonomous provinces was notorious not just for the sort of maladministration Sidney describes but for real tyranny and violence as well, and the lands of the Duc de Bouillon in particular.[46] Indeed Mazelieres was so notorious and hated that three and a half years after Sidney's letter 'several Neracais, outraged by his crimes and victims of his injustices, assassinated him'.[47] Perhaps, then, we should not discount the effect of more than four years living in one of the remotest and most lawless reaches of southern France on the view of the fragilities of human society that we eventually find expressed in the *Discourses*. (Given that the experience of England that preceded it was that of the civil war and interregnum the point is rather emphasised than diminished.) It is even easier to see how the alpine critical perspective appropriate to Sidney here as a large fish in a small sea (and which led him to lecture one of the greatest aristocrats in France on how to run his own affairs) transferred itself later to the political landscape of England. It illustrates how Sidney's Republic was less a place than a state of mind, applicable to politics or partridges as the case might require it; and how here the second son who could not be a lord or king in his own country became a lord, according to the *Discourses* equal to a king, in the rural fastness of somebody else's. In this respect Sidney's role in relation to de Bouillon's lands in France was simply a continuation (mentally if not legally) of that earlier adopted towards Strangford's in England; that of a hitch-hiker on other people's estates.

The final thing of great interest about this letter is its reference to de la Rochefoucauld at Verteuil. We cannot be certain Sidney visited him but such detailed knowledge of the running of his estate is unlikely to have been acquired any other way. The enigmatic Duc was not only a retired frondeur but, of course, became in his retirement one of the period's most celebrated writers as well. De la Rochefoucauld's *Maximes Morales* were first published (illegally) in the Netherlands (1664) and then a year later in France (1665) at the time Sidney's own *Court Maxims* were being written. Like Sidney's *Maxims*, and as one would expect from an aristocratic frondeur in retreat, they were a work of sceptical interest theory.

For the human condition the central reality they posit is '*amour-propre*', self-love: 'it makes men idolators of themselves and tyrants of others . . . Nothing is so impetuous as its desires, nothing so hidden as its designs.' This is like Sidney's 'private interest', and similarly the link between '*amour-propre*' and the world is '*interet*'. 'Interest is the soul of *amour-propre*.' 'Since it is unlikely that a number of persons should have the same interests, it is at

---

[46] John Lough, *An Introduction to Seventeenth Century France* (London 1954) pp. 68–9.
[47] Agen R.O., Lagrange-Ferregues p. 182.

least necessary for the smooth operation of society that they do not have contrary ones.' 'Luxury and excessive politesse are a sure sign of increasing decadence, because as all individuals become attached to their private interests [*interets propres*] they turn away from the public good.'[48]

If de la Rochefoucauld's interest theory was classically French, and more sceptical than Sidney's would ever be, it is, nevertheless, a reminder of the continental flavour of Sidney's own, and of the fact that the two ageing aristocratic rebels would have been able to speak the same political language.

In Nerac Sidney himself had visitors. On 13 May 1674 two English travellers, Suzanne 'Groundon' and Oliver Cheyney, were married there by a huguenot pastor in 'Le Comte de Sidney' 's own house.[49] In Nerac, too, he must have met the huguenot Joseph Ducasse (son of Jeremie Ducasse, *avocat en Parlement*) who was to flee to England in 1682 to escape the religious persecutions and become Sidney's 'valet' in London. It was Ducasse who waited on Sidney throughout the ordeal of his imprisonment in 1683; who was responsible for the hiding and safekeeping of his final *Apology*; and who appeared with it before the committee of the Lords set up to investigate his 'murder' in 1690. The records of a huguenot church in London in 1685 show him married to 'Marie' and eventual father of a number of children. The point is of interest since a letter from James Vernon to the Duke of Shrewsbury in 1697 includes a startling description of Ducasse (who had petitioned Algernon's brother Henry, then Earl of Romney) as the Frenchman who 'married Algernon Sidney's daughter'.[50]

This is the most intriguing of all Sidney mysteries since aside from this letter there is no other trace of such a person. If Vernon is correct we have no idea where or when 'Marie Sidney' came into the world; whether Ducasse met her in France or in England; and whether he married her before or after Sidney's death. Of Sidney's social life in the south of France in general we know nothing else, though he retained correspondents there after his return to England in 1677, sending packages and receiving the traditional Bordeaux gift of wine, and maintaining his intention to return there finally when his legal troubles were over. In his *Apology* in 1683 he wrote that 'when a favorable decree, obtained in chancery [1681], gave me hopes of being freed from such a vexatious business, I reassumed my former designe of returning into France; and to that end bought a small parcell of ground, in a friend's

---

[48] Keohane N., *Philosophy and the State in France* pp. 289–93.

[49] Agen R.O., Registre des mariages benie en l'eglise reformee de Nerac 4E 199/17.

[50] Agen R.O., Lagrange-Ferregues, *Notes Sur Nerac: Familles* I pp. 316–9; James G. P. R. ed., *Letters Illustrative of the Reign of William III* (1841) p. 273; London Huguenot Soc. Pubs. vol. 16 *Registers of the French Church, Threadneedle St London* vol. III (1906) pp. 52, 61, 79, 91, 116, 141, 188, 241; Bibliothèque Nationale FM 2366. My thanks to Dr Paul Hopkins for this discovery.

name, with an intention of going immediately unto it'.[51] In a letter from his prison cell to his fellow-prisoner Hampden in the same year he wrote:

I did yesterday receave a letter from a freind in Guascony, whoe [having told another friend there that] I would goe unto that Country as soone as I could get free of businesses heare, he bid him let me know, that he had tow houses besides that in which he lived, either of which should be at my disposall: One of them I know very well, and it is a good one, about twelve leagues above Bourdeaux, the other which I take to be much better, and in a better country, is eight or ten leagues higher. If you can for a while content yourself with a country life, and it please God to deliver us from hence, wee may probably expect as much peace, safety, and convenience ther[e] as in any place I knowe.

Who these people were we will probably never now know; Turenne had died in 1675, de la Rochefoucauld in 1680.

14.6 PARIS–NERAC–PARIS, 1676–7

The visit to Paris mentioned by Sidney in his letter to Bafoy took place in the autumn of 1676. There as usual he took the opportunity to see English (and other) friends and relations, and it was from one of these meetings that there suddenly emerged the prospect of his return.

The opportunity came through a meeting with his grand-nephew, George Savile, Lord Halifax's eldest son. Like Sidney's own father, Halifax had sent his son to be educated in France, and the boy had just returned to Paris via Saumur among other places. He was accompanied in Paris by Harry Savile, his jovial and irreverent uncle, and Sidney's future correspondent and friend. Savile's servant Du Moulin recorded:

Wee waited off Col: Sydney in the afternoone who was extraordinary kynd to mr Savile [jnr], and who approved much of the design to make the Tour of France by the way of Augeres, Nantes, La Rochelle and Bordeaux in march and april next . . . but he said once he got mr Savile at Nerac in Guyenne where he lives, and whether he intends to return shortlie, he would keep him as long as he could before he would let him go to Montpellier.[52]

It was presumably at Sidney's own request that soon after his subsequent return to England Henry Savile made enquiries of the Court through secretary Henry Coventry about the possibility of a pass to visit England. Sidney stayed on in Paris another month, and wrote to Savile from there on 14 November to enquire after progress in that 'business'. He then left for Nerac some time in the following two weeks.

One month later, back in Nerac on 18 December, he wrote a joyful letter to

---

[51] *Apology* p. 4.
[52] Chatsworth, Devonshire MSS Halifax Papers: Du Moulin letters 21.9 (21.3.76); 21.20 (4.3.77); cf. Foxcroft H., *Life and Letters of Sir George Savile* (1898) pp. 136–7.

Savile. In it he acknowledged receipt of three letters and the promise of a pass for an initial period of at least three months.

my obligation unto you is [so great] and I so far acknowledge it to be the greatest that I have in a long time received from any man, as not to value the leave you have obtained for me to return into my country after so long an absence, at a lower rate than the saving of my life.

Sidney promised to

put myself entirely on the kings word; and desire you only to obtain a pass to signify it ... I have no other business than what solely concerns my person and family ... I desire not to be a day in England unknown to the King, or his ministers ... I think it no ways reasonable that I should stay in England, if the King do not see I may do it without any shadow or possibility of prejudice unto him; and unless I can satisfy him in that point, I desire no more than to return on this side the sea after the three months, where I intend to finish my days, without thinking any more of living in England.[53]

Two months later Sidney wrote to Savile from Nerac again. Had he not been determined to accept whatever the King offered, he said,

the letter I writ [from Paris] in answeare unto yours of Novr 2nd, would have argued more of indirectnesse, than I hope any man, shall ever finde in my proceedings. The truth is, ther is hardly any worldly thing in my prospect, that I doe soe earnestly desire, both in regard of seing my freinds, and setling my private affaires, as my hope that my intentions having bin ill understood at court, I shall be able to explaine them soe well unto the King, or his ministers, if I may speake to them, as to make it appeare, that my remaining in England, shall be in all respects harmelesse, if not usefull, soe as not to doubt, but I may have the leave continued, as much as I shall desire.[54]

With regard to the pass itself:

I am not curious in words, and remit thoes matters to the iudgement of my freinds upon the place, and though I could wish, there might be somme difference made betweene me, and many meane fellows to whom passes have bin granted, and perhaps the King may think it not unreasonable, I will insist upon nothing of that kinde.

He told Savile he would remain in Nerac only until the winter receded sufficiently for him to 'repaire into England, with such diligence, as my health and strenght [*sic*] will permit'. Once in London he would wait on Coventry, and then

My first remove from thence, shall be to Penshurst, where I will conforme myselfe to such rules as shall be imposed upon me, in avoiding to my power any thing that is like to give occasion of offence: The three moneths being expird, I will againe repaire to the secretary, and returne one this side the sea if the King doth not consent that I continue in England.

Sidney's only request was that he might be protected from

a businesse I have depending with Sr Robert Honnywoods heires, for a publike debt in

---

[53] Sidney, *Works* (1772) 'Letters to ... Savile' pp. 56–7 (wrongly dated 1682).
[54] Longleat, Bath MSS Coventry Papers app. ii fols. 134–5.

which he and I weare engaged ... this Pa[rliament] having overthrowne, what the former had orderd for the payment of it out of the publike treasury ... [yet even] that shall not hinder [me] ... but if you secure me from being molestd ... upon pretence of matters relating unto the state, I will secure myself as well as I can from such inconveniences, as may arise from this private one.[55]

Two months later in mid April Sidney received a letter from Coventry. It promised that

you may come into this kingdom with all safety and Security and there so abide for so long time as his Majesty shall find Convenient ... and ... during that time you shall be by his Majesties Royall Authority protected against all manner of Molestations or prosecution for any Act done ... by you at any time before this present 16th day of April 1677 agt his Royal father or the Government and for this you have his Royal word.[56]

Sidney replied on 4 May: '[I] neither doubt of the security ... given, nor think any can be greater, then the word of a king [! this is Sidney at his most courtly], deliverd by a Minister, that was never suspected of any thing, that agreed not, with the rules of honour, and iustice, but it not being acompanied with a pass, I feare I shall be stopped every wheare.' He therefore requested that a pass be sent to him via his sister Sunderland, presumably in Paris, 'and in the meane[time] beginning my journey, I hope ere long, to let the King see his favour unto me, is not ill imployed'.[57]

Sidney arrived back in Paris, then, in mid 1677. The English ambassador Ralph Montagu reported:

Mr Algernoone Sidney is heere at pasing upon his return for England. When he was last heere in the fall of the yeare, he sent to know when he might see me; I told him the king having refused him leave to come into England ... it was not proper for one in the station I was in to convers with one that then lay under ... my Master's displeasure. It seems he took this ill, though when I was last Ambassador here, and he was at Paris, he was contented to ask the King's leave before I saw him. But now he has never come at me tho' he has been twice or thrice to versailles.[58]

It was on this last visit to Paris that Sidney had the conversations with Jean-Baptiste Lantin that have been extensively quoted in earlier chapters.

'I had often dined in Paris with le Comte de Sydney in 1677', wrote Lantin. 'I had been staying in the rue de Tournon, and I used to take my meal with the Comte at l'hostel d'Antragues.' The mention of the street is interesting, since this is the only street that Sidney himself is on record as naming in connection with his earlier life in Paris with his father. In 1661 he had described to his father a Portuguese friend in Rome who had been with the Portuguese

---

[55] *Ibid.*
[56] Add MS 25,124 fol. 122.
[57] Longleat, Coventry Papers II fol. 105.
[58] Longleat, Coventry XXXIV fol. 226. Sidney could have been visiting de Bouillon, who had a residence at Versailles.

'ambassadors [in Paris], when your Lordship did visit them in the Rue de Tournon'.[59]

Lantin, member of the Parliament of Dijon, was about the same age as Sidney and a 'Grammarian, Orator, Historian, Poet, Mathematician, and Philosopher' as well as a recorder of other people's conversations. He had published a number of books on subjects ranging from Euclid to the setting of thirty Horatian odes to music, and his other (recorded) conversation partners in Paris over the years included Liebniz, Hobbes, and his close friend Salmasius. He particularly enjoyed discussing politics and political philosophy and in drawing out from his (preferably foreign and exotic) conversation partners accounts of intriguing developments (and personalities) in their own country. Thus it was that he managed to extract from Sidney stories about Selden and Milton (of particular interest as the opponent of Salmasius), as well as of Cromwell and the English Republic.[60]

What is most interesting about Sidney's conversation with Lantin at this time is the telling counterpoint it provides to what we have just heard him saying to the English King. For if the letters to Savile evidence a genuine desire on Sidney's part to stay out of political trouble, the diatribe to Lantin shows how much that desire would be up against it once it relocated itself in an active political context. Lantin set Sidney at his ease, and gave us one of the most relaxed and private views we have of him – it could not be said that he ceased to perform; rather that he had only to perform for an audience of one. The result for Lantin was genuine bemusement at what a spirited (again that word *esprit*) *republicain outre* his guest was. Nostalgia it may have been, but the belief informing it was still alive.

What Sidney said makes it clear that he believed he had been involved, not simply in a great struggle for English liberties, but in an historic political experiment which had made the whole of Europe look Westwards with alarm. That experiment had been destroyed by Cromwell but not before it had conquered everything to which it had laid its hand. It was as one of these still-amazed continentals that Sidney assumed Lantin wished to know all the details. And it was by this belief that Sidney had maintained his *espirit* for so long in a world fallen calm again. Needless to say this was a dangerous situation. When that calm proved to be fragile in England Sidney's promises proved fragile too.

In September the English government received a report from Castle Elizabeth in Jersey.

[O]n the 4th arrived here a person of quality, who concealed his name; I went to his

---

[59] Paris, Bibliothèque Nationale Fr. MS 23254 ('Lantiniana') pp. 99–101. Sidney, 'Letters ... from the Sydney Papers' in *Works* p. 47.
[60] 'Lantiniana' – a manuscript well worthy of modern publication.

lodgings, he told me his name was Sydney, and that he was bound for England. I offered him convoy: he said he had sufficient and showed me the king's pass.[61]

When he stepped ashore in Kent Sidney had been away for eighteen years. He was fifty-five years old, and this was his first experience of adult life under an English monarchy.

[61] Longleat, Coventry Papers no. 55 p. 247.

INDEX

Lightning Source UK Ltd.
Milton Keynes UK
UKOW04f0702200717
305685UK00001B/50/P